No More Mondays:
A Nautical Odyssey

LaVonne Misner

No More Mondays:
A Nautical Odyssey

LaVonne Misner

For my dear friend Penny Johnson Martin

LaVonne "Hanb" Misner

Lighthouse Press Publication
a division of ProStar Publications, Inc.

© **2002 by LaVonne Misner.** All rights reserved. Except for use in a review, no part of this book may be reproduced or utilized in any form or by any means, electronic or mechanical, including photocopying, recording, or by an information storage and retrieval system, without written permission from the publisher.

ISBN: 1-57785-298-2

Printed in the United States

Published by:

Lighthouse Press
a division of **ProStar** Publications, **Inc.**

3 Church Circle
Suite 109
Annapolis, MD 21401
(800) 481-6277
Email: editor@prostarpublications.com
Website: www.prostarpublications.com

Cover Design and Production:
Ron Ligrano
Book Design and Production:
Carole Ann Thomas

I dedicate this book with love and admiration to my husband, Tom Olson, who had the courage to follow his dream. While I thought I was merely going along for the ride, he helped to stretch my horizons beyond that which I thought was possible, even to the point when I eventually put it all on paper.

ACKNOWLEDGEMENTS

I want to thank all the cruisers who were and were not mentioned in this book. Each of them added to the joy and completeness of our daily lives while on the sea, in shared anchorages, and in ports.

Thank you as well to the many local people we met throughout our travels who selflessly shared the highlights of their country, city, or island with us so that I was able to share their culture with you, the reader.

Heartfelt thanks go to the Ham Radio community, especially to those who freely shared their time and skills by facilitating phone patches so that we were able to stay in touch with family members who were left back home.

Loving thanks are given to Elinor Reiss, Diane Rider and Shari Pagnotta from the Scripps Ranch Literary Group who tenderly edited and offered encouragement when I needed it.

Grateful respect and appreciation are given to my neighbor Richard Louv, a talented writer and author of many books, for his constant encouragement and commiseration.

Deep respect and appreciation are given to Dale Fetherling, a talented author and journalist, for his editing and guidance. Working with him has been both an education and a joy.

Thank you to Peter Griffes, Publisher with ProStar Publications, for his faith in the book, to Diana Hunter for the attention she paid to details and the respectful manner she treated my manuscript, to Carole Ann Thomas for her tastefully appropriate graphics, and to Ron Ligrano for choosing my painting for the cover.

CONTENTS

PROLOGUE 8

Part One: Outward Bound
Chapter 1 Goodbye Duluth, Hello World 13
Chapter 2 Onward to the Atlantic 53
Chapter 3 Migrating South 101

Part Two: Life in the Tropics
Chapter 4 To the Bahamas and Beyond 139
Chapter 5 South America Calls 189
Chapter 6 A World Awaits Through the Canal 231

Part Three: The South Pacific
Chapter 7 The Galapagos & Crossing the South Pacific 271
Chapter 8 Enjoying Life in Polynesia 287
Chapter 9 Winding Down after the Passage from Hell 321
Chapter 10 How Long Do We Tempt Fate? 347

Appendix A: Growing Leaf Lettuce On Board 353
Appendix B: Making Beer On Board 355
Appendix C: Pavlova Recipe 358

Color Photo Insert . . . . Book Center

PROLOGUE

Tom and LaVonne married in 1977, a second marriage for each. Their combined families formed a combined household of six children (grade-school age through high school); two cats and a small black dog appropriately named Inky. With two careers and a large household, their lives were complicated and there were days when it seemed the only family member with no complaint was Inky. Getting meals on the table, laundry done, grass cut, snow shoveled, bills paid, and homework completed all contributed to scheduling problems requiring communication and negotiation skills.

Tom graduated from the University of Minnesota with a degree in mechanical engineering. He had always been physically active and often was more interested in the doing of things as opposed to studying them. His exuberance worked well for him in the corporate world and his career took off. He quickly moved up the corporate ladder into middle management. His energy and ability to make hard quick decisions coupled with his slim tall stature and dark features enhanced the fact that he was a man in command of most any situation. There was never dust in his cup of life; instead it was full of life yet to be lived. People liked that about him, and when he offered his large friendly handshake it encased the other person's hand and they instinctively trusted him. He was good at what he did and for nearly thirty years he was immersed in business where Mondays represented the first of five or six consecutively tense and demanding days.

LaVonne was a nutrition professor and a supervisor for a federally funded program called The Expanded Food and Nutrition Education Program run by the University of Minnesota. She loved her job, valued her career, and was proud of having been the first college graduate on her side of the family. Her position afforded her the luxury of being her own boss with a pleasant office and loyal secretary. Each day her ethnically mixed staff consisting of American Indian, Black, Causasian, Hmong, Iranian, Lao, Spanish, Thai, and Vietnamese taught her new things.

LaVonne and Tom's busy unpretentious home was located on 165 feet of lakeshore in a bedroom community called New Brighton, a northern suburb of St. Paul, Minnesota. The home was large enough to accommodate the blended family and they thought it the perfect haven for the growing children. They had three old boats: a beat-up runabout used primarily for water skiing, a 16 foot Hobie Cat sailboat, and a rather unshiny dented aluminum canoe. As one might imagine, their summers were packed with family water activities. But the season was short and soon winter whistled down from the north and the lake was frozen. Winters in Minnesota are cold and when the lake ice was deemed to be strong enough to be walked upon safely, the entire family enthusiastically shoveled the snow off a very large area for an ice skating rink. With each new snowfall and as the winter lengthened, family enthusiasm for shoveling decreased and the ice rink became smaller and smaller until finally the lumpy outline of the original rink was hardly visible.

The children grew, as children do, and Tom and LaVonne talked about their futures and their dreams. They wanted to visit foreign countries, see old ruins, visit the Seven-Wonders of the World and great historical spots, taste great wine, and touch life as it was lived in other cultures.

"Once the children are all grown up, we'll do it," they promised each other and began saving for when that day would come. The first step in their plan was to live on one income and invest the other and without realizing it, they adjusted their purchases in anticipation of their departure. When they needed to replace their family-room furniture, Tom told the salesman they did not need furniture to last a lifetime – it only needed to last a few years. When Sara, their youngest child, graduated from high school and had plans to enter college and a dorm room, Tom and LaVonne launched on their trip.

PART ONE
Outward Bound

CHAPTER ONE

Goodbye Duluth, Hello World

SHIT BY A TORNADO

"*VONNIE-T, VONNIE-T, do you read? If you are still in radio range, this is the Duluth Bridge Captain. A tornado has been sighted. Return to port!*"

Our trip of a lifetime was threatened to end nearly before it got started. We were faced with making a major decision, and doing it fast! The sky was still sunny and clear overhead but a black horizon was rolling toward us. We considered turning back and trying to outrun the tornado as the bridge captain suggested, but we feared the storm might catch up with us just as we were negotiating the ship channel. Worse yet, the storm could catch us after arriving in the harbor where we would be near rocks, docks, and other boats with almost no room to maneuver. If that happened, our lives would probably be saved, but the likelihood of doing damage to our boat and others around us was highly probable.

One alternative was to stay out on the lake and take our chances. What should we do? That was the question.

On July 21, we departed from the Duluth harbor for what was expected to be our final exodus from the port. We checked on the weather, but knew it was always a gamble. Lake Superior is the largest body of fresh water in the world. It is as large as a sea, 400 miles long and 200 miles wide. It creates its own weather, making it impossible to get a reliable long-range weather forecast.

One dramatic aspect that early morning was the growl of the lift-bridge gears as they thundered across the icy cold water of Lake Superior while the bridge was being raised for us to sail underneath.

Tourists in nearby shops stepped outside to watch the sight. The sounds of moving steel girders and gears were accompanied by the gentle clang of bells that were attached to long wooden arms with flashing lights that stretched across the street at both ends of the bridge. I looked up from our deck and saw lines of cars orderly threading themselves along the narrow street in both directions, knowing we were the cause of the traffic jam. While the sounds reverberated off the water and the traffic delay may have been an irritant to some, we knew most Duluth residents relished seeing their bridge in operation. The bridge was almost an antique, and it was loved like an elderly grandmother representing dignity, pride, and wealthier times. Often residents could be heard reminiscing about the glorious shipping days that transported grain from the Midwest and iron ore from Northern Minnesota. They remembered when Duluth was a great port and this majestic little lift bridge, dating back to 1929, fueled those memories.

"That was big business in these here parts," they would say. "That's when people stood tall, when they said they were from Duluth, Minnesota."

I had mixed feelings on the day we slid out under that bridge, and I suspect Tom had a few of his own. The reality of taking our sailboat out of that marina for the last time caused a quivery frightened feeling in my stomach.

Tom's eyes glistened with excitement — or were they moist with tears? Duluth had been homeport for VONNIE-T, and the bridge, like our family, was just one more thing we were leaving behind. When we said goodbye to that bridge, our philosophical shore, we said goodbye to security, safety, family, friends, jobs, and nearly everything from our previous lives. We were proud of our courage, yet frightened that we might be overly confident. How fitting it was for the bridge to play a role in our departure, for it was the last tangible thing we saw of Minnesota.

Water view of the beloved Duluth lift-bridge on Lake Superior from the bow of VONNIE-T.

SHIP'S LOG, TOM'S ENTRY
46°North Latitude, 92°West Longitude, July 21, 1987

MAN CANNOT DISCOVER NEW HORIZONS WITHOUT THE COURAGE TO LOSE SIGHT OF THE SHORE. **We are leaving our home for the last time. Goodbye, Duluth, Minnesota.**

I wondered if Tom felt as brave as the words that he wrote. Was it perhaps his way of giving himself a pep talk? We had done our very best to prepare ourselves for the trip and we hoped we had done everything right. We even put guns on board in the event we would have to protect ourselves from pirates. We had Tom's old shotgun, a rifle, and two stainless steel handguns – one handgun was mine, the other was Tom's. The retired policeman who gave me lessons on how to shoot my .357 Magnum said he thought I was ready to use it if I ever needed to, but I hoped I'd never have to test my marksman skills.

We were proud of our financial ability to leave, but scared that we might have overlooked something and may need more money than what we planned. We were equally proud to know "DULUTH, MN" was in big bold letters on the stern of our boat indicating our homeport, yet nervous about the time when we would be crossing oceans. We had a thousand mixed feelings.

On the day of our departure, I was at the steering wheel while Tom stood on the bow where he could see well. Based on what he could see, he gave me steering and speed directions. He looked a little like a hood ornament standing erect with one hand on the roller-furling halyard, gazing out to the water in front of the boat. I didn't realize it then, but these would be the roles we would each perform thousands of times over for the next six and a half years.

"Keep her slow and steady," Tom said to me with a Mona Lisa smile showing a flicker of self-satisfaction in the corner of his mouth. "Stay to the center of the channel," the old lion said with pride, while trying not to gloat. Clearly, he enjoyed his Captain role.

I followed his directions, noting that my stomach muscles had tightened. While he enjoyed every moment, I was apprehensive and on the verge of throwing up.

"OK, put her in neutral," he said. "I can't tell if the mast is going to clear the bridge yet. OK. It looks good. Put it in gear, but slowly! Keep moving forward VERY SLOWLY!"

Tom carefully scanned the distance between our 62-foot mast and the bottom of the bridge. A lot was at risk. If we didn't clear the bottom of the bridge and our masthead hit it, our rigging would come crashing to the deck, and with it would come all our hard work and dreams. Finally, we slid under the bridge, clearing it by at least a foot. I took a deep breath and gulped for air after unknowingly holding my breath.

We had talked to the bridge captain on the radio and told him of our plans and when he saw us come out from under the bridge and appear on the other side, he said over the VHF radio, "May the seas be kind to you, VONNIE-T." The moon- shaped lines around

LaVonne proudly displaying her amateur ham radio call sign, NØHWB, from the side-deck of VONNIE-T

Tom's mouth deepened as he finally broke into a full smile. Then we heard the Great Lakes salute: three long and two short blasts from the bridge horn for all the spectators to hear. That salute was the greatest send-off anyone could possibly have given us!

Happily, we waved to the spectators standing along the ship channel wall - some were strangers, others were friends. It's hard to know what they might have been thinking, but it didn't matter. We were embarking on an adventure that most of them would never experience in a lifetime.

"Looking good, VONNIE-T," said one of our ham radio friends over the two-meter radio.

Learning radio, the Morse code, and getting an amateur radio license had been some of my more time-consuming, pre-voyage tasks. Unbeknown to us at the time, our amateur radio would become a major asset to our travels for a variety of reasons we were too inexperienced to recognize.

At that moment, we could think of nothing but our bursting pride. One look at Tom said it all. His back was straight and his face nearly glowed. When the tension in my stomach began to ease, I became aware that my cheek muscles ached from the smile that refused to leave my face.

I listened to the soft gush of the water as it pushed past our hull while we glided out from behind the channel wall. The surface water was glassy and with the sun high overhead, I was able to look straight down into the cold deep. All aspects of the day looked friendly.

After clearing the wall Tom instructed me to turn upwind so he could raise the mainsail. With practiced confidence he guided the sail up the mast and set the sheets.

"Fall off the wind and hold a steady course," he instructed while rolling out the jib and winching in its sheet.

He became totally absorbed in trimming the sails to achieve perfection, tinkering with a little more here and a little less there. He walked the deck with the look of a king surveying his kingdom of sheets, lines, and sails. Each had a purpose and he intended to do them justice. The task was clearly a labor of love. When he could find no more sail trimming to do, he joined me in the cockpit where we sat together and savored the beginning of our special day. Each of us was lost in our own thoughts.

We sat in silence, not a loud silence where the ears are edgy or uncomfortable while they listen for a voice to soothe them, but a peaceful, contented silence. It allowed me to think about the excitement I felt and to try to push down my fears. The challenge of being self-sufficient, living off the sea and making the wind work for us seemed perfectly natural to Tom. He was comfortable with these things. On the other hand, I loved the notion of travel, enjoyed meeting new people and seeing new places, but the skills involved in sailing and the ordeal of facing oceans frightened me. My biggest fear was of Tom falling overboard. It was difficult for me to even be rational about that topic. I knew a person's survival time in Lake Superior was about ten minutes before hypothermia set in and the heart stopped beating. If I was the one to fall into the water, I felt Tom might have a chance of saving me by getting back to me in time. If Tom fell in, however, I very likely would not be able to get the boat turned around in time to find him and get him out of the water. Because he did all the deck work, he was the most likely to fall overboard. That fear nagged at me in spite of my every effort to stifle it, but it was too beautiful a day and too nice a sail to dwell on the negatives or the "what ifs." The sky was a bright paint-box blue and the sun was out in all its glory. The winds were soft, the water sparkled, and the air was cool and crisp with a comfortable 15 knots of wind. What could be better?

That was when everything changed and when we received the startling call from the Duluth bridge captain. We had hardly been out on the lake for an hour when his agitated voice jarred us from our daydreaming. It seemed preposterous to think bad weather could be heading our way, but then we saw it. Off in the distance the horizon had become black and it formed a dramatic contrast to the sun that still shown brightly overhead. It had the appearance of being a brutal storm, and the bridge captain wanted us to return to the harbor immediately.

It was not an easy decision to make and we quickly considered all the options. As Minnesotans, we knew a lot about tornadoes. Before my marriage to Tom, I had lost the roof of my house to a tornado. The winds had plucked it off and slammed it down next to the garage in the neighbor's yard, so I knew first hand the destructive powers of a tornado. Heading back to port would not free us from risk either. On a more positive note, there was seldom lightning with tornadoes, so the likelihood of our tall masts getting hit by lightning seemed remote. Finding ourselves dead center in the "eye" of the tornado where we would take a direct hit did not seem very probable either.

After quickly analyzing our options, we decided to stay out on the lake and take our chances.

When the dark sky closed in on us, it brought powerful winds that whistled through our rigging. I had to squint to protect my eyes so they would not get wind cuts. With each new gust of wind the boat was shoved over onto its side, requiring us to grab onto anything within reach. We had to get the sails down before they filled with water and caused us to take a knock-down. We quickly put on life vests and safety harnesses. Tom turned on the engine, and without a single word he crawled out on deck to take down the sails he had so carefully put up less than an hour earlier. While he secured the sails, I drove the boat head-on into the wind and rising waves in an effort to take the pressure off the sails. As the sails eased to the deck, they snapped like bullwhips while loose sheets and halyards were left to jangle and clang. I feared Tom might slide off the deck, or fall each time we got a new gust, but he managed well and I was greatly relieved when he had finished the job and was back in the cockpit. Once the sails were down and stowed, we put up our vinyl cockpit enclosure, a tent-like structure with clear isinglass sides.

Tom turned on the radar switch and I noted his annoyance at the delay while it warmed up. He selected a compass heading that would face us toward the Wisconsin shore, and told me to steer that heading. Unfortunately, it was directly in the path of the stormfront, and we experienced increased wind and rain. An artificial night enveloped us with a veil of black wetness. There were no stars and no moon in the middle of the day — only darkness and wind. The rain spiked loudly on the fiberglass decks and the vinyl cockpit enclosure. I worried that the enclosure may not survive the brutality of the storm because without it I would be the one receiving that pelting.

Tom stayed below with his head pressed up against the radar screen. From there he called up new headings for me to turn the boat into the storm and rising waves. He wanted to avoid having a high wind catch us on our side. As I steered, I watched the cold water froth across the deck and push its way up the front of the cockpit enclosure where it caused a whiteout within the darkness around us. I could see nothing beyond the boat, and sometimes I couldn't even see our bow. Tom remained vigilant at the chart table with his forehead pressed against the light shield of the radar screen, making certain we didn't hit another boat.

He continued shouting directions to me and asked, "What are you clipped to?" My safety harness had a large, stainless steel clip (like a big safety pin), on the end.

"I'm clipped to the steel tubing of the cockpit enclosure," I shouted back through the noise.

"Unclip, and re-clip to the slide on the track behind you," he said, "and be sure the slide is locked!" I was in the process of doing that when he added, "That cockpit enclosure may not hold, and if it goes, you need to be prepared to duck out of its way."

He paused, and must have thought more about the hazard the cockpit enclosure could be.

"Remember, if that cockpit enclosure rips off, duck behind the wheel and just let it go. Don't take a chance on getting hit by the aluminum tubing by trying to catch it."

The thought of losing the cockpit enclosure and having all that water coming at me was frightening enough. I had not even considered what a hazard the jagged metal could be if it broke away from its hinges. I found myself mentally pleading for it to survive the beating, as its survival was also mine. It was the only thing keeping me dry and it was the only separation between me and the violent cold water. It could harm me only if it let loose and flailed its stainless tubing at me like multiple flying swords.

The first round of the storm was fierce, but it was over quickly, as most tornadoes are.

The winds peaked at 50 knots, but the front passed through us within 15 minutes or less. It only seemed longer.

"That wasn't bad at all," we agreed, feeling rather pleased with our decision to ride out the storm.

We commented on how well the boat took the impact, and we were very impressed with our isinglass cockpit enclosure. It was comforting to know that neither of us panicked or over-reacted, and we basked in complimentary comments about one another's cool-headed actions. I was proud of Tom and knew I would be able to trust his judgment again and again. He had to make a quick decision based on the best information he had at the time, and he proved that he was capable of doing it. I was pleased with myself too because I did not waste time arguing with him or questioning his decision. We were able to operate as a team and that knowledge felt good. We knew that would be important for our survival in the future, and we gloated a little more before Tom raised the sails again.

The day, however, did not remain that simple. The storm cell clocked around several more times and gave us problems all day. It grew in strength each time it came through, bringing stronger winds and higher waves each time. It kept us so busy that I did not bother to look at the anemometer. We were each involved in doing what we had to do in order to keep the boat and ourselves safe, and that required all of our concentration, time, and energy. What began as a beautiful sailing day turned into an exhausting test of stamina as we battled the cold wet waves and the power of the variable winds.

Not until 4pm did the winds stop, and then they stopped dead. What a contrast that was! We were becalmed. We sat in the cockpit exhausted, listening to the rigging as it clanged from side to side. The sails, that we did not have time to take down during the last time the storm came past us, slid abrasively against the shrouds. We knew we should attend to them, but we were too exhausted and hungry. We had not had time for lunch. We needed time to rest the tired muscles in our hands and arms that were not used to that type of work, time to rest our jangled nerves, and time to eat something. We sat, each with a soda, and shared a can of Pringles. It was all I had the energy to produce for lunch that day. What a pathetic excuse for lunch it was from someone who had taught nutrition for 15 years!

When Tom had the energy to move, he turned on the radio seeking information on what was coming our way next. We expected anything by then, but before we got a weather forecast the sun came out, and we began getting light sailing winds — nice comfortable gentle winds! The storm had finally blown itself out or had moved on. We took our time trimming the sails and set our course heading for Bayfield, Wisconsin. Later that day, we heard the storm report from the Duluth Airport where it had recorded winds of 60 knots (69 MPH). That was enough wind to blow a cow from one Minnesota farm to another.

Once we were on a comfortable sailing tack, I went below and made spaghetti and a salad for dinner. We ate in the cockpit while sailing through the pine forested Apostle Islands. After dinner we had a few hours of early evening sunshine, gentle breezes, and of course, full tummies. I cannot remember spaghetti ever having tasted so good.

We arrived at Bayfield before dark and tied up at the public dock. Putting my feet on the ground again felt great. It had been a hard day and we rewarded ourselves with a walk downtown for an ice-cream cone. Afterwards, I called a friend who lives in Flint, Michigan, and requested permission to have our first batch of mail forwarded to her. I told her we would be arriving in Port Huron in about ten days. She was surprised at the adventure we had undertaken but willingly agreed to watch for our mail. That mail arrangement had been easy, but we still had not worked out how we would get mail after we were out of the United States. That would require more creative planning.

We walked back to the boat feeling good about our days accomplishments, but the walk became long and cold, and I was asleep the minute my head touched the icy cold pillow and damp sheets. I did not even want to think about what might be in store for us the next day.

HAM RADIO – "DO YOU COPY?"

I woke with the sun glaring in my eyes through the large porthole over our bunk. Sluggishly, I remembered where I was and stretched under the fluffy down blanket, appreciating its warmth. I considered pulling the sheet over my head and going back to sleep, but instead I snuggled over to Tom's side of the bunk. On my way over, I glanced at the small battery operated clock affixed to the bulkhead and was shocked to see it was nearly 8am.

How had the morning arrived so quickly? If I had slept any longer I would have missed my very first radio schedule and that would have been unthinkably insensitive. I knew each of the men who helped me study for my operating license were eagerly waiting for my report, and after yesterday's tornado we would have caused a lot of needless worry if they did not hear from me.

I stepped out from the warmth of the bunk and pulled on yesterday's clothing that was still lying where I had peeled it off the night before. While I brushed my teeth, Tom tuned the radio and started the coffeepot. Then I turned the dial of the ham radio set to our prearranged frequencies and listened for familiar voices, but none could be heard. I dialed up and down the band slowly, listening for my call sign.

Finally I heard a male voice, "NØHWB, this is WBØKIS. Do you copy?" Wow! That was the first time I heard my call sign on the air.

I pressed the microphone button and said, "Yes WBØKIS, this is NØHWB. I have light, but clear, copy on you."

Being able to talk to someone over the radio from the boat was very exciting! I told WBØKIS (Warren Koppy) all the details of yesterday's storm, where we were that morning, and how I had almost overslept for my first contact. While we talked, Warren called another of my instructors, WØFCO (Ralph Andreas), on the telephone that is referred to as a "land line" in radio jargon. Warren encouraged Ralph to come up on the radio and join our chat, and the three of us had a wonderful conversation. My first radio contact had been a success, and they agreed to call our family to inform them that all was well aboard the VONNIE-T. Tom laughed and told me that I was radiant during my conversations with Warren and Ralph. I guess I was pretty pleased to have made that radio contact.

MAKING DELICIOUS LOVE IN THE COCKPIT

We set sail shortly after breakfast, anticipating a comparatively easy day. Our destination that night was the Upper Michigan peninsula at the Keewana Canal. We had been there twice before, and found the towns of Houghton and Hancock, on opposite sides of the canal, to be charming. Originally, the canal had been dredged so that large lake boats could escape the vicious storms that frequently blew up unannounced on Lake Superior. How well we could relate to that! The canal also provided the added bonus of shortening the voyage from Duluth to the Sault Saint Marie locks on the eastern end of Lake Superior. When we had sailed to Houghton/Hancock previously, we thought that was an ambitious undertaking. Now, it was only the second day of a more epic journey!

Everything about the day was beautiful. The wind was smooth and steady at 10 to 15 knots, the seas had only a slight chop, and the sky was milky blue with no clouds on the horizon. All morning we moved along at a steady, uneventful clip. As the sun rose high in the sky, and later when it slid down the stern it warmed the cockpit and the boat interior. The daytime warmth was a delicious contrast to the cold nights.

It was not long before my long-sleeved flannel shirt was uncomfortably warm. I slipped it off allowing my bare arms to soak up the rays, and lazily stretched out on the back cockpit cushion. How strange, I thought to be lounging in the same spot where only yesterday I was clenched to the wheel during the storm. And the same cockpit enclosure that we didn't think would survive the storm now had all the plastic windows rolled up to allow the maximum breeze into the cockpit. Whoever wrote the song "What A Difference A Day Makes" must have been a sailor.

Theoretically, the entire boat could be run while sitting on the bench in back of the cockpit, and it was probably designed with that in mind. I'm equally sure it was only accidentally the most comfortable place to sunbathe, and I enjoyed the luxury of having discovered that by accident.

Tom had never seen me act so lazy and he finally said with a smile, "There're no other boats in sight, so why don't you do it right and take off your bra too?"

"Hmm," I responded, nearly half asleep, not wanting to move.

Tom was on watch for other boats while we sailed. He occupied himself with a crossword puzzle while I lounged like a lizard, lost in the pleasure of doing nothing. I woke slightly when I became aware of him opening the belt on my jeans.

"You can't get a tan with blue jeans on," he said.

"No, I guess not," I answered and allowed him to pull off my jeans.

"I think this underwear needs to go too," he said slipping it off as well.

Before I could object he had a soft terry cloth towel ready to put under me and was nibbling on my ear. The autopilot was on and he stood in the center of the cockpit with a little boy grin waiting for me to undress him. I did it slowly, one button at a time.

When neither of us was wearing anything, Tom gently guided me back down onto the soft towel. My head rested on a life preserver on the high side of the boat while one foot rested gently on a winch and I closed my eyes in delightful anticipation allowing myself to feel his every touch. His hands cupped my face and I listened to the soft slosh of water as it rushed passed the hull. It seemed to match my shallow breathing. I could feel his warm breath next to my ear just before he kissed my neck and worked slowly across to my lips. Our lips parted and we kissed — deep, warm, and wet.

For the first time in our lives, time was not our enemy. Time on the boat did not need to be parceled out into small pieces to accommodate the needs of others. There were no telephones, no work schedules, and no kids. There was not even another boat or a sign of humanity in sight. We had all the time we wanted. There was no rush at all.

The realization that it was perfectly okay to use as much of the day as we wanted to enjoy ourselves and take pleasure in each other was an amazing awareness. Time had become a new gift, one that would allow us to invest in each other's pleasure.

GETTING READY FOR THE BLUE WATER

All our laborious preparations for the trip seemed worth it on that day. We had spent almost every weekend the previous summer working on the boat. Tom sanded off all the blistered gel-coat. He replaced the fancy fold-out doors with solid two-part hatch boards. We had the compass checked and carded, and all the rigging, lights, through holes, and tubing inspected. Replacement parts were ordered for the engine, the generator, the refrigeration, and the dinghy motor. Tom ordered a heavy-weather drogue chute that we hoped we would never have to use. He ordered bright yellow, Henri Lloyd rain gear, blaze orange survival suits, and several sets of safety harnesses. We had our six-man lifeboat opened and repacked, and we mounted an EPIRB under the chart table near the hatch. We installed a man-overboard pole, and an inner-stay for a hank-on sail in the event our roller-furling jib ever gave us problems. We had Loran C for navigation, radar, an autopilot, and a single sideband radio on board. We established a long-distance telephone credit card, and a VISA account so that we would be able to draw out money and pay bills. We had complete physicals that included shots for yellow fever, typhoid and tetanus. We got fitted with new eyeglasses with extra UV protection, studied the medicines our doctor recommended we have with us, and filled our first aid kit with all the items he suggested. In short, we had prepared ourselves as thoroughly as we could.

THE EVENING SKY DANCED

Later that evening, while anchored in a cove near the canal a few miles west of Houghton, we languished in our newfound contentment, sitting topside together with our backs propped against the mast. We were at total peace, with one another and with our new lifestyle. The cool, damp evening air required that we wear jackets, and I was aware that my nose had an icy chill, but the rest of me was toasty and warm. I felt great! I breathed in the fresh smells of the water and enjoyed the soft cool breeze on my face.

We were completely alone in the cove, and the conspicuous absence of noise from people, cars or anything resembling civilization was awesome. Still, it was not that there were no sounds – just different sounds. There was the hypnotic slap of water against our hull, the buzz of nighttime insects, and the breeze tickling the trees on the nearby shore. They were good sounds, sounds we seldom heard back home.

The most spectacular event of the evening made no noise at all. The Aurora Borealis, often referred to as the Northern Lights, put on an award-winning performance. Streaks of white light shot silently across the sky as we watched, sipping our after-dinner wine. The entire sky served as a movie screen for the panoramic show that included billions of twinkling, dancing stars. The Milky Way shimmered as if several chiffon scarves were being pulled through the sky by a ballerina. Such a spectacular show deserved an audience. It was unlike anything we had ever seen from the city where only a few of the most prominent stars could be seen because of the competition from city lights. Even after going to bed I watched the stars through the hatch over our bunk and I thought about what a lucky woman I was. Not only had it been a great day, it was also an incredibly beautiful night!

PARTNERS FOREVER?

Early the next morning we sailed to Houghton/Hancock. We anchored in front of the town, took the dinghy into shore, tied it to a dock piling, and walked into town where we made a few purchases. My most exciting purchase was a camper toaster, a wire configuration that sat on a stove burner and would toast one side of four pieces of bread. When one side was toasted, the bread would have to be turned. It was not as easy to use as our old electric toaster back home, but it didn't take up much space and it would work on the boat without the need for electricity.

Our walk led us to the Soumi Restaurant/Bakery for breakfast where, from past trips, we knew we could expect Finnish charm and excellent food. Tom said his mouth watered at the thought of their big cinnamon rolls, the ones with the thick white frosting that dripped and oozed while still warm from the oven.

Three years ago we had met Kenner, the owner of the restaurant and he seemed genuinely delighted to see us again. "Can we see your boat from here?" Kenner asked then, perhaps not believing we had actually sailed there from Duluth, Minnesota.

"I think so," Tom said. "Do you want to see it?" He said he did, so Kenner, his wife,

Tom, and I walked toward the window on the waterside of his restaurant to have a look. "It's that one over there, with the two masts and the brown sail covers," Tom said, pointing in the direction of our boat.

"Oh, it looks like it's a big boat," said Kenner. "How big did you say she was?"

"Fifty feet," Tom answered, trying to disguise his bursting pride.

"Well," Kenner said with a glow, "Take a look over there, at the right. Do you see that plane anchored out there next to those two small boats?

THAT'S MY TOY!"

Tom and I admired his seaplane, knowing he had as much pride in it as we had in our boat.

We had searched long and hard for our boat, and it was not easy to find one large enough to live on yet small enough to handle by ourselves. At one point we even considered having one built for us so "we could have exactly what we wanted," but the humbling reality was that we did not know what we wanted. The more we looked, the more confused we became. Even the boat salesmen provided different advice concerning the ideal "blue water" sailboat. I learned that a "blue water" sailboat is one built well enough for heavy-duty ocean sailing as opposed to one merely suitable for day sailing. Nearly all the boats that I liked were not suitable. I looked at a boat as a floating home and evaluated it based on its maximum living comfort, while Tom's evaluations were based on safety, speed, handling, and maneuverability. At the time there did not seem to be a boat available that would meet both of our needs.

After many heated and frustrating discussions we agreed to hire a boat surveyor to help us sort through our many contradictory ideas of an ideal cruising boat. At the time, we had been looking at boats in Braintree, Massachusetts, so we made an appointment with a surveyor listed in the telephone yellow pages. We relied on him to tell us which boats were strong and seaworthy, and we valued his opinion knowing it was based on years of experience and the fact that he had no monetary motivation to recommend one boat over another. That turned out to be one of the wisest things we ever did because the surveyor helped us prioritize.

After our meeting with the surveyor we looked at boats up and down the East Coast, checked several places on the West Coast, searched the marinas in Annapolis, and even flew to Hawaii to check out a boat. There were many times when our search challenged our marriage and compatibility, but our tenacity and the adventure in our souls carried us through. After our long and detailed search, we became the euphoric owners of a 50-foot Gulfstar ketch purchased in Fort Lauderdale, Florida.

We sensed the Kenners had a spirit similar to ours, and that they were a team in everything they did. We instinctively knew it did not matter if it was a business commitment, a big social adventure, or the owning and operating of a seaplane. They were partners in all of life's experiences, and we knew they sensed those same characteristics in us, but during that last meeting I secretly wondered how much of a team we would be after living on the boat together for an extended period. Would our relationship be strong enough to endure?

We made a commitment to one another to go cruising for one full year. If either of us wanted to quit at the end of that year, then that would be the end of it. At that point we would sell the boat, be happy with our year's experience, and not place a guilt trip on the one who wanted to quit. At least that was what Tom told me, but I wondered. Would Tom really be willing to stop cruising at the end of one year? Deep down I knew it would likely be me who would want to stop, and that Tom would want to continue sailing. I wondered if he would stick to his promise, and I wondered if we would still be a team at the end of the year.

"CAN I TRUST YOU, MOM?"

After breakfast we fueled and raised our anchor and were on our way by 11 a.m. I steered while Tom tackled one of the many items on his "jobs to do" list. He kept the list on a clipboard hooked under the chart table. Each time he thought about something else that needed his attention, he wrote it down. That enabled him to select a job based on how much time he anticipated it would take, and he could use the clipboard as a reminder of the supplies he needed.

On that day he decided to take on the task of running coaxial cable through the boat for my two-meter ham radio. It required lifting floorboards to run the cable and thread it up behind the paneling and cabinets on the port side of the main cabin. While he worked, I was left alone on the wheel through the eastern end of the Keewana.

"Can I trust you, Mom?" Tom teased. "The last time you had the wheel at this end of the waterway, we went aground, remember?"

"Yes, I remember," I said with an embarrassed smile while promising to pay close attention to the red and green buoys.

I had taken the boat much too close to the side of the channel and managed to get our deep keel stuck in the mud. To get us out, Tom had to repeatedly take an anchor out to the center of the channel by dinghy. Each time we winched ourselves out a little more toward the deeper water, a process sailors call "kedging." That mishap was more than three years ago, but Tom still loved to tease me about it. Though I felt terrible about it at the time, we later realized that the whole experience had given us the opportunity to deal with a grounding that was not serious. Still, I didn't want to repeat the performance, so I used the binoculars to scan for the next set of buoys, far in advance of coming close to them.

The winds were 20 knots from the SW as we left the Keewana Canal and entered the east side of Lake Superior. We had been sailing in the canal with just the jib, but once we entered the open lake, Tom hoisted the mainsail.

"Sailing doesn't get much better than this. We're moving 8½ to 9 knots," he announced after checking the Loran C.

We had several hours of fast sailing, but by mid-afternoon the wind let up and we slowed down. Tom called the nearest marina over the VHF to reserve a slip and asked if the water was deep enough to accommodate our six-foot draft. He learned we could tie up to the gas dock when we got to the marina and another cruiser, called SNUFFY, would have our head (toilet) keys. I could see it would be well past the dinner hour before we would arrive at the marina, so I prepared our dinner while Tom sailed the boat. Once again, we ate while underway.

Soon the winds died even further. We turned on old Iron Mike, our trusty diesel engine. At 8pm cruiser SNUFFY called on the radio, asking if we were still coming. Tom assured him we were still on our way and hoped to be there soon. Time seemed to slide past a lot faster than the water was sliding under our keel. An hour later cruiser SNUFFY called us again wondering how we were doing, and I appreciated the patience in his voice. The temperature had dropped rapidly and even with a jacket on I felt chilled. Finally, at 10pm we called cruiser SNUFFY to let him know we were entering the harbor.

Some harbor! My relief at having finally arrived vanished when I saw what we had to face. The bright city lights reflected on the water around us, making it nearly impossible to pick out the navigational lights. By sheer luck we were able to steer around the large rocks at the mouth of the harbor because none of them was lit or marked. We inched our way through the entrance and once we were inside we were finally able to see a red navigational light, but no green one to indicate the width of the channel.

We used our spotlight and inched our way toward the red light. The night was dark and damp and a fog was setting in. Neither of us liked this situation. We could barely see the shadow of the large break-wall as we passed it on our way in, and we kept about six feet away from it as we inched our way forward while keeping a careful eye on our depth meter.

"What's the depth?" Tom shouted, with that tone of voice he used when he was nervous about something. He went to the bow with the spotlight in hand and scanned the water.

"Twelve feet," I said, while the boat continued to slide forward. The words barely left my mouth when the depth meter changed. "Ten feet," I shouted, then in almost the same breath I yelled, "Eight and a half feet."

"Put it in neutral," Tom screamed back to me.

I did, but the depth meter indicated smaller and smaller numbers as the boat glided forward. I just continued shouting out the depths to Tom, "Seven and a half feet," "seven feet," "six and a half feet!"

"Reverse," Tom shouted back at me. "Reverse with hard left rudder and give it some juice — we're grounded!" He was already running back to the cockpit. He grabbed the wheel and pushed me aside.

I didn't know what I was supposed to do, so I went to the bow with the spotlight. We were very close to the pier – so that in spite of the fog I was able to see the outline of someone standing on the pier with a flashlight. That person was trying to tell us something and finally, even over our engine noise, I understood him. He told us to monitor another VHF channel on low power. I put the spotlight down, went below and switched our VHF to that channel. He told us he was cruiser SNUFFY and began giving us directions, which we happily and obediently followed. He guided us past the rocks and around the sandbars. Without him we could never have entered that harbor in the dark. Even in daylight we might have had trouble.

There seemed to be so much to learn. That night we learned the value of local knowledge. Without that it is often impossible to avoid newly-formed and ever-shifting sandbars, and we learned the importance of avoiding going into a strange anchorage at night.

Once inside the marina, there were six to eight people on the gas dock, each ready to give us a hand tying up. Once our lines were secured, we introduced ourselves and thanked everyone for their help. Then we learned the cruiser SNUFFY was originally owned by the creator of the cartoon character, Snuffy Smith. The present owners, David and Amy Carter, chose to keep the boat name when they bought it. There are superstitions about changing boat names. David was a retired harbormaster and had many years of experience on several Great Lakes ships. Amy was a tiny woman who taught 5th grade, and together they lived on their boat in the harbor.

Strange lifestyle, I thought, when I learned about each of those couples living on boats. Then I had to laugh at myself because that was exactly what we were doing; VONNIE-T was our only home as well.

After much-appreciated hot marina showers, our tired bodies once again eagerly crawled into our bunks. Sleep had become a wonderful reward at the end of each day.

BLACK FLY ATTACK

By the fourth day, we had settled into somewhat of a routine. Our emotional antennas were no longer peaked for action, adventure, or lust, and we began learning to work together in small spaces. Sometimes we stumbled over one another, but mostly we enjoyed the close proximity.

What was difficult, however, was the idea of being responsible to no one but ourselves. After years of being accountable to so many others in both family and work, we found ourselves at loose ends over not having accomplished something tangible at the end of each day. Learning how to enjoy leisure was not an easy transition and we felt a sense of guilt when our only accomplishment was in putting miles under our keel.

Guilt had always played a major role in my personality. During my working years I remembered feeling guilty when I took time out of my busy day for something as pleasurable as leisure reading. To avoid guilt in those days, I limited my reading to material that was either work-related or helpful in preparing for our trip. On the boat I found reading solely for pleasure to be tainted with guilt too. I could have used a handbook to teach me the art of leisure, but of course none existed. At least none existed on the VONNIE-T.

We had been given several books as going-away gifts. All were stacked neatly on a bookshelf in the main cabin, so I selected one called *Racing Through Paradise* by William Buckley and took it topside. I made myself comfortable on a sail bag and rested my back against the mast. "With a little practice," I instructed myself, "I could get used to this."

I had just begun reading about William Buckley's Galapagos Island adventures when something bit my ankle. Without taking my eyes off the page, I brushed aside whatever it was. Then something began crawling on my neck. There was no way I could ignore that, so I looked up from my book and discovered I was covered with masses of large black flies. They were everywhere: on my jeans, on my chest, and walking down the arms of my shirt. Then I heard them buzzing angrily in my hair. Frantically, I tried to brush them off, but all my cries and body gyrations only caused them to buzz with yet more disgruntled anger. Humming, pulsating colonies – some the size of dinner plates – were quickly forming on the decks and sails. The scene could have been in a science-fiction thriller, but it was real and it made no sense. Though we were miles from land the black swarms continued to arrive from the sky.

In the cockpit, Tom swatted at them with a newspaper. "Didn't you buy some fly swatters?" he shouted at me. He killed a lot of flies with each swat, but each one left inky smudges along with yellow fly guts and blood on the white fiberglass. Yuck!

"Hurry up, I'm losing the battle," he yelled.

I found the fly swatters and quickly closed the hatches to prevent any more from invading our living quarters below decks. Tom and I joined forces, killing as many flies as we could while standing in the cockpit.

"Wow! Look at that, a triple," Tom bragged with satisfaction at having killed three flies in one swipe while millions more seethed and circled our heads.

We slapped at them as fast as we could swing our arms and soon we realized we could get more flies with less arm movement and a little more wrist action. As we gained in proficiency, the volume of fly carcasses on the cockpit floor grew. Some stuck to the sides with their squashed innards acting like glue while others fell through the grating on the floor. It was a nauseating scene, and we were demoralized by the futility of fighting a losing battle. Not only that, but we began to wonder if the dead flies would leave permanent stains on the fiberglass.

It seemed like a long day. A little after 6pm, with flies and all, we pulled into Grand Marias, Michigan. Several other boats were already tied to the large pier and we lost interest in the flies while we negotiated our way into a space barely large enough for our boat. Not until after we were completely tied up and all the fenders were in place did we realize the flies had gone. How could they have disappeared so quickly after being such beastly pests for hours?

When the people on the neighboring boats came over to meet us, they all had a good laugh when they saw the fly graveyard stuck all over the VONNIE-T. "I see you met up with our Great Lakes resident flies," they chuckled. "Nothing you can do about 'em, you know. Just have to learn to tolerate 'em," one man said. "Pesky things, though, I gotta admit that."

Folks on one of the neighboring boats told us they planed to walk "up to town for a dinner of white fish," and they invited us to join them.

"Hey, we'd like that a lot," Tom said. "Just give me a minute to put on a clean shirt."

"Oh, yeah," our new friend said. "I forgot to tell ya, you'll need to wear a shirt with a collar at this restaurant."

I had to smile. During our working lives the question would have been "Does Tom need to wear a tie?" Our new lifestyle only required a shirt with a collar.

SHIPS OF ALL SIZES CAN SINK

The next several days slipped by uneventfully. We did not have a repeat encounter with the flies, and once the dead ones had been washed off the fiberglass, the sun bleached the stains with no further effort from us. The winds remained comfortable, the harbors were well marked, and I was delighted when it appeared that life aboard VONNIE-T had the potential to continue with no new excitement.

One evening we tied up at White Fish Point, made famous by the November 1975 sinking of the 729-foot iron ore carrier the *Edmund Fitzgerald*. The lyrics of a haunting sea chantey retold the story, *"thirty men tried and thirty men died ......"* and I was once again reminded not to become complacent about our sailing life. If the *Edmund Fitzgerald* could sink in these waters, so could the VONNIE-T.

The following day we planned to go through the Sault Saint Marie Lock, which was a 20-foot drop. It's often called the "Soo" Canal and in its heyday not so many years ago, it transited more tonnage than the Panama Canal and Suez Canal combined. Iron ore was the principal cargo, and was transported from the Mesabi Range in Northern Minnesota to the Detroit steel mills to meet the demand of the automotive business.

We had planned to transit on the Canadian side, rather than go through the American lock, as we heard the Canadian lock was better equipped to handle smaller vessels. We motored into the narrow holding channel, saw the red light, and tied up in the proper place to wait our turn. While we waited a man shouted to us from across the channel.

"You over there, . . . that Canadian lock is closed. You'll have to go through on the American side, if you want to go through."

"That's just great!" I grumbled under my breath. "Now what do we do?"

"We're going to turn around," Tom said cheerfully. "It's going to take a little planning, but we can do it."

I could not imagine how we were going to turn a 50-foot boat around in that narrow channel, especially with the current that was typical around all locks. We would need to back up, and because sailboats have only one propeller they do not back up straight! Ours was no exception. VONNIE-T backed to starboard but Tom enjoyed every moment of that little challenge. He managed to turn VONNIE-T around by making our starboard reverse situation work for him instead of against him. I was impressed! We motored out of the Canadian channel and into the American lock and entered with one of the Sault Lock Tour boats.

The tour boat was packed, and I believe every pair of eyes on it watched us. Of course we stared back at them because there wasn't anything else to look at once we were in the lock, and I found it fun to speculate what each pair of eyes might be thinking:

"I wouldn't do that on a bet — too dangerous." Or, *"Oh boy, I wish I could do that someday."* Or, *"I wonder what HE did for a living in order to afford a boat like that"* (never "she" or "they," always "he"). Or, *"I wonder how they make those things go up-wind."* I knew those were thoughts among the group because we often heard similar remarks by passers-by at piers.

It was a Sunday when we arrived at the St. Mary's River which connects Lake Superior to Lake Huron. The winds were perfect for sailing so we were not surprised to see a lot of weekend day-sailors on the river. Due to the large amount of local boat traffic, we needed to stay alert, so we took turns hand-steering the boat and each did projects from our respective "jobs to do" lists when not steering. I oiled the exterior teak while Tom steered. He repaired an assortment of things while I steered.

During our working years Tom had often announced that he enjoyed repairing things. Before living on the VONNIE-T he claimed, "Boats are a fixer-upper's dream and an unhandy man's nightmare," but after living on the boat for only a few weeks the constant need to repair something had begun to take its toll on him. When things broke faster than he could keep up, he would clam up and become moody. We also began arguing about the safety harness. I wanted him to wear it when he did deck work. But not only did he think that he didn't need to wear one, he hated having me tell him what he should do. I knew the safety harness slowed his deck work and restricted his movements, but I felt the safety factor outweighed the nuisance factor. The issue became a major dispute with no apparent resolution.

We made good time that day: 6½ to 7 knots, but even with the strong and steady winds we would not arrive at our destination of Roger City until 10pm or later. I began cooking dinner early so we could eat in daylight and just as I started to rattle the pans in the galley, we heard a MAYDAY on the VHF. I stopped what I was doing to listen more carefully, thinking I had heard wrong. Tom heard it also and turned the radio up. Unfortunately, we had heard correctly. It was a Mayday from SOUTHWIND, a black-hulled Canadian sailboat that had passed us going in the opposite direction several hours earlier. We listened intently.

"What is the nature of your problem, and how may we assist you?" The Coast Guard asked the SOUTHWIND.

"I have a man overboard." There was a pause, then the man's voice cracked. "And . .

. you can't help cause he's drowned."

"Where is your location, sir, and do you wish us to assist?"

"Yes, of course. My location is by Old Fort St. Joe Point, North 46 degrees 04 minutes, by West 83 degrees 55 minutes." There was another pause, and then we heard his distressed voice add, "My God, he just went overboard and disappeared. I've looked and I've looked, but I can't find him anyplace."

An excited voice broke into the transmission. "Coast Guard Sault St. Marie, Coast Guard Sault St. Marie, this is the sailing vessel ORION. I am 10 or 15 minutes away from those coordinates. Do you wish for me to assist?"

"Roger, ORION," said the Coast Guard. "That is a roger! Proceed to those coordinates and keep your radio on channel 16."

Soon, the Coast Guard ordered other craft off channel 16 and queried the SOUTHWIND for more information such as what the man was wearing, his age, how long he had been in the water, plus identifying information about the boat. We knew survival time in water that cold was short. Tom and I had talked about it many times. My worst fear was that Tom would someday fall overboard and it would be my voice calling a MAYDAY.

We were hours away from SOUTHWIND. There was nothing we could do to help so we continued on our way while listening to channel 16. I finished making dinner and we ate in the cockpit in silence, but our food had no taste that night. Our appetites were lost in thoughts. Any words spoken by either of us would have sounded inappropriate. We sat emotionally numb, knowing a man had just drowned.

Neither of us was paying attention to the conditions around us, and it came as a surprise when we finally noticed the wind and waves had built on our stern. It was getting dark, and we were not happy about the change in weather. Without my having to say anything about a safety harness, Tom went below and put one on before going out on deck to shorten the sails. Safety was the first thing on both of our minds that night.

EXERCISING MIDWESTERN DENIAL

As the novelty of our new lifestyle wore off, we struggled with its sameness. Facing each day without having a productive purpose continued to be troublesome, and the joy of living on the boat had begun to fade. I didn't like Tom's dark moods, and I began to resent the constant motion of the boat. Once I had thought the boat motion was charming, but now it compounded the difficulty of doing even the smallest task. With so much idle time I began reminiscing about the things I missed such as comfortable chairs, soft sofas, hot showers, and also my friends, and the respect I once had. I knew those thoughts were the first signs of resentment about the present. I gave myself a scolding and tried to avoid negative thoughts by seeking to concentrate on the enjoyable aspects of boat life. I told myself it would not only be the good days, but also the not-so-good days, that would provide the memories and experiences that I would appreciate some day. Until we both totally adjusted to our new lives, I would just have to give myself regular pep talks.

The day we motored under the Detroit Bridge we were traveling at an average of six knots. Six knots is a dignified speed for a sailboat but very slow by land standards, but as we neared the bridge we saw the traffic above us was barely moving because of a morning traffic jam. With a big grin on his face, Tom said, "Look at that, will you! We're going faster than any car on that bridge!"

I smiled in acknowledgment, pleased that he was in a good mood. While I knew that my attitude still needed a lot of improvement, his was far from perfect as well. When he was not sulking or all clammed up and not talking to me, he was swearing at something he was working on or snapping orders about something that I was too inept to handle.

"I'll bet those guys are wearing neckties!" he added and shouted up to the traffic, "Hey, you guys, we have no more Mondays."

Grateful for the mood of the moment I added, "and the women are probably trussed like sausages in pantyhose." While speaking, I noted that I was slouched in my usual corner of the cockpit, not even attempting to suck in my stomach. Shoot, I did not even know that it was Monday until I heard Tom shout to the cars.

We watched humanity creep across the bridge locked in their cars and seat belts while we smugly sat in the comfort of our jeans, tennis shoes, and flannel shirts. We knew we were acting childlike and somewhat arrogantly, but we savored the moment. Neither of us wanted to acknowledge the many days we had been cold and miserable, nor the days that we lived in our foul-weather gear. In our effort to think positively we selectively chose not to ponder those times. Nor did we note the days we could not take showers, the days we barely combed our hair, or the days we wore the same dirty clothes. Neither of us mentioned the fact that Tom no longer shaved and that he had begun to look like a derelict. In true Midwestern fashion we were skilled at denying discomfort. Without ever speaking of it, we both knew it was important to focus and appreciate the days when our lives were pleasant. And, on that particular day all was well with us on VONNIE-T, and the saying of "no more mondays" took on a prophetic ring.

A COLD SPLASH

As we were about to get underway from a small marina on Lake Erie, a neighboring 38-foot Morgan returned to the pier shortly after it had set sail. We were surprised and a little concerned when we saw it return and assumed it was because of boat problems. We stopped what we were doing and walked to the end of the pier ready to assist with docking.

"We didn't expect to see you back so soon," Tom said, while catching the bowline.

"The seas are wild out there!" said the Morgan captain. "Much too high to be out on that lake today. My God, when the dog starts looking for a place to hide, you know it's plenty rough."

When the man's black Scotty knew he could safely make the leap from the boat to the pier, he jumped and was clearly happy to be off the boat just as his captain had indicated. I remembered reading someplace that "inside each of us is another person – one we wish to keep hidden, especially from ourselves" and I thought it aptly applied to this captain. He was relieved to be able to claim he returned to port because of his dog and he did not wish to acknowledge that it was he who did not want to be out sailing that day.

He was a robust man of medium height with a ruddy, weathered look and jerky mannerisms. He must have weighed well over 200 pounds which he carried mostly in his barrel chest and short, hefty arms. As he talked, his arms made staccato movements providing emphasis to his every word, and he chuckled nervously while telling us how anxious the dog was to get off the boat. We smiled knowing it accurately described *his* feelings. He talked continuously to no one in particular while securing his lines in big figure eights around the pier cleats, piling on more and more unnecessary line. Mentally, I questioned if he knew what he was doing, but who was I to judge? I was still learning what sailing was all about, myself. I was tempted to neatly coil the excess lines, but sensed he would not approve of a woman helping him.

When he and Tom had the boat secured at the pier, the captain stood up straight and took a big step backwards. I felt an adrenaline surge, knowing immediately what was going to happen but was powerless to prevent it. He didn't miss a beat in his dialogue as we watched him step out of sight and splash into the icy water.

My hand went over my mouth in an attempt to avoid laughing, but even his dog thought it was a game. He barked and wagged his tail while standing on the edge of the pier looking into the water. I knew falling into Lake Erie could be very serious! A person of his weight and build could easily have had a heart attack, and I scolded myself for having laughed. Still, it was a hilarious scene to have witnessed.

He must have gone down a long way because it took a while before he surfaced. Several people came running over when they heard the splash, so there was a lot of manpower to help Tom lift him out. He was cold, wet and embarrassed, but seemed no worse for the icy dip.

When we were sure the wet captain was all right, we got underway. True to what he said, the lake was not pleasant that day. Lake Erie is shallow by Great Lakes standards and when the weather kicks up, it develops a miserable, short and choppy wave action. The conditions were not particularly dangerous for a boat of our size, just unpleasant. In the early afternoon, fog set in adding poor visibility to our discomfort. When we could no longer see either shore, we used the radar to scan the horizon and navigated by Loran C.

We heard the sound of a distant motor and watched a small boat head toward us on the radar. It turned out to be three men in an open sport fishing boat with no radio or navigational equipment. They had become lost in the fog and asked for the direction to reach land. My God, I thought, were these guys courageous or just plain stupid to be out that far

Port Dover, a fishing community where the name Misner, my last name, is seen on the side of a major fishery.

on Lake Erie in those conditions? We pointed them in the direction of the shore. They thanked us and off they went.

PORT DOVER AND CANADIAN WATERS

Our favorite place on Lake Erie was Port Dover on the Canadian side. It was here that we were invited to dock in front of the Yacht Club on a calm, narrow river within sight of a small lift bridge that opened every half-hour. Port Dover was a sleepy fishing village where the name Misner, my last name, was visible on several large fishing boats. The dockmaster told us the Misner family owned the town. I wasn't sure what he meant by that, but I wished that I could have met one of the local Misners. In lieu of meeting them, I photographed the bold lettering "Henry H Misner, LTD." on the side of a major fishery with the Canadian flag flying proudly on top.

That evening we went out for dinner. We were encouraged to order the yellow perch and found them to be delicious. They were firm, lightly battered and had no bones — fantastic eating! We liked the fish so much that we decided to stay in Port Dover a second night so we could go to the same restaurant and eat the yellow perch again. Being able to get off the boat and go out for dinner improved my attitude immensely.

Tom appreciated the quiet water and took the opportunity to make several boat improvements. The main task was to install two sets of lazy-jacks, a system of lines that would catch the falling sails, thus making them easier to take down and prevent them from falling into the cockpit. This required me to use the electric windlass to hoist Tom up both masts so he could drill holes and mount the necessary fittings. This was not an easy job under any conditions, but the quiet harbor at least made it possible because he was able to work without being swung on a swaying moving mast.

A SHAKESPEARE RECITAL ON OUR BOAT DECK

On the eastern end of Lake Erie is the Welland Canal consisting of two sets of locks. The first set of seven locks drops from Lake Erie to Lake Ontario. The second set of seven locks goes to the upstream end of the Gulf of St. Lawrence, a direct passage to the Atlantic Ocean.

When we pulled into Port Colborne, just south of the Welland Canal, we planned to spend the night and transit the canal the next morning. The harbormaster provided detailed directions over the radio on how to get into the harbor and where to tie our boat. We followed his directions to the letter, but as we came through the cut, we still bumped and scraped along on something on the bottom. Luckily, we bounced up and over the obstacle with no serious problem.

Once in our slip and all tied up, Tom mentioned our having touched bottom at the harbor entrance to the harbormaster. The harbormaster's eyes grew large and he slapped his forehead, "Oh, yea," he said. "I keep forgetting about that sunken crib right there. We don't get many big boats, ya know. I'm real sorry bout that, cap'n."

The customs woman standing on the pier overheard the conversation. She welcomed us and explained that Port Colborne used to be lovely until two years ago when a storm destroyed it. "No one has taken the time or money to rebuild it," she said, "but you'll like the town." She recommended that we walk "uptown" along main street about four blocks for marvelous Italian food at Ralph's! She recommended the fettucine alfredo, which is one of my favorite dishes. So we walked, and we walked, and we walked perhaps four miles, not four blocks, before we found Ralph's. The old town looked depressed and unkempt. We ate our okay, but not marvelous, Italian food and walked back to the boat.

The harbormaster sauntered over to inform us that we would be required to have a third person aboard in the canal. We told him we'd heard from other boaters that three line handlers were required to come up the canal, but only two people were needed to go down the canal.

"Yea, that's true for small boats," said the harbormaster, "but I don't think that's true for a boat the size of yours. Do ya want me to call for yea?" He disappeared back into his shack and re-emerged a few minutes later. "Yep, 50 footers needs three people both ways."

"Well, what do you suggest we do?" Tom asked. "There are only two of us?"

"I don't know," he said while taking his hat off to scratch his head. "I suppose you could try to hire someone."

"What would that cost, and where would we find someone?" Tom asked.

"One of the guys in our welcoming group would do it for $100, but you'd hafta wait for two days. That's when this guy I know has his day off," he said.

We both felt a little sick to think we might have to stay a couple of days in such a depressing place. As we were standing there discussing the problem, three young people walked past. They had just come up the canal that day and were returning to their boat after having taken showers. The boat owners were going to continue sailing the next day while their cousin (their third line handler), planned to return to Toronto by bus the next morning. Imagine the coincidence!

"How would you like to go back through the canal with us?" Tom asked excitedly.

"Well," the cousin said, "I don't know. I have to be at work in Toronto tomorrow night by 7:30pm."

He seemed like a nice young man. We were trying to quickly size him up to determine how reputable a character he was, just as I'm sure he was doing the same with us. After a few minutes of small talk Tom said, "Oh, come on, we'll have breakfast ready for you and leave at whatever time you're comfortable."

"OK," he said. "Why not? I'll see you at 7:45am. Let's leave by 8am." He stuck out his hand and said, "By the way, my name is Scott."

With introductions done we each excused ourselves and went to bed early. The next morning, true to his word, Scott was at the boat at 7:45am He toured our boat, ate breakfast, and asked if his friends could have a quick tour as well. We agreed. They brought over several fenders made of plastic garbage bags filled with straw. "You'll be glad you have these in the locks," they said. "You can just give them to another boat coming through the next direction if you don't want them. That's how we got them."

"OK," Tom said. "That's great. I've just the perfect board to use as a fender board with them." He invited them to have breakfast with us as well and we got a later start than what any of us had intended.

It was at least 8:30am before we left the dock. As we motored toward the first lock. Tom tied the new fenders onto the stanchions and he dug out the old plank that had been living under a bunk in the side cabin and secured it over the fenders. All of a sudden, I understood what a fenderboard was. That entire side of the boat was protected by the fenderboard that was cushioned by the fenders. Now, wasn't he the clever one, I thought.

When we approached the first lock we were told to tie up to a holding dock while the canal accommodated several large ships coming through the locks in the opposite direction. We sat in the hot sun at that holding dock until 11am. During that time, we learned a lot about Scott. He was a charming and entertaining young man, an actor with a baby face perched on top of a 6-foot-7-inch body. He enjoyed talking and acting out even the most mundane things. Scott's present job was acting at a medieval dinner theater in Toronto.

Finally, the lockmaster called us and told us to break away from the dock quickly and follow one of the ships into the canal. We were to relay these directions to the two smaller boats tied to the holding dock behind us. One was a 30-foot sailboat, the other a 20-foot powerboat. They were to follow us into the first lock. We were all proceeding as we were told when we heard, "VONNIE-T, VONNIE-T," over the VHF radio.

Tom ran down to the radio by the chart table. "This is VONNIE-T," he said.

"VONNIE-T, there has been a change in plans. We want you and the other two boats to tie up on the 'wedge' on your port side, until further notice."

"Roger, roger," Tom answered.

Scott and I quickly scrambled to get the lines switched to the other side of the boat. We had not anticipated having to tie up outside each lock and wait. Even that would not have been so bad if we didn't need to keep switching sides and if there would have been low walls for us to tie up to. But all the holding places were designed for large ships. That meant high walls and large bollards, some of which were two feet in diameter. Already, I was appreciating having 6-foot-7-inch Scott with us. Tom and Scott, both with long legs, did all the jumping on and off the boat, climbed up the cement walls, and tied lines while I stayed at the helm and steered.

In the first lock we needed our fenders on the port side of the boat. The second lock required our lines to be changed to the starboard side. The middle locks were close together and the boats needed to go directly from one lock to the next without tying up outside. Scott correctly anticipated another long wait before we were allowed to enter that set, as each lock needed to be prepared for us before we could enter. He was a wealth of information after having gone through the locks in the opposite direction the day before.

Outside each lock, while waiting at a holding station, we were able to listen on the radio to the positioning and repositioning of the large ships coming through from the other direction.

We anticipated seeing the ships and tug boats as they came out of the upbound locks, but we did not expect the tremendous rush of water and turbulence we got from them. As the lock opened and the ships passed, VONNIE-T was thrown violently first on one side and then the other as she strained at her dock lines. Her starboard side bounced on and off the cement pier several times, while our fenders, that were intended to protect the boat from harm, jumped up and down so rapidly that they ended up sitting on the wall, thereby exposing the side of the boat with no protection. Tom, Scott and I worked frantically with our arms and our feet to keep VONNIE-T off the wall as best we could.

When we got the boat under control, we looked back at the boats behind us. The small sailboat had enough people aboard to hold it off the wall as we did, but the little powerboat was pitching in every direction imaginable and bounced several times onto the wall. The waves sloshed on all sides and it looked as if it might capsize any minute.

Luckily, the violence subsided and none of the boats was seriously damaged. However, because the small sailboat behind us did not have Channel 14 (the Canal channel) and the little powerboat had no radio at all, I felt a responsibility to report the incident. So, I did.

"VONNIE-T," answered the lockmaster, "do you or the others have damage that requires assistance."

"Negative," I answered. "Luckily we are all OK, but I just feel such poor seamanship needs to be commented upon."

Before the lockmaster could respond, the ship that had just passed denied having done any wrong. "Ma'm, I was doing as I was told — just going dead ahead at five knots. I deny having done anything wrong," said a deep and tired sounding voice of the ship captain.

I felt my face flush, but before I could say anything, we heard another voice on the radio.

"I'm afraid it was my fault," said the second male voice. He identified himself as the tug captain who sped up to go around the ship.

"Thank you for the apology," I said, feeling terribly embarrassed at having taken on two captains who do that work every day. In my haste I had forgotten that they would both be able to hear my complaint and conversation with the lockmaster.

Finally, it was our turn to enter the triple lock. All went smoothly, but ever so slowly. There was a large group of people on the observation deck at the middle lock. Scott loved an audience, so as the water filled the lock he filled his time by reciting Shakespeare. His big voice resonated with depth and drama in the lock chamber and his audience was captivated! As we rose closer to the group, he used more body, hand, and facial expressions. When we finally arrived at the same level as the group, he finished with a dramatic bow and invited them to come see him at the downtown dinner-show restaurant where he worked. The crowd loved him and clapped enthusiastically.

We knew he was enjoying himself, but we also knew he was getting nervous about how quickly time was slipping away. He began looking at his watch frequently, and we knew he was worried about getting to work on time. "When you're in a play," he explained, "you simply can't call in to say you'll be a little late."

We felt badly for him but powerless to do anything about the slow process of going through the locks. I put out a call on the two-meter radio. A fellow ham operator named Chuck answered. I asked if he could help us by finding out the bus and airplane schedule to Toronto from St. Catharine's where we would come out of the canal. He agreed to call and get the information.

Within minutes he called me back, saying, "The Gray Coach leaves every hour, 10 minutes before the hour, and you arrive at Toronto two hours later. There are no commercial flights tonight from St. Catharine's to Toronto."

It was already 5pm and we were still in the canal. Clearly, the bus would not get him there on time. "What about a private plane?" I asked Chuck. "Would that be possible and how much would it cost?"

"Hold on," Chuck answered with excitement in his voice. He enjoyed helping us with our dilemma and he knew we appreciated his efforts. He quickly made a few telephone calls and was back to me with the bad news. "Due to bad weather in Toronto, all private planes are prohibited from landing there," he said. Finally, he arranged for a taxi to meet us on the south side at the next lock. We pulled over and Scott got ready to jump off onto the pier.

"How much all the way to Toronto?" Scott shouted to the cab driver as he jumped off the boat with his overnight bag.

"Sixty-five to the airport, Seventy-five to downtown," answered the cab driver.

Tom quickly handed him a hundred-dollar bill. We thanked him for his help and good company and we wished him well.

"Well," Scott said merrily to the taxi driver, "call your company and tell 'em you're going to downtown Toronto." Off they sped, leaving the two of us to complete the last two locks alone. We did so with no problem, and we wondered if Scott made it to work with as much ease as we were able to handle the last two locks.

When we reached the last lock, the lockmaster informed us of nasty weather moving in from the direction of Toronto. He advised us not to cross the lake that night and recommended that we stay at Port De Louse, a nearby marina. I called Chuck again on the two-meter radio and asked if he would call Port De Louse to see if they could accommodate us for one night. He not only called, but he also arranged for the yacht club commodore to meet us at the pier.

The commodore was a thin, elderly man and at first I thought he was the perfect host. He helped us dock, greeted us warmly, and insisted on walking with us up to the yacht club where he bought us each a welcome drink. While Tom drank his beer and I sipped my wine, he poured out his sad divorce story. We soon realized we were expected to be his captive listeners for the night. I felt sad for him, but also disgusted at the same time. This was not what I had in mind when we set out to meet interesting people!

I HATE MY LIFE ON THE BOAT!

We woke the next morning to a cold gray Saturday. Even though it was only 24 miles across Lake Ontario to Toronto, we could not see even a hint of the Toronto skyline. The lake was gray soup! Everything seemed wrong about the day. Even the wind, though it was light, was out of the wrong direction. We knew the crossing would be mean and uncomfortable, and neither of us looked forward to it.

As a delay tactic we took a walk downtown to mail letters and postcards and call various family members in Minnesota. Since it was Saturday we reached several of our six adult children suspecting that we had gotten them out of bed. Sara and Andy were still in college and probably had not even gotten to their beds until very late. Still, it was the best time to reach them if we wanted to talk with something other than their answering machines.

We hoped that by the time all our conversations had been completed the gray storm system would have lifted and the weather would have improved. A little sunshine would have been welcome, but mostly we hoped the wind would clock around so it could work for us instead of against us. The break we hoped for did not happen, and we finally made the crossing anyway, and it wasn't as bad as we had anticipated. We had to motor all the way, but the lake was fairly flat so we were not taking water over the bow as we often had in the past. That meant the water stayed out of the cockpit and we were able to stay dry. As long as we were dry we were able to keep warm, and by then I had learned to appreciate even the simplest basics.

About half way across, we felt and heard a thump on the bottom of the boat. When we looked behind to see what had caused it, we saw a tree trunk floating by. It had to be at least 14 feet long and I shuddered at the thought of how much damage something like that could do if it spun off the top of a big wave when the seas were riled. A log that size could easily put a hole through our decks and sink us.

My stewing about the log was short-lived however, because we were soon able to see a faint outline of the large buildings in Toronto. It had been several months since we had been in a city with tall buildings and I was surprised at the excitement I felt at the mere prospect of being able to go shopping, since I had never considered myself to be a big shopper in the past.

We pulled into an incredibly beautiful harbor called Ontario Place. It is a family wonderland with a marina in the middle. The grounds were well planned and nicely kept. It offered a wide assortment of family entertainment including a water playland for young children and a six-story I-MAX screen for educational movies. We were fortunate to have been there while the Royal Canadian Ballet performed *Sleeping Beauty* at The Forum, an outside amphitheater on the grounds. The performance was marvelous and the costumes nothing short of superb.

Cruising life was again looking good to me, for I realized I would not have had the opportunity to see that impressive performance or those lovely grounds any other way. We were allowed to stay at the marina for two days, so when the sun came out the next morning bathing us in its warmth, we became motivated to tackle another major boat maintenance project on our long list.

The staysail tracks had been giving us problems. The track on the port side did not allow the car to slide, and the one on the starboard side leaked when it rained or when we took a wave over the bow. The leak was the bigger of the two problems because it leaked above the chart table near our navigational instruments. We had been putting clear plastic bags over the instruments in an effort to keep water off of them, but this made it inconvenient to use them. The problem needed to be addressed.

We started the project by first removing the large bolts from the track. Tom hammered and swore at the port track while pounding it into shape. Finally, the car on the track grudgingly slid. That took nearly an hour and during that time we had not noticed the build-up of flies. Unlike the flies we encountered before, these could not be ignored because they viciously bit at our ankles. I was kept busy with the fly swatter while Tom removed the other track. Even with fly swatter in hand, however, it was another losing war. The flies were winning again, and I wasn't sure if Tom was swearing at the track, the flies, or me.

Finally, he had both tracks ready to seal with a polysulfied sealant, a white tar-like substance that would waterproof the track and the bolts. The plan sounded simple. Tom would squirt the sealant down the holes and then drop in the bolts. I would be below in the cabin and put a washer and a nut on the end of each bolt. We planned to begin aft and work forward on each side. Then we could tighten them together as we worked. That sounded simple enough and we thought we would be done in no time at all.

But, before I saw anything, I heard Tom: "LaVonne, get up here and bring the paper towels."

When Tom called me by my name instead of "Mom," I knew it was serious. I grabbed the entire roll of towels and scrambled up on deck. When I got there, I broke out in laughter. He had white sealant smeared all over both hands, the front of his shirt, and his jeans. There was sealant on the deck and around the bolt-hole, but not a single drop in the hole where it should have been. I tore off a couple of pieces of toweling and handed them to him, but they just stuck first to one hand and then the other.

"Give me the whole God damn roll," he demanded while unwittingly spreading the stuff around even more. The sealant seemed to grow before our very eyes. Each time he slapped at a biting fly, the sticky sealant was spread around even more than before. The only way to cope with the flies was to try to ignore their bites.

Once he got most of the sticky stuff off of his hands we returned to our original plan. With renewed determination and focus, he succeeded in getting the sealant down the holes. He pushed a bolt through each hole, and then just to make sure they would never leak again, he gave each hole a couple of extra squirts. The sealant had nowhere to go but down — down to where I was looking up, trying to slip on the washer and nut. Large globs of it plopped downward, first on my hands that were in the process of putting the nut on, then down my arms, unto my upturned face and down the front of my shirt. But I didn't have any paper towels because the entire roll was up on deck with Tom. I yelled as loud as I could, "Stop! Stop squeezing that stuff and bring me the paper towels!"

Instead, I sensed he was working faster and faster. I knew he wanted to finish before the flies ate him alive. I also realized he could not hear me because I had closed all the hatches to keep the flies out. In his frantic rush to finish, he continued squirting the sealant down the holes completely oblivious to my plight. I made a feeble effort to plug the sealant holes but the stuff just oozed down my arms and more of it dripped onto my face. I pushed it off with my forearm and knew immediately that I had unwittingly mushed it into my hair. There was nothing I could do to stop it, and increasingly larger globs started plopping down onto the chart table, the sofa, and on the galley cupboards. Everything under the track holes was squirted with the thick, sticky white goo. What were at first singular globs soon began to run together into a thick long white trail.

I grabbed a cupboard door where I knew we had paper dinner napkins. That smeared sealant on the cupboard door handle as well, but the situation was so out of hand I did not even care. I wiped the thickest amount off my hands and stood on the sofa to open the side porthole closest to where Tom was working. I unscrewed the two hand-bolts on the porthole as quickly as I could, forgetting that each had a spring latch. The porthole sprung open with a powerful snap and hit the bridge of my nose with a whap! The pain was excruciating and when I yelled that time, Tom heard me and came below.

At first, everything went dark, but then I began to see bright flashing lights before my eyes. I held my aching face and nose while I whimpered, swore, and stomped my feet. I wanted to curl up in a ball and sob, but I was such a sticky mess I did not dare even sit down.

"Oh my gosh!" Tom said. "Is it your eye?"

"No, it's my nose," I sobbed.

"Let me see, do you think it's broken?" He asked and reached over to examine it.

"Don't touch it!" I snapped.

He looked at me with horror because I'd never snapped at him like that before, but then he began to laugh. "My God, look at you! You look like a white tar-baby." How dare he laugh at me! I didn't see anything funny!

He got the mineral spirits out and I reluctantly let him help me get cleaned, but I did not think he was being a bit gentle. It felt like he was cleaning me with about as much care as he would show a used paintbrush. My nose eventually stopped throbbing and I realized it was not broken. Knowing that helped me calm down, but my earlier panic began to be replaced with a deep, dark anger. In spite of my vile mood, I knew we still had to finish the job because the sealant tube had already been opened and would not keep for another day.

First, we removed the sealant from all the things on the interior of the boat before it set. Getting it off the sofa fabric was no easy matter. It seemed to just smear into an increasingly larger spot. When the interior was cleaned as well as we could manage to get it in a short time, we returned to our original job. It was still a messy task which required me to stand on various things while reaching up over my head to tighten sticky, slipping nuts. Tom, meanwhile, had to contend with flies biting his ankles during the entire process, but I could tell that he was being much more careful about the amount of sealant he sent down each hole. We were both miserable and like noble martyrs we silently did our jobs.

By the time we finished, our moods were equally dark and heavy. Our very breathing filled the air around us with a thick depressing cloud. Neither of us spoke, and we moved carefully around each other to avoid accidental touching. I felt unloved, unappreciated, and badly used, and I neither cared nor acknowledged the fact that Tom might have felt the same. I wanted him to love and comfort me. I wanted him to appreciate all that I was doing, and I wanted him to realize this was a difficult life for a woman – at least it was for this woman.

He seethed with his own anger, and I sensed he felt he had been bearing all the responsibility while I had not been pulling my fair share. I knew he still also carried the concern of what he would do with the rest of his life if we did not live and travel on the boat. We became dramatic in our efforts to maintain a stony silence, and each fueled our own slow burn, self-righteous manner, and indignant composure.

Physically, I ached all over! My hips, my nose and even the skin on my knees felt worn and raw from all the crawling around. I nursed my dark mood by telling myself I simply was not cut out for life on a boat. The job we did that day was not only messy, but it was physically hard work. I knew there were people who thrived on that sort of thing, but I was clearly not one of them!

I took a mini-shower and longed for one of those long, hot, luxurious showers that I used to take for granted when we lived in a house. I poured myself a brandy and sat on our stiff settee wishing for a soft easy chair or sofa. I took a healthy gulp and thought about the many tender and romantic evenings we used to have together sipping wine before a crackling fireplace, and I pitifully caressed those memories of the comforts and of our house. I remembered being useful back then, of looking decent with combed hair, manicured nails and fashionable clothes. I was lost not having something that I was in charge of and by not having structure in my day. I longed for almost any personal accomplishment that might give me a measure of my own self worth.

Tom, on the other hand, thrived with his new charge and the cruising environment. He had the resourcefulness and willingness to put up with all manners of danger and discomfort, and he structured each day exactly the way he wanted it. The notion of having no more Mondays provided him with satisfaction and all the self worth that he needed. While he thrived, I became increasingly depressed and each day I felt worse about myself. I missed so many things from my former life. I missed going to work each day, I missed spending time with women friends, I missed going to plays, I missed driving along a road with a beautiful view, I missed dry sheets and fresh hot towels from the dryer, but mostly I missed being in charge of things and being considered a "person-in-the-know." In contrast, I didn't know a damn thing on the boat. I was pathetic, and I did not even attempt to avoid my negative thoughts – I enjoyed my sulk and foul mood and in some ways it felt really good to feel sorry for myself. I wanted to go back home where a sissy like myself could live a comfortable life! I had had it! I hated boat life!

TRYING TO GET THAT BEAVER CLEAVER ATTITUDE

By morning my attitude had improved. Perhaps, having slept really well made the difference. In some ways, the previous day's anger had been a relief, like a volcano that needed to erupt. With the new day I was able to look at things more objectively. I hoped that with time I would toughen up and be able to do more without constantly feeling like the victim. I could almost admit to seeing humor in the previous day's fiasco, providing I didn't look at my banged up face or touch my tender, swollen nose.

Through an unspoken agreement, neither Tom nor I wanted to open emotional wounds. So rather than discuss what had happened, we spoke to one another with excessive politeness, each doing our own version of a delicate verbal dance while pretending yesterday's events had never taken place.

That afternoon we met a live-aboard family, and for some reason, perhaps because I was searching for good role models, they affected me positively. Dean and Janice were teachers who, with their three grade-school age children, spent the entire summer on their boat. They said the kids "benefited greatly." I was envious of their up-beat attitudes and admired how physically fit the entire family was. Perhaps the thing that impressed me the most was observing the children's curious minds. They had great verbal skills, and their knowledge of nature and local geography was as sophisticated as most adults I knew. The only thing that alarmed me was the parents' complacency about allowing the children to use the boat mast as a jungle gym. They let the kids crawl up and down without the use of safety harnesses and seemed oblivious to what I deemed a potential danger.

"Because the children live on the boat every summer they've learned to entertain themselves by exploring and reading," Dean told us. "They've learned how to enjoy their own company and for a few months each summer they don't miss television or friends." As teachers, he added, "We see too many kids who complain of boredom because they don't know how to enjoy their own company. We feel those children have been short-changed in their ability to learn who they are."

I could not help think that even as an adult I was not doing very well at enjoying my own company. As far as our children went, at similar ages their major interests were based on peer pressure and having trendy labels on their little rumps. I think Tom had done some soul-searching of his own because I heard him tell Dean that it bothered him to think he did not know what he was going to do with the rest of his life.

When Dean learned we planned to go through the Murray Channel the next day, he shared their experiences and provided several useful tips. He assured us the channel would be deep enough if we stayed in the center, but cautioned us to pay close attention to the navigation markers.

"Any error in judgment will put you aground," he said. "And then there is the matter of several bridges. Three long blasts on your boat horn will alert the bridge-master to raise the bridge for you. A person will come down to meet you with a metal cup on an extended wooden handle the length of a broomstick. You'll be expected to put $2 in the cup and remove your receipt."

The entire family had that sunny "Beaver Cleaver" attitude that was contagious and it fortified me with a new desire to make our cruising life together, work. It was obvious how much they enjoyed the Murray Channel and life on the boat in general, and I made a promise to myself to be more like them in the future. I suspect they had a similar impact on Tom because after having met them our life aboard the boat improved.

Our sail eastward along the Canadian side of Lake Ontario went extremely well and we found the Murray Channel to be just as interesting and picturesque as Dean promised. At each bridge someone did indeed run down to the boat and thrust a tin cup in our direction on a long wooden stick, into which we deposited our $2, and then the bridge was opened for us.

The landscape around us was green – "Jolly Green Giant" green. The lawns were neatly manicured and clipped to prevent encroachment on the narrow cement sidewalks that led to steps and screened-in porches. Shrubbery snuggled against the front of each house and majestic oaks lined the street. All the box-shaped wooden homes were painted white with the only variation being the brightly colored trim around the windows and along rooflines. Backyard gardens flourished with what looked to be tomato plants, parsley, zucchini, and pole beans. Some yards had bright pink children's bicycles lying on the grass while others had red and yellow swing sets planted securely inside white picket fences. Many had dogs stretched lazily in spots of shade, and I wondered how the families felt about the boats that went through their town. Did they wish they could go someplace or were they content with their "Norman Rockwell" lives?

At night we anchored, and I devoted the evening to "chewing the rag" with other hams in the area. During one of those evenings in the Murray Channel we were gifted with another spectacular showing of the Northern Lights, and hams all over the region compared notes on the breathtaking imagery in the sky.

CANADIAN WATERS

We continued eastward toward the St. Lawrence Seaway. The east end of Lake Ontario joins with the St. Lawrence at the Beaurnouis Lock where we met an older couple on a powerboat. Pesel was sensitive to the sun, so before entering each lock she put on a wetted gauze suit before going up on deck to hold the lines. The suit enabled her to tolerate the sun and stay cool when there was little or no breeze at the bottom of a lock chamber. She was a quiet person and only spoke to strangers with caution, but from a reserved distance I was impressed with her ingenuity.

By contrast, Marty was friendly, outgoing, and curious, especially about a sailboat with "Duluth, Minnesota" painted on its stern. First, he asked if we were *really* from Minnesota, then where we were going to spend the night. It was early in the evening and we knew we should not travel those waters after dark, so Tom told him we would either anchor or tie up on the other side of the lock.

"No, no, I will not hear of it!" Marty said with elaborate hand motions. "You must come with us and spend the night at our club."

"That would be very nice," Tom said. "How far is your club?"

"Not far," said Marty. "Can you keep up with six knots?"

"Yes," Tom said, "We can handle six knots."

"Okay then, you just follow us. Keep as close as you can so you don't cut any corners and go aground. Some places get real shallow, and fast!" Marty said.

When the lock opened, Marty pulled his boat, SHAYDA II, ahead of us and we dutifully followed. It was nearly dark when we arrived at "their club," The Royal St. Lawrence Yacht Club at Dorval, a suburb of Montreal. We were thrilled to be guests at this beautiful yacht club with its many amenities.

The next day, Marty and Pesel took us around Montreal in their car to see the sights. Part of our tour included a stop at Marty's favorite bagel shop where we watched bakers take a dozen bagels out of a brick oven in one swoop with a long wooden spatula resembling a wide boat oar.

The following day, we experienced the Montreal subway, and we were impressed with the cleanliness and the quality of the freelance musicians who played for donations. We took the subway to the Isle of St. Helen, the home of Expo 67 and the Olympic Stadium. While most of the buildings were closed, the grounds were dressed to park standards with blue flowers and cascading water fountains.

Two days was not enough time to see that city, and we promised Marty and ourselves that someday we would return. Saying goodbye to him included a promise to stay in touch through the ham radio, and he made note of my morning schedule: 7:30am on the Waterway Net, and 9am on the North Carrs Net.

While heading toward Quebec City a few days later, we had another pleasant surprise. Near Deschailliones, Quebec we were startled by whistle blasts from a large ship ahead of us. We became alarmed at first, not knowing what it meant or what impact it might have on us. But then we learned the ship was saluting a retired seaway pilot (a Captain) who had a home on the river. The response from shore was the raising of the ship's country flag on a large, land-based flagpole. While the flag was being raised, the country's national anthem reverberated across the water from huge speakers built into the steep earth riverbank. We were amazed at the pomp and circumstance. When the music stopped, Tom clapped enthusiastically and dipped our flag in salute. Next, we saw Old Glory going up the flagpole, and the Star Spangled Banner echoed majestically across the water. It caused tears to well in our eyes. That touch of home felt very good!

We entered the Quebec harbor by going through a small lock into Basin Louise. The

A lock at the entrance to Basin Louise at Quebec City allows boats the luxury of ignoring a 15-foot tide.

tides at Quebec can run as much as 15 feet, and the lock brought us up to the harbor height. Once inside the harbor we were able to tie to a dock without having to calculate the amount of slack needed in our lines to accommodate tide changes. The local people were justifiably proud of it.

Basin Louise is in an area referred to as Old Town, Quebec. French is the first language, but many people spoke English as well. The Basin Louise had been refurbished in 1984, the 400th anniversary of the founding of Quebec City by Jacques Cartier. "Jacques Cartier was Quebec Province's equivalent to our Christopher Columbus," one man explained.

In spite of our inability to speak French, most people were kind and helpful, but occasionally we met Separatists who believed Quebec should be a separate country from Canada. The Separatists refused to speak English as a matter of principle, and they demanded "Quebec Rights" which included the right to use French exclusively in the schools, on street signs, and in all of Quebec. When we had a question and accidentally asked a Separatist, "Do you speak English?" the response was always a stern-toned "non" as opposed to the non-separatists who would politely say, "only a little." We did not encounter many Separatists, but when we did their icy reception put a memorable damper on the moment.

One of the kindest men we met in Quebec was Marcel Coté, who had a cruising dream similar to ours and was preparing for an October departure. Marcel built his boat and unlike most homemade boats, his had graceful lines and a finished interior. We traded sea stories, dreams, plans and charts. He especially liked the "lazy jacks" Tom put on our boat, and took detailed notes on how to add them to his.

One evening he and his wife Suzan invited us to their condo for dinner. The condo had an impressive view overlooking Place de Paris in the center of Old Town, and we could not help notice Suzan's reluctance to give it all up. Marcel, on the other hand, was so excited about his dream of cruising that he saw none of Suzan's concerns. He told Suzan, "Sail away with me my dear, and you will never grow old." She put on a weak smile but said nothing.

The harbor, with its floating docks and close proximity to the old city offered the freedom of being able to step off the boat at will and stroll aimlessly through shops and beautiful courtyards. Each building, walkway, and café depicted old-world charm and I drank it all in. One day Tom went for a walk with me and we treated ourselves to lunch at a small café. We ordered what we thought would be a simple meal of soup and salad without having any idea how special the experience would be. First, we were invited to help ourselves to the "toast bar" which consisted of a wide assortment of bread and several large crocks of herb-flavored butter, each seasoned differently. Then we were encouraged to toast our choice of bread to the degree of brownness we wanted on a long charcoal grill. When it was toasted to perfection we buttered it with wooden spatulas from the assorted crocks of herbed butter. Of course, then we had to taste several of the herbed butters, each of which melted sinfully into the freshly grilled toast. We were stuffed when we left, and I knew both the memory and the calories from that lunch would stay with me for a long time.

Each day while in port we tried to complete at least one repair or maintenance job from Tom's clipboard repair list, and on some days, we did several. Still the list seemed to take on a life of its own. Tom would no sooner get something repaired and crossed off the list before he would have to add one or two new chores. I knew the list had begun to gnaw and nag at him when he started swearing under his breath each time he added something new. Still, I was amazed at his ability to tackle the projects whether they were plumbing, electrical or mechanical.

Each job was important, but none more important than when he tightened all the wires on our main engine. A few days earlier when we were in a narrow area with fast current, we lost our wind. But when we needed the engine, it refused to start. Luckily, just before we got pushed into a buoy, we got a gust of wind that allowed us to sail through the rest of the channel. I hated hair-raising episodes like that, and if I was going to stay on the boat with him he had to do everything he could to avoid those near misses. So, he gave all the engine wires a thorough checking and changed the filters.

Engine work was always messy and time-consuming, and I had learned to stay out of Tom's way unless he needed my help by handing him tools or supplies while he worked in our cramped engine compartment. While he worked on the engine that day, I oiled the exterior teak, and cleaned the heads, treating the toilets with hydrochloric acid. Then when it was time for me to cook, Tom had to find something else to do because his feet would have been sticking out of the engine compartment right in front of the stove. Gradually, we learned to mesh our activities and share space in a way we never needed to do in our spacious home.

THAR SHE BLOWS!

When we left Quebec City through the friendly little lock and entered the Gulf of St. Lawrence, many of the jobs on our clipboard were finally completed. It was a wonderful feeling! That evening we stopped at Tadoussac on the north shore where the Sagunay River flows into the St. Lawrence. The Sagunay is the only fjord in North America and is reported to be 600 feet deep with 400 to 800 foot mountains on each side creating a spectacular view. We were told cruise ships go up the river but we did not see any that evening.

The Sagunay, at 40 to 45 degrees Fahrenheit, is a cold tidal river all year around. Dealing with the tidal current of any river is a challenge for a sailboat, but dealing with the rip tide current was an even greater challenge. When we first read the words "rip tides" on our chart we were not sure what that meant, but when we actually encountered them there was no doubt about what they were! Rip tides are the result of two currents entering a junction from different directions. The water appeared to be boiling in the rip tides and it literally danced straight up and down, unlike the singular direction of waves.

We tied up next to a 38-foot sailboat at the Tadoussac Marina, and at first I was amazed to see seven people on board, but later we learned the boat was a sailing school. Six were students and one was the combination captain-instructor. There were no electronics on the boat, and the students, all young men, were learning to sail and navigate by charts, sextants, and stars. They planned to be back at Quebec City by Friday. This was Wednesday evening. They told us they were "two tides away from Quebec City."

"On the seaway, we never refer to how many days we are from something," the captain-instructor said. "Instead, it is a matter of how many tides we are away from something." He went on to explain how fortunate we were. The tide we needed would begin at 6:30am, while the tide they needed in order to sail in the opposite direction would begin at 12:30 midnight. The tide ran at about six knots, so going with it we would run 12 knots over the ground and against it our speed would be zero. It was perfectly logical and routine for them, but not for us. The information was new, interesting, and frightening because we recognized our lack of skill and confidence to make the tides work for us. We were barely at the stage of coping with tides so they they would not hinder us.

One of the young men expressed his surprise to find only two of us on a 50-foot boat, while they had seven on a 38-foot boat. Not knowing what to say I finally said, "Maybe more people keep your boat warmer."

"Ah yes," he laughed in the French manner of throwing his head back to get his long dark hair out of his eyes." More horses in the barn, so to speak."

We thanked them for the valuable information and wished them well on their journey. We set our alarms for 6:30am and crawled under our down quilts for the night. Actually, for the first time I had to admit that I was eager and a little excited for the next day's adventure because we anticipated seeing whales.

A different type of current is responsible for bringing whales to the Gulf of St. Lawrence. The Labrador Current flows in a continual southwesterly direction from the Arctic, and then flows into the gulf until it feels the effect of the Sagunay and the St. Lawrence. Once there, it wells up from 2000 feet, bringing nutrients from far away, and the whales that we looked forward to seeing all fed on those nutrients.

At 6:30am, after what seemed like only moments, the alarm rang. I had thought the night air was cold, but the morning air was almost freezing. My poor sore nose felt icy, and our breath was visible when we talked. There was no problem getting dressed quickly that morning. I pulled on long underwear, two pairs of socks, a wool sweater, an insulated survival suit, gloves, and a wool hat. A quick glance at the thermometer informed us that it was 42 degrees. Tom made coffee and locked the pot on the stove. I started the engine, and Tom came up to untie our lines so we could shove off from the little dock.

We were both excited about the day, knowing we would be sailing through a whale feeding area. During the months of July and August, 10 different species of whales swim up the Labrador Current to eat plankton as it flows east from the Sagunay River, and we hoped to see great blues, fins, humpbacks, and maybe, if we were very lucky, belugas.

We were told the area made its own weather because of the cold water, and not to be disappointed if we encountered heavy fog, as it was present in the area 30 to 40 percent of the time. When we saw the sun burn through the haze on the horizon, we felt luck was with us. We put our cameras in the cockpit and motored down the river, turning northeast at the last red buoy. Tom put up the sails and we turned off the engine hoping the whales would come closer if we did not make any engine noise.

We scanned the water in all directions but saw nothing but water and seagulls. Hours passed while the scenery remained the same, and we grew impatient with disappointment. Then when we least expected it, we heard a big puff of air and a short snorting sound. We turned our attention towards the sound on our starboard beam and there was a big whale! It slid back into the water for a short time and resurfaced again with a graceful dive and soft blow. It swam parallel with us, not more than 100 feet away. Then we began to see other whales near us. We knew there were some under the boat too because the depth meter that had been showing 190 feet of water for the past two hours began flashing 15 feet. The realization that we had whales only 15 feet under the boat was not something I had bargained for. Our presence did not seem to matter to them at all; if we were in their path they swam around or under us, but they did not touch us. They were gigantic, but they were also graceful and their sense of space was obvious when we saw how close these huge creatures could swim next to one another without getting in one another's way. They almost seemed polite.

They had a distinct breathing and eating pattern. They surfaced in three long graceful glides, each time producing a soft "blow" prior to sliding back into the water. They remained under water only a minute or two after each of those dives, but when they surfaced for the third time, they lifted themselves high out of the water, made a loud "blow" and dove deep. After the deep dive, we did not see that particular whale for a long time.

All the whales we saw during the first sighting were of a dark blue-gray color, and to our untrained eye, they seemed similar except for size. Our book indicated that fin whales were about 21 meters long, humpbacks were 15 meters long, and minke whales eight meters long. Still, it was difficult for us to gauge those lengths when we saw only part of the whale out of the water at any split second.

Then we saw something new. At first, I thought one of the whales had rolled over exposing its white belly, but then I realized we were looking at a white beluga whale. The belugas were smaller than the others (about four meters long) and did not seem as shy. They surfaced closer to us, and swam within a few feet under the keel of the boat! Our depth meter alarm rang several times notifying us something was so near the keel that if we had been close to shore we would have expected to go aground. They swam much too close for comfort and made me edgy.

At the height of my concern, I saw a flat spot on the water four feet from the boat. Out of the flat spot emerged a beluga whale that acted like a surfacing submarine. It was so close we could see the lines and texture of its white skin fold into ripples in front of its tail. The experience was so exciting that I actually forgot to be afraid. The belugas did not stay with us long. They swam on and went about their business of feeding, but it was exciting

On one of the few sunny days LaVonne hung hand laundry on the lifelines with the hope of it drying.

during the short time they were there.

When the wind let up, we turned on Iron Mike, our engine. The noise seemed to cause the whales to stay away from us, so we began our crossing to the south shore of the seaway. We motored for several hours, seeing little with the exception of a few orange ball floats. Knowing the floats were part of fishermen's nets, we gave them a wide berth to avoid getting the net caught in our propeller.

After the excitement of the whales, we settled into our routine of doing little projects. I did hand laundry and hung it on the lifeline on the sunny side of the boat. Tom started designing a larger cockpit table with ruler, pencil, and graph paper. We were each involved with our tasks, not anticipating any excitement when we heard a loud snort.

There was no doubt what that sound was! It was a deep "blow" from a whale and it was louder and more powerful than any previous sounds. We didn't know where the sound came from because our engine noise confused the direction of sounds, but the whale had our attention regardless of where he was. Within seconds we saw and heard it off our port bow. He was magnificently huge! He was much larger than the whales we had seen earlier and he did not appear to be the least bit concerned about the noise of our engine. He headed straight at us slipping under the water and under the boat. We turned off the engine and waited for him to resurface. Questions raced through my head. "Why was this whale by himself? Why wasn't he afraid of our engine? Did the sound of our engine anger him? Is that why he swam toward us? How close would he come? Would he touch the boat — and if he did, what would happen?"

Tom stood on the side of the boat with camera in hand. I was in the cockpit with the binoculars. We waited, expecting to see this beautiful creature surface next to the boat. Instead, we heard a loud "blow" off the stern and saw a waterspout burst from him that looked much like a fountain. He slid gently back into the water and left. We heard his "blow" and saw his spray far off in the distance later, but he never came close to us again. Apparently he just wanted to look us over, and after having done just that, he left. I doubt if either of us will ever forget that whale! He made an indelible mark on my memory helping me to realize we only borrowed a little space in his environment as we explored, while he owned it!

CHAPTER TWO

Onward to the Atlantic

THE WHALE KEPT ITS EYE FOCUSED ON CLAREMONT

Autumn was fast approaching with the temperatures dipping lower each day. This was partly because of normal seasonal changes but it was also the result of our continued northeastern direction. We sailed farther and farther north up the St. Lawrence River toward the Atlantic Ocean.

Occasionally, in the middle of the afternoon we were able to shed our mittens and hats for a short time if the sun came out. Mostly, the days were gray and the sky drizzled a chill into the air and deep into our bones, especially my arthritic joints. Each rain lasted only a short time, never long enough to wash the dirt off the decks, but long enough to make everything, including our clothing, damp.

The damp and cold were not the only unfriendly elements we experienced. The water under our keel had also become less friendly. We were getting the full motion of white caps on top of three-foot rolling waves and, as we got closer to the mouth of the seaway, I knew what we were experiencing was the first ominous taste of the North Atlantic. The current was amazingly swift and forced the brightly colored fishing floats to pull and strain at their hidden tethers. Seeing the power of that water increased my dread of facing the cold North Atlantic. Neither of us spoke of it because neither wanted to cause the other additional stress, but I knew Tom had a similar anxiety. He, of course, had the added pressure of having to make all the decisions, and I wondered if he questioned his ability to meet the challenge. It must have been worrisome.

There were no marinas that far north so we settled ourselves in fishing harbors each night. The fishermen were always kind to us and we tried to be respectful of their dock by not taking the best place. Often they insisted on putting us in what they felt was the choice location, and they helped us secure our lines knowing we were unfamiliar with their tides.

We were a novelty, and they were justifiably curious about us. They wanted to see the interior of our boat and showed particular interest in our navigational equipment. So, after we tied up to a dock, I automatically made a pot of coffee, knowing Tom would invite them on board for a tour. In spite of the language barrier we were surprised at how easy it was to communicate when everyone made an effort.

Our first experience with the seaway tides without the help of the fishermen was at a stationary pier at Sainte-Anne-des Monts off the north coast of the Gaspé Peninsula. Our tidetables indicated there would be a seven-foot tide, and Tom tied our lines with what he hoped would be enough slack to accommodate a seven-foot drop in the water. He did this by bringing the bow and stern lines 20 feet down the pier before and aft of the boat. The idea was to create a 10-to-15 degree angle with the lines from the pier. At high tide the boat floated a long distance from the pier, but a long mid-ship line made it possible for us to pull ourselves over to the pier when we wanted to get on or off the boat.

The pier we tied to that evening was a crumbling old cement wall and periodically we heard small pieces of cement splash into the water when our lines rubbed on the edge. We were already nervous about trying to deal with a seven-foot tide and we did not need the crumbling wall to add to our anxiety. With each new noise we charged up to the deck to see if it was really only another piece of crumbling cement and not a chaffed line or a pulled-out boat cleat. It caused a restless night, and Tom and I met up on deck several times during that night each with flashlights in our hands. We checked the status of the boat after every little noise because if it got loose while we were asleep we would surely have faced some degree of catastrophe. Our bunks were always cold and damp by the time we returned to them, causing us to shiver before we could get back to sleep. When morning finally arrived, we were relieved to leave that place.

We set sail for Percé, a small town at the eastern tip of the Gaspé Peninsula where we had the surprise pleasure of meeting a friendly fisherman who spoke English. Claremont was full of exciting stories and was happy to have us as his audience. He was a net fisherman who set his nets each day and when he emptied them the next morning he reset them for the following morning. The entire process took the better part of each day, depending on how full the nets were. I thought it sounded terribly boring and repetitive, not to mention backbreaking, but he did not feel that way at all. He claimed every day offered new and exciting experiences. "You just never know what will happen the next day," he said with a twinkle in his eye.

Claremont's most fascinating story had to do with a whale. While tending his nets one morning, he noticed a large whale that did not exhibit the same feeding pattern as other whales. The whale circled his boat and seemed to watch him as he worked the nets. Claremont's little fishing boat was a rough, 28-foot wooden boat held together with a few nails and many coats of paint. It would not have taken much of a nudge from a several-thousand-pound whale to make his little boat a pile of floating splinters. Claremont told us he began to be a bit concerned but didn't know what to do, so he continued pulling up the nets. Finally, he saw what the problem was. A baby whale had become trapped in his net, and when the baby whale could not escape to come up for air, it drowned. At that point, Claremont told us, he became frightened. He worked quickly to free the baby and let it fall away into the ocean and as the baby whale sank, the mother whale dove down to follow it. He said he left the rest of his nets alone that day.

"I just figured those fish could stay in the net another day," He said. "I knew that the mama whale could have given me a big bump right away when she saw me and I just didn't think I should hang around to tempt fate. You know what I mean? Anyway, I just thought it's time for old Claremont to take a day off work. So, I did!"

We listened to Claremont's stories late into the evening and when we woke the next morning we found a package, wrapped in newspaper, on the side of our boat. In it was an assortment of fish, and we knew Claremont had put it there for us to find. That evening we put together a little package of our own: a canned ham, a bottle of wine and fresh corn on the cob. We carefully placed our package on his boat, as he had done to ours, for him to find the next morning. After tending to his nets that day, he stopped by our boat to tell us about the strange little people who lived around there.

"You see," he said with a broad crooked smile, "They come out mostly at night. Yup, there are these funny little people who leave things in the night, and then ahh, it's Christmas!"

We feasted each night on the fish Claremont left for us and because we were still unfamiliar with the differences in fish, each was a pleasant experience of new taste and texture. As a home economist from the Midwest, I knew the name of every cut of meat, but I knew practically nothing about fish. Fish was simply referred to as fish when we talked about it in Minnesota. We seldom differentiated one from the other as a menu choice, and I was surprised at the differences in the color, taste, and texture of the fish flesh. Some were pure white, others were tan or light yellow, and some were even a little blue or gray in appearance. I thought all of them tasted great!

Each fish was a bit of a surprise but none was more puzzling than the dark red one that looked like old beef. Claremont told us everything in the package was fish so I did not try to second guess his word. I prepared the red fish for our dinner by frying it a few minutes as I had the others, but it didn't cook the same at all. It got tough with the fast cooking, not tender and flaky as the other fish did, and it had a strong wild flavor similar to venison. Neither of us liked it, and slowly it dawned upon us and we knew what it was. It wasn't fish at all. It was a porpoise that got caught in his nets and drowned, just like the baby whale did. It should have been cooked with slow moist heat and lots of onions or a sauce as I would have cooked a piece of venison, or better yet I should not have tried to cook it at all.

At low tide the next day we walked to Gaspé Rock on the sand bar connecting it to land. We timed our walk carefully so we would be back before the tide rose and would ultimately cover the sand bar. Ordinarily I love to go on long walks and I should have enjoyed that one too, but instead I became a worry wart who spent most of the time checking her watch. I didn't want to take a chance at spending a cold night on that island while waiting for the next low tide.

On another day we motored VONNIE-T around Bonadventure Island, which is the summer home to some 50,000 gannet birds that migrate there from the Caribbean to have their young. The gannets are large birds about the size of a duck. Their bodies are white with black tipped wings, and they all look as if they dipped their heads in a can of yellow paint. The birds have an unusual mating dance that includes fencing with their long beaks. A successful mating produces only a single egg that is turned over every 10 to 20 minutes and kept warm by the mother and father who take turns at wrapping their feet around it. Our trip around Bonadventure Island was interesting, but the noise and smell from so many birds made us happy to return to Claremont's rickety little pier.

We were surprised to see another boat on the pier when we returned. Claremont told us it was the doctor. "He's in town making his usual rounds," he said. "He comes by every couple of months, and that big dog on board protects his supplies." Claremont winked at us while going through the motions of pretending he was injecting himself with drugs. We looked at the boat and saw a large black Labrador on board. He did indeed look like an effective security system for the doctor's medical supplies.

We really enjoyed Claremont's company and realized we had bonded with him in the short time we knew him. It was a sad moment when we had to say goodbye, and this was one more aspect I found difficult about our sailing life. Claremont had moist eyes when we told him we would be leaving, but being a good strong Gaspien man, he kept a stiff upper lip. "If you wouldn't have said goodbye to other people, we would never have met," he said. "And besides, we won't be able to meet again, unless we say goodbye once." Such beautiful, uncomplicated thinking brought tears to our eyes.

SHOOT, THE SHEET WAS IN THE PROP!

It was a rare sunny day when we left, but the winds were strong: 15 to 20 knots. Our teary goodbye with Claremont caused us to get a late start, so we were actually happy to have the wind. We had a long way to go to reach a safe shelter for the night and the wind would enable a faster sail.

At first, we moved along at eight knots. Then the seas mounted and the wind clocked around 30 to 40 degrees off our bow causing us to beat hard into the wind. The seas continued to build and soon we experienced six-foot black waves with vomit-green spume flying off the top, each dropping our speed to five knots. Some winds gusted to 30 knots making our goal of crossing the Chaleur Bay before dark not likely, as we would have had to average 6 ½ to 7 knots.

Tom shortened the mainsail by reefing it, but he left the jib up, hoping the gusts would let up soon. When it became apparent that the winds were continuing to build, we knew he had to bring in the jib, a 150% roller-furler. It was a great sail under most conditions, but it was too large for the conditions we faced. Unfortunately, we had left it up longer than we should have, because we dreaded the task of rolling it in. It took the strength of a bear to bring that sail in and we did not have a winch on the furling line so it was an even tougher task. Added to the problem was the incredible sound of the wind and the crashing waves making communication between us difficult.

When it finally became apparent that we could procrastinate no longer, Tom readied himself to pull in the jib. He shouted for me to let the port jib sheet (a line fastened to the rear corner of the sail) loose, but when I tried to loosen it I discovered it was jammed. I guess he thought I didn't hear him when the sheet didn't release from the cleat, so he shouted the order at me again a little louder. Since I was downwind from him I was able to hear him easily, but of course he did not know that. Meanwhile, he couldn't hear me shout back, upwind, at him, so he kept shouting louder and louder, "Let it loose! Let it go! God damn it, let it go!"

I continued to shout back, trying to tell him I had already let the sheet go, but it had gotten caught on the roller. I worked at freeing it, but he couldn't see what I was doing, and he couldn't hear me. It was a terrible situation, and the weather was getting worse. The noise was ferocious, and we had six-foot waves crashing across the deck soaking everything in their path. Soon we were screaming at one another out of sheer frustration.

Tom was red in the face and I could see he had his jaw clenched hard. His face was scrunched, and he looked mean as he single-handedly fought the power of the jib. Finally, I got the loop knot out of the port sheet and in less than a blink, the sheet flew out of all the guides through which it had been laced. My first thought was "thank God", but almost instantly I realized a very bad thing had just happened.

The sheet I had just freed flew overboard. That was bad enough all by itself, but the wind whipped the sail with such a violent force that both jib sheets, not just the port sheet, flew out of the guides. The only good thing about the episode was that neither of us was hit with them because a loose 5/8-inch thick flying dacron rope could be as deadly as any whip. The starboard sheet flew into the air and wrapped around the shrouds. Luckily it did not break anything, and we were able to retrieve it from there, but the port sheet went overboard and sunk into the sea. Tom turned on the engine, thinking the sheet would straighten out next to the boat and then he could bring it aboard with the gaff hook. Instead, the engine killed in seconds. I did not understand what had happened, but Tom knew immediately. All the color that had been in his face drained from him, and he sat down with slow deliberate movements and said, "shit!" I knew I shouldn't say a word, so I just sat next to him waiting for my lecture about what I had done wrong. Finally he spoke. "Do you know what happened?"

"No," I said.

"We have the sheet wrapped around the propeller," he said.

I felt sick to my stomach and totally incompetent. I was sure he meant that I should have somehow been able to hold on to that sheet and not let it go overboard, but before

I could begin playing the verbal "kick me" game with myself he said, "I want you to know none of this is your fault. I shouldn't have turned on the engine and I should have had figure eight knots tied at the end of those lines. It's my fault, not yours. There was nothing you could have done differently."

I sat dumbfounded. I looked at him and saw a giant. How many men, captains if you will, would be big enough to admit errors when there was someone else available to dump on? Tom could have blamed me and I would not have known the difference, but he didn't. He had too much integrity for that. For a few moments, we ignored the seas, the wind and the unsettling noise, and took the time to hold one another and apologize for having yelled at one another. It is hard to explain, but in spite of the violent elements all around us, we experienced a few moments of peace and harmony. But we could not afford to languish in that feeling very long as we still had a big problem and it needed to be solved. Although we were a sailboat and not a powerboat, being without engine power was a serious problem because we could not trust ourselves to enter a fishing port under sail alone. Most of the ports were so small and shallow that entering them with the added maneuverability of an engine was enough challenge.

"THE DIVING SERVICE EES MY PLEASURE"

Our second concern was more immediate. If the winds continued to build, we would want to head straight into them to avoid having the boat broach or take a roll-over. But it was impossible to head into the wind under sail-power alone, especially with a jib able to function on only one tack. We tried several methods of getting the sheet off the propeller, but none of them worked. It became evident that someone would have to dive beneath the boat to untangle the thing. We had dive gear on board but our wet suits were "shorties" (short sleeves and no legs), and that water was too cold to dive in with only a "shorty."

The next logical step was to hire a diver who was equipped for the cold water. We remembered seeing a dive shop in Percé, so in spite of the hard miles we had already put in toward New Brunswick, we turned around with the intent of returning.

Once we were turned around the wind was on our back and so were the rolling, churning steely gray mounds of water. The result was a feeling of calm. The motion became more comfortable and we seemed to fly as we sliced through the top of the water. I called the Coast Guard on the VHF radio and asked them to telephone our friend Claremont and request that he find a diver for us. The Coast Guard called back, informing us that Claremont was "nowhere to be found." Neither his father nor his wife was able to locate him, but the Coast Guard kindly called the dive shop and located an English-speaking person for us.

The process took several hours, but that did not matter because we were still en route to Gaspé under sail. We had a lot of time that day. When we were six miles away, we saw the Gaspé Rock and it looked glorious in the low early evening sunshine as it glowed from under the heavy purple clouds. The wind had let up and all signs indicated a lovely evening. Soon, there was hardly enough wind to sail those last six miles, and we wondered how that could be. All day we had fought fierce winds, and when we had a diver waiting and no engine, the wind became nothing more than a soft breeze. One would have thought it was Friday the 13th.

Tom carefully trimmed the sails to capture every little puff of breeze and with great skill he managed to bring us into the Gaspé Harbor where a zodiac dinghy with a diver waited to meet us. The diver spoke only French, making communication difficult. He made up-and-down motions with his hand but we did not understand what he was trying to tell us, so we continued sailing toward shore. Again, he made an up-and-down motion with his hand. We still did not understand. Finally, he made large dramatic up-and-down motions with both arms before we understood that he wanted us to drop our sails. As soon as we had the sails down, he rolled off the zodiac and dove under the boat. It was dark by now and I felt sorry for him in the cold dark water, but he was fast and efficient. It took him only a few moments to free the line. He brought it up to us and took one more dive to check for damage on the bottom of the boat. Within minutes he resurfaced. In English, with a heavy French accent he said, "Okay, follow me." We dutifully did. He led us around the rocks and motioned for us to tie up at the main pier.

"When you ready, go restaurant — second floor," he told us in a heavy accent. Both the restaurant and dive shop were owned by a man named George Mamelont, a sophisticated, hard-working French businessman. He ran a charming restaurant and was a marvelous cook! He was also a diver and he dove early each morning for fresh lobster, sea urchins, and other items on his menu that included sea urchin soup.

When Tom and I entered his restaurant the warmth from the fireplace, the soft music, and the comfortable chairs caressed our tired bodies and battered spirits. We ordered a carafe of wine, fish chowder, and a pizza that was baked in a brick, wood-fired oven. We did not even want to think about how expensive the day would be, considering the diver, dinner, and wine. Somehow, by then it didn't matter. We were warm, safe, and finally able to relax. We paid for our dinner and asked to see George. He still had not told us what we owed him for his diver. Finally George came out of the kitchen wearing a tall chef's hat. "How did you like your meal?" He asked in perfect English.

"Oh," Tom said truthfully "It was a very fine meal!"

They chatted together for a short time, trading sea and restaurant stories. We learned of George's unique method of having lobster on his menu year around. He bought live lobsters in season for his restaurant, kept them in a large cage 50 feet underwater and fed them daily. That way he had an ample supply of fresh lobster for the restaurant long after lobster season closed. He seemed to enjoy talking with us and listened with interest about our adventures, but the evening was late and again we asked about our bill. "The diving service," he said, "ees my pleasure." What he wanted instead of money was to visit our boat the next day. We were more than happy to provide that and invited him to sail with us.

That night I snuggled very close to Tom in bed, but I can remember only about 30 seconds of his warm skin before we both fell into deep needed sleep.

The next morning George sent word that his busy schedule and the demands of the restaurant prevented him from sailing with us. Here was another kind and generous person I suspected we might never see again.

LOBSTERS, LOBSTERS AND MORE LOBSTERS

Just when we thought we had nearly everything under control, Arthur (the autopilot) pooped out and we had to take turns hand steering through the North Humberland Straits. Normally, we would have set the autopilot for a desired compass heading and through electronic wizardry, it would gently adjust the rudder to keep us on course. We fondly referred to the autopilot as Arthur because we relied upon it as we might a third crewmember. Most of the time Arthur was actually better than having a third person aboard because it did not complain, get seasick, act moody, or require food. When Arthur didn't work, however, our fond feelings for it ceased to exist and it became just another piece of bedeviling machinery. Tom placed the word "autopilot," not "Arthur," at the top of his clipboard list as one more burdensome task needing his attention.

While I prepared breakfast that morning, Tom steered the boat while struggling to look into the glare of the sun on the water. I brought him a cup of coffee and just as I was about to hand it to him I saw a stick with fisherman's floats attached to it rush past our hull. With the sun on my back it was easy for me to see the water as it passed our hull, but Tom was facing east and was blinded by the brilliance reflected on the water.

I let out a startled gasp when I saw how close we had come to it. My gasp caused Tom to jump and follow my line of vision in time to see the fisherman's float slide past our stern. I plopped the coffee cup down onto the cockpit floor next to me. This was no time to worry about coffee, and breakfast would have to wait. We cupped our hands to shield our eyes from the glare as we squinted and strained in search of more floats. Sure enough, there was a whole string of them! Most were on the surface, but some were water-logged and floating a few inches below the surface.

We figured each of the floats held nets, similar to Claremont's. He told us his nets floated eight feet under the water, were 300-feet long, and had a lead rope running through the bottom to weigh them down. While he was fastidious about keeping his nets repaired so they wouldn't be a problem for boat propellers, we could not assume all fishermen were as careful. Nor could we be sure that other fishermen's nets would be eight feet under the water. We wanted to stay as far from the fish floats as was possible so we would not foul our propeller. The sheet episode at the Gaspé had been bad enough.

We both watched the water intently, steering wide of each float, but in the process we lost our advantageous wind angle. Tom guessed one string of nets was nearly two miles long. Soon we noticed brightly colored flags in the water. Each flag was attached to a stick buoy, with an additional oval float of two or more colors that looked like large pill capsules and were attached by a thin line. Some were red and white, some yellow and green, others were orange and blue, every color combination imaginable. We had never encountered that type of buoy before.

We studied the water with binoculars and were horrified to discover these colorful obstacles were everywhere. As far as we could see there were colorful flags attached to floating sticks and two-toned buoy floats. There was no obvious way around them, so with lumps in our throats we zigzagged through them trying to allow a distance of approximately 10 feet. If anyone had tracked us on radar that day they might have thought the helmsman was drunk.

When the sun rose higher, we found it easier to see the flags, but the vast number and density of them demanded that we both stay alert. It made a long tense day, and by 6:30pm we were fatigued, irritable, and beyond the point of hunger. We headed for the leeward shore with the intent of dropping our anchor in New Brunswick for the night, but as we approached we were surprised to see what looked like a fishing harbor. We thought our eyes were deceiving us because our charts did not show a harbor in that area.

We took the sails down, turned the engine on, and motored closer to take a look. We speculated that the harbor was for shallow-draft boats and that was the reason it did not appear on our chart, so we turned away intending to find a place to anchor when a 45-foot fishing boat emerged from behind the breakwall. When the captain waved to us, I motioned for him to come over toward us. "Do you think we can tie up in there?" I shouted over the noise from our two engines.

"How deep do you need?" He shouted back with a French accent.

"Six feet."

"Ya, sure. You can fit if you keep close to wall," he said before speeding off with a goodbye wave.

His advice to stay close to the wall was not to be taken lightly. Tom inched us as close as possible while nervously watching the depth meter. The small harbor was packed with fishing boats, most of which were rafted to one another to save space. If there would have been room to turn around we would have left, but once through the mouth of the harbor there was no option but to go forward. We felt like a lobster entering a trap.

There were many people on the pier and they helped us tie up. They put us in the fish broker's spot next to the large fish scales. It was Sunday, the one day of the week when there would be no commercial fishing or buying. We would not be in anyone's way that evening.

When we were tied up, with fenders in place, I looked up at the rows of people lining the pier watching us. We were the town spectacle — the Sunday evening entertainment in a town with a population of 200. Apparently we were the first cruising yacht to have graced their harbor, and they were fascinated. They looked into the cabin through the portholes, seemingly unaware they were looking into the windows of our home. I even had to put a towel over the porthole in the head in order to use the toilet in privacy. We could hear a buzzing of French and knew they were talking about us. We knew they all wanted to come aboard but that would have been impossible. There were simply too many of them!

We were famished but it was impossible to begin dinner while being watched like an animal in a zoo. We decided to get off the boat and explore the harbor, figuring that would give the people sufficient time to gawk at the boat. We had just stepped off the boat when three fishermen walked toward us with a cardboard box. It was the same fishermen who gave us directions into the harbor. The soggy wet box held crawling, live lobsters. They were lobster fishermen! "You know how cook lobster?" one of the fishermen asked Tom. "You want these? I make gift to you." The fisherman shoved the box into Tom's hands. Tom was thrilled and thanked them, then handed the soggy, quivering box to me and suggested I take both the lobster box and the fishermen aboard to show them our boat.

I was surprised to find only one came with me. His name was Elmo, the boss. Later we realized Elmo told the other two not to come aboard, but I didn't know that at the time and asked, "Where are your friends? Tell them they are welcome to come aboard, too!"

He signaled that it was all right for his father and the hired man to come aboard. Tom provided each of them with a beer and a tour of the boat. They were mostly interested in three things:

- How much did the boat cost?
- How big and what kind of engine did we have?
- What kind of Loran C did we use?

The hired man spoke English most comfortably of the three so he did most of the talking. Elmo said very little at first, but he listened intently so we figured he understood. When he began to talk we realized he spoke English very well. He explained that each different color combination of float we saw that day was a single lobster trap, not a net. Each color combination belonged to a different lobster fisherman and they kept track of their traps by a Loran C, the same gear we used for navigation.

After sizing us up, he began telling sea stories. The story Elmo enjoyed telling most was about a fisherman he found hanging on one of his traps. His whole face became animated when he started his story: "We were out tending the traps as usual on this particular day. The seas were high and it was hard to see them things, even with our red markers. Anyways, we just motored over to trap number 82 and there was someone a hanging onto my marker. He just was a hangen on, all cold and wet — the water was cold at that time of year. I guess he was pretty happy to see us," Elmo said with a little chuckle at remembering the incident. "Anyways, we just hauled him out just like he was a lobster trap. He came up on that board and plopped down on the deck just like he was a lobster too — all wet and surprised like, only I think he was a lot happier to be on our boat than any of those lobsters are. It turned out he was one of Jake's men so I took him over to Jake's boat. He climbed onto Jake's boat while he was still dripping water from his clothes. His boots made sounds as he put his weight down on each foot. Jake was happy to see him I guess, because they was a huggen one another as soon as he climbed aboard and the tears was a rollen down their faces. Yup, it would be hard to lose a good man like that," Elmo said trying to sound more casual about the experience than what we surmised he actually felt.

We learned that the event took place nearly eight years before, but Elmo still enjoyed telling the story. After Elmo finished his story, he stood up indicating that it was time for them to go. They chugged the last of their beer and we thanked them again for the lobsters. They bid us "bon appetite." They had barelygone when two more fishermen came by to give us a mackerel. Of course we dug a few more beers out of our refrigerator, provided another tour of the boat and listened to more fishing stories.

It was 10pm before they left and, thank goodness, there were no more people on the pier. Our empty stomachs were flat against our backbones; we were famished! I cooked all 10 of the small lobsters in a pot that had previously only cooked corn on the cob. I opened a bottle of wine and we ate in pure delight and gluttony. We didn't have lobster tools aboard so we used the same pair of pliers Tom used on the engine. They worked just fine and did not detract in any way from our wonderful feast.

When we woke the next morning we were amazed to find all the fishing boats were gone. Each of them had large diesel engines, and we wondered how we could have slept through their departure without hearing them. It seemed strange to leave the harbor without saying goodbye to anyone, but at least the empty harbor provided easy maneuverability. The sun was on our backs making it easy for us to see deep into the water, thus our exit was far less stressful than our entrance.

EXPLODING GLASS

Late that afternoon, we sailed into the Summerside Yacht Club on Prince Edward Island. Again friendly people greeted us only this time everyone spoke English. I was surprised and a little embarrassed at how many people found us worthy of their interest. Perhaps they were fascinated with us because we were living their dream. Many told us they had fantasized about cruising like we were.

The people at Summerside took us under their protective wings. One man, upon learning of our broken autopilot, made every attempt to locate someone who might be able to repair it. Another took the trouble to fashion a 32-inch stick with a notch on one end that could serve as a table leg for the new cockpit table Tom had recently built. We immediately felt a warm comfortable bond with the people, especially with T.G. and Beverly Grove, musicians who lived in Summerside each summer while playing in the operetta "Anne of Green Gables." They invited us to the next performance, but with much regret we had to decline because the next performance was not for several days. With cold autumn weather nipping at our heels we knew we needed to keep moving forward. When they learned we eventually planned to stop in Halifax, they told us they lived there during the winter months when they played with the Halifax Symphony Orchestra. He played the bassoon, she the violin, and they gave us their Halifax telephone number, making us promise to call them when we arrived.

Summerside had something else that made me extremely happy — a nearby grocery store that carried fresh produce. We had been out of fresh fruit, vegetables, and milk for several days and I was eager to restock them, but I was not prepared for what happened in the grocery store. While walking down the aisle past the soda pop, one of the bottles erupted. Sticky cola sprayed all over the floor, the soda display case, and anyone near it. The glass bottle laid in several pieces on the aisle floor where I stood with my mouth open in total disbelief. Before I could compose myself a young man in a store uniform arrived carrying a mop and a bucket. He saw my confused look and said, "Oh, this happens all the time."

"But why?" I asked. "Why is the soda pop in glass bottles?"

"There's no plastic allowed on the island," he explained, knowing I was a visitor. "It's against the law to use plastic on Prince Edward Island. You see, we wouldn't have any place to put it."

"Has anyone ever been hurt from one of those bottles when they explode?" I asked.

"No, I don't think so," he said with a smile while he proceeded to mop up the mess.

At the checkout counter everything was put in brown paper bags — no plastic. I was glad I did not need to take the groceries out to the boat via a dinghy because I am sure everything would have been soggy and wet.

Many people came to the dock the next morning and each in their own way encouraged us to stay another week or so. If the weather forecast had not been so bad, we would have been tempted. But there was a nasty front moving in behind us, with predictions of 30-knot winds for the next day. If we had remained, we probably would have had to stay for several days until the front passed, and we knew at that time of year similar fronts would most likely be coming closer and closer together. The only safe thing to do was to get going!

ROCKS AHEAD!

The day of departure was gray and cold, and we dressed in our full raingear suits with plenty of warm wool clothing underneath. We wanted to leave three hours before high tide. The plan was to time our departure from Summerside to take advantage of the tidal current as we sailed toward the midway point. If we arrived at the midway point at slack tide, we could expect the reverse tide to work with us past that point. It was our Summerside friends who explained to us in great detail the importance of using the tide to work for us, yet it was they who delayed our departure by several hours mostly because they did not want us to leave.

When we finally pulled away from the dock, the winds were already stronger than predicted, and to make matters worse we were exactly two hours late to take advantage of the tide change. Our anemometer showed 20 to 25 knot winds by noon. We were four hours out when it began to rain, and from that point on it never quit! Everything on the boat became wet. Waves crashed against the bow and burst across the deck and up the front of the cockpit enclosure, before oozing through the seams and zippers of each panel. Sometimes we received an additional surprise of cold water rushing down inside our boots, especially if we found ourselves too close to the grooved track where the hatch slid and where the water found an easy path.

The winds continued to build! By 3pm we had 25-to-30 knot winds and still had a long way to go before reaching Wood Island Harbor on the southeastern end of Prince Edward Island. The rain pelted us horizontally, forcing itself through any and every opening of the boat. Tom and I were cold and we began taking turns going below in an attempt to warm up.

Tom checked the chart again looking for a closer port to duck into, but the absence of deepwater ports was discouraging. We had no alternative but to continue toward Wood Island Harbor. The current, which worked against us due to our late departure, was strong and made progress slow. Even when we turned the engine on we did not make good time.

My wet feet felt stiff and frozen in spite of having wool socks inside my rubber rain boots. My leather sailing gloves were soaked, and the joints in my hands and fingers ached. I decided my hands might actually be warmer without wet gloves, so I hung them on the compass cover to let them drip. I stuck one hand in my pocket and steered with the other. The only good thing I can say about the day was, that for some unknown reason, I did not feel seasick. Could I have finally gotten my sea legs?

But the cold, the wet, and the struggle with both high wind and strong current in unfamiliar water were almost more than we could handle. The water felt like broken, buckling cement slabs that continually slammed into our hull at evenly spaced intervals. We knew we were in trouble but we had to continue the best we could. Visibility, which had been poor all day, became worse in the darkening gloom. There were no stars or moon, and by early evening we could see the bow only faintly. We opened the front of our cockpit enclosure to try to see something ahead, but there was nothing but blackness. The open enclosure only let in more water. In some ways I felt like I was inside a washing machine with a load of dark socks. The high-pitched screech of wind as it whistled through the shrouds was shattering to our nerves. Our U.S. flag on the stern, the Canadian courtesy flag halfway up a shroud on the starboard side, and the Seven Seas Cruising pennant half way up a shroud on the port side all sounded like bullwhips as they snapped in the wind. We knew they would be torn to shreds but I did not even consider going out on deck, and I did not want Tom out there trying to rescue them either!

The wind and waves threatened our fragile existence. We worked together without complaint knowing our lives were at stake, and we were determined not to lose the battle. When we were still five miles away from Wood Island Harbor, I asked Tom to call the Coast Guard to "give them our position, just in the event that —" I couldn't bring myself to finish the sentence but he knew exactly what I meant.

"I don't want to go through all the routine questions they're required to ask," he said. We were both so tired that even the smallest task seemed monumental.

"Look," I said with more determination than I actually felt, "these are bad conditions — much worse than what was predicted — and anyway, what's wrong with answering a few routine questions?"

"All right," he said reluctantly as he went below to call. He was back in the cockpit in less than a minute.

"Well, aren't you going to call?" I asked in a demanding tone.

"I did," he said. "They didn't ask any questions at all."

"Well, what exactly did they say? Thank you for the information?" I asked in disbelief.

"Something like that," he responded and went on to take another fix on our progress.

We were barely inching our way along. We had the engine on full throttle but with the wind, waves, and current working against us we barely maintained four knots headway. It was discouraging because when each wave smacked the bow, our speed dropped even more and with each new smack it felt as if we paused momentarily on top of the wave. At that slow pace, I was afraid it might be dawn before we got to the harbor — if we got there at all. Once again, my thoughts turned dark. I was discouraged and I wanted to cry each time I got a new burst of cold salt water in my face. From there it ran down my neck and into my thermal underwear, causing my whole body to feel as if it was wrapped in a large, wet diaper. The wetness was bad enough, but the saltwater also left a scratchy residue similar to fine sandpaper on my face, my neck, and around the elastic of my panties and bra.

I began asking myself why I was battling these elements when I could have been home comfortably sitting out on the sundeck Tom had built on the back of our house. From the deck, we had a serene view overlooking Pike Lake. We used to sit there together for hours watching the families of mallard ducks walk casually across our yard and the night herons hunt in front of our house. Then my mind meandered to my colleagues at work and the person they hired to fill in for me. I wondered what would happen if I went back to work before the end of my year's leave of absence, that is, if I lived long enough to reach land. The next slap of cold water reminded me where I was and I knew I had to stop that kind of thinking if we were going to survive the night. I momentarily snapped out of my depression when Tom asked from below, "What's our speed now?"

"Four knots," I answered.

"I'll take the wheel for a while," he said. "You go get warm."

I went below and pulled off my wet gear with the intention of making myself a cup of hot cocoa. But even that was anything but simple on a boat, especially on that particular day. Salt water had oozed though portholes, hatches, and around the boot of the masts causing the sole (floor) of the boat to be slippery. Plus, the pounding of the boat caused all manner of things to emerge. Dishes, pots and pans, canned goods, and our video camera had all spilled out. For a brief second I considered trying to pick them up, but decided I would not know where to put them. I knew I needed to do a better job of securing things in the future. Meanwhile, I put water into a pot. I secured the pot by locking it in place on the gimbaled stove and lit the burner while standing at a 30-degree angle with my knees bent to absorb motion and I readied myself to duck any flying objects from our cabinets.

While the water was heating, I worked my way back toward the head. We had two heads, one port and one starboard. Two heads on a boat may be unnecessary except in bad weather conditions. I had my choice of using the one on the port side where I would have had to put my hands on the door in front of me to avoid slipping off the stool. With that option I had the problem of keeping the contents in the toilet. Or, I could use the starboard head where I would be nearly lying on my back while using it. I chose the starboard head and somehow managed to get my jeans and raingear leggings down, take care of nature's call and get all that clothing back up without falling down or hurting myself. Clearly, a woman's anatomy was not designed for sailing.

I inched my way back to the galley, carefully holding on to something with each step. I took a dirty cup out of the sink (this was not the time to worry about cleanliness), put instant cocoa in it, and poured hot water. Seeing a dirty spoon sitting in the sink, I considered giving my cocoa a quick stir but changed my mind. Stirring required two hands, which left none for hanging on. I sipped my lumpy cocoa hoping it would warm my stomach and not splash or burn me. If nothing else, the cup felt wonderfully warm in my hands.

The hours dragged on with Tom and me changing places. One toilet break, one cup of cocoa, one "fix" on where we were, then back to the wheel was the routine and, as bad as it was, it seemed almost acceptable as I became more used to it, except for the winds. They continued to increase, and we were getting gusts of 45 knots.

Finally, we could see the golden fuzzy glow on the horizon of the Wood Island Harbor ferry landing. How wonderful that soft glow looked to us! We continued toward the lights while keeping a close eye on the depth meter because our chart showed a shoal on both sides of the entrance. Finally, we found the first red buoy. It seemed dimly lit, but we thought it might just be that way because of the bad conditions. Then, we saw what looked like a green range, a pair of lights indicating the correct entrance vector.

We started motoring into what we thought was the harbor: red buoy on our starboard, green range on our port. Luckily, we also checked our way with a portable spotlight because all of a sudden we realized we were heading straight into a breakwall of large rocks! We threw the engine into reverse and gave it a shot of power. We turned just in time to miss the rocks and returned to the red buoy. We looped that buoy several times, round and round we went buying time for our hearts to stop pounding. When we finally conjured up the courage to try again we shined the spotlight toward shore in search of the harbor entrance. It looked as though we needed to enter with the green range on our starboard, but that was against all navigational protocol so I called the

Charlottetown Coast Guard. "Charlottetown Coast Guard, Charlottetown Coast Guard, Charlottetown Coast Guard, this is the sailing vessel VONNIE-T," I said into channel 16 on the VHF radio.

"VONNIE-T, this is Charlottetown Coast Guard. Switch to channel 11," a lazy male voice answered.

"VONNIE-T switching to channel 11," I answered as properly as I could. After switching channels, I said, "VONNIE-T on channel 11."

"Yes VONNIE-T," the voice said, "This is Charlottetown Coast Guard." He sounded as if I had awakened him from a nap.

"Charlottetown Coast Guard, we are a 50-foot sailboat trying to enter Wood Island Harbor, but we are confused about the entrance. It appears we are to enter with the green range on our starboard. Since this contradicts most harbor entrances, and because of the poor visibility, I wonder if you could confirm this."

"VONNIE-T, I'm not familiar with that harbor and I don't have any charts to check it on," he answered.

"Well, is there someone you could call to check with?" I pleaded. "Conditions out here are very bad and we're not sure how to enter the harbor."

"There is no one I can call," he said flatly. "The ferries don't run at this hour of night and there is no regular staff on duty at the harbor."

I was angry, but because of some stupid pride I tried not to show it. "Thank you Charlottetown Coast Guard. VONNIE-T is returning to channel 16." I responded as politely as I could, but I was burning mad at his unwillingness to even try to assist us.

I put the VHF back to channel 16 and went topside. We took one more loop around the red buoy and directed the spotlight on what we thought was the opening. We decided to inch our way forward. Eventually, we saw that the opening was indeed on the left of the range, and that there was a car on the breakwall with its high-beam lights shining on the harbor entrance trying to assist us. We crawled forward until we saw we were heading for the opening. We passed through it safely and saw the substantial rocky breakwall on both sides. What a relief! Rain and fog were so thick that we could not see things until we were nearly next to them. We couldn't see where to tie up, and nearly hit one of the big red buoys. We looped it until we could determine where to go next.

The car drove from the breakwall to another spot in the harbor. We hoped it meant we should head toward it, which is what we did. We put our fenders down, got our lines ready, and moved slowly toward the car headlight. As we neared the pier, we saw an elderly man and two young men standing in the damp of the night ready and waiting to assist us. Thank goodness they were there! Without them we could not have entered that harbor, nor could we have tied up. The winds were so strong that it took all five of us to get the boat secured. We later learned the elderly gentleman was the night watchman for the ferry service. He sat next to a telephone all night. The Coast Guard could easily have called him to ask for information. One of the young men lived with his father in the lighthouse run by the Coast Guard, so the Charlottetown Coast Guard voice could have easily called the lighthouse as well. We also learned there was no green range, that the light we thought was a range was actually something on shore and completely unrelated to the harbor.

We invited these three angels of the night on board for a beer and our sincere thanks. The old man looked at the long leap required to get on and off our boat and declined, but the two young men eagerly jumped aboard. They enjoyed looking at every inch of the boat, and before leaving, the son of the lighthouse caretaker asked if we would adopt him. He seriously wanted to go with us, and I was very tempted to invite him to take my place. If I would have had a home to return to, I think I might have done it!

Before collapsing into bed that night, I promised myself I would do two things the next morning. First, I would mop the sole of the boat with fresh water to remove the residue from the salt water in an effort to save the teak finish. Second, I would write to the Charlottetown Coast Guard to register a formal complaint of incompetence against the man on duty the evening of Wednesday, September 9, 1987.

"HE RIPPED OFF THE LEGS AND DISCARDED THE BODY."

Several days later we tied up at a small yacht club in Port Hawkesbury. The club was a sparsely furnished, wooden one-room drinking club for members who were all involved in various water sports. The grounds were overrun with weeds and tall grass, but the members compensated for the unsavory first impression with a warm and friendly welcome. They asked many questions and showed a genuine interest in our adventures, and when they returned to their homes that evening, they left the clubhouse door unlocked for our convenience so we could use the showers and bathroom. They even presented us with an honorary membership card and listed our names on their membership roster. We felt very honored!

From there we sailed through the Straights of Canso where there is a small lock that prevents the rush of high current between lower Nova Scotia and Cape Breton Island. The lock is only a 1 foot drop, making it a lot easier to pass through what otherwise would have been a difficult tidal river. We had gone through 16 different locks by then, and dropped a total of 600 feet from Lake Superior to sea level: the Sioux Saint Marie lock, seven locks at the Welland Canal between Lake Erie and Lake Ontario, seven more locks in the upper St. Lawrence River, and now the Straights of Canso.

It was nearly noon, and we stopped at Melford, Nova Scotia for fuel and ended up watching the fishermen unload their day's catch of cod, blue fish, red snapper, and queen crab. What a spectacle it was! I had never seen so many fish in one place, nor had I seen queen crabs, which are about three feet in diameter. We had eaten smaller versions of crab but we had no idea there was such a variety.

Our curiosity piqued, we purchased several queen crabs from one of the boats tied to the pier. The fisherman tried handing the crabs up to us as we stood on the pier next to his boat. Neither Tom nor I knew how to handle live crabs whose arms were nearly as long as ours, so we didn't put our hands out to receive them. When the fisherman saw this his eyes grew large with surprise. The leathery lines in his face quickly folded into deep half moons around a smile of stained and broken teeth.

Without a word spoken he stopped his work and made a spirited graceful leap up onto the pier. He took three legs of a crab in his right hand and the other three in his left. Then he knocked the front of the shell off by striking it on the cement wall next to the pier. He ripped off the legs and discarded the body into a large smelly barrel while screeching seagulls hovered overhead trying to steal what they deemed a feast. He split each of our crabs in this same way within a matter of seconds with no indication of squeamishness about tearing the appendages off a living, moving creature whose two post-like eyes rotated around to look at him while he did it. I knew I could not have done what he did, and Tom obviously couldn't have either. But once the dastardly deed was done we had no problem with the concept of cooking or eating something that had been alive only moments before.

While Tom pulled away from the fuel dock, I dug out our large pot from its resting place under the salon bunk. When I had insisted on bringing it with us, Tom had questioned the wisdom of trying to stow such a large item in our limited galley. However, it had already served us well. First, it was a corn-on-the cob pot, then in New Brunswick it was a lobster pot, and now it would serve as a crab pot. I filled it with water and locked it onto the stove with the long stainless steel stove arms. When the water came to a boil, I dropped in several legs, cooking them only a few minutes until they turned a bright red. I lifted each leg out of the water with a bottle tong and put two on each of our plates while the others stayed warm in the pot.

Tom cracked open the first one and tried to eat it while steering the boat with his knees, but we soon realized that was not going to work, so we began trading off steering while the other ate, one leg at a time. It made for a long delicious lunch! The crab was sweet and fresh, and our appetites were continually whetted as we patiently watched the other eat.

By the time we finished our long lunch we were on our way out of the protected area of Canso where we got our first glimpse of the North Atlantic. For a long while I had been dreading our entrance into that brutal ocean, and as we entered it, I immediately noticed a different wave action. The Atlantic waves were long and rolling because of the great distance they traveled. We gazed out over the ocean at miles of lumpy wet moguls built from over 2,000 miles of water with Europe someplace on the other side. The very thought sent shivers down my spine.

We rounded the last tip of Canso and I was awed at the high craggy coastline, rugged from years of being brutalized by the powerful North Atlantic. In Nova Scotia, refuge from the violent waves that pounded the coast could be found only by sailing several miles up an inlet into a harbor. Our charts indicated that those extra miles could result in an additional hour of sailing just to get in or out of an inlet.

THE SKINNY SICK SHARK

That afternoon, we entered the first of those inlets by rounding a buoy marker and sailing through a nearly invisible slit in the land with steep banks on each side. Eventually, we reached a small fishing harbor called Murphy's Cove. There was only one dock in the harbor and several fishing boats were already tied to it, so we tied to the opposite side. It was not an ideal place for us because the wind pushed us hard against the dock, but we put all our fenders out to protect the side of the boat and resigned ourselves to adjusting them every couple of hours as the tide changed.

When the fishermen saw our situation, they insisted that we move to the protected side of the dock. Tom thanked them, but said we were content to be where we were because we did not want to disrupt them in any way.

"Fishing, after all, is your livelihood, while we're sailing solely for pleasure," Tom said. Some pleasure, I thought to myself.

They were gracious hosts, however, and would hear no more about it. They jockeyed their boats around to make a favorable place for us next to one of the boats that was not scheduled to go out fishing the next morning. Our new place was ideal! Not only was it on the downwind side, but we were also tied to something that floated, which meant we did not have to concern ourselves with the rising and falling tide.

Like all fishermen, they were fascinated with our boat, so we invited them aboard and enjoyed the opportunity to become acquainted. They had a full load, 13,000 pounds of fish including three sharks, ready to sell to the broker later that afternoon. We also learned that the youngest fisherman, a skinny little man, got seasick every day. "Do either of you get seasick?" he asked.

"Tom never seems to get sick," I answered. "But I often do. I don't actually get sick, I just get feeling really rotten but I've found eating soda crackers helps."

"For the first hour of each day, I just hang on to the side and puke my guts out," he told us.

"How can you face doing that every day?" Tom asked in amazement.

"It's easy," the young fisherman answered. "Do you see the orange house over there? That's my house. Nice huh? I painted it bright so I can look at it when I'm out there. It's not finished yet, but when it is, it will be all paid for. I have a wife and two kids. Fishing is how I earn my money."

"Yes, but there must be something else you can do to earn a living. I can't imagine getting up each day knowing you're going to be sick," Tom said.

"Yea, it's tough some days," he said. "But, I'm lucky 'cause I've got an understanding boss."

The boss, a heavy set man who owned the boat just ahead of us, nodded and said, "After he gets all his puking done, he's a good worker."

We asked the boss about the five-foot shark hanging on a rope by its tail on the stern of his boat. It hung several feet above the water, exposing its fierce teeth. "Oh, that," he said, glancing at the shark. "I think that one is sick, so I don't want to sell it. We'll take it back out with us tomorrow and dump it when we're away from the harbor."

He explained they were paid only 25 cents a pound for shark, so it wasn't a large financial loss. "The only reason we bring shark in at all is because they're such a big problem to us, and we're happy to kill a few. They tear up our nets, or hang around snappin' their big old jaws when we're bringin' the nets in. We just gaff 'em and add 'em to our day's catch. But, that one there," the boss said, "I don't know about him. He just seems too skinny for his length. I think he's probably sick."

I was very impressed by the integrity of those fishermen and had never thought about what would happen should less reputable fishermen sell sick fish to a fish broker. I realize now that it would in all likelihood end up on someone's dinner table, and the unsuspecting diner would have no way of knowing what made him ill.

The fishing boats left early the next morning and we left shortly after. Our destination was Halifax, hopefully before nightfall.

TOM CAUGHT A SEAGULL ON HIS FISHING LINE

It was another of those rotten days: a gray, depressing, drizzly sky with rolling waves the color of graphite. September was much too late to be in these waters. The boat was in constant motion, up and down, back and forth with 30-knot winds on our bow. My mood, once again, became dark. I felt sorry for that young fisherman facing each miserable day of his life knowing he was going to be cold, wet, and sick because he had no alternative. But I was angry with myself because I had an alternative and did not exercise it. My resentment of life on the boat mounted each day, and I wondered why I continued to stay.

The need to hand steer had become a festering irritant as well. Actually, I was able to keep my seasickness somewhat at bay while I steered, and I guess I didn't mind the mechanics of steering as much as I hated having to tell Tom each time I needed to go below to use the head. Nothing was totally satisfactory. Every little thing irritated me, and it didn't help when the morning Dramamine began to wear off, allowing the all-too-familiar nausea to reappear. As a matter of routine I had begun putting soda crackers in a small plastic bag and slipping the bag into my jacket pocket so I could munch on them as needed like when I was pregnant and ate them to help with morning sickness. The combination of pills and crackers helped ward off some of the nausea, but still I lived on the edge of vomiting. Sometimes I wished that I could throw-up and get it over with, but at the same time I hoped I would not.

Tom was so damned cheerful! He was enthralled by the fishermen's stories and could hardly wait until we were in the open ocean so he could put out his fishing line. That irritated me too, because: (1) I did not want him to catch a fish because I did not want to cook or eat another fish. I was tired of fish! (2) I did not want to smell the thing when he pulled it out of the water. They always flopped all over the deck, leaving their slimy odor. And (3) I did not want him out on the stern deck risking his life and mine over a fish.

He was either completely unaware of how I felt or was determined to ignore my feelings because he happily chattered on about his hope of catching something with his "green artificial squid." God, just the words "green squid" nearly made me puke. "Maybe I'll catch an Atlantic blue for dinner. Would you like that, Mom?" he asked happily. I didn't answer, because the question did not deserve an answer as far as I was concerned.

We sailed all morning with no action on the fishing line. I had nearly forgotten it was out, and my mood had begun to mellow as my nausea tapered. At midday, however, the fishing reel

Tom, shown here wearing a safety harness on stern of VONNIE-T with a freshly caught Dorado fish.

sang — zeeeeeng —as it unreeled at a fast clip. I looked back to the stern of the boat in time to see Tom grab the rod out of its unattended holder.

Each time Tom caught a fish, the script was always the same. He screamed at me to slow the boat down. I bellowed back, "I'm doing the best I can." He became exhausted while fighting the fish and thinking I was not cooperating. I remained tense and nervous about the likelihood of a jibe, or worse yet, I worried that he might fall off the stern without wearing a lifeline. We both hated the script, yet we continued to play our respective roles again and again. Tom was usually so excited about landing the fish that he forgot about all the previous yelling. The incident was therefore never talked about and the problem never resolved.

What I expected to be a repeat script turned out to be entirely different that day because it wasn't a fish on his line at all. It was a seagull. The seagull must have thought the green squid lure was something good to eat and swooped down to grab it. I'm sure that was one surprised gull when he discovered the "squids" sharp hooks were planted firmly in his beak. We were surprised, too, as the seagull began flying around with the fishing lure and line attached to the rod in Tom's hand. The line continued to zeeeeeeng out faster and faster while Tom stood holding the rod, laughing. The seagull alternately dove in the water, then flew high in the air squawking loudly while trying to shake the lure out of its mouth. Each time the gull began a dive there was a little slack in the line and Tom used the opportunity to reel in several more feet. "I don't know what to do," Tom said. "If I cut the line, I lose the whole works. He can have the lure, but I don't want to give him all my line."

We hoped the gull would become tired, but he gave no indication of it. Instead, he continued squawking and flapping his wings. He flew! He dove! He flew again and dove again head first, deep into the water. Each time he surfaced, he seemed to fly again with renewed determination. Tom gained a few more feet of line before each dive, but many yards of his 20-pound test line remained in the air with the seagull.

Finally, the line broke and the gull became quiet. Tom reeled in the rest of his line and was thrilled when he realized it broke not far from the seagull and he was able to retrieve most of it. I, too, was relieved when the fiasco was over. I put us back on course and was happy not to have another fish to cook. I hoped there would be no more excitement that day, but before I could even formulate the thought we heard more squawking and screeching and looked back to see what the problem was. "Did you see that?" Tom said. "Another seagull tried to steal the lure away from the first one. What greed! No wonder they are called the "rats of the sea."

FERMENTED LAUNDRY

As we approached Halifax we contacted Halifax Traffic on the VHF radio in accordance with the directions in our chartbook. Halifax Traffic, like the Canadian Coast Guard, assists ships and boats as they enter and leave the harbor. They were very helpful. They watched us on their radar and knew our exact speed, heading, and location. They told us about navigational markers before we could see them, and, as we neared the city, they invited us to tie up at the Maritime Museum wharf where we would be allowed to stay four days without charge. They even called our friend, John Hughes, whom we had met in Montreal.

John was a BOC racer who sailed his 40-foot boat around the world in 1986. This hearty young sailor was known for having lost his mast in the South Pacific, but he never lost his confidence or his determination to finish the race. He rounded Cape Horn under a jury-rig made of spinnaker poles. I knew finishing a race would not be what I'd have been thinking about if we had lost our mast in the South Pacific!

Feeling happy and having something to look forward to had been a rare occurrence for me the past several weeks, so the feeling of happiness as we rounded the last sea buoy was memorable. As we continued heading further up the large ship channel, I knew we were heading toward a friendly harbor away from the miserable sea conditions. Halifax Harbor was notable for its World War II history. Because the outer harbor is more than a mile across, it was large enough to assemble 40 large merchant marine ships and had been used as a staging point for merchant marine supply convoys that fed the Allied effort even before the U.S. entered the war.

As we approached the pier, we saw John Hughes waving a welcome to us, as he stood in the rain waiting to help us tie up. After the boat was secure he offered to take me to a laundromat. Now that was Canadian hospitality! Most men I knew would never think of offering to take anyone to a laundromat. Only people who had sailed long distances could appreciate the need for a laundromat when coming into port.

I quickly gathered our dirty clothes. I pulled the sheets, damp from the salt air, off our bunk and stuffed them into the laundry bag with the sour towels and other items that had each acquired their own level of fermentation. I think the laundry bag should go into the trunk," I told John as I handed it to him. "It's a little ripe."

He laughed, knowing exactly what I meant. "Been there, done that!" he said.

The next day, two other fellows from Halifax Traffic stopped by to see us. One was Doug Conrad, a ham radio operator. We had never talked before, but he said he had been listening to me on the morning radio net since we were in Lake Ontario and had been following our progress. He knew all about us. "I knew you would get here eventually," Doug said, "So I just listened and waited to meet you in person."

Doug gave me a ride to one of the large grocery stores in the area, another kind act appreciated by sailors. By having access to his car I was able to buy as many heavy items as I wanted. What a pleasure not to have to base my grocery list on what we were able to carry in our arms or on our backs as we walked back to the boat.

WHALE BREATH

After completing all the basic household tasks, we called TG and Beverly Grove, whom we had met in Summerside, Prince Edward Island. They said they had been waiting for our call and arranged to pick us up the next afternoon for dinner at their home.

Their home was along the Halifax coast in an area called Duncan's Cove where winters seldom got below 40 degrees Fahrenheit because of the warming effects of the Gulf Stream. They had built several houses on their property, not unlike "The House That Jack Built." Each home was built of unpainted rough wood with the grain in a vertical direction. TG believed if wood were kept vertical it wouldn't ever need paint because the rain would be able to run down it freely. "Keep the wood grain in the same direction as it grows on the tree is what I always say, that way we can keep everything natural and maintenance free," he told us.

They lived in one house and rented the others to artists and musicians, thus making up an idyllic little artist community. Beverly told us her husband had another interesting hobby as well. "He flies a small private airplane — a two seater Piper Cub that we use to go back and forth to Prince Edward Island. We land it on the grass over there," she said pointing to a lumpy grassy field. "Sometimes it feels like the fillings are going to shake right out of my teeth when we land," she said with a wink. She loved her husband deeply and enjoyed each of his little idiosyncrasies. He was a man of many interests — an aviator, a carpenter, and a musician.

There were many aspects of Halifax that we liked. The city is clean and tidy with 18th Century buildings and dormer frame houses. It was the most pedestrian-friendly place we had ever been. The first time we walked into the city we just wanted to stand on the corner and look around, but as we did so all the cars stopped. At first we didn't know what happened, and we wondered why the traffic stopped. We looked at the cars and saw that the people in the cars were looking back at us, and slowly it dawned on us that they were waiting for us to cross the street. Wow! That would never happen in the United States.

We knew TG was itching to go sailing, so we invited Beverly and him to sail with us to Lunenberg. It would be a four-to-six hour sail but would only take an hour by car. They arranged to have their neighbors drive to Lunenberg to meet us for dinner. That way they could sail with us during the day and drive home with them that same evening.

The weather was pleasant that day. It was, in fact, a rare beautiful day. Beverly sat in the cockpit and talked with us comfortably. TG had been unusually quiet, however, and after a short time he got up and stood outside the cockpit while hanging on to one of the shrouds. I was a little uncomfortable with him standing back there, but I did not want to sound like his mother, so I avoided commenting since conditions were not threatening and he obviously preferred standing out there.

Suddenly, I heard a big "blow." Tom heard it too and we looked at the water around the boat, but before either of us could tell our guests, we heard it again. That time we ALL saw it too! It was a 40-foot whale, and he was very close to us. He dove down under the boat and surfaced on the other side. Each time that he surfaced, he "blew." When he surfaced on the downwind side of the boat we tried to get a picture. We all babbled in excited anticipation of the next time he would surface. Then we heard him on the up windside of the boat, and we got a whiff of the most God-awful smell we could ever imagine! It was whale breath. "Good God," said Tom. "Does he ever have bad breath!"

'That's what I have been smelling for the last hour," said TG. "I thought it was your toilet, or something. That's why I stood out there on the side of the boat. The smell was making me seasick." We all laughed while he came into the cockpit and found a comfortable place to sit down.

The whale stayed nearby and played with us for nearly an hour. He surfaced on one side, then up in front, behind, and then on the other side. Sometimes, he surfaced on the same side several times in a row, but we could never accurately predict where he would surface and, as a result none of us got a good picture of him in spite of the many times he showed himself. All we have are pictures of large black slicks on the surface of the water where the whale was only seconds before the shutter snapped.

When we got to Lunenberg, the Groves' friends were already at the pier waiting for us. They helped us tie up and we all walked downtown to the restaurant. It felt wonderful to be able to walk on solid ground, and the restaurant food was great. It was fun for us to hear the Groves tell their friends about the whale and the day's sail because all the little things that I had begun to take for granted sounded new and exciting when they talked about them. It was good for me to hear about the day through their stories.

WHO MOVED OUR BOAT?

It was early evening when we left the restaurant and stepped out into the chilly air. The last of the sun could be seen low on the horizon, making wonderfully long artistic shadows of the trees along the road. As we approached the pier, I looked for our boat masts but could not see them. "Tom, shouldn't we be able to see the masts from here?" I asked.

"Tom looked towards the pier. "We sure the hell should," he said.

We picked up our pace and began to half walk, half jog up the road towards the pier. Still we could not see the boat masts. As we got closer, we could see a Nova Scotia Coast Guard vessel tied to the pier where we had left our boat, but not VONNIE-T. It was nowhere in sight!

We ran to the stairs that led down to the pier and not until we were half way down could we see VONNIE-T. Someone had moved our boat forward so the Coast Guard vessel could tie up to the dock, and the hill was so steep that it completely dwarfed our masts. We were relieved to see the boat, but we were concerned that whoever moved it might not have tied it securely so we checked all the lines and re-belayed them. When the Coast Guard vessel captain saw us board the VONNIE-T after adjusting the lines he came over to express his concern. "Did the owners of this boat give you permission to get on it?" he asked us.

"We are the owners," Tom said.

"Well, who were those other people who moved the boat?" The captain asked.

"I have no idea," Tom said. "We arrived here a few hours ago, tied up where you are now, and walked into town for dinner. We were quite concerned when we didn't see our masts until we were half way down the stairs."

"Oh, I am so sorry," said the captain. "I would never have let anyone else move your boat for us. I would have anchored out. I thought they were the owners."

"Well, no harm done, I guess," said Tom trying to be good-natured about it.

"Please accept my apology and come to lunch with me tomorrow in the officers' lounge," he said. "Shall we say, 12:30?"

We agreed and said good night to him, and after saying goodbye to our friends we turned in for the night. Before falling asleep I wondered, "How long could new things keep happening to us?"

WHAT'S A LUNENBERG ELBOW?

We awoke to the sound of hammering, and Tom stood up on our bunk so he could investigate the cause of the noise by looking out of the hatch directly overhead.

"Incredible! You're not going to believe this when you see it," he said, while standing with his upper torso stuck out of the hatch. "There are two guys putting a cedar shingle roof on that run-down old building next to the pier."

The weather-beaten structure he was talking about had such a steep roof that the mere thought of being on top of it would have terrified me, and it seemed ridiculous to put a new roof on such a dilapidated building. The exterior wooden slats were exposed with no evidence of paint having ever touched them, and next to the building was scrap wood piled high in the barren yard. Even weeds were unable to grow in the hard-packed dirt, yet the two workmen seemed oblivious to those things and concentrated solely on the roof. They stood on long boards that were nailed lengthwise across the roof with their bodies nearly lying on the roof as they hammered each nail into the honey-colored cedar shingles.

We got dressed and watched them work while we ate breakfast in the cockpit, making wild guesses as to what the building might be used for. When we finished eating, we walked over with a thermos of fresh hot coffee as a friendship offering. They expressed gratitude for the coffee and said it was an ideal time for a short break, and as Tom poured each cup, we learned the building was used to build dories for fishing boats.

"Many of the larger fishing boats have at least a half dozen dories," one of the men explained.

"The dories go out with the mothership and are lowered into the water each night. There's usually several men fishing from our dories most every night. Sometimes they fish in the daytime, but mostly they fish at night 'cause they can shine a light down in the water and attract the fish to their lines. In the morning, the fishermen return to the mothership with their fish. Then, the fish are gutted and put on ice til they get to market. Sometimes, those fishermen are out there for a month or more," he explained.

"We build really solid wooden dories here," the other man boasted. "Our dories are strong and heavy — good an safe in rough weather, not tippy neither. You see, we use tree roots for the elbows in our dories. It's our Lunenberg elbows that makes 'em so strong."

"Did you say you use tree roots?" Tom asked with a puzzled look.

"Yup, just like the ones right here on this pile," he said while lifting one off the pile next to where we stood.

To our untrained eye, the pile looked like unusable tree remains that someone just piled up in an effort to clean things up. It seemed preposterous that dirty tree roots could be of any value, but we had not paid any attention to the shape of each individual piece.

"Do you see the perfect elbow?" he asked, while showing us a root with dirt still hanging on it.

"Yes," Tom said. "I can see they're elbow shaped, but I still don't understand how you use them."

"We use em for ribs to make both sides of our dories strong. The root is sawed into two-inch wide curved timbers and screwed to the sides and bottom of the dories at 16-inch intervals. You see, the tree root elbow is the perfect shape and there ain't no joint to break. They're just naturally strong!"

He held a root up and brushed off some of the dirt as he showed it to us, but when the coffee thermos was empty, we knew we needed to let them get back to work. We thanked them for our lesson on dory building and walked up to town to find a telephone. While we walked, we talked about our experience with the two men. They were intelligent, hard working men with little or no formal training, yet very set in their ways. They preferred to do things in "the good old fashioned manner" and probably learned their skills as apprentices, perhaps under a grandfather or an uncle. When Tom asked if asphalt shingles might not have been easier and cheaper than the cedar shingles, he was left speechless by their reply: "Yes, but that's not the right way to do it, now is it!"

RUMPS ALOFT

The walk was great, because the day was one of the few glorious sunny ones we had in Nova Scotia. We found a public telephone in working condition. It was graffiti free, didn't smell of urine, and still had its receiver. Even the phone book was intact – a nice contrast to many we had seen. Tom made several calls and finally located a mechanic who agreed to help him with an assortment of small engine repairs. We walked back to the boat, arriving shortly before the mechanic.

Tom removed the hatch stairs, opened both doors to the engine compartment, and the two of them spent the rest of the morning with their heads in the engine compartment while their rumps stuck out into the boat interior. That left no room for me to be down below, and I knew it was best if I just stayed out of their way. Besides, they kept themselves deep in conversation about things of which I had no interest or understanding.

At noon they were still at it, each in their awkward positions. I reminded Tom that we were expected on the Coast Guard vessel at 12:30 for lunch with the captain. "You better get ready and go," he told me. "I'll get there as soon as I can." He put the stairs back on, so I could get below and back into our cabin so I could change my clothes. I looked forward to the opportunity of getting dressed up. Dressed up by boat standards meant clean jeans, combed hair, and lipstick.

LUNCH WITH THE CAPTAIN

At 12:30, I went over to the Coast Guard vessel. Tom was still in the engine compartment with the mechanic, both covered with grease. I made apologies for Tom to the captain and explained there was a mechanic aboard our boat and Tom would join us as soon as the mechanic was finished.

The captain made no attempt to hide his annoyance that Tom wasn't there, but tried to act the part of a gentleman and suggested that one of his officers give me a tour of his ship while we waited for Tom. I smiled in agreement, feeling immediately uncomfortable with the tension of the situation. I tried to act casually and told him I would like a tour very much.

The tour turned out to be a lot more interesting than I had expected. I learned the vessel was a 200-foot Coast Guard buoy tender and its job was to check all the buoys in a given area to make sure the lights and batteries or solar device on each was functioning. Each buoy was systematically lifted out of the water and a functioning replacement put in its place.

The buoys are hoisted out of the water with a crane bolted to the deck, and it takes several men using ropes to guide it into place. A wide variety of barnacles and sea-life cling onto each as it is lifted out of the water, and the crew removes the encrustations with long-handled scrapers before power-washing the buoy. Each buoy is then given a fresh coat of paint while another crew repairs the electronics before the buoy is placed back into the water.

I hadn't realized just how cumbersome each buoy was until I saw one on deck. Each is a large, steel object, perhaps four feet in diameter and 10 feet tall, and lifting one out of the water is a big task all by itself. We had seen many since we started the trip, but I had no idea until then how much was under the water and never seen.

The tour took nearly 45 minutes and still there was no sign of Tom. Finally, I was ushered into the captain's dining room and told lunch would be served.

"We can no longer wait for your husband," the captain announced crisply.

"I understand," I said, wishing that I was not there either.

The small dinning room was handsome but smelled musty. The heavy, wooden chairs and sideboard were old with scars and scratches, but had been rubbed and highly polished, giving the entire cabin a rich, old-world look. There was freshly ironed linen on the table and heavy, high-quality silverware for three persons placed on it.

When I was seated, a young woman entered the room with our salads. The fresh green salads were crisp and topped with seasoned croutons and a light vinegar oil dressing. The salad was delicious, and I told the captain what a treat it was to have fresh lettuce since our refrigeration did not lend itself to keeping lettuce crisp. He did not seem interested in that conversation, so I tried another.

"I was surprised to see a woman on your vessel," I said. I used the word vessel because I didn't know if he considered this to be a boat or a ship. We considered anything small enough to fit on a ship to be a boat. "For some reason I thought there were only men aboard," I said.

There was no response, and I wondered if he was going to eat his entire lunch without speaking to me. Finally he said, "Yes, we have one woman aboard: the cook."

"How nice," I said, not knowing if I thought it was nice or not. I had to say something

He made no response for what seemed like several minutes. Finally, he asked, "Do you get seasick?"

This was not what I considered desirable lunch conversation, but I was so relieved to have him talk to me that I was happy to answer. "Often," I said. "Do you get seasick?" I asked in return, thinking that we finally found a topic that he wanted to discuss.

"Yes," he said. "That's because the captain's bridge is so high off the water." There was another long pause of uncomfortable silence. "Most of the men get seasick," he said. "The only one who never gets sick is the cook. I think it's because she's always down below, low in the boat where it is more stable. There is less motion in the galley area." Clearly, the galley was not where I would want to be in rough weather. The galley was exactly where I would get seasick, but I didn't think this is what he wanted to hear so I changed the subject.

"Are you married?" I asked.

"Yes," he said. "I have two young sons. One of them will start school this fall."

"It must be very difficult to be away from your family for long stretches of time when you are out to sea," I said, smiling my warmest innocent smile.

"Not really," he said. "The boys act as if they're afraid of me when I'm home." Silently, I empathized with his sons. "They're a couple of mama's boys, and I can't say I am particularly proud of them."

"They're still very young," I said. "I'm sure you'll be very proud of them someday when they're a little older." He made no response. I felt increasingly uncomfortable. Each minute, each silent second felt like an eternity!

Finally, the captain looked up from his plate. His cold brown eyes stared into mine. I was not sure what I was in for but the knot in my stomach tightened. I knew I was perspiring and hoped it didn't show. Finally, he spoke to me in a slow, low voice. It was the coldest voice I ever heard. I had never witnessed such controlled anger in a person before. I sensed that at this moment I represented every woman he ever knew, and it was clear he did not like women. "When we were first married," he said, "My wife didn't understand my job. She said she hated the sea and was afraid of it. With time she learned to respect my job. Now she understands it's necessary for me to be gone for long periods of time. Most women just don't have an appreciation for the sea. Now she has her boys, and you may believe me or not, but she doesn't need me or miss me any more than I need or miss them."

He just finished his little tirade when Tom showed up. Thank goodness, I thought! Tom was ushered to his seat. He shook hands with the captain and apologized for being late. The cook brought in the main course. The captain and Tom immediately fell into a conversation about engines, ignoring me entirely. I was grateful and ate in silence. I had never before met anyone who hated me just because I was a woman, and why, I wondered, was he irritated with me and not Tom? After all, it was Tom who was late, not me.

TOM AND THE RAW SCALLOPS

That afternoon I spent hours trying to make radio contact with our ham friends in Minnesota. I knew they were trying to do the same on their end because it was one of the prescheduled times when they patched us through the telephone system to various family members. Radio conditions were not good that day and Tom got restless watching me search through the different frequencies, so he went for a walk and let me "play radio" by myself.

He walked along the harbor front talking to people. He could hardly believe his good fortune when he was invited aboard a scallop boat that had just returned from Georges Banks. "It was a very impressive operation," Tom said later. "There were only seven men on board as crew. They had been out on Georges Banks for eight days, dragging the bottom for scallops. Some of the men talked about the gales they had. It didn't sound like it was any picnic, that's for sure."

I learned that Georges Banks was only 100 to 200 feet deep and full of marine life. The depth was suitable for dragging. We knew from our experience on Lake Erie that shallow water not only can, but often does get very choppy. "The scallop boats drag large rakes over the ocean bottom to scoop up anything of legal size while allowing the small scallops to drop back through to the ocean floor," he explained. "All seven men work continually, either pulling in and emptying the rakes or processing the scallops. The men work long, hard hours and sleep only a minimum amount of time."

"Why so few men?" I asked.

"I asked that, too," he said. "They told me they prefer it that way because they split the profits. If there were more men, the profits would need to be split further. This way everyone works hard and they know their efforts will be directly proportional to what they'll earn." I could see by the smile around his eyes that he was excited by what he learned, so I listened and let him tell me at his speed. "The inside of the boat is one big, stainless steel kitchen. It's spotlessly clean with no fish smell. You would have been impressed with it," he said. "As fast as the men pull in the scallops off the rakes, the other men open up the scallops with a heavy duty knife. The shells are thrown back overboard and the meat is washed and put into large bags. Each bag weighed about 30 pounds. As soon as the bags are filled they're immediately put into shelves in the large, walk-in refrigerators. That way each scallop is chilled within minutes of it being removed from the sea. A portly government fisheries inspector was aboard when I got there, and he was sampling from randomly selected bags."

"Do you mean he tasted them raw?"

"Yea, they all eat 'em raw," he said. "I ate some raw too."

"How did raw scallops taste?"

"OK, I guess, but I still prefer them sautéed with a little garlic and butter," he said. "But the really amazing thing," he added. "is that they had 23,000 pounds of solid scallop meat, all cleaned and ready to be sold. Those seven men did that in only eight days. They stay out until the refrigerators are full. Of course they worked damn hard, but now they will rest for several days before they go back out again." I was glad Tom enjoyed that adventure and equally happy to have missed it. Eating raw scallops was not high on my list of desired experiences.

A POLICEMAN CAME ABOARD

The next day we sailed to Liverpool, Nova Scotia. The weather gods were kind to us by providing strong, beam-reach winds. We easily made 8½ knots. The entire trip took a little over five hours. After making the turn into the fjord toward Liverpool, a school of porpoises played next to us and surfed on the waves. What could be a nicer welcome than that? We tied up to the government pier, allowing enough line to accommodate the tide. Tom wrote in the log: "Sailed 2300 nautical miles since leaving Duluth."

The next morning we awoke to rain. It rained all that day, the next day, and on the third day it was still raining. It seemed there would be no let-up and the winds were high each of those days also, although we suspected we were not getting an accurate reading from our anemometer because the wind that whistled up the fjord, between the steep land banks, would likely be different from wind out on the open ocean.

The boat was damp and cold from the back-to-back days of rain and we were both miserable! We began to worry there would be no break in the weather and winter might set in immediately following the rainy period. If the rain turned into sleet and snow, we were afraid we would not be able to make the crossing to the United States. The very thought of spending an entire winter on VONNIE-T in Liverpool, Nova Scotia was depressing.

That concern was furthered by our inability to get a marine weather report at Liverpool. Something about the way Liverpool was situated between hills created a radio vacuum from the weather station. We preferred to get our weather information firsthand, but since that was not possible, I put out a call on the ham radio for a second-hand report.

Howard Henderson responded to my call and told me he had listened to me on the radio before. He expressed an interest in meeting us and asked if I knew that my signal was weak. I acknowledged that I had been having trouble with my signal and told him that I did not understand why. That was all Howard needed to hear. He came directly over to the boat with his ham-testing equipment ready to solve the mystery of my weak signal.

Our boat antenna system at that time consisted of a set of Hustler whips mounted on the stern. The whip antenna was changed each time I used a different frequency band. Each of the antennas had been tuned in Duluth before we left, and my signal then was strong and clear. However, it had become increasingly weaker each day regardless of how well our boat batteries were charged at the time. It was a puzzle!

Finally, it dawned on us. The whips had been tuned when we were in fresh water, and as we progressed up the St. Lawrence Seaway the water became increasingly salty, thus altering the grounding conductance. Once we figured that out, Howard helped us retune them for the new saltwater environment, and we were amazed at what a big difference it made! I immediately received reports that my signal had improved. Still, we were unable to get a marine forecast because we were in some sort of radio black hole for that frequency, but I considered myself fortunate to be able to talk to the sailboat KATHLEEN, another American sailboat in Novia Scotia. They said they were several days behind us and were equally concerned about the weather, eager to move south. I talked with them daily to get their weather information, and although we never met, we became radio friends. Tom and

I appreciated the weather information, and I told them we looked forward to the day we would meet in some harbor.

With the dual purposes of occupying myself and attempting to dry out the interior of the boat during those rainy cold days, I baked and cooked everything I could in the oven. I made several batches of cookies, baked bread, and made most of our evening meals in the oven. While I baked, Tom rented VCR movies and played them through our camcorder and on our nine-inch television. He did a few inside repairs, but for the most part, we were restless and eager to get moving south. Neither of us enjoyed living like moles down in our hole.

One afternoon, we heard a knock on the hull. We were surprised there would be anyone outside standing in the rain. Tom slid the hatch back and poked his head outside. He found himself looking into the face of a uniformed policeman holding up a badge.

"May I come aboard?" he asked.

"Yes, of course," Tom said, "but what's this all about?"

The policeman slipped his shoes off and backed down our stairs. He introduced himself and held his hand out to Tom, then to me. I asked him if he would like a cup of coffee and freshly baked cookies. Tom invited him to sit down. He sat down carefully on the settee across from the cabin table, but declined the offer of coffee and cookies. He was all business and wasted no time getting to the reason for his visit.

"How well do you know the boat KATHLEEN?" he asked me.

"We've never met them," I said. "I've only talked with them on the radio. I've been getting a marine weather forecast from them each day because we can't seem to get one from here. Why do you ask?"

"Do you know where they are now?" he asked me.

"I think they are about three days behind us — at least that's what they told me. I don't think they ever did tell us the name of the harbor they're in. It didn't really matter to me because I probably wouldn't have known it anyway," I answered.

"Ah, yes! They wouldn't have told you. That's their pattern," he said. "They're wanted on drug trafficking charges. We've been trying to monitor all their conversations and when we heard them talking to you we hoped you could lead us to them."

"I can assure you we have nothing to do with the drug scene," Tom said loudly.

"I know, I know, I checked with Howard first. He told me you folks were straight as an arrow. I only hoped you could provide some information," he said. "Look, do me a favor though," he said. "The next time you have a radio contact with them, try to find out where they are. If you get any information, give me or Howard a call." He handed us his card with a local telephone number.

"I don't think I'll be having any more radio conversations with them," I said. "We don't want to be associated in any way with drugs or anyone who uses them."

"Yeah, I was afraid you were going to say that," he said and stood to leave. "Thanks for letting me come aboard," he said. "You have a nice little boat here."

He calmly shook our hands, put on his shoes and raincoat, and left. We were rattled!

Liverpool did not seem so friendly anymore and the next day we left for Shelborne, Nova Scotia. It was a cold, wet, miserable passage, but because we anticipated the worst it did not actually seem so bad.

SAILING ALL NIGHT – 250 MILES

At Shelburne, we were finally able to receive marine weather forecasts firsthand. That itself was cause for improvement in our spirits despite the lousy weather. Still, I was blue and procrastinated before getting out of my bunk each morning, dreading to face the cold, penetrating dampness of the morning air. My only luxury was to be snuggled inside my down blanket. I heard Tom up early that morning making coffee in the galley.

"Hey, you'd better get up and see this day." He said with laughter in his voice. "There's a big orange sun coming up over the horizon."

Was he teasing? Or could we really have a day of sunshine to look forward to? The mere thought of sunshine was exhilarating.

"We'd better take advantage of this break in the weather and begin our crossing," he added.

If he was telling the truth, and not teasing as he so often did, I wholeheartedly agreed. We needed to head south, and I was eager to get going in that direction. At the same time, however, I dreaded and feared making the required 250-mile crossing.

Prior to that day, we had done only what sailors refer to as "day hops", which meant we sailed during the daylight hours and stopped someplace for the night. We either tied to a dock in a marina or fishing pier, or, at the very least, we anchored someplace for the night, thus allowing us both to sleep.

We were neophytes when it came to overnight passages, which would require us to sleep in shifts while one of us sailed the boat and stayed on watch. The person on watch needed to make sure that we continued sailing on course and that there were no hazards such as other boats in our path. With our autopilot not working, it also meant either steering by hand or locking the wheel in place. Both options required paying very close attention to the compass heading and the position of the sails.

Not only were we about to make the longest passage we had ever attempted, but our route would be exposed to the rage and furry of the North Atlantic and the powerful current flowing out of the Bay of Fundy. We would be out of sight from land until we approached Provincetown, Massachusetts.

"I think we should have a big breakfast before we start," I said, "because I'm not sure if I'll be able to cook anything once we're out to sea." Tom agreed, knowing that when I became seasick I was useless. I quickly prepared a hearty breakfast of scrambled eggs, toast and fresh cantaloupe. Ironically, making toast was the most difficult of these to prepare. I used the wire camping toaster that we purchased at the beginning of our trip.

I washed the dishes after first wiping them off with a paper towel so as to use as little water as possible, and then we each took a hot mini-shower, again using a minimum amount of water. We dressed in comfortable, clean, warm clothing, knowing we would live in those clothes for the next few days and nights.

Tom appeared excited and I think he actually looked forward to the sail. He removed the sail covers, checked the lines on the deflated dinghy that we stored on deck forward of the mast, laced the halyard through the lazy-jacks, and put it on the main sail ready for hoisting. I stowed the things below and secured all the cabinet doors with small bungee cords. I wanted to avoid having things fly out of the cabinets as they did during our wild passage to Wood Island. I made sandwiches, wrapped them individually, and placed them on the top shelf of the refrigerator within easy reach.

We welcomed the friendly sun and found it not only warmed the cockpit but also our spirits. When we arrived at the ocean we discovered light winds and fairly flat seas. What a delightful surprise and contrast from the previous days!

At 9am, I went below to check into the Waterway Net on the ham radio and that morning, I filed my first "float plan." A float plan is filed verbally by boat name with the net coordinator before beginning a long passage. Once a float plan has been filed, the boat provides daily reports of its exact position (loran coordinates) and ETA (estimated time of arrival). The net coordinator keeps the phone number of a family member so if a search is required he has a way of contacting the family and requesting permission to initiate it. It was comforting to know someone would notice if we disappeared, and that they would have the authority to call the Coast Guard to provide information on where we might be found.

The net format is organized for maximum efficiency. First, a current marine weather report is provided, followed by float plans and position reports. After all the business is processed, the net coordinator then takes what is called "general traffic." During the general traffic portion, the coordinator assists individual ham stations in their quest to meet one another on a different frequency so they can converse. Lengthy individual conversations are never allowed during the net on the net frequency.

We admired the efficiency of that net and the integrity of the boaters who maintained the high standards of ham radio. Many of the participants had been cruising for years and were far more knowledgeable than we. They sounded pleasant and charming and willingly shared a wide assortment of helpful cruising information with each other. We had not met any of them in person, but hoped to. Even the most experienced among them had not sailed as far north as we were, and they seemed genuinely interested in hearing about our experiences. I was a little surprised by that because I just wanted to get into the warm waters where they were.

After the net was finished, I returned to the cockpit. So far, the morning had been comfortable and rather uneventful. We sat in our respective places adjusting to the new motions, neither of us saying anything. It wasn't like we weren't talking to each other, it was more like neither of us had anything to say. I wrote notes about our travels and did a little reading. Tom worked crossword puzzles and periodically went below to take a new Loran C fix. He wrote the Loran information in the log and placed a small X on the chart in the precise spot where we were.

There was no sight of land ahead and the outline of Nova Scotia behind us became grayer, smaller, and more difficult to see as the hours passed. By late morning, no land was visible at all. For 360 degrees, there was only slate-colored water with a light blue horizon line. There was absolutely nothing in sight, no boats and no birds. Tom and I were alone on VONNIE-T in the middle of the ocean — it was like nothing I had ever experienced before!

Sometime during midday, I brought sandwiches up into the cockpit. We ate them in silence. Eating was pleasant and it helped to pass the time, so I concentrated on making the act of eating my sandwich take as long as possible. Back in my days at the university, I remembered hearing elderly people say they had to "work at finding things to do." I was so busy in those days that I could not even relate to what they were saying, and I admit I made no effort to understand them because I thought they were rather pathetic and not worth my time. Now, I found myself one of them. My God! I was eating a sandwich just to have something to do!

After finishing our sandwiches, I suggested one of us try to take a nap since we would continue sailing through the night. Tom actually jumped when he heard my voice. For hours the only sound was the droning engine and the rush of water as it passed our hull. I guess the sound of a human voice was startling. "Sure," he said. "If you think you can sleep go right ahead. I know I can't sleep in the daytime."

I had no experience with taking naps, but I figured I would be able to sleep so long as my feet were at the same level as my head. I settled into the main cabin where Tom could wake me easily if he needed me. I yawned, closed my eyes and got as comfortable as possible on the low side of the boat. I kicked off my shoes, stretched out my legs, and waited for sleep. I put a second pillow under my head and tried again. While listening to the monotonous rush of the water under the hull I pulled the blanket up over my shoulders, took a deep breath and told myself to sleep. I did not obey. My left side felt worn out, so I sat up and plopped the pillows to the opposite end of the settee and lay on my right side. I waited but still sleep didn't come. Finally, I realized the futility of trying to sleep and went back up into the cockpit to sit with Tom.

"That was a quick nap," he said.

"I couldn't sleep," I answered.

"Oh, what happened to the feet-and-the-head-on-the-same-level theory?" he chided. The question clearly didn't deserve an answer, and since I couldn't sleep, Tom decided he would try, but he was no more successful than I. When the wind built, he got up to raise the main and yankee sails, and he set a new course, heading to take advantage of the wind. As the winds increased, so did the height of the waves.

Because of the Bay of Fundy tidal current, which is caused by the gravitational effect of the moon pulling masses of water up into the bay, we were experiencing slippage to port and had to set our course heading to compensate for it. Water, I learned, tries to follow the moon, and when it reaches the throat of the Fundy, there is nowhere for it to go but up. That "up" in Fundy means a vertical rise of 35-feet, and when that water ebbs back to sea, a troublesome current forms. The Loran C, however, kept us well informed of where we were, and Tom carefully charted each new position, adjusting our course to compensate for our slippage.

By late afternoon, clouds began forming in the sky, and we saw less and less of the sun as the cover became thicker. Finally, the sun disappeared completely and the sky looked dark and unfriendly. By early evening, a fine mist fell giving the air its all-too-familiar chilling dampness. Soon, a cold, black uninvited night arrived. Again, there were no stars and no moon, only darkness all around us.

I insisted that we shorten sail for the night. To keep peace with me, Tom put a reef in the main and rolled in the jib half way. He turned on the running lights and put on another layer of warm clothes and suggested that I try to rest while he took the first watch. I took a seasick pill, wrapped my fully clothed body, shoes and all, into a wool blanket and lay down once again in the main cabin. I had a fretful sleep, but I did sleep and was surprised when I felt Tom's hand pat me on the leg.

"You need to take over," he said. "I can't stay awake any more." He kissed me with icy lips. Not only was he tired, he was cold!

"OK," I said. "Give me a minute in the head and I'll be right up." I worked my way back to the toilet, heated water for hot cocoa and began the laborious task of putting on my Mustang survival suit. It was a big, blaze-orange bulky one-piece suit with zippers, Velcro flaps, and built-in floatation. I hated the struggle of getting into it, but I knew it would keep me warm. By the time I got the suit on I had worked up such a sweat I wasn't sure I wanted the hot cocoa any more. The water was ready, however, so I made a cup and climbed up the ladder into the cockpit. The icy, damp air swept across my face, and the reality of how miserable the night had become was a shock. "My God, I can't see a thing up here!" I blurted out, while struggling to get over the hatch boards that were up in case we took a big wave into the cockpit.

"Yeah, it's soupy all right. You'll need to check the radar every 20 minutes," Tom said.

He handed me a small pen-light flashlight to keep in my pocket and showed me where we were on the chart while instructing me on the compass heading. Then he disappeared below to the warmth of our cabin without a second kiss. I knew he was tired and cold, and that I was alone. I had never felt so alone before in all my life!

As usual, we were headed up-wind, pounding into the sea. We had only a reefed mainsail up to steady ourselves and the engine was on full power. We were making six knots until we hit a wave, then we dropped to 3½ knots. I could hardly believe how freezing the night air had become and I really appreciated both the Mustang suit and the cup of hot cocoa.

I squeezed my eyes shut for a few seconds in an attempt to get my night vision. Still I could see nothing, just darkness all around. It seemed as if the world ended at the edge of the boat; beyond it was nothing but a black void. It was a desolate feeling!

When I finished my cocoa, I wedged the cup between two cushions while mentally noting where I put it. I checked my watch: 10:35pm I slid my rump along the cushion to the bench behind the instruments, not wanting to take a chance of falling by trying to stand up. All the readings on the instruments were in order. I did a 360-degree "look-around" and scanned the darkness while staying seated. I saw nothing. Seeing nothing was good, I reminded myself. Seeing nothing meant we were in no danger of colliding with anything. I checked my watch. It was 11pm, time to check the radar.

I slid the hatch open and clawed my way down the ladder toward the chart table. I switched on the radar, positioned the sweep hand to begin at the bow of the boat, and let it take a 360-degree sweep. The radar read the horizon in a 13-mile radius. I was comforted to see it picked up nothing around us. I flipped the radar switch back to the standby mode and could hear Tom snoring in the back cabin.

I returned to the cockpit, feeling my way up the ladder and over the hatch boards. It was 11:05pm Already, it was a long night! I let my thoughts float freely from topic to topic. I thought about my job, the kids, and our mothers who were back home wondering where we were. I thought about my father who would have enjoyed this adventure much more than I. I thought about being alone and cold in the cockpit all night! Enough of that, I scolded myself.

I stretched my neck and moved my arms in an effort to change the pattern of my thinking. I found myself thinking about how pleasant it would be to take a long, hot shower and to sleep in a big bed that didn't pitch, rock and roll — one with smooth dry sheets. I thought about a comfortable chair, the kind I could sink into permitting it to wrap around my tired body. I thought about getting dressed in feminine clothes. I was fed up with jeans and flannel shirts!

Again, I scolded myself for being such a namby-pamby. I had not liked myself the last several weeks and I thought about how different I was on the boat from when I was on land. On the boat, I felt sick much of the time, frightened each time Tom went on deck. I had developed a "victim" attitude. On land, I had felt strong and healthy. I had had a positive attitude and had felt in charge of myself.

I clearly needed to work on my attitude – I needed to take charge of myself. Why did I think I shouldn't take care of my appearance just because I didn't go to an office each day? I decided that from then on I would get myself fixed up every day! I would put on clean clothes, comb my hair and even put on lipstick. I would do it just for me. I felt better having had that little pep talk with myself!

With that new resolution, I pulled the pen light out of my pocket and checked my watch. It was 11:25pm, time to check the radar. I went down through the hatch, turned on the radar and did the sweep. Good, nothing was around. Back to the cockpit, checked the instruments. All was well. I found a place to sit in the cockpit where I was out of the wind and settled in for another 20 minutes. Time crept by. I stood and tried to do a few stretching exercises, but found it impossible with so much boat action.

I went below and got an orange. I peeled it slowly, throwing the peels over the side into the darkness. It seemed as if they were thrown into a vacuum because once they left my hand I could not see where they went, nor could I hear them hit the water. Beyond the edge of VONNIE-T was nothing – nothing at all. It was eerie! I put a section of orange in my mouth and sucked on it slowly. It not only tasted good, but it also became a tool to help me stay awake and alert. I wondered how long I could suck that particular section of orange before I had to swallow it. It was a positive game I was playing and it was a refreshing taste in my mouth. Eventually, I had to put a second piece in my mouth, but I tried to make it last longer. When I had eaten the entire orange I checked my watch: 11:58pm.

I brought a packet of soda crackers up to the cockpit with me after checking the radar. I hoped my pocket would protect them from the wet night air. I ate them slowly, as I did with the orange, and was surprised to realize I was no longer afraid of being alone at night in the cockpit. With that realization I acquired a sense of control over myself, and I began to actually enjoy my time alone. It gave me time to think my own thoughts. I had not realized until then that private time was something I had missed, too.

The crackers made me thirsty, but I waited. At 12:16pm I heated water for tea and checked the radar and instruments. All was well. Nothing in sight. The night crept by in 20-minute intervals. I thought about things, sat in different areas of the cockpit, sang some of the old songs when I could remember the words, and checked the instruments and radar on schedule.

After several hours I needed to use the toilet. Good God, how would I use the toilet in a Mustang suit? I thought about it for a while, hoping the need would go away. It didn't! I went below, feeling my way back toward the head because I didn't want to turn on a light or disturb Tom's sleep. I pulled the Velcro flap open, unzipped the front, pulled my arms out, slid the suit down, unbuckled my jeans, slid them and my underwear down and nearly fell onto the toilet. All of that had to be done with one hand, the other was needed to hold on and keep my balance in the pitching, rolling boat. When I was seated, the entire pile of clothing was bunched at my feet, preventing my feet from being used for balance. To get dressed, the entire process had to be reversed and then the toilet had to be pumped out by hand. The whole process was fairly aerobic, and it helped me get warmed up. I returned to the cockpit and resumed my 20-minute routine and was startled when the hatch slid open.

"Is everything all right?" Tom asked.

"Yes," I answered. "Did you sleep well?"

"Yeah, surprisingly I feel pretty rested. I'll be up in a minute so you can get some sleep."

Unknowingly, we had established a night watch pattern that we would follow for the rest of our cruise. Unlike the navy's four hours on and four off, we slept whenever we were able to fall asleep and only woke the other person when too tired to function.

I heard him put on the teapot, check the radar, and pump the head. I checked my watch. It was 4am I was rather pleased with myself and I decided that I would try to do more night watches in the future and give Tom the opportunity to sleep at night. After all, it was more important that he remain alert for all the deck work and navigation. I must have gone to sleep the minute my head hit the pillow because the next thing I knew I smelled coffee and opened my eyes to daylight.

SAD AND SEASICK!

"It's almost time for your radio check-in," Tom said, carefully handing me a cup of coffee while firmly gripping the bulkhead handrail with his other hand. The boat continued to pitch and roll. I sat up slowly, holding the coffee cup away to avoid getting burned if any sloshed out of the cup. I sat on the edge of the settee with both feet planted firmly on the sole of the boat and sipped carefully. At first it tasted wonderful, but soon it didn't even smell good. I left the blanket in a heap and slid across the cabin to the radio on the other side. I brought my half-drunk cup of coffee with me.

Tom handed me the ship's log. He had entered our latest position and included all the information and details the float plan report required. All I had to do was report the information at the appropriate time. Tom poured himself another cup of coffee and went back up into the cockpit. I waited at the radio for the net coordinator to call VONNIE-T.

As I waited I felt myself becoming queasy. At first, I thought it was because it was stuffy down in the cabin. I looked back towards the hatch. Tom had already removed all the hatch boards and I could see into the cockpit with ease, yet there did not seem to be any fresh air down below in the cabin. I broke out in a sweat; beads of perspiration formed on my back, forehead, and neck. "God," I thought. "it can't be hot down here."

I sat very still, hoping the feeling would pass. I put my head back and closed my eyes while listening to the other boats give their reports. I marveled at how cheerful and carefree each of them sounded. If I did not know better I would have suspected they were talking to the net coordinator from their living rooms instead of being tossed about in a boat on the Atlantic. They made little jokes and laughed as they reported high seas and strong winds. Not a single one sounded seasick, uncomfortable, or frightened. I admired them and felt unworthy. I felt sicker by the minute, but I could not leave the radio because I knew they would call on me soon. I sipped my coffee and waited. The coffee was cold now and tasted terrible, but I was too sick to turn around and pour it in the sink. I heard a light buzzing in my ears. I closed my eyes and commanded myself not to get any sicker. I waited, and I continued to listen for the net coordinator to call on me. Finally, I heard the radio say, "VONNIE-T, how do you copy and what is your position today?"

I put the microphone up to my mouth and said, "This is VONNIE-T and I have good copy on you."

"Good, VONNIE-T," the net coordinator said cheerfully. "We have good copy on you as well. Go ahead with your position report."

"We are at 42 degrees 29 north; 68 degrees 32 west; steering a magnetic course of 242. We have 25-knot winds from the southwest and an eight-foot swell. Our barometer is 30.22 and rising. We're averaging six knots.

"OK VONNIE-T, we have you at . . . ."

He repeated all of what I had reported. I knew I was supposed to listen and make any corrections in case he did not copy my report correctly, but I was so sick by then I could not even focus my eyes on the data Tom had so carefully written in our log. I just wanted to close the conversation and get up in the cockpit where there was fresh air!

When he finished, he asked, "Are there any corrections, VONNIE-T?"

"No, no corrections," I said with great effort.

"What is your ETA VONNIE-T?" He asked.

"Tell him we have 110 miles to go and should be in sometime tomorrow morning before net time," Tom shouted down into the cabin at me. I repeated Tom's words to the net coordinator.

"OK, VONNIE-T, I will look for you tomorrow at this same time. We will close out your float plan tomorrow after your report. Have a safe sail," he said.

"Ask him if we can expect any change in this weather, or at least a change in wind direction." Tom shouted down at me once again.

Oh my God, I thought, please do not ask me to be on this radio another second. Willpower is an amazing thing, however, and I managed to ask the question.

"Stand by VONNIE-T," the net coordinator said. Within seconds he added, "It doesn't look like you can expect any positive changes. If anything, the winds may increase a little but I don't see any hope for them changing direction."

"Thank you," I said as cheerfully as I could. Instantly, I knew I could not stay below for another second. I dropped the microphone letting it hang from the cord. I tossed my coffee cup toward the sink and scrambled up into the cockpit for air. I could hear the net coordinator continue to talk to me but I had no idea what he said.

I was sick! I knew I was going to vomit, and there was no stopping it! I tried to make it up to the cockpit so I could do it overboard, but I did not make it. My feet were on the bottom of the ladder, my head level with the cockpit floor, and up it all came. Vomit was all over the floor. It got caught up on the floor grate and oozed down into the scuppers. It was awful! I couldn't stop it, and I couldn't move. All I could do was hang on to the ladder while I vomited again, and again, and again. Finally, there was nothing left in me. I felt weak and my mouth tasted like the bottom of a birdcage. Strangely, however I felt better.

Poor Tom! He sat there helpless, watching me and knowing there was nothing he could do. I was embarrassed about the unsightly show I had put on. "I'll clean it up in just a few minutes," I said weakly. He smiled kindly and helped me up into the cockpit. I sat down and he instructed me not to move.

"If you think you can keep a seasick pill down, I'll get one for you," he said.

I swallowed the pill and sipped the water slowly. Tom lifted several buckets of seawater from the ocean and splashed them into the cockpit. The mess washed down the scuppers and into the ocean. Neither of us said anything for a long time. Finally Tom said, "You know, if you would have let me put up more sail we could have fallen off the wind and the boat would have been a lot more stable. We would have done a few tacks across the water and you wouldn't have gotten so sick."

I knew he was right. My big pep talk with myself last night was ridiculous. I was worthless, physically sick, and emotionally whipped. I could not even take care of myself, let alone pull my weight on this boat.

A GLOW ON THE HORIZON BECKONED TO US

The seasick pill stayed down and did a fair job of settling my stomach, but it also caused drowsiness and dryness in my mouth. After a short time I was able to eat, but only if Tom was the one to go below and prepare the food. I needed to stay in the cockpit and tried to avoid moving my head in any direction. If I went below, even to use the head, my stomach roiled.

The day dragged, and it was the longest of my life. At one point, I thought about dying — not with dread, but with desire. Death would have been a pleasant alternative to the misery I felt. The pills provided only marginal relief, and when their effects wore off, it was still two hours earlier than the label recommended taking another. Somehow, I got through the day because there was no alternative, but I dreaded facing a second night at sea. I saw it as an extension of the misery I already felt.

Luckily, our second night was not nearly as bad as our first. When the stars came out, the night immediately appeared friendly. They sparkled and twinkled on the rippling waves, giving the ocean the appearance of a large disco stage. Later, the moon rose and painted a silver streak across the water as if it were a road enticing us off to the end of the earth.

By 10pm, we could see a yellow glow from the lights of civilization. Our Loran C confirmed the glow came from the direction of Provincetown. In spite of being many miles and hours away from it, just being able to see it was encouraging for we knew we could look forward to being in protected waters sometime that night. Neither of us attempted sleep. We stayed in the cockpit together and occasionally saw a small green or red light flicker on the horizon. We knew they were the lights of another boat, probably a fishing vessel far enough away so we did not need to alter our course.

Tom kept a close check on where we were by taking a "fix" and charting our position. We needed to clear the Cape before making a port turn. He studied the charts carefully and made small, but necessary adjustments in our heading. Soon, we would need the

Provincetown chart, so Tom pulled it from its storage spot. Looking at the clean, still-unmarked chart reminded me of our planning days back in Minnesota when our plush, blue living room carpet was fully covered with charts and guidebooks for our voyage. There were charts of the Great Lakes, the St. Lawrence, the eastern seaboard, and all the Caribbean islands, each in enough detail to get us safely across passages and into protected anchorage areas. Before leaving Minnesota, Tom folded each individual chart and filed it in a sequence of use. We had thousands of dollars invested in nautical detail.

AN UNWELCOME RETURN TO THE UNITED STATES

The city lights, far off on that horizon, seemed to beckon to us. The glow increased in intensity as time passed and we got closer. When we were within radio range of other boats we began to overhear conversations on the VHF. Mostly, they reported on the status of their fishing. At one point we listened to a "Pan-Pan," an urgent call to advise the Coast Guard of a problem. A Pan-Pan is not as serious as a Mayday, but still it is not to be taken lightly.

The Pan-Pan we listened to was from a fishing vessel taking on seawater. They had not located the leak when the captain alerted the Coast Guard. His crew was checking all sea-cocks and hoses. Meanwhile, with extra pumps they were able to pump as much overboard as was coming in. The captain said he did not think he was in immediate danger of sinking. He felt confident his crew would locate the problem and be able to repair it, but in case the situation got worse he wanted the Coast Guard to know of his predicament and his location.

The Coast Guard maintained radio contact with the boat every 10 minutes, requesting an update on the situation. The captain finally reported finding the problem. It was a broken engine hose that could easily be repaired. He thanked the Coast Guard and canceled his Pan-Pan.

Listening to the drama of the Pan-Pan unfold helped us stay awake and alert. It was rather like listening to a live radio soap opera. It also reinforced the importance of regular boat maintenance on things such as sea-cocks and hoses, and I noticed Tom adding a few more items to his clipboard "to do" list.

When we were 15 miles from land, we turned on the radar. Even on a clear night we could see things on radar we could not with the naked eye. When the harbor buoys showed up on the radar, Tom adjusted our course and headed straight for them. Soon we were able to see the sea channel clearly. We cherished the sight of the red and green buoys and followed them in according to their numbers in descending order.

We motored past the sea wall and into the large harbor. As we did, the motor coughed once, then twice, then stopped. We knew immediately what had happened, for we had heard that sound once before. We had run out of fuel!

Luckily, Tom had a spare five-gallon can of fuel in the lazarette. He dug it out, poured the fuel into the tank, primed the engine and it started right up. He did not even glance at the manual before he primed the engine that time because he had mastered the procedure during our trip across the Gulf Stream when we first bought the boat. Still, it was not a pleasant task after having spent 42 hours at sea.

With five gallons in our tank, we motored slowly into the main harbor and could hardly believe our eyes when we arrived. The harbor was jammed with boats! All the boats were on moorings and none of the moorings were empty. We didn't know what to do. It was 2am and we were tired beyond the point of being able to think clearly. We had finally arrived in a safe comfortable harbor, but there was no place to park. What a joke! Then we saw the gas dock. There were no boats there so we motored over and tied up. Finding it was a relief! We would get fuel in the morning anyway so it seemed the most logical place for us to spend the rest of the night.

I brushed my teeth and washed my face for the first time in two days, dropped my clothes on the floor next to the bunk and crawled into my bunk naked. The sheets were cold and damp at first, but soon they became warm from body heat. I fell asleep, a deep, wonderful, motionless sleep.

"Hey, you guys, get the hell off my dock! Who do you think you are? Wake up down there! You want me to call the police? Get your asses out of here! Do you hear me?"

I was sound asleep and there was a male voice shouting something during a bad dream. I did not want this dream, but the voice continued its tirade. I remember waking enough to think how strange it was to dream about someone yelling, and if I was dreaming, why was I not able to visualize what the man looked like. Most of my dreams had detail. That dream had none. The yelling and shouting grew louder. I wanted it to stop. I wanted to start a different dream. I needed restful sleep, not this.

"VONNIE-T, or what ever the hell your name is, get off my dock! Wake up down there, God damn it!" When I heard our boat name, I immediately snapped out of my troubled sleep. That angry male voice was actually yelling at us. We had spent several months in friendly Canadian waters and now, hey, welcome to the USA. I jumped out of my bunk feeling very much like a scared rabbit. I stood stark naked with my insides rattling and grabbed at the closest thing, a bath towel, and wrapped it around myself. I gave Tom a hard shake and demanded he awaken. Then I ran to the hatch to see what the problem was.

When I got to the hatch I saw we were at low tide — very low tide! Our boat was far below the gas pump. The man doing all the shouting was standing on the gas dock that was now nearly 10 feet above our decks. Fortunately, we had tied the boat to a set of floating dock rings, the type that moved up and down with the tide. At the time however, I did not feel particularly lucky to find myself on the receiving end of verbal abuse and lecherous glares, especially when I nearly lost my towel while reaching up to slide the hatch open. Shivering from the chilly outside air was the least of my concerns.

"Hey lady, what are you doing on my gas dock?" He asked a little nicer when he liked what he saw. "If you don't want no gas, you'll hafta get off of it. It's so my customers can come and buy gas. This ain't no marina slip, you know," he said.

By now, Tom was awake and standing behind me. I stepped aside to let him up into the cockpit until I realized he had not bothered to grab a towel. He was totally naked. "Do you have diesel?" Tom asked loudly, irritated by the man's rudeness.

"Yea," the man said. "You wanna buy some diesel?"

"Yes, we want a fill with diesel," Tom shouted up to him.

"Go get my pants," Tom said to me softly. "And get the key to open the fuel tank, too."

I scurried back to our sleeping cabin. I saw my jeans on the floor and pulled them on. I picked up my flannel shirt and slid one arm into it, while snatching Tom's jeans in my other hand. I handed him his jeans, slid my other arm into the shirt, and managed to get a couple of buttons fastened. This was not the time to worry about the lack of underwear.

Tom already had the fuel key in his hand. He pulled on his pants, went to the fuel tank cap and opened it. Not until then did I realize the man on the fuel dock was standing in a cage made of chain-link fencing. There was an opening facing us, with a locked gate on the dock entrance side of his cage to protect him from thieves. With a rope he lowered a small, wire mesh basket. What sort of a place was this that required fenced security?

"Put your money in the basket," he directed. "After I see your money I'll lower down the gas hose." Tom placed some bills in the basket. The man pulled the basket up and lowered the hose. The pump handle barely reached our tank opening.

"Is this diesel?" Tom asked.

"Yeah! You said you wanted diesel, didn't you?" he answered coldly.

"Yes," Tom said. "I just wanted to make sure. I'm not used to pumping anything into our tanks when I can't see the pumps."

The man did not answer or acknowledge that his gas setup was the least bit unusual. Tom pumped the fuel into our tanks based on the blind trust of that character's word. When the tank was full, Tom stopped pumping. "That's all she takes," Tom said facing up to the gas dock attendant.

"OK, I'll bring up the hose and send down your change," he said. The dock man hauled up the hose, letting it clunk against the dock post several times en route and lowered the wire mesh basket. In it we found our change and a receipt for the fuel we purchased.

"How do we get a mooring?" Tom asked.

"I don't know nothing about those things," he said. "I just run the gas dock, and as soon as you get your boat off my dock, I can start selling gas to some real boats. I can't make a living offa sailboats. Besides, you take up too much room. I can get two powerboats up here, fillin' up in the same space as you take. Now get going! You got your fuel! So, get off my dock!"

MUSTACHES KISSING

Tom told me to start the engine. He untied our lines and pushed us off the pier. We slowly motored away from the gas dock, not knowing where to go next. Tom came back and took the wheel while I called on the VHF radio requesting information on berthing. After motoring around in the harbor, we were assigned to a temporary spot on the pier. After all the wonderful experiences and friendly people we met in Canada, we felt this was a sorry welcome back to the United States.

When we were tied up in our temporary berth, we showered and put on clean clothes in preparation for a walk into town for a big breakfast. It not only felt wonderful to be clean, but it also felt great to have my feet on firm ground. We walked down the pier and were totally unprepared for what we saw. The pier was populated with gay men! They held hands, embraced, and kissed, and nearly all took photos of one another.

That was our first exposure to homosexuality, and I found the scene hysterically funny. I began to laugh, and I could not help staring. I almost expected someone to jump up and say, "Smile, you're on Candid Camera," but nothing of the sort happened. It was not a joke. It was real!

I was surprised when Tom didn't find humor in the situation; instead it made him angry and irritable. He announced we were to return to the boat and that we would eat breakfast on board. It was not a suggestion; it was a command!

We returned to the boat after our "almost" walk. I changed the sheets on our bunk, gathered the laundry, and reorganized the galley cabinets that had been jostled during the passage. Tom filled the water tanks, hosed the crusted salt off the exterior of the boat, and put up our Seven Seas burgee.

The burgee was a small triangular flag that indicated our membership in the *Seven Seas Cruising Association*, an organization we joined two years prior to moving onto VONNIE-T. As members, we received a monthly bulletin featuring articles written by other cruisers. Each article addressed topics pertinent to cruisers: port check-in procedures, customs information, ham radio reciprocal directions, docking and harbor data, plus the locations of domestic services such as laundry, groceries, fuel and propane in various ports. We loved reading about the faraway ports in distant lands and dreamed of the day we would be there. The *Seven Seas Cruising Association* motto is LEAVE A CLEAN WAKE. We liked the motto. It was how we felt about travel in general, regardless of the traveler's mode of transportation.

By the second day, we were out on a mooring. The boat was neat and tidy, and we had gotten over our shock of seeing gay men display their affections. The next morning we heard a knock on the side of our hull.

"Good morning, VONNIE-T. Are you folks awake yet?" A gentle male voice asked. Tom stuck his head out and saw a young man standing in a dinghy next to our boat. "Hi," the young man said. "I saw your SSCA burgee and noticed that you're a long way from your home port. I thought you might like the use of my car."

"Well, that's very nice of you," Tom said. ' How much do you charge for a day?"

"Oh, no," he said. "I don't want to rent it to you. You can just take it. I'm an SSCA Commodore. I live over there on that boat. I've been working on boats here all summer, trying to build up the old sailing kitty." He gave us a big smile. "When I first got here, I bought an old clunker just to get around in. It'll just be sitting over there in the parking lot all day. When I saw your SSCA burgee, I thought you might want to use it to get groceries and stuff. Just replace any gas you use, that's all," he said. "Hey, I gotta get going," he said. "Here are the keys."

He handed the keys to Tom, told him where to find the car, and sped off in his dinghy. We used the car to tour the town and surrounding areas and restocked groceries. Before returning the car to its parking place, we filled it with gas and put a case of beer in the trunk with a thank you note. Later, that afternoon, the car owner stopped by our boat for his keys. We thanked him and invited him on board for dinner.

"Gee, thanks folks, but I've got to meet this guy I've gotten to know pretty good," he said with a dreamy sigh. "Glad you got some use out of the car, though. If I don't see you again, may the seas be kind to you."

He sped off in his dinghy toward the dock. We didn't get his name and we never saw him again. His gracious act was a big contrast to our gas dock welcome and resulted in our being a little less judgmental about gay men.

We left the next day with a 10-knot wind out of the northwest. How pleasant! We sailed all day and stopped overnight at Buzzards Bay. The following day was another long but pleasant sail. We did not stop until we arrived at Newport, Rhode Island, where we rested and played tourist. We visited the old historic mansions, took a bus tour, and enjoyed the atmosphere of the town.

It was early October and late in the season to be that far north, so after only a few days we headed for Niantic Bay on Long Island Sound. We arranged a rendezvous with Linda and Ron Turner on MOONSHADOW that evening. We had never met them, but I had talked with Linda on the radio nearly every day and felt as if we were old friends. Those two "salts" had been cruising the eastern U.S. waters and the Caribbean for nine years.

Shortly before entering the harbor, we saw a boat with dark red sails sailing a similar course heading. Linda told us they would be easy for us to sight, as they had new red sails. Sure enough, it was them!

We entered through the swing bridge opening, motored up to a quiet area and anchored. I made a big pot of spaghetti and they brought dessert. We drank lots of wine, ate till we were stuffed, and shared sea stories late into the night. We knew we had made long-term friends.

A CHASE SCENE

The next day we set sail for Port Jefferson, New York, on Long Island. We planned to anchor and visit that lovely area, but the weather became dirty and stayed that way all day. After anchoring, the thought of pumping up the dinghy, lowering it into the water, and trying to get the motor on it in rough water was not appealing. Besides, we knew we would be soaked with saltwater spray by the time we arrived on shore. So, we remained on board and cooked dinner in the oven to take the damp chill from the boat.

It was not a comfortable night. The boat motion made sleeping difficult, and both of us were cranky and irritable the next morning. By midday, the sun began to peek through the clouds, bringing the temperature up to 60 degrees and helping to thaw our moods considerably.

We were sailing a soft beat and making fairly good time up the sound toward New York City. We noticed several sailboats off to our starboard raising their sails, but paid little attention. It was a weekend, and I suppose we both assumed they were trying to get one last day of sailing in before they hauled their boats out for winter. We continued our course heading, 165 degrees, cruising at 7½ knots. We were rather pleased with our progress and never gave another thought to the sailboats we passed.

Suddenly, a powerboat came zooming past us blowing a painfully loud horn that was blasted directly at us. I jumped and covered my ears. Tom swore at the boat when it startled him. We didn't know what to think of the situation. Why would he buzz us and give us a horn blast? We watched the boat in disbelief! It made a short turn and doubled back at us again! "What the hell?" Tom said. "What is that son of a bitch trying to do?" The powerboat came toward us and blasted its horn again. It circled, and we saw two men making hand motions for us to go away. We could not figure out what was happening! We asked what the problem was, but apparently they could not hear our voices over their loud engine. They sped away.

At first we thought they were trying to tell us something was wrong with our boat. Maybe there was smoke coming from our engine or something equally terrible. Tom checked everything quickly, but all seemed in order.

He sat back down in the cockpit; ready to return to the crossword puzzle he had been working. Suddenly, he sat up straight and said. "Oh shit! I turned around to see what had upset him. There was a fleet of racing sailboats coming up our stern. They were fast boats and now we understood what the powerboat was trying to tell us. We were sailing through the middle of a regatta!

Tom turned on our engine. We tried desperately to get ahead of them and out of their way. He increased our engine power, but still the regatta gained on us. We looked back realizing there was nothing we could do. It looked as if we were in a "cops and robbers" scene, we were the robbers being chased by the cops. We made a tack, thinking that would help us get out of the regatta path. No such luck! No matter what we did we were in someone's way. Our tacking only put us in the path of the second leg of the race. There was nothing we could do, so we continued on our way, steering a direct course. At least that way the racing boats could anticipate where we would be when they got close to us. We wondered if VONNIE-T was on their local sports news that night. If we were, I am sure we were not spoken of in favorable terms.

That night we pulled into Flushing Bay at the head of Long Island Sound, adjacent to Shea Stadium and La Guardia Airport. Our guidebook indicated a marina there. When we were within radio range I called the marina and inquired about slip availability.

"Yea, we have a slip. How long are you?" the marina operator asked.

I told him we were 50-feet and asked how much it would cost.

"A hundred bucks," he answered.

CHAPTER THREE

Migrating South

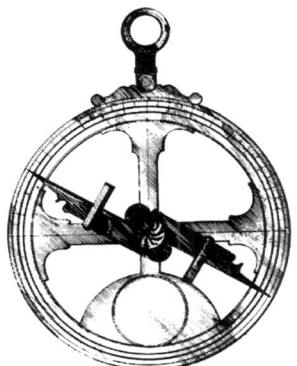

SAILING PAST THE STATUE OF LIBERTY

In the early morning sunshine we motored down the East River past Riker's Island Prison. "I'll bet you need to be a real bad-ass guy to get in there," Tom said, pointing to the prison as we passed. We knew there was status among New York thugs who boasted of having served time at Rikers. We also knew New York held the worst and the best of many things.

Manhattan is linked to New England by the East River that flows from the Hudson to Long Island Sound, while the northern end of Manhattan is defined by the Harlem River flowing from the Hudson in an easterly direction to the East River. The juncture with the East River is appropriately named Hell's Gate, and presented a challenge for us because of its strong tidal currents. The tides cause the currents and switch direction every six hours. At Hell's Gate, there can be a seven-knot, easterly, Harlem River current meeting a six-knot westerly current in the East River. The resulting confused waters can be extremely dangerous for slow sailboats to navigate. We timed our entrance to Hell's Gate to be near "slack tide," when the tide direction was about to change and not yet flowing rapidly in either direction. Our timing was good, and we had an easy passage.

We continued down the river with Manhattan Island on our starboard side and Queens on our port. The enormity of one tall building after another was awesome. As cornstalks sit in perfect rows on the farms in Minnesota, so do the miles of buildings in New York. We knew we were sailing past the beehives of American finance, each in its own house of steel and glass reaching high toward the sky. We could barely see the Empire State Building, once the tallest building in the world, but now dwarfed by newer taller structures.

The silence we had known at sea was lost to the discord and clamor of the most populated city in the United States. We listened to the drone of traffic, honking horns, and the chopping sound of helicopters delivering important people to the city. New York is where money and ulcers grow simultaneously. Down-river we motored under the Brooklyn Bridge, an impressive, heavy cabled structure from any view, but especially so when looking up from the water.

We experienced a feeling of nostalgia as we passed Ellis Island and thought about our ancestors who had landed there on arrival to this new country called America. We realized that we knew almost nothing about our ancestors, those brave people from France, Germany, Ireland, and Sweden and we regretted our ignorance. Most stirring of all was motoring past the Statue of Liberty. What memorable stories could that Grand Lady tell? What secret tears of joy and loneliness has she seen?

We were tempted to anchor and take a ferry into New York later that evening to sample some of the nightlife. But the river traffic was heavy, and we could not bring ourselves to leave VONNIE-T unattended in all that congestion. We knew we would not have been able to enjoy ourselves worrying about the boat, so instead we motored on admiring the skyline and realized we no longer missed the hustle and bustle of big city life.

We had plenty of our own immediate traffic concerns to contend with. The water highway we traveled had plenty of excitement on it and required that we stay alert. There were buoys every place we looked. Each one marked either the port or starboard side of a river traffic lane. There were about 20 different types of buoys because several lanes crossed here forming major water intersections. We adopted the philosophy of "might makes right" and assumed all others had right-of-way over us, even though we knew that was not officially correct. The blue-and-gold Staten Island ferries, large working boats, and a wide variety of pleasure craft used the water highways daily. Each of them was familiar with the water lanes. We were not, and they were each much bigger than we were.

We continued under the Verrazano Bridge connecting Staten Island to Brooklyn and noted with surprise the volume and variety of flotsam. There were wooden planks, life preservers, tennis shoes, plastic bottles, and many unidentifiable floating objects.

We arrived at Great Kills Harbor and entered the Richmond Yacht Club. It was the end of the sailing season so we had no trouble getting an empty mooring. We were pleasantly surprised to learn that the reasonable cost of the mooring included water taxi service to and from shore, so we did not even need to go through the hassle of inflating our dinghy and lowering it down off our deck.

Earlier in the season, this would have been an ideal anchorage, but it was cold this time of year. The night temperatures dipped lower and lower each night, and weather reports of impending storms increased in frequency. We knew we needed to push ourselves as far south each day as possible. Unfortunately, the wind had been blowing from the south all day and we did not relish the thought of heading directly into it.

We went to bed early, unsure of how long we would be forced to stay in Great Kills Harbor waiting for the wind to clock around. Neither of us slept well that night nor was it immediately apparent why we both woke at 4:30am Tom turned on the radio looking for a weather report and we learned the wind had changed and was no longer coming from the south. Since we felt rested and ready to face the day we dressed, ate breakfast, slipped our line off the mooring, and headed out of the harbor.

We motored slowly through the darkness, being careful to avoid buoys that might be slightly submerged. Tom stood on the bow with a flashlight and directed my steering. By following his directions and keeping our speed slow, we inched out of the harbor safely. Once outside the break-wall, we met 15-knot winds out of the west. The offshore breeze meant light seas and easy sailing. Tom raised our sails and we headed south.

ALL DRESSED UP IN MUSTY CLOTHES

We had an easy trip down the Jersey Coast and arrived at Atlantic City late that afternoon. We ate dinner on board and took short naps to prepare for the gambling nightlife. Later, we dressed in our fanciest clothes. Tom had a navy sport jacket, tan dress slacks and one pair of leather shoes on board. I had a skirt, wool blazer, black flat leather shoes and a pair of panty hose. That was the total of our finery. While dressing we discovered our clothes smelled musty from the dampness on the boat, but we did not let that deter us. We looked the best we could possibly look, despite the odors. We stepped off VONNIE-T onto the dock and walked into Harrah's where the glitz provided a sharp contrast to our nautical lifestyle! Many people were beautifully dressed but we did not feel out of place, and after a few minutes in the smoke-filled rooms, everyone's clothing smelled the same. A slight musty odor was the least offensive of all.

It didn't take me long to deposit my gambling allowance into the various slot machines. Each slot consumed my money just as fast as I chose to feed it. Occasionally, one of the machines would tease me by giving back a portion of the coins I fed it, but never did one give back enough to cause elation. Tom went to a black jack table. The end result was the same for him, only faster.

"I still feel I'm ahead," he told me after losing his $50.

"How do you figure?" I asked.

"Because I enjoyed myself and I was at a 'No Smoking' table," he said.

"Isn't the human rationale an amazing thing?" I thought.

What I liked most about the casino was not the elaborate surroundings, the glitter, or the gambling. It was the warmth! For me, temperature control had become a wonderful luxury. We both loved the warmth of the room but it also made us sleepy and soon we looked forward to getting back to our bunks. We walked back down the same chilly pier, climbed aboard and hugged one another in our cold bunks until our shivering stopped and we fell sound asleep.

The next morning the weather report announced snow had fallen in New York that night. Boats at Great Kills Harbor reported waking to ice on their decks. The realization that snow and ice were only one day behind us caused another early departure.

That night we anchored at the Cape May New Jersey Inlet. As we left the following morning we saw a sailboat up on a reef near the inlet. It looked as if the captain either misjudged the inlet or did not have enough power to go through the breakers. It had been a lovely fiberglass boat and we presumed the crew got off safely as there were many people standing around watching the boat pound itself unmercifully on the rocks. The sight gave me goose bumps. I could not help thinking, "That could have been us."

OUR MIGRATION SOUTH

Our drive to head south was so strong that we felt like birds in migration. We had sailed 3,249 miles since we left Duluth and still we needed to push forward. The following night we were at Upper Delaware Bay. By then we had developed a sound anchoring routine, and I appreciated Tom's care with it. He made sure the anchor seated itself well, as neither of us wanted to wake in the middle of the night too find we were floating away.

Typically, Tom would take down the sails and motor around the anchorage until he found a suitable depth. When he found the spot he liked, he put the boat in neutral and went forward to lower the anchor. After the anchor was down he directed me with hand signals to put the boat in reverse while he watched to see if the anchor chain tightened. A tight anchor chain indicated the anchor was holding, while a bouncing one indicated the anchor was dragging. If the anchor refused to take hold, he would raise it and we would start over again in a new place.

On that particular night, we were near the shipping lane in the Upper Delaware Bay and the anchor refused to seat itself. Tom raised it three times trying to find a place where it would hold. Each time we backed the boat down the anchor slowly dragged in the soft mud. He finally gave up and decided it was the best he could do. "I'm not very happy with the anchor tonight," he said, while I headed below to begin dinner. I paid little attention because I knew he had always been overly cautious on that point. I did not give it another thought until I saw how close the ships passed us as they entered the C & D Canal that joined Delaware Bay to the Chesapeake.

"Wow, look at how close that ship is to us," I said, implying poor seamanship on the ship's part.

"I know," Tom said. "That's the shipping channel."

"We're *that* close to the shipping channel?"

"Uh-huh," he said. "Maybe we should do anchor watch tonight," he added.

We went to bed shortly after dinner, but every two hours I awoke automatically to check where we were. Tom slept soundly knowing all he had to do was say, "Maybe we should do anchor watch tonight." Guess which one of "we" he had in mind?

FINALLY WE MET SOME OTHER CRUISERS

Luckily, our anchor did not drag that night and early the next morning we went through the C & D Canal. When we reached the Chesapeake we thought we saw an enor-

The Annapolis inner harbor is almost always crowded with big expensive boats.

mous rectangular structure moving along the water. From a distance it looked like a five-story cement building and we thought it was an optical illusion, something that looks as if it's moving when it really was not. As we got closer we saw lettering on its side that read TOYOTA. Not until then did we realize it was no optical illusion, we were looking at a gigantic rectangular ship carrying thousands of Toyota cars. Later we learned those ships carry a payload of 5,000 cars worth $100 million. We realized they were moving slowly because of the confined space, but I shuddered at the thought of running across something that large in open water when it was moving at its normal speed. I knew there would be no way for it to stop or maneuver around us if we were in its path. Our lives would depend on us getting out of its way.

We sailed down the Chesapeake and anchored at Annapolis for the next five days while we attended an *Seven Seas Cruising Association* party and the famous Annapolis Boat Show. We looked at many larger and more expensive boats on display, but anything larger than 50-feet would have been too cumbersome for us to handle by ourselves. Somehow, we purchased the perfect boat for our needs and it was comforting to be able to reinforce our decision.

While attending the SSCA party we met many cruisers and cruiser hopefuls. Among the people we met for the first time were Todd and Dianne Williams, a couple from Duluth, Minnesota on a boat called LADY DI. They had left Duluth three weeks before we. Imagine having traveled all that way to meet someone from the same homeport! Unfortunately, while we were at the SSCA party, Todd was lying in his bunk because of an injury. Diane confirmed that he was doing the absolute most difficult thing in the world for an active sailboat captain. "Nothing is the thing he does least well." We knew exactly what she meant.

We also met many of the people we had talked to on the ham radio over the past several months, enabling us to put faces with names and call signs for the first time. One of the more memorable was a single-handed cruiser who had already been around the world. He was lamenting about being back in the United States and kept saying he "should never have left the South Pacific." He became the center of everyone's attention because we all wanted to know what was so special about the South Pacific, and we eagerly listened to him wide-eyed and child-like.

When the SSCA party broke up, I thought it might be difficult to say goodbye to our new friends, especially considering all the months I had looked forward to meeting those voices on my ham radio. But after several days of seeing people and being on land, we were both ready to move on. Perhaps I had begun to adjust to boat life because I no longer liked large doses of stimulation from crowds.

We continued heading south, stopping at Gwynn Island the next night, and Sarah Creek, across the York River from Yorktown, the following night. We sampled a piece of American history at Williamsburg by attending the 206th Anniversary of the surrender of Cornwallis. Tom was enthralled. "This is just fine, fine history. Very educational," he kept repeating.

I guess I enjoyed the history too, but I appreciated even more the warm spell of Indian summer. The temperature ranged in the low 70s and the trees had just begun to change color. The golden, green, yellow, and red leaves of autumn were gorgeous. Those were happy colors and happy days! But then, just when I thought I would be able to rely on comfortable weather we had a day of fog. Three miles of visibility of was not a problem for us navigationally speaking, but it robbed us of seeing all the natural beauty around us. Everything took on a dull gray appearance.

At the lower end of the Chesapeake, we entered Norfolk, Virginia, a major U.S. Navy base, and were awed as we sailed past the stern of the carrier John F. Kennedy with its flight deck a little higher than the top of our mast. We saw many warships and even a squadron of submarines. We anchored across from the main Navy docks and it was there that we discovered our anchor light had burned out. We knew having a light on at night when we were that close to the ship channel was crucial. Tom clipped a bosun's chair to the main halyard, put a few tools in a canvas sack that he tied to his belt, and instructed me on how to hoist him up the mast using our electric anchor windlass. (See Color Photo Insert, page 7.) What he thought would be a simple bulb replacement became more complicated because each time a ship passed, it left a large wake that caused VONNIE-T to roll. It was not a problem for me on deck, but the top of the mast swayed from side to side 10 feet or more while Tom was left hanging on for dear life. When he saw a ship approaching he quickly put his tools back into the canvas bag and wrapped both arms and legs around the mast until it stopped swinging. He didn't seem to mind it, and claimed it was better than most carnival rides, but I sure was glad it wasn't me up there.

THE DISMAL SWAMP

The next day we investigated the feasibility of transiting the Dismal Swamp Canal. We read that it had been engineered by George Washington in 1793 and took 12 years to complete the 22-mile long waterway. It connects the Chesapeake Bay in Virginia via the Elizabeth River and the Albemarle Sound in North Carolina via the Pasquotank River. We asked other cruisers about it, but not many seemed familiar with it. There was no shortage of opinions based upon hearsay, but no concrete data, so I called the Corps of Engineers to inquire. I learned The Dismal Swamp Canal had been dredged that spring and was told that if we stayed in the middle of the channel we could rely on seven feet of water. "Depth won't be your main problem," the engineer told me on the telephone. "Your main problem will be keeping your rigging free from the trees. How tall is your mast?" he asked.

"We have two masts," I told him, "The main mast is 62 feet off the water."

"Well, I think you can do it," he said, obviously delighted to have us consider using his beautiful canal. "Just make sure you stay in the center."

Tom and I talked it over that night and decided to give it a try. We anchored in front of the first lock so we would be ready to go through when it opened the next morning. We had fog again but the night was lovely, not in spite of the fog but because of it. The fog added an aura to the whole setting and I could appreciate the legend that Edgar Ellen Poe wrote "The Raven" from this very spot. We knew there were trees on both sides of us and that they were very close, but they seemed far away, almost not there at all. The sounds were both fantastic and eerie. It was a symphony of low buzzing, humming, and croaking from the nighttime insects, frogs, and birds.

Early the next morning, the fog was still lying on the water with patches snuggled in and among the trees, but it all burned off quickly as the sun rose. We entered the first lock, just a mini-lock compared to our previous experiences, and tied up to the small cleats. There were several other boats in the lock with us. One carried a motorcycle on board below decks and used it as a means of land transportation when needed. To get it on and off the boat they hoisted it out using a four-part block and tackle line under the boom. We were impressed with their method of hoisting it but thought it unusual that they were willing to sacrifice so much living space for a motorcycle. Tom had an old bicycle strapped topside on our stern deck, and sometimes we felt that was a poor use of space, especially since we had not used it and it was showing signs of rust, leaving orange stains on the fiberglass.

As the boats slipped out of the first lock, we each motored toward the second lock at a comfortable speed of six knots while the smaller boats quickly fell behind. The canal is only 50 or 60 feet wide and a lush, thick, wooded area continues down both sides. Wooden posts were used as retaining walls to hold back the soil, and the tops of each old post had collected enough dirt and seeds over the years to sport an assortment of wild flowers.

Several blue herons flew out of the thicket to sit on the stumps and watch us pass. Our previous experience with the blue herons in New Brighton was that they would fly away when approached, but here in the Dismal Swamp they came out to look at us! The trees were spectacular—each displayed an assortment of red, gold and orange. It could not have been lovelier, and I felt like we were floating through a child's picture book. It had been reported that Edna Ferber based her novel *Showboat* on her experiences in the Dismal Swamp Canal. Later, the novel was rewritten as a musical, becoming the famous production that we all know today.

After we completed a lock, the lockmaster jumped into his car and quickly drove to the next lock to prepare it for us. In spite of going our slowest speed we passed several smaller sailboats as we motored from lock to lock. One boat caused us to break out in laughter as we took a second look at it. There was no one visibly steering the boat. In the absence of a captain, a parrot was perched on the steering wheel and hopped to the top of the wheel each time it turned. We realized the captain was below in the cabin steering by remote control, but the illusion was that the parrot was steering the boat. It was great!

I felt sad when we finished the entire lock system and we were sorry that we had rushed through it in one day. We should have savored that precious experience a lot longer, but we discovered the perfect way to stay and enjoy the beautiful scenery. At the end of the canal was a small cove and Goat Island. We anchored near the small island for the night. There was absolutely nothing there except beautiful flat water and colorful trees and no signs of humanity. The weather was unusually warm and pleasant, and we had no urge to push on the next morning. We wanted to stay right there! We rationalized it every way we could, and finally justified staying a few days while we did some needed boat projects. Would we never get rid of our strong work ethic?

The project we decided upon was the exterior teak. When we purchased the boat the varnish on the exterior teak was in pathetic shape. It had begun to peel which left the raw wood gray from sun exposure. We thought oiled teak would be easier to maintain so we stripped all the varnish off, sanded it, and oiled it. The oiling improved the appearance from what it was, but still it never looked really great like nicely varnished teak. Now, after months of being bathed in saltwater spray, the oiled teak looked dingy and dirty. Not only did the oiled teak look bad it was no easier to maintain. We discovered that we should have been cleaning the teak prior to each oiling to avoid its muddy appearance. If we needed to do all that, we decided we might just as well give it a light sanding and varnish it.

We spent the next several days varnishing the teak and enjoyed the beauty of our private little estuary as well as the beauty of the varnished teak as it took on a golden luster finish. We worked hard each day, but it was satisfying work and we were at peace with ourselves and with one another. In many ways it was like a honeymoon. Each late afternoon, we took a rest from our work and watched the new parade of boats coming out of the Dismal Swamp lock system. None of them stopped to anchor as we had done and we were

Tom gave the deck a finishing rubdown after we varnished all the exterior teak.

pleased with our solitude. Days later we had three coats of varnish on all the exterior teak and VONNIE-T looked downright spiffy. We could not have been more proud.

THE ROSE BUDDIES

When we could procrastinate no longer, Tom pulled up our muddy anchor and we headed to Elizabeth City, North Carolina. The hospitality of that town was exceptional. We were given a berth for two nights, free of charge. That evening two men who called themselves The Rose Buddies greeted each new boat. They gave each boat captain a copy of the local newspaper and presented each lady with a fresh long-stemmed rose. They set up a portable table and spread it with an assortment of wine, cheese and crackers. All the new boats were welcomed and encouraged to participate in the party.

Because of the warm hospitality, we stayed both of our allotted days. We ate all our meals in the local restaurants, restocked our groceries, did laundry at the local launderette, dry-cleaned our winter jackets and sweaters, and purchased shoes and other things that we had not taken the time to buy during the past several months. In short, because Elizabeth City made us feel so welcome we stayed long enough to spend our money there. I appreciated the welcome so much that I wrote a short editorial, pointing out the money each boat spent in Elizabeth City as a direct result of the Rose Buddies welcome. I dropped it off at the local newspaper and it appeared in print the next day.

Two days later we were heading south again, along the ICW (Intra Coastal Waterway). Most of the eastern seaboard from Norfolk to Miami has seaward islands stringing the coastline like pearls. Inside the islands and protected from the Atlantic is the ICW. Sometimes it follows rivers, but elsewhere it consists of a series of man-made canals. Many bridges cross the ICW, and most of them swing up or away to allow boat traffic to pass. Only a few are actually high enough to allow sail boats to pass under. We found the ICW attractive and interesting, but not as charming or as pleasant as the Dismal Swamp. For one thing, we did not like the powerboats that zoomed past us. At first, we moved over to accommodate them, but after getting our keel stuck in the mud a few times, we stayed in the center of the channel and forced the shallow-draft boats to go around us. Most were rude and made it clear they were annoyed by this small inconvenience. They probably were not even aware that sailboats have deep drafts and could not safely leave the center of the channel. Often they did not slow down at all, or if they did slow down, it was just enough to cause maximum wake. The wake caused water to slap violently against the shore. Often we saw large pieces of sod and dirt sucked from a homeowner's back yard and fall into the water. The situation must be a constant nightmare for them.

CAN HORSES SURVIVE ON SALT WATER?

One night, we anchored at Beaufort, North Carolina, near a small island populated by a group of wild horses. There was no obvious source of fresh water on the island, and there was much speculation as to whether the horses had adapted to survival on salt water.

The horses were not the only ones facing the challenges of nature. Anchoring in the tidal river next to the island was an interesting challenge as well. Safe anchoring in tidal conditions called for two bow anchors — one to hold while we pointed in one direction, the other to hold us when being swung with the tide in the opposite direction. Tom understood the principles of the tricky maneuver and we never had trouble with that anchoring technique. He would point to the place he wanted the first anchor and I would motor over to the spot. When we got there he dropped the anchor. We backed it down to set it and then drove forward to drop the second anchor. The second anchor needed to seat itself so it would hold in the opposite direction while not pulling up or unseating the first anchor. The difficult part was to accomplish this while avoiding the entanglement of the first anchor line. Tom had a good grasp on the whole procedure, and while he stood on the bow ready to drop the anchor, he used hand signals directing me where to steer the boat. We had the entire process finely tuned and seldom had any trouble with the task.

That was not the case for some of the other first-year cruisers. One of the couples we planned to have dinner with in town that evening anchored and re-anchored several times and got their anchor lines twisted in the process. When they finally got settled, she called us on the VHF. "We won't be joining you for dinner tonight," she stated. "We're not fit to be with other people."

"Oh, come on," I coaxed. "You'll feel better once you get off the boat and get some hot food in you — anyway, I'm sure you don't want to cook after all that."

"No," she said. "You're right about that! I have no intention of cooking for that man!

I'm opening a couple bottles of whiskey and putting a straw in each of them. That's dinner as far as I'm concerned and if he wants anything else he can cook it himself. I've had it!" She clicked off the radio mike and we did not hear or see either of them until the next day, and even then things seemed cool between them.

THE THORNY PATH

We spent six days in Beaufort talking with other cruisers, visiting a maritime museum, and exploring the town. The marina most graciously loaned us a beater car that we used to visit several chandleries to buy boat equipment. There were several long-term live-aboard cruisers anchored near us. They were waiting for favorable winds to make a 10-day passage directly to the Virgin Islands. They explained that was the easiest way to get to the Caribbean. I remembered all too well our one overnight passage, and I could not even imagine going to sea for 10 days and nights! What were those people thinking? Why did they want to do that when they could have easily made several day trips and have a nice place to anchor each night? They kindly smiled patronizingly, knowing I had a first-year cruiser's normal fears of being off shore.

"During our first year of cruising, we did the same thing you're planning to do," one of them told me. "I know you don't believe me now, but what you're planning to do is actually going to be a lot more difficult. From Florida, you'll have the wind on your bow the whole way. We call that 'going down the thorny path'."

He was right about one thing; I didn't believe him! There was absolutely no way I was going to go to sea for 10 days and nights! Absolutely not! Thank you very much!

We continued our passage south, one day at a time. I often thought sympathetically about those other cruisers when we were putting down our anchor for the night. I appreciated being able to get a good night's sleep. Besides, we enjoyed seeing the rest of the ICW and there was an endless assortment of interesting things to see.

We saw our first pelican in North Carolina as we passed Camp LeJeune Marine training ground, a swampy undeveloped area full of bird life. We also saw a hydraulic dredge working to keep the waterway open by sucking up bottom silt and pumping it ashore through a large pipe. We guessed that was a continual process, for we often touched or bumped along on the mud bottom. We saw shell fishermen who must have been going deaf from the noisy flock of sea gulls hovering overhead and squawking as they gleaned bits of marine life from the catch.

It was November 9 and 80 humid degrees when we arrived in Beaufort, South Carolina. Just above the town, I called on the radio for directions into the marina and apparently I mispronounced the name Beaufort because a southern gentleman broke into my conversation. "Ma'm, you-all are in South Carolina now, and Beaufort is pronounced as in the word 'beautiful,' not like the word 'boat' as North Carolina pronounces it." I was taken aback but apologized for my error. Was this "kindly" correction an example of old southern hospitality? It seemed to be anything but hospitable.

In the center of Beaufort was a section dating back two centuries. There were large brick mansions with handsome, authentically preserved white pillars from the 1700s and 1800s. These were the plantation homes typical of the wealth derived from agriculture and made possible by slavery. As we walked the narrow streets we could almost feel the time when the streets were of brick and dirt and residents traveled by horse-drawn carriages. The streets now, as then, were lined with stately, old oak trees with Spanish moss dripping from their massive branches.

Our next stop was Hilton Head Island, a big contrast to Beaufort in that the homes and condos were all modern. This former plantation land had no historic mansions, but the wealth of modern day was apparent. We loved the trees. A mixture of pines, oaks, and palms standing guard on every acre. The only open land was the golf course, and even there homes lined the fairways. Tom remarked about the absence of a source of productive income. Everyone, it seemed, was living off of retirees by providing services for them.

Our main reason for stopping at Hilton Head Island was to visit "shirt-tail relatives." It was a pleasant visit, and we offered them a day sail, but they declined because of other obligations. We felt they were shackled by the money game. They lived an image, and they needed to keep working in order to maintain it. They were nice people and we were happy to have had the opportunity to visit them and see their island homes. But we knew their life was not a life we could live, any more than they could live part of their lives on a boat.

We left Hilton Head in the rain, the first rain we had in weeks, and we discovered leaks. The cockpit cover leaked in several places and the mizzenmast leaked at the deck joint. Tom knew what he had to do to solve the leak at the mizzenmast though it would be a lot of work, but we didn't know what we were going to do about the cockpit cover. We didn't like the idea of having a new cover made. Not only would it be expensive, it would force us to stay in one place for however long it took to get it completed. On the bright side, the rain was warm and getting wet was no longer such a serious matter.

WHERE DID THE ANCHOR GO?

Once we were south of the lovely historic city of Savannah, the ICW became more challenging to follow. It looked wide and appeared to hold a lot of water, but only the center channel was deep enough for us. We needed to follow the numbered buoys very carefully as the ICW had a lot of curves and bends. If we would have missed a buoy, we could have easily become lost and found ourselves up in a dead-end inlet and unsure how to exit.

Each buoy was numbered but many were spaced far apart requiring the use of binoculars to find the next one. Even with a detailed chart of the ICW, it was not easy to anticipate where that next buoy might be. In most places, the swamp grass was too high for us to see over. Our utmost concentration was needed to be sure we were going in the right direction.

As we motored along looking for our next buoy, we heard an elderly male voice on channel 16 of the VHF, "This is the sailing yacht JULIEL. Where can I purchase fuel?" Another voice answered him, requesting that he switch channels. "I can't switch channels," said the elderly voice. "I'm all alone and I can't leave the wheel to go below to my radio. I have a hand held microphone up here in the cockpit with me, but I can't change channels on it."

"Okay," said the younger man. "Where are you now?"

"I'm not sure," said the elderly man. "Just tell me which number buoy I should turn at to get fuel and I'll find it."

It was unusual for a conversation of this type to be taking place on Channel 16 because it is considered a "calling" station. People were expected to make their contact on Channel 16 and then switch to another channel for their conversation. In theory, that made their conversation more private, but mostly it freed up Channel 16 for others to make contact. Under the circumstances no one objected, so the conversation continued. We listened to the conversation and the events as they unfolded, as if on a radio play. Finally, the elderly man said he thought he knew where he was. We could hear the elated tone in his voice as he announced his revelation to the younger man. The younger man told JULIEL to turn around and go back four buoys, to buoy number 127. The elderly man said he understood. They signed off the radio and all was quiet.

A half-hour later, we heard the same elderly man on Channel 16 again. Not only was he unable to find buoy number 127, he was now completely lost. For all he knew he was not even on the ICW because he had not seen a numbered buoy for some time. The chatter was still going on when we came around a bend of tall swamp grass and saw the sailboat JULIEL anchored on the side of the ICW. We anchored next to him and Tom put our dinghy in the water and rowed over to him. His name was Charles, and he was an elderly single-hander. He was lost, confused, and said he was nearly out of fuel.

While Tom was still talking to Charles, a Coast Guard boat came by. I called it on the radio and requested spare fuel for the elderly gentleman. They agreed and anchored, while one of their small boats brought fuel to JULIEL. They asked if we would let him follow us until he got out of the tricky part of the ICW, and we agreed.

We told Charles he should follow us and that we were going to keep going until dark. Tom asked him what speed he could hold and he replied, " five knots." We agreed to maintain that speed. He seemed happy with the new situation and did a good job of following. At dusk, he must have been having a difficult time seeing us, because we heard him give a long blast on his air horn. We figured he wanted us to stop so we looked for an anchorage.

We anchored for the night at Buttermilk Sound and invited Charles to join us for dinner. He readily accepted. Watching him eat was like watching one of our boys eat when they were teenagers — we could not seem to fill him up. That skinny little man ate a huge dinner! He even ate the skins on his sweet potato. Later, he told us he had not eaten anything since breakfast. He was an interesting man, an 83-year-old retired doctor who was taking his boat from New Bern, North Carolina to Stuart, Florida. We learned his wife and son had hired a captain to go with him, but the two of them had not gotten along. "He didn't know what he was doing," Charles told us. "He just wouldn't listen to reason, so I told him to get off."

"Oh," we said, trying not to smile.

"Yes, but he just called my son and complained. My son made me take him back again. I tried it one more day with that guy, but he just didn't learn. He wanted to do it his way, or no way at all. So, I put him off again, and that time I didn't take him back on."

Charles had a need to talk, so we didn't interrupt him. We listened with curiosity and respect for this old man who was willing to do what he wanted to do, in spite of his frail, elderly body. "My son is worried I'm going to die out here all alone on the boat. I keep telling him I know how I'm going to die. Some day my pacemaker will just run its batteries down and that will be the end of it. That's not a bad way to go," he said. "Not if it happens while I'm doing something I like doing, like running the JULIEL."

He told us of his experiences as a volunteer doctor in Africa and many other stories. We found him to be charming and alert for his age. He captured our hearts, and his head seemed to work very well after he had had some food. He hardly seemed like the same man we had listened to earlier.

When dinner and a litany of sea stories were finished it was time to part. The current had changed now, so Charles would have to row against it to get back to his boat. He thanked us for the dinner, got in his dinghy, and started rowing through the darkness toward his boat. Thank goodness he had left a cockpit light on. At least he could row toward the small light. As he rowed against the current we thought about his pacemaker and became worried.

"I can't stand this," Tom said. "I just know I am going to be looking at his cockpit light an hour from now, wondering if he ever made it back to his boat. Then I'm going to be the one rowing all over this swamp looking for him." With that, Tom got in our dinghy and rowed toward Charles. When Tom caught up with him, he towed Charles back to the JULIEL. When Tom got back to our boat he said, "Good, now I can sleep comfortably." I gave him a kiss, turned off the VHF radio and we went to bed.

The next morning we were surprised to see the JULIEL was gone. "He's a spunky old coot," Tom said. "He probably was ready to go by sun up." We ate breakfast and got a fairly early start. At 9am Charles called us on the VHF.

"Good morning, VONNIE-T," said Charles. "You folks must really sleep sound. I tried calling you on the radio last night, but I guess you didn't hear me." I apologized to Charles and explained that we always turned the radio off at night to avoid having the chatter between fishing boats wake us. "Well," he said. "Someone came by and stole my anchor last night. I woke up bumping on the shore. Lucky, there was a little early light and I was able to get off before I got good and stuck. I was worried about you folks. Did they steal anything from you?"

"Charles, I'm sure no one would steal your anchor. Perhaps the anchor wasn't tied securely," I said.

"No, it was secure," he said. "I know because I did it myself!"

FLORIDA

The Georgia waters were a rich fishing grounds, and in St. Andrew Sound we saw the intricate silhouettes of shrimp boats. They waltzed across the water with nets spread out on long arms, giving the appearance of some mystical aberration holding out the skirt of a long flowing gown.

In Florida, we anchored for the night at St. Augustine, the first permanent settlement in North America established in 1565 by Pecro Menendez as a Spanish colony. The next night we anchored at New Smyrna Beach, the place where Ponce De Leon landed in 1513, 107 years before the Pilgrims from England arrived at Plymouth Rock. Though they landed a hundred years later, the English were better colonizers than the Spanish because they brought families, while the Spanish sent all-male contingents who could only fight for territory. Apparently, the stability of English family life outlasted Spanish military ambition. As we continued, we passed from old history to history in the making at Cape Canavaral, where we saw the NASA Vertical Assembly Building and the Apollo and Challenger pads.

Further south, we sailed through Boca Raton, a wealthy community of pink-and-white homes with sprawling lawns, private tennis courts, and connecting indoor-outdoor swimming pools. Power boats hung gracefully over the water, but there were no signs of people living there. We saw only workmen trimming hedges and on riding lawn mowers.

VONNIE-T'S EARLY HISTORY IN FLORIDA

We had purchased our boat two years earlier in Fort Lauderdale. My father, who was terminally ill with a brain tumor at that time, lived there. Tom named the boat VONNIE-T for the nickname of Vonnie, my fathers pet name for me when I was a child, and the "T" represented Tom. My father was estatic when he learned about our purchase, and he could hardly wait to go for a sail. We were inexperienced at the time, but we willingly invited my father, step-mother, sister, and brother-in-law to go with us on our test run. With everyone on board, we motored out of the canal and entered the channel carefully staying between the numbered red and green buoys until we were in the ocean. After clearing the congestion of other boats, Tom put up the sails and I turned off the engine. We sailed and tacked back and forth several times, pleased with the performance and handling of the boat.

My father sat tall and proud on his side of the boat, obviously thrilled with the whole experience, while my stepmother dutifully sat next to him, white knuckled and holding on to a nearby cleat. My sister, Tracy, eagerly took the wheel when given the opportunity. She enjoyed steering and feeling the power of the wind in the sails. Her husband, Mark, sat next to her and tried to be a good sport, but soon became pale. When we realized he was becoming seasick, we decided to go back into shore.

"Better start the engine," Tom said, "and I'll take down the sails." I turned the key to start the engine, but it would not start. We were stumped as to why. Tom went below to prime it, but that did not work either. My Dad and Tracy were nonplussed by the situation, but my stepmother became increasingly tense and jittery, and Mark became sick and vomited over the side. Tracy removed his glasses and we helped him step out of the cockpit and onto the side deck where he lay down and continued to vomit. We put a lifeline on him so he would not slip off the boat but could do nothing to ease his discomfort. The poor guy lay there like a big, miserable beached whale.

Meanwhile, Tom was down in the engine compartment trying to prime the engine and could see Mark's vomit slide past the porthole next to him. It was a terrible situation, not a dangerous one, but an extremely uncomfortable one.

Finally, Tom solved the mystery. "LaVonne, see if that black button next to the gear shift is pushed all the way down," he said. I checked and found it was up. "Push it down," he instructed, "and turn the key again." Sure enough, the engine started right away. The black button was a kill switch and it needed to be pushed down before the engine would start. We would *never* forget the kill switch again!

Tom took the sails down, and we motored in through the red and green buoys, back through the canal, and up to our slip. Mark was the first one off the boat, and he felt better as soon as his feet touched land, but then he was hungry. That was probably the emptiest his stomach had ever been. My stepmother was the second one off the boat while my Dad was in no hurry at all. He decided to take a little nap in one of the bunks until dinner was ready. I do not know if he slept or just savored being on the boat. I know he enjoyed every moment of that day.

THE GERMAN BUMBLE BEE

This time we arrived in Fort Lauderdale a few days before Thanksgiving and requested a boat slip. The SSCA was scheduled to hold its annual meeting the following week, and we knew there would soon be a shortage of slips and anchoring space. The slip assigned to us was under the Las Olas bridge and I was ecstatic to have the luxury of being able to step off the boat and onto a dock. Without a slip we would have anchored, and that would have required sharing the dinghy each time one of us went ashore. There would also have been the added concern of dinghy security, as there had been reports of dinghy thefts in the area.

Nothing is perfect, however, especially a boat slip under the Las Olas bridge. We soon discovered there was a constant *thumpity-thump thump* from the cars as they crossed the bridge and frequent shouting of unpleasant verbiage from rowdy teens who seemed to take pleasure in harassing boat live-aboards.

On our starboard side was a tiny boat with a meek couple and two yapping dogs. He, a retired doctor, hardly spoke loud enough to be heard. She, a nurse, spoke in a soft little girl's voice. The dogs seemed to make up for their owners' meekness by barking at the teens. On our port side was a high-decked sailboat flying a German flag. The man was a large, burly sort with a good sense of humor. He was easy-going and nonchalant about anything life presented to him. His wife, by contrast, was a large, no-nonsense woman. She did not think living on a boat was utopia, but out of duty to her husband, she did so.

Late one night, four or five rowdy teenage boys were making a lot of noise on the pier directly in front of the three boats. When the teens became louder and used obscene language, the German woman refused to ignore them. She got up from her bunk, marched down the dock in her night clothes and approached them with every intention of correcting the situation. She scolded them and called them "young punks" in a loud voice heavy with German accent. I was sure she could be heard all across the waterway.

"Vat do you think you are doing? Do you think nobody else is trying to sleep?" she screamed at the boys, who were tall and muscular. They loved it! It was the best fun they could have hoped for. They laughed and jeered at her and made obscene gestures. The added gestures only infuriated her more and increased her intent to discipline them. "Vere are your mothers? Vat do you think your mothers vould think of you boys if she could see and hear you?" she scolded with hands on her hips.

We watched her husband step off the boat, walk toward her and size up the situation. He realized they were delighted at the prospect of a physical fight. His very size would have made the fight a lot of fun for the boys, but of course it would not have been a fair fight, and we were relieved to see he had no intention of fighting. "Vooman," he roared! "Get back on the boat! Now!" His deep resonating voice hung in the air.

The scene was over in seconds. She stopped when she heard her husband's command. She turned and walked down the dock, stepped past him without saying a word, and returned to their boat. He did not speak another word either, not to her, not to the boys, and not to any of his neighbors who were in their cockpits watching. He followed her back to their boat and closed the hatch. The boys, like all the rest of us, were left with mouths hanging open, while his roar echoed in our heads. It took the boys a few seconds to realize they had lost the opportunity for some fun, and when the boys left we went back to bed. The rest of the night was peaceful. Even the sound of cars going over the bridge seemed less loud.

The next morning our German neighbor introduced himself. His big strong hand, while totally enveloping my hand offered a gentle handshake. He was not one of those people who needed to impress others by a painfully strong handshake. I liked that about him, and I liked how he took care of a potential problem.

"Gooten morgan," he said cheerfully. "My name is Ziggy. I vant to apologize for the little commotion last night."

"You needn't apologize to us," Tom said with sincerity. "I was impressed at how you handled those bullies. Your wife was pretty impressive, too."

"Ya, she's a tough vooman. I guess she's alright!" he said with a big laugh.

The conversation was light and pleasant. Ziggy's wife, Gertrude, brought up beer for the men and they used the drinking time to get acquainted. Sharing a beer together was a male form of German camaradrie at any time of day. I sympathized with Tom who was not used to drinking beer at 8:30 in the morning, but Ziggy didn't seem to think anything of it. While it did not matter what time of day he drank beer, it did matter what container the beer was in. Ziggy did not think beer tasted as good when it came from a can, or a "tin" as he put it. He drank only bottled beer.

Tom asked about the large circular structure lashed on his deck. It was huge and took up the total deck space on the bow of their boat. We had been curious about it from the moment we saw it. "Oh that," Ziggy said smiling and saluting it with his beer bottle. "That's my bumble bee. I've had more God damn fun vit that thing!"

Tom and I still didn't understand what it was, but Ziggy's laugh and delight with his bumble bee held our interest.

"It's vhat I think you Americans call a hovercraft. It goes fast as hell!" he said.

Gertrude said, "Von time he nearly killed himself on his bumble bee!"

"Yah, dat vas really goot," he told us. "I took the bumble bee out to see a big cruise ship dat vas anchored. She vas a good looking ship and I vanted to see her up close. I vas going real fast and looking up at the ship. Lots of people ver looking down at me, ven all of a sudden I saw der faces get a big vorried look on dem. I vondered vy they vas so vorried. Then, just in time, I saw vat they vas so worried about! I vas headed straight for the ship's big anchor chain. If I vould have hit that big anchor chain, vile going fast like that vith the bumble bee, I vould have made a big mess of myself and a lot of paper vork for the ship." Ziggy laughed again when he said, "Yah, I almost shit my pants that time. I tell you no lie."

CATCHING UP ON THE MAIL

We rented a car and eagerly drove north 200 miles to pick up our youngest son, Andy, and his roommate from the Orlando Airport. Andy planned to take a quarter off from college and spend it with us on the boat, and we couldn't have been more pleased. We felt it was a once-in-a-lifetime educational experience for him, one he couldn't get at school. We were not sure how much time his roommate, Ken, planned to spend with us, but whatever time he wanted was fine with us. We knew he had purchased an open-ended airline ticket because he wasn't sure, either.

As we drove toward the airport I noticed how good it felt to be in a car again. I had forgotten how comfortable car seats were. There was no place on the boat where either of us could sit that comfortably. I had also forgotten how fast cars were until I saw the trees fly past us along the side of the highway. Fifty-five miles per hour was a lot faster than six knots!

The boys' flight had been changed, and it took several hours to connect with them. After a mirthful reunion, Andy handed me a box wrapped in brown paper. "Here," he said. "This is your mail." As we walked he filled us in on the news from home, "Grandma is doing just fine. . . . Clark says hello. . . . Sara is still planning to come over

Christmas. . .. It was 32 degrees in Minnesota when we left. . . Boy, is it ever hot here! What's the temperature?"

We started the drive back in rain. Within a half hour all the family news had been shared, and the chatter stopped. It was dark. Soon we heard snoring from the back seat and there was no more talking. The windshield wipers made the only sound. Tom concentrated on the road and I concentrated on helping him stay on the road.

That night we read our mail until late into the night. Several months of mail takes a long time to read. Bills were placed in one pile, social correspondence in another. There was no rush. We wanted to savor each letter for as long a time as possible.

SEND THE GUNS HOME!

The next day, Tom and I went to the annual meeting of the Seven Seas Cruising Association (SSCA). I was amazed to see so many cruisers living on their boats at an anchorage, or at a slip or on a pier. All of them dreamed of the distant day when they would be able to sail to foreign shores. There were also many weekend or vacation sailors who looked with envy at those of us who were no longer chained to a five-day work week. We were most fascinated with the live-aboards who had actually sailed to those far away places, especially those who were willing to share stories about their expeiences. Each person we met was interesting and unique in their own way, and willingly shared what information they had.

One of the topics discussed was the dilemma of whether to have guns on board. Most of the old-time cruisers said, "Send them home or get rid of them." First off, they felt most people couldn't actually shoot another person if they were called upon to do so, and felt guns would only end up being used against the boat owner. Second, they said there were no reported incidents where having guns on board was justified or needed. Consensus was that they were a major inconvenience and not worth the bother of checking them in and out of each country. Based on that information Tom called his brother Mike and asked if he could send the rifle and the shotgun back to him. Packaging them and securing all the proper permits and paperwork was a feat in itself, but he finally got them mailed. We learned later that to receive them, Tom's brother needed to deal with more bureaucratic procedures. We kept the two handguns on board.

WATERPROOFING

Another timely thing we learned at the meeting was how to waterproof our leaking cockpit cover. It was a simple matter of painting it with Thompson Water Sealer, a sealer normally used for driveways. "It's sticky stuff, so it's best to avoid doing it on a windy day," we were told. "It will make a mess everyplace it hits."

We bought a big plastic container of the sealer and carefully painted it on the fabric with a brush. It worked beautifully and didn't leave the fabric stiff as I feared. The end result was a dry waterproofed cockpit. What simple, yet valuable advice.

PREPARATIONS TO LEAVE THE U.S.

While we attended the SSCA meeting, Andy and Ken got acquainted with chores on their new home. The boys were both great sports about all the tasks Tom assigned. They washed and waxed the fiberglass, cleaned both heads, put a fresh coat of paint inside the lockers, and scrubbed the anchor chain and chain locker. The anchor chain was a smelly mess, full of all sorts of decayed stuff from the many days of anchoring in the ICW. To wash it they spread its entire length out on the dock, scrubbed it well with heavy-duty brushes, and allowed it to dry in the sun before they planned to feed it back into the chain locker. But for some unknown reason the chain started to slide over the edge of the dock, and there was no stopping it. Once it started moving it was like a greased weasel. After a big laugh and a lot of muscle power they were able to bring it back up onto the pier.

They did a lot of physical work after they arrived, but they didn't seem to mind. I think they actually enjoyed working together in the warmth of Florida's weather. Their biggest challenge was in trying to deal with the limited space on the boat. They were both big, tall kids and they may have previously thought their dorm rooms were small, but the boat presented a new meaning to the word "small." In spite of having traveled fairly light, they were at a loss as to where they could keep their gear. We told them they could have the entire V-berth for their "stuff" and they could keep it as neat or messy as they wanted. They could sleep any place they wanted on the boat, but all their bedding and gear had to be stowed in the V-berth during the daytime hours. With four people living together on a boat, we needed to make every effort to keep the main cabin as clean and orderly as possible.

Tom and I already had a long list of tasks to accomplish before we left Florida, and our list lengthened considerably after talking to the old time cruisers at the SSCA meeting. We were encouraged to provision everything we thought we might need for the next several months because once we left Florida, we would be in foreign countries and would lose the convenience of stores and repair facilities. We bought more navigational charts, spare boat parts, and provisions such as food, paper, and hygiene supplies. Even the most mundane items required thought such as how much toilet paper would the four of us need and where was a dry place to stow it. Our next major provisioning would not take place until we reached the American Virgin Islands. As we brought aboard more provisions the task of stowing it became increasingly difficult and required creative sorting, stacking, and condensing.

Our most expensive and perhaps most important purchase was a satellite navigational system (Sat Nav) which would take the place of the Loran C we had been using. Once we left the U.S. coastal waters, we would no longer be within Loran C range. The Sat Nav was designed to allow us to navigate any place in the world via satellite.

Before we left the United States, I also took the test for my advanced ham radio license. Much to my relief, I passed. The new license allowed me to talk on a wider range of radio frequencies, and I hoped it would make phone patches with family members easier. It was important for us to frequently let them know where we were and that we were all right. It was even more important with someone else's son on board. I was sure Ken's family would appreciate hearing the "all okay aboard VONNIE-T" message as frequently as possible.

After 10 days of boat maintenance, shopping, stowing things, taking tests, and listening to the cars overhead on the Las Olas bridge, we were more than ready to go sailing! On the day when the weather and wind direction were favorable, we said goodbye to our neighbors and left the slip that had begun to feel like home—a noisy home, but home nonetheless.

TO "HERD" OR "NOT TO HERD"

We motored out from under the bridge. Tom raised the sails as we passed the breakwall and we sailed into the Gulf Stream through the buoyed channel. It was a wonderful relaxing sail with perfect 15-knot winds and lots of sunshine that sparkled friendly little smiles on the rippled water. Our destination that night was Key Biscayne. We planned to anchor at No Name Harbor and from there cross the Gulf Stream and sail to Cat Cay in the Bahamas the next day.

Apparently, others had a good plan as well, because the harbor was packed. It was much too crowded, and many boats were already anchored outside the harbor. There was no possibility of us anchoring inside the harbor and we considered ourselves lucky to find a comfortable place outside.

After we anchored Tom studied the charts and determined we should begin sailing shortly after 4 am. To figure our passage time, he calculated the distance, our typical speed, and the side slip from the Gulf Stream. The goal was to arrive at Cat Cay during daylight hours while the customs office was open. Shortly after dinner, we set our alarm and turned in for the night, feeling secure with our plan.

At midnight we were awakened by a steady stream of boats sailing out of the harbor. It looked like a parade, each neatly spaced the proper distance from the boat ahead, following along the same invisible line in the water. The night was lit from the nearly full moon and sky full of stars, and in the gentle breeze each boat seemed to silently entice the next one to follow. It was beautiful yet eerie to see so many boats following one right after the other into darkness.

"My God," Tom said. "It looks like a graduation procession where the lines of robes never seem to end. This time it's a line of sails." I could hardly believe there were that many boats in the little harbor. "It's tempting to pull up our anchor and go with them, isn't it?" Tom said.

"Yes. We may be the only boat left here if we don't."

We discussed the possibility of following the group. Then we remembered a discussion we had with our friends Linda and Ron on MOONSHADOW. After nine years of cruising they told us, "There will be times when you will have very logically planned your next move, when suddenly you will be tempted to do something illogical just because of the momentum of what other boaters are doing." Their advice was "to avoid succumbing to the temptation and stick to your plan."

We realized this was far from the life-or-death situation they spoke of. They told us the "herding" pheonomenon often happened when storm warnings were broadcast and "herding" took precidence over logic. We realized it would not have mattered if we had left then or a few hours later, but it was a good opportunity for us to practice doing what we *planned* to do, by not picking up the anchor to follow the flock. So we went back to bed and avoided second-guessing ourselves. When the alarm went off, which seemed like only minutes later, we were the only boat left in the anchorage.

We ate breakfast, hoisted anchor, and set sail into the darkness following the course Tom had previously drawn on our chart. We were proud of ourselves. The other boats were hours ahead and therefore our risk of collision with any of them was lessened.

It was a pleasant sail across the Gulf Stream, and Tom did an admirable job of charting our course to take into account the North Equatorial Current that flows into the Gulf of Mexico. It is a massive warm-water river in the sea that has been calculated to be 25 times greater than all the combined flow of the fresh water rivers in the world, and it passes the northern end of Cuba and the Bahamas on its way to the North Atlantic where it is squeezed into a 90-mile width between Florida and The Bahamas. With our typical 6-knot speed forward combined with the 2-knot stream current, Tom calculated we would be pushed northward by 30 miles. To compensate, he set our course to steer southward 20 degrees off line to allow for the side slip.

OUR ARRIVAL

Tom's calculations had been correct. We arrived during normal working hours and cleared customs at Cat Cay. Doing all the paper work was time consuming, but not a problem, as we had avoided a lot of confusion by not being there when the mass of boats arrived all at once. We used our seal with our boat name and the U.S. Coast Guard registration number for the first time. Some of the SSCA members told us they experienced smoother check-ins once they got a boat seal, so we had one made before we left Florida. I could hardly keep a straight face while watching Tom dramatically press each document with the seal in a flamboyant act of self importance, but the officials loved every minute of it and our check-in could not have gone better.

SALT WATER BATHING

For the next several days, we sailed early every morning and anchored in the afternoons allowing time for swimming, island exploring, and spear fishing. Tom and I thought the days were paced nicely, but the boys had a difficult time adjusting to the early hours. We were used to getting up before the sun and going to bed as the sun set. The boys were not! On a typical day we were up at 5am. Tom started the coffee, checked on the weather, and turned on the ham radio. At 6am I checked into the Caribbean NET followed by the

Waterway NET at 7:45am.

Andy chose to sleep in the main cabin where the radio and navigational station were located so there was no way we could insulate him from the sounds of our morning, and he made it clear he had no intention of getting up at that "ridiculous hour of the night." He would roll over, give a deep disgusted sigh and put the pillow over his head. Ken gave it his best effort the first few mornings by getting dressed, putting himself in an upright position, and sitting with his eyes wide open in a glassy gaze. Typically he sat on the low side of the cockpit like a statue, unable to speak, or even blink. Occassionally I tried to initiate a conversation with him, but I was lucky if it lasted more than a few brief sentences.

They didn't realize it, but their adjustments had just begun. While we were on the dock in Florida, there had been no problem with each of us taking a daily shower. When our boat water tank became empty, we simply filled it with a garden hose from the faucet at the end of the dock, but after we left the dock, the boys continued taking daily showers. When I checked our supply I became alarmed at how much water we had used since leaving Florida. In the Bahamas, we could not continue our daily practice of showering because in a salt water environment fresh water was scarce.

That evening I shared my concerns with everyone. I thought the boys understood, but apparently they had not grasped the seriousness of what it would mean if we ran out of water as that evening I saw both of them head toward the shower with towels in hands.

I said, "Wait a minute, where are you going?" They stopped in their tracks and just looked at me. "Remember," I said, "we are short of water and there can't be any more fresh water showers. All bathing from now on must be done in the ocean."

They did not move nor did they say a word. They stood looking at me with blinking eyes. I think they were waiting for me to laugh and say "April Fool" or something. "The fresh water we have left in our tanks needs to be used for cooking, drinking, and brushing our teeth," I explained.

When they realized I was serious and not joking, they looked at Tom. They didn't say anything, but their eyes asked, "Is this right? Do you really expect us to go without a shower?"

"We're not short of water yet, but we may be if we continue to use it for showers. The truth is, we don't know when or where we will be able to replenish our supply so we need to conserve," Tom explained in support of my announcement.

"But, if we take a bath in the ocean, how do we get the salt off of us, Dad?" Andy asked.

"Just towel it off," Tom answered.

"What about our hair?"

"Same thing," Tom said. "Just towel it off."

They both laughed hysterically thinking they had just heard the most absurd thing ever. In a mocking tone Andy said, "Well, Kenny let's go take our salt water bath."

"Okay Andy, it's probably going to keep our skin soft and youthful forever," Ken responded, while glaring at me out of the corner of his eye.

I knew it was going to be a big adjustment for all of us and decided not to let their disrespectful tone bother me. It would be better if I went along with their remarks rather than take offense so I said, "Well, it probably won't do that, but we'll all get used to it. I've found dish detergent or shampoo works a lot better than soap in salt water, so help yourselves to either." With that I dropped the topic. I was aware the boys would watch me closely to see if I was going to continue taking fresh water showers, but within a few days salt water bathing was no longer an issue, and we all did it.

STEERING AROUND THE CLOUDS

One afternoon Andy cast his fishing line off the stern of the boat. He caught some little fish, but since they were not big enough for eating he used one as bait. The water was about 12 feet deep, but crystal clear, so he could see when something came near his hook. All of a sudden he began laughing and called for us to come up into the cockpit. We looked into the water off the port bow and saw three barracuda, each about 36 inches long lying near the bottom.

"Watch this!" Andy said as he put another small fish on his hook.

We didn't have to wait at all. As soon as he dropped the fish and hook back in the water one of the barracudas took the head off the fish so fast we did not even see him bite on it. It took only seconds for the other two to clean his hook, but they were very careful not to touch it.

"Did you see that, Dad?" Andy asked. "Are those sharks?"

"No, but they're just as mean as sharks. They're barracudas and they're sneaky bastards." Tom said. "I don't much like them."

"Are they good to eat? There sure are a lot of them around." Andy said, thinking he would try to outsmart them and catch one.

"No, we don't want to eat those guys. We learned about them at the SSCA meeting. They are the most likely fish to have Ciguatera poisoning. The small fish eat reef vegetation containing ciguatera, and the big fish eat the small fish. We learned that ciguatera doesn't make the fish sick, but it accumulates in their systems. If people eat fish with ciguatera it stays in them too, and when a person accumulates enough he or she can become sick. The illness affects the nervous system and acts like the flu during the first few days, but when the flu symptoms are gone people are left with a reversal of hot and cold. One man told us he burned his mouth drinking hot coffee because the coffee felt cold to him while he was recovering from ciguartera," Tom explained. After that litany of information Andy lost interest in fishing for the night.

We needed to put miles under our keel each day and as we did so we also needed to carefully read the milky blue shallow water carefully. Dark spots in the water usually meant coral heads and it was crucial that we steer around them because our deep keel would surely hit them if we tried to go over one. One day, there seemed to be an unusually large number of coral heads and I steered an erratic course to avoid hitting them when finally Tom asked, "What are you doing?"

"I'm steering around the coral," I answered.

"There's no coral ahead," he said. "Where do you think you see coral?"

When I pointed out the dark areas on the water he began to laugh. "What's so funny?" I asked.

"That's not coral," he said, "it's just clouds casting shadows on the water. You're steering around the clouds."

Boy, did I ever feel like a big fool! I'd obviously been behind the wheel too long and we agreed it was Tom's turn. It was important to arrive at Nassau in time to meet Sara, our youngest daughter, and steering around clouds only slowed our progress.

Sara was a freshman at Mankato State College and she planned to spend her Christmas break with us. We would be a little more crowded with five on board, but the boys had adjusted so well by then that we felt adding Sara would go smoothly as well. We would be a very full boat, perhaps even crowded, but we were thrilled to have all of them with us over the Christmas season.

DOUBLE WHISKER RUBS

Two days before arriving at Nassau, I received a message on the Waterway NET from Warren (WBØKIS), one of our ham radio friends in Minnesota. Through the net coordinator, a frequency and time was scheduled for me to talk with him. We wanted to think it was good news, but we were afraid it might not be. With intrepidation, the boys and Tom sat listening quietly while I contacted Warren at the scheduled time. Our fears quickly evaporated. Warren had great news! Clark, our oldest son, was also flying into Nassau to spend Christmas with us. Clark's plane would arrive two hours before Sara's.

Wow! We would have half of our family with us for Christmas! I was both pleased and worried; worried because I would need to provide three meals a day for six people in an area of the world where grocery stores were few and far between. Even as a home economist who once taught others how to plan meals and stretch their food dollars, I was concerned, since I had provisioned for four people, not six. The shortage of space was another concern. How were six of us going to live, eat, and sleep in close quarters? The potential for friction was high.

We arrived at Nassau on time and anchored close to the Bahama Search and Rescue Association (BASRA) dinghy dock. On the way to meet Clark and Sara's airplanes we stopped at the Nassau Telecommunications Office where I picked up my reciprocal Bahamas ham radio license. I knew that I had to get a reciprocal license to operate the ham radio legally in each country, so when we were in Florida I mailed my check and a copy of my US license to the Nassau Telecommunications Office expecting it to simplify the process when we arrived. When I picked up the license, however, I was disappointed to learn there was no "third party traffic" allowed in the Bahamas. That meant I could not send or receive messages from family members (a third party) through the ham radio while we were in the Bahamas. While I understood the intent was to encourage use of their telephone system, the rule was ridiculous because the Bahamas was made up of many uninhabited islands where telephone service did not even exist. I complied with the law of the country, however, and informed my ham friends in Minnesota of the restrictions when I talked with them.

Clark's plane was right on schedule and when I saw him I almost didn't recognize him. He had grown a beard. His beard, like Tom's, sprouted an assortment of colors, but Clark's had a color range from reddish brown to blond. "Clark," I yelled and waved to him. "I nearly didn't know you behind that beard."

"Well, look at you, Mom. You look like a native with your dark hair," he answered. I had forgotten he wasn't accustomed to seeing my natural hair color. I had been a bottle blond for years and let it grow out only a few months before we moved onto the boat.

"And who is this old scrub brush with you?" he asked when he saw Tom with his new beard.

"You just mind your manners there, Honey Boy," Tom said.

Honey Boy had been Tom's nickname for Clark ever since we married. It was based upon my calling Clark "Honey" when he was a young boy, but after Tom and I married I found myself calling him "Honey" as well. Clark naturally became "Honey Boy."

"This scrub brush is a sign of dignity," Tom teased as he gently pulled on Clark's beard. "Hey, this is going to be a good handle to grab any time you get out of line with the captain."

There was a surplus of new beards and hair color at our mini-family reunion, and after I became accustomed to seeing Clark with his, I thought it looked good on him. It added years and a touch of maturity to his young face. He was our oldest child, the most mature of the six, yet the least sophisticated. He dressed in old jeans worn thin at the knees and a light blue cotton knit shirt. His tennis shoes were partially laced to allow his foot to slide in and out, loafer style. He had spent six years in the Navy and had recently started working at a refinery. He was the only one of our six who was self-sufficient with a responsible job. He had quick-witted humor and an easy attitude, and looked upon life as something to be tasted and enjoyed. People liked Clark.

Our two hour wait for Sara became a three and a half hour wait, and seemed even longer in the heat of the small airport in Nassau. When her plane finally arrived we were relieved and happy to see her, as we did not want a repeat of Andy and Ken's arrival in Florida when they had been transferred to another plane without our knowing it.

Sara, our youngest child, was at the other end of the spectrum from Clark. First of all, she was perfectly groomed and looked absolutly great! She had always been a pretty child, but as I watched her step off the plane I was struck with how grown-up she had become. She wore her long blond hair in a single French braid which started on the top of her head and ran down the center of her back. She wore no make-up to accentuate her natural beauty, and she carried her tall, slim body with elegance, seemingly oblivious to the mystique she presented. To her, life was a serious matter: something to be treated with care and caution.

When she walked through the gate, I said, "Sara, we are over here." She heard my voice and walked toward us gracefully and without hurry.

"Dad, is that really you?" Sara asked. "Oh, my gosh!" She said while trying to avoid laughing out loud.

"How about a little whisker rub from your old dad," Tom said while reaching out to give a big hug.

"Oh ick, dad!" Sara said, while smiling and trying to hold Tom at arm's length for fear his beard might actually touch her. "Why did you grow THAT?" Sara barely got the words out when she realized that the other bearded character was her brother, Clark.

"Hello sister, this is your lucky day — double whisker rubs," Clark teased as he gave her a hug.

Our happy reunion continued as we climbed into a cab and headed back to the dinghy dock, about fifteen miles from the airport. We loaded the luggage and ourselves into the dinghy and motored out to VONNIE-T where Andy and Ken waited for us. I couldn't help thinking how different Sara's first Christmas holiday from college would be compared to her classmates'.

Her brothers and sisters wanted to be on their own as soon as they finished high school, and it seemed perfectly natural for us to begin our adventure soon after Sara's graduation. We helped Sara into her new home (dorm) at Mankato State College and provided money and anything we could to ease her transition.

Later we realized the burden we had placed upon her. When the other kids in her dorm went home for the occasional weekend and returned with clean clothes, a box of cookies and good memories, she felt abandoned. Our reassuring phone calls were not the same as sharing tribulation and success first hand. We felt badly for pushing Sara out of the nest so soon. On the other hand, she quickly matured from a self-centered teenager to a responsible adult. Emotionally, she grew faster than her classmates, and we saw that she had acquired a self-respect and sensitivity for others. She had become a joy to be around.

Life aboard our crowded floating home with adult children was wonderful. Our sailing became more relaxed once everyone had arrived, meaning we did not get up until 7:30am and didn't get underway until about 9:00am Some days we didn't sail at all. Sometimes we stayed a day or two at an anchorage, especially if the water was clear and there were fish to catch and things to see and explore. There was the constant sound of laughter, healthy teasing, and caring inquires about school and future plans. Sara helped me cook, the boys took turns doing dishes. Everyone assisted with sailing, bringing the dinghy aboard and keeping things neat and orderly. We all snorkled, fished, and laughed often. There was an attitude of helpfulness and sharing. Our children had become adults.

ONLY TEETH AND EYES WERE VISIBLE

On Boxing Day, the Bahamians celebrate their independence from the English, in 1973, with nighttime festivities called Junk Canoe. It is a big cultural event, and we all looked forward to experiencing it, so that night we went to bed right after dinner and set our alarm clock for 2am.

It seemed strange going to shore and walking to the bus in the middle of the night, but many Bahamians were out on the street heading to Junk Canoe, as well. The bus was packed, but we were the only white people on it! Everyone was in a festive mood and they kindly squished together to make room for the six of us. We got off when everyone else did and followed the group along the poorly paved streets until we ran into a wall of people who stood along the parade route, and we could walk no further. Judging by the laughter and chattering of voices, everyone was having a great time, but it was difficult to see how many people were there. There were no street lights and their dark skin blended into the night. Only eyes and teeth were visible when they laughed.

We heard clanging music off in a distance and when the music grew louder we saw it came from a large papier-mache' dragon float. There were many floats after that one and many bands with homemade instruments. Hardly any of the instruments were designed to produce a pleasant sound; apparently they needed only to be loud and to pound out a beat. Next came a dancing group composed of tall slender young women in costumes made of crepe paper, sea shells, and cocoanut shells held together with green vines. Their long muscled brown legs and arms glistened with perspiration as they danced to the loud beat. It was a spectacular event, especially considering the limited access to any of the things we would think necessary for a parade of that magnitude. After Junk Canoe, we returned to the boat hungry, and I made a big breakfast of pancakes before we all went back to bed.

It was early afternoon when we woke feeling sluggish but not really tired, clearly not up to par. We were tempted to lie around the boat and be lazy, but instead we went back into Nassau to see what the day after Junk Canoe looked like.

CHEW THAT CONCH

It was hot that afternoon and many people were resting. Still, there were a number of peddlers down by the wharf, but because the crowds were thinner we were able to watch Bahamian men clean conch. They were very fast at it! They picked up the entire conch shell, made a small hole with a machete a short distance down from the pointed end, and severed the muscle from the shell with a small knife. Then they reached in and grabbed the claw, or the foot, of the conch and pulled the live critter out.

The conch was a slippery gray-black glob of muscle. The head was jet black, the shape of a human thumb, and on it were two thin slimy posts with eyes perched on the ends. The body of the creature was various shades of shiny black and dark gray and at the end was the clawlike foot used to move the conch and its big heavy shell around the ocean floor, as it searched for food.

As the Bahamians cleaned the conch, they discarded the shells on a large growing pile. What a shame! They were the type of shell tourists liked to put up to their ears to hear the ocean. The pile was not only an eyesore, its stench was a haven for both flies and rats.

We saw men walk over to the cleaning tables, converse briefly, and take some part of the conch from those who were cleaning them. They put whatever it was in their mouths and walked away. The process was repeated often, always by different men, and it aroused our curiosity. Those who cleaned the conch were professionals; they were fast and made it look easy. One of them handed Tom a part of the conch that was the size and shape of an earthworm, but it was clear and dripped slime. Not all conch had this thing, but I still did not understand what it was until we asked.

The man we asked had one big yellow eye and the other was milky and didn't focus well. He talked to us through large thick lips, exposing an equally thick tongue. Several teeth were missing, leaving a lot of gum line visible as he smiled and spoke to us in broken English slang. In spite of the heat and humidity he wore a multi-colored knitted wool hat over thick, bushy, black hair that stuck out around the edges. While he talked, his thick fingers and large hands continually worked on a conch and didn't miss a stroke. His smile seemed sinister as he told us the slimy clear worm was the male conch organ and that if men ate it they would acquire greater potency. When I realized that was what we saw those other men putting in their mouths, I nearly gagged. It didn't appeal to Tom either, and he declined the offer, but we saw the local men continue to stop for them. They popped the raw slimy thing into their mouths and went on their way, no doubt feeling much more manly.

The conch itself could be tasty if prepared properly. The easiest was to chop it and put it in a small plastic bag with peppers, onions and vinegar, which became a salad. But the best way, we were told, was to pound it and then fry it, thus making a dish called cracked conch.

We left the waterfront and decided we should at least taste a typical Bahamian cracked conch meal, so we entered the first local restaurant we saw. It was a small wooden structure that showed evidence of once being painted green. The rickety door squeaked and sagged as we opened it and it was dark inside. It took a few seconds for our eyes to adjust before we saw three empty booths on the right side of the room and tables covered in worn plastic with a floral pattern. Across from the booths was a wooden bar with a few rickety bar stools pushed up against it. At the other end of the room was a pool table with torn felt. There was a cotton print curtain hanging from the doorway to the kitchen. The place was empty, but we were immediately greeted by a large Bahamian woman who appeared from behind the curtain. All six of us squished into one of the booths.

"You wanna eat or just drink?" she asked.

We told her we had heard that cracked conch was a specialty in the Bahamas, and that we would like to try it if that was possible.

"Yeah. Dat be no problem. You alls wana have cracked conch? Dat gona take me maybe 20 minutes or mo. You wana have sompin to drink whiles you waits?"

We ordered soda and beer and waited. We heard tremendous pounding sounds coming from the kitchen followed by the sounds of hot sizzling grease — then more pounding followed by another hiss from hot grease. Finally, our meals came. The cracked conch had been fried in a light fluffy batter and looked more like big pieces of Japanese tempura. Each plastic plate held two large pieces of conch, a cabbage and tomato salad, and a baking powder biscuit. There was a pot of margarine and another pot of honey on the table for the biscuit. Everything was delicious, and the best part was, I didn't have to cook it!

We were stuffed and when we got back to the boat we were ready for a game of cards. We had begun a pattern of playing cards each night, something everyone seemed to look forward to because it was a venue for sociability. Some nights we had so much fun that Tom and I managed to stay up until 11pm, several hours past our normal bedtime.

Over the next few days we sailed to several small anchorages where we could swim and fish, and in one we were surprised to find a plentiful supply of conch. Tom, Andy, and Clark dove down to get them. They had a great time diving, each time stretching themselves a little further until they were free-diving to 15 feet with no trouble. Soon we had a lot more conch than we could possibly eat, so we kept the largest ones and threw back the smaller ones. Everyone looked forward to having cracked conch for dinner that night, as it would be a welcome change from fish.

Tom got out his hatchet and made a small hole in the shell. He reached in, grabbed the foot and gave it a pull, just like the Bahamians did, except the critter did not come out! In fact, it pulled itself up further into its shell. Tom made another hole and tried again. Still no success. He tried again and again. Finally, he got one out, but the shell was nearly pulverized and fragments were all over the stern of the boat. With much effort he smashed several more shells and removed the critters. I cut the eyes, head, and foot off of each one and took them below to cook. We were told to pound them to tenderize them, so I pounded each of them several times with an empty wine bottle. I sliced them into half-inch-thick strips, dipped them in egg and seasoned flour, then dropped them into a fry pan with hot oil. The conch curled up in the pan and turned a dark brown. Humm, they didn't look the same as the ones in Nassau, but the galley smelled good and everyone looked forward to dinner. I put a big platter of conch in the middle of the table and smaller bowls of side dishes next to it. Everyone sat down, contined their chatter, and served themselves as usual. We each had big piles of conch on our plates, but soon the usual chatter stopped. I looked around the table and saw rolling eyes and chewing jaws. We chewed, and chewed, and chewed. Eating my conch was like trying to eat thick rubber bands. The conch simply would not allow themselves to be chewed into small enough pieces to be swallowed, but no one was brave enough to say a word. The kids looked at each other while trying to talk to one another with only their eyes. They silently continued chewing.

Finally, it was Tom who broke the ice. "Boy, these conch suckers are really tough," he said. "Mom, I think you need to go back to the Bahamian lady and ask her to show you how to cook these things." Under any other circumstances I would have been hurt to have Tom talk about my cooking that way, but this time even I had to laugh. They were awful! I didn't have a clue as to what I had done wrong, but whatever it was, it was disastrous.

Two days later we were back in Nassau to purchase fresh food supplies. I made a trip back to the restaurant and told the cook I wanted her to teach me how to prepare conch the way she did. I told her I would buy a conch dinner, but I wanted to watch her cook it in her kitchen. At first she didn't want me in her kitchen. She wanted to tell me how to cook conch. I said no, I needed to *see* her cook it. Finally, she relented. She told me to return in two hours and I realized that she wanted to clean the kitchen before I saw it. When I returned, she took me back to her kitchen. I can not imagine how bad the kitchen must have looked before she cleaned, because it was still filthy! The floor was dirty linoleum, the walls were dark with greasy smoke stains, the wooden table which was also the cutting board had deep cuts in it, filled with dirt and old food. The only light in the kitchen came from the back door and a single light bulb hanging from a long filthy cord over the table. The stove was old, with only two of the four burners working. She had the conch all ready for me. The black little critter laid on the center of the table.

"The first thing yous got to do, is remove da skin," she said. She took a large knife, made a slit in the skin and pulled it off. No wonder my conch was tough; I had completely skipped that step and fried the conch with the skin on.

"Da next ting is to get da grease good'n hot." She lit the stove with a wooden match and put the pot of old grease on the burner to heat. I wondered how many conch that old grease had cooked. It looked gross. "Whiles da grease is get'n hot, wes got to pound da conch," she said. "You sees, conch is mighty tough, an it do need a lot of tenderisen. It shor enuff do need dat." She took out a meat tenderizer hammer and pounded that small conch until it looked like a lace doilie. "When you gets it nice an thin, like dis, den you is ready to cook it.

First, she dipped it in seasoned flour. Next, she dredged it though a whipped raw egg. Then she dropped the conch into the hot fat. It sizzled and puffed up and she used a wire spoon to remove the conch from the fat. "Dats all de is to it," she said. "It really ain't no trouble. You's just got to pound it a little, honey child."

It was delicious, and oh, so tender. I praised her, paid her, and thanked her. We parted as two happy women, realizing we did not know anything about each other's worlds — only that we had become friends.

THE GRINCH STOLE CHRISTMAS

On Christmas Eve Day, we sailed into Staniel Cay, Bahamas and were greeted by Kathy and Dave Jones on the sailboat PERIGRIN. We first met them in Beaufort, North Carolina, and had been surprised when they already knew so much about us. Kathy explained she had relatives in Duluth and sailed there last August. They had rented our slip at the Lakehead Marina. By the time we met them, they had heard all about us from the neighboring boats in Duluth. It was good to see them again here at Staniel Cay. They had their college son, Jay, with them for the holidays.

Jay told us about a marvelous cave to swim in. "The fish are tame and swim toward people, expecting to be fed. They're really colorful and they actually brushed up against me looking for bread or crackers. Two movies were filmed in the cave: a Walt Disney film and 'Thunderball', one of the James Bond movies."

Of course we all checked out the cave. It was just as nice as he promised. The fish were great and there was even a nurse shark lying on the bottom. After swimming in the cave, I invited the Joneses over to VONNIE-T for drinks and snacks.

Everyone was wet, cold, hungry, and thirsty. While the dinghies were tied up quickly, I got out towels, beverages, and snacks. We chatted about future cruising plans and searched the fish books to try to identify the fish we had seen in the cave.

"Did you see the shark on the bottom?" Jay asked Sara.

"Yeah, but I thought sharks were bigger than that," she answered.

"That was just a baby," Jay said in a macho tone.

"It was just a nurse shark," Andy added, all puffed up. "Nurse sharks never hurt people."

"I liked the little yellow and blue fish," I said. "They're so pretty."

"They're called surgeon fish," Andy said and showed me a picture of one in our fish book.

"They're pretty," said Kathy, "but I don't like it when they rub up against me."

"Oh, that's what's so neat," said Clark. "I liked having the fish swim around me. The only thing is, I know they're just begging for the bread."

We continued socializing about the fish, the cave, and each of our little water-related phobias. The kids became better acquainted with Jay, sharing information about schools and college classes. At one point I heard Sara ask Jay, "How do you explain to your friends that your parents live on a sailboat?"

"I just tell them," he said. "They don't understand, but they don't really care much one way or the other."

"Yeah, but don't you feel bad sometimes when everyone else goes home for weekends and holidays?" Sara asked.

"I did at first, but I'm used to it now," he said. There was a pause during which all three college kids were thinking about how different their lives were from their college friends. Then Jay added, "Sometimes I go with my friends to their homes. That's usually pretty nice. My friends' parents are always interested and surprised to learn where my parents are. They usually want to know more about my parent's travels than I can answer."

Meanwhile, Tom and Dave looked at charts and marked the good anchorages. The whole day was pleasant and everyone enjoyed themselves and one another's company. When the sun began to drop, Dave, Kathy, and Jay said they needed to get back to their boat which was anchored around the corner and out of sight. For safety reasons they wanted to dinghy that distance while there was still daylight.

After they left, we went below for our Christmas Eve dinner. Sara helped me make lasagna for the special night. Making lasagna is a lot of work under the best of circumstances. Making it on a boat compounds the difficulty by at least a factor of two. The effort was worth it though; it was delicious and every last square was eaten.

I felt wonderful, not only because the lasagna turned out well and was praised, but because our kids were appreciating everything. In the past they seemed to have the attitude that life owed them everything. None of that old attitude showed on the boat. The difficulties and scarcities of everyday living aboard made them value things they had previously taken for granted. Both Tom and I were proud of these three. They had become happy, sensitive, caring adults.

The talk at the dinner table was, as usual, on a jovial note. We talked about Santa being a little slim this year in the gift department, but we told them he had a small gift for everyone, which we would open in the morning. There was great reminiscing about Christmases of the past. They were wonderful memories, discussed and re-discussed, with much laughter and good humor. We could hear the music on shore from the little festivities, so the kids asked if they could take the dinghy into shore after dinner.

"Sure," Tom said. "Mom and I could use a little time alone too. Just be sure you tie it up well. The dinghy is like our car, you know. Without it we can't get into shore."

"Okay, no problem! We'll be careful," they all agreed.

"First we'll do the dishes." Sara said, "Won't we, guys?"

"Oh, yeah, little sister, good idea," Clark said with a silly smile, but immediately started to clear the table.

They all pitched in with the dishes and they were done in a flash. They freshened up: Sara combed her hair and the boys put on clean shirts and money in their pockets. As they climbed out into the cockpit, Tom teased Sara "Sara, when have you ever had three bodyguards before?"

"Really!" She answered with a big smile, while pretending not to like it.

"Have fun, but try to be quiet when you come back because Mom and I will probably be sleeping," Tom instructed.

While Tom said this, the kids stood topside on the port side near the cleat where we tied the dinghy. Each peered into the water, but no one untied the dinghy or got into it. They stood and looked into the water. Then they looked at one another and back into the water. Sara was the one to finally break the silence. She said, "It's gone!"

"What's gone?" Tom and I asked in unison.

"It's gone," she said again. "The dinghy is gone!"

I heard the words, but somehow couldn't believe it. I quickly flipped on the deck lights and went up to look for myself as if I were looking for a misplaced mitten or a sock, and maybe they couldn't find what was right before their eyes. I peered into the black water which was rapidly moving past the hull of the boat and realized the current had taken our dinghy and motor out to sea. Somehow with all the commotion and excitement of the afternoon, the dinghy had not been tied securely. Clark took full responsibility. "I was the one who tied it up," he said remorsefully.

Everyone felt sick about it. Our perfect day and Christmas Eve had turned into a nightmare. No one dared speak; we went below and sat in heavy silence. Tom walked over and flipped off the deck light. Then he sat down with the rest of us.

Finally, Tom spoke. "As captain, I should have checked the dinghy. It was my responsibility, no one else's."

"Shit," Clark said. "I'm the one who tied it, or thought I tied it."

"It could have been any one of us," Tom said.

No one could think of anything else to say or do. Everyone felt terrible and there did not seem to be any way to fix the situation. It just was not fixable! Ken looked frightened, almost as though he was expecting someone to have a temper flare-up. After all, he didn't know us very well and he certainly had not seen how we reacted in stressful situations.

Andy looked like he wanted to cry and Clark looked like he would like to crawl into a hole someplace. Tom looked tired and spent. I don't know how I looked to the others, but I felt sick to my stomach, and it would not have taken much for me to throw up all the lasagna I had just eaten. Sara remained hopeful and suggested, "Maybe we could ask someone on the radio to look for our dinghy." Her helpful suggestion was followed by a long silent pause. "Well, I'm only trying to help," she said defensively when no one responded to her suggestion.

Quietly, and with almost no expression Tom said, "That may work if we offered a reward."

"Do you think that would be possible?" I asked with renewed hope.

"I don't know, but it might be worth a try," he stated flatly.

"Should I call on the radio?" I asked.

He agreed, and I felt a hopeful excitement as I went to the VHF radio and called the Yacht Club where all the island activities were taking place that evening. I told the woman who answered that we had lost our dinghy. I told her we would be willing to pay a $200 reward to anyone who found it. I asked her if she thought anyone on the island with a small boat might be interested in looking for it tonight.

"I dona know, but I axeses around da place," she said in Bahamian English. "Whats da name of your'n boat?"

"This is the VONNIE-T," I said, and spelled it for her: "Victor, Oscar, November, November, India, Echo dash Tango."

"OK, BONNIE-T, someone'l call you later."

"Thank you," I said, encouraged. "How soon do you think we will hear from you? It is important that they start the search as soon as possible."

"Maybe ten'er twenty minutes," she said, and promptly closed off.

I began to feel positive until Tom said, "No one is going to want to look on

Christmas Eve."

I did not want to believe that. I went up to the cockpit to think, and be on the lookout for some good samaritan who would want to look for our dinghy. Pretty soon Sara came up to join me. What perfect little Pollyannas: We actually thought someone would be willing to leave their family and friends on Christmas Eve to help us find our dinghy. The guys were far more realistic. They seemed to accept the idea that no one would help us. Andy went to bed. Ken and Clark sat solemnly on their bunks and I'm not sure what Tom was doing. Whatever it was, he stayed below.

Sara encouraged me to call the yacht club back again after 20 minutes had passed. I called, feeling much less encouraged than I was 20 minutes earlier. Much to my surprise, I learned one of the local men would be interested in trying to find the dinghy. Yes, he had a boat. Yes, he would come right out to our boat if we would turn on our deck light so he would be able to identify our boat.

Before I even signed off and hung up the microphone, Tom had the deck light turned on. He had a flashlight in his hand and was putting on a windbreaker. Clark had his jacket on and was in the process of putting on his second shoe. It was clear they both intended to go on the search.

I dug out two flotation belts and told them they needed to put them on, while giving one of my typical little lectures which went something like: "Please be very careful and don't do anything that will risk your lives. Your safety is far more important than any old dinghy. I want you to wear a safety flotation belt, because if anything happens, you will have to stay afloat until daylight before anyone would be able to find you."

I expected an argument, but I did not get one. They put on the belts and got into the tired little wooden boat which appeared at our boat side. As they motored off into the darkness I thought, "Oh please, please don't let this night turn into a worse nightmare than it already is."

My only comfort was knowing they were wearing flotation belts. The belts consisted of a small pouch on a belt. The pouch was designed to spring into a horseshoe life preserver when it hit the water. If for any reason the pouch did not explode upon impact with the water, there was a small rip cord which was supposed to activate the CO_2 cartridge when it was pulled.

It had already been a long night, and I suggested to Ken and Sara that they go to bed. I started a pot of coffee. While the water was heating, I dug out two hundred dollars from our secret compartment to pay the man in the event he found the dinghy. Once the coffee was done, I took a cup up into the cockpit and prepared myself for a long wait. I had not even finished drinking my first cup when I heard the small boat motor. It came closer and closer but I could not see it. It was a very dark night — no moon and no stars. I strained my eyes in the direction of the sound but saw nothing. The air was gray soup. I was surprised when the small boat appeared next to our boat since I couldn't see it until it was right there. There was no dinghy with them but everone was safe. I didn't care about the dinghy any more; I was just relieved and happy to see Clark and Tom back safe and sound. Clark pulled his own money out of his pocket and paid the man for his time and gas and thanked him for trying.

"It's so dark out there, we would have to bump into the thing by accident before we could even see what we hit," Tom said to me, as he crawled back onto our boat.

Clark didn't say a word. He went below, got undressed, and went to bed. We knew he felt terrible, but there was nothing any of us could do about it. He wanted no comfort!

Tom and I sat in the cockpit for a long time, sipping hot coffee and discussing how our relationship with the kids was so much more important than the dinghy and motor. We probably talked for an hour or more. Finally, Tom said firmly, "We just can't let the Grinch steal our Christmas."

With that statement he stood up, gave me a kiss and said, "Voman, (trying to mock our German friend Ziggy) "It's time we put these tired bodies in bed."

The next morning we had our small Christmas, as planned. We had breakfast and exchanged small gifts. Then we got out the charts and developed a new plan to sail back to Nassau where we would purchase a new dinghy and motor.

PART TWO
Life in the Tropics

CHAPTER FOUR

To the Bahamas and Beyond

DEPARTURES

The two-day trip back to Nassau turned out to be a lot more fun than we had anticipated and we quickly adapted to life without a dinghy. Come evening, we anchored in 15 feet of water close to coral formations, where we were able to snorkel, spear fish, and of course, take our salt water baths.

Tom used the VHF radio as we neared Nassau, to request a slip with a dock so we could get off the boat without having to swim to shore, and fortunately dock space was available. The time had come for the family exodus from Christmas vacations. Clark was the first to leave as he needed to return to work, but before he boarded his airplane he made us promise to let him pay half the cost of a new dinghy and motor. Reluctantly, we agreed, knowing he would never feel good about the dinghy incident if he was not allowed to pay what he felt was his fair share. We were proud of him and his integrity.

Ken decided to leave with Clark. We knew that Ken had grown from his experience and that he had acquired a new appreciation for creature comforts that he had previously taken for granted. After Ken left, Tom and I joked about the potential for establishing a business providing sailing experiences for pampered suburban children. We figured there might be many parents who would gladly fund such an experience.

Sara left a few days later, leaving only Andy, Tom, and me, and the boat seemed empty without the laughter of the group. On the positive side, however, Andy was still with us, and we appreciated his company.

Our first order of business in Nassau was to buy a new motor and a dinghy. We purchased a soft-sided hard-bottom Avon dinghy, an Evinrude 10-horsepower motor, and a large carbine stainless steel clip for the end of the painter to ensure that we would never lose another dinghy because it wasn't belayed properly. The dinghy was entirely gray yet

Tom insisted it only *looked* gray, but was really *gold* — his way of saying they were both very expensive. Only as a last resort would cruisers buy a dinghy or motor in the Bahamas; they are simply too expensive there.

NORMAN'S CAY

We left Nassau on January 6th while most other cruising boats stayed in port in avoidance of a 30-knot wind. Strong wind or not, it was blowing on the beam and Tom wanted to take full advantage. After months of beating into the wind, he had no intention of passing up an opportunity for a fast, easy sail. The boat sliced smoothly through the water creating a frothy, gurgling wake. Tom loved it. I endured it.

"Is Andy sleeping?" Tom asked me.

We had not seen him for about a half hour. I figured he had curled up in the V-birth and was taking a nap, but I decided to check on him anyway. He was not in the V-birth, and neither was he in either of our two heads. "He's not here," I told Tom with a sick, panicky feeling.

"What do you mean, he's not here?" Tom asked, hoping I was playing some sort of a joke. "He's not on deck, so he has to be down below deck!"

"Well, he's not!"

Tom turned the wheel over to me and went below to look. He opened both head doors and slammed them shut, checked the V-birth, looked in our stern cabin, and the side cabin where he kept his tools, and even peered into the engine compartment. Andy was not below decks! He came up to the cockpit looking ashen, and his eyes bulging like those of a trapped beast.

We both started talking, trying to remember if either of us had heard a splash in the water that might have been Andy falling overboard, but neither of us could remember having heard anything different from the constant flow of water being pushed past our hull. Still, if he wasn't on board then he must have fallen overboard.

I turned on the engine and Tom prepared to release the sails so we could turn the boat around and begin our search. I released the genoa sheet while Tom readied himself to roll it in. As we entered our turn the boat healed to the other side with a sudden jerk and then we heard Andy's voice coming from the spreaders half way up the mast.

"Hey, what's going on?" he asked, while hanging on tightly as he began to descend from his perch.

"What are you doing up there?" Tom asked with both anger and relief.

"I was just sitting up there and watching all the fish."

With all the innocence of a boy, he had no idea how panicked we were, or that we were even looking for him. He had not heard our calls because he could hear only the wind as it glided off the sails, and of course we could not see him as the sails blanketed him.

With Andy in the cockpit with us we continued sailing on our original heading with a 30-knot beam wind, and arrived late in the afternoon at Norman's Cay, one of the northern islands in the Exuma chain. We came up to the mouth of the harbor, dropped the sails, and anticipated an easy motor through the pass. Instead we came to an abrupt stop. What a jolt! One moment the boat was moving along nicely and the next moment all three of us were thrust forward in the cockpit! Fortunately, no one fell or was injured. We knew right away what had happened; we had sailed onto a sandbar. After a quick check, Tom determined nothing was damaged. Then, he studied the tide tables. He learned the tide was rising and decided to wait for it to lift us off the sandbar. While we waited, the boat was slightly heeled over in an ungraceful position. It was one of those moments when we hoped no one would notice us, but we had no such luck. Someone anchored on the inside of the harbor saw our tilted mast and called on the VHF.

"Hello to the sailboat outside Norman's Cay," the chuckling male voice said. "Do you copy?"

Tom refused to answer. He was embarrassed, his captain's ego was bruised, and he was in no mood to accept heckles from another captain. I knew if we ignored the call they would assume we were in trouble and come out in dinghies to check on us, so I answered, "Yes, we copy," I said while carefully avoiding to give our boat name.

"It looks like you found that unmarked sandbar out there. Do you need help?" the jovial voice asked.

"Thank you for the offer," I said, "but the tide is rising and we should be able to free ourselves soon."

I hung up the microphone and sat down in the cockpit with Tom and Andy to wait for the rising tide. Waiting for a tide to rise is about as exciting as waiting for the grass to grow. The more we watched for it to rise the slower the process seemed to take. In fact, it looked like nothing at all was happening. Tom and Andy are both "doers." Neither is long on patience, and waiting for that tide to come up was nearly impossible for them.

When Tom lost his patience he said, "If we don't get this show on the road soon, we're going to run out of daylight. LaVonne, start the engine, but leave it in neutral. Andy, stand over here on the low side of the boat. Hang on to the shrouds and lean your weight out as far as you can. I'm going to raise the sails and maybe we can heel over far enough to float off this sandbar."

We did all the things Tom directed us to do. At first nothing happened, but then under full sail power we began to inch forward. Tom sheeted the sail in tight to promote more heeling, and we finally floated gracefully off the sandbar. Tom quickly dropped the sail, put the boat in gear, and headed through the harbor entrance into the beautiful calm blue waters of Norman Cay. We anchored next to a boat whose captain advised us in a friendly manner about the holding and tide considerations for that anchorage. We appreciated his nonjudgmental assistance.

The next day we took our new dinghy around the bay and noticed a seaplane cabled to a cement block on the opposite side of the harbor. On shore were beautiful large palm trees; each perfectly spaced to please the artistic eye. Since palm trees were not indigenous to the Bahamas, we knew it was the location of an old resort and that the palm trees had been hauled in, planted, and tended carefully in order for them to survive. We motored over to shore, pulled the dinghy out of the water near the abandoned resort, and walked around to explore the grounds and empty cabins.

Our cruising book explained that the resort once operated as an elegant summer vacation spot for the wealthy, but was actually a cover for a drug smuggling operation. With each group of paid guests, the plane took a load of drugs to the United States until the Bahamian Government closed the operation five years ago. All the buildings were still there, as were the tennis courts and cement airstrip, but all were in ruin. Weeds grew between the cracks in the cement, dusty canned goods remained on shelves in the cabin kitchens, and mattresses rotted on the beds serving as present day homes to rats and lizards. It looked as if the people had left in a hurry, because some cabins still had clothing, cooking equipment, and personal items. That was the closest thing I had ever seen to a ghost town.

We walked the grounds, picked up fallen coconuts, and watched in fascination while some of the other cruisers did their laundry from the intact fresh, deep-water-well at the resort. The laundry operation was made possible by siphoning the water with a garden hose, using a series of five-gallon buckets placed at various levels. The clothing was washed in the top bucket and passed down through a series of rinse buckets. At the bottom, someone sorted the laundry by boat ownership. Men and women from three or four boats were laughing and socializing while doing their shared laundry.

It happened to be our wedding anniversary and we decided to celebrate by inviting the friendly people on the boat next to us for a spaghetti dinner. We had drinks before dinner and wine with dinner, but after I served coffee and dessert we expected they would return to their boat. Instead, they went back to their boat briefly to bring a bottle of whiskey back over. They drank, and drank, and drank, and I was having a difficult time staying awake.

"How long haveyooou been marrrried, anyways?" she asked.

"Ten years," I answered while Tom gave me a look that I read as how are we going to get rid of these people.

"Wowww, that's a looong time," she slurred. "I've never been able to stayyy with a guy one full year."

On cue Tom said, "Well, guys, before this evening turns into another year I've got to go to bed. We'll see you tomorrow." That was exactly what it took. They blinked and it finally sunk in that it was time for them to return to their own boat.

A SURPRISE BIRTHDAY PARTY

The following day we made a return sail to Staniel Cay where we had lost the dinghy, but there were no reports of a dinghy having been found. We were still there on January 11, my 47th birthday. I had not expected a gift from Tom, but I did think he would have

LaVonne (left front) in VONNIE-T cockpit celebrating her surprise birthday with cruising friends.

Guests for the birthday party arrived in their only transportation, their dinghies.

at least remembered to wish me a happy birthday. He didn't.

I hadn't had any negative feelings since we had left the cold weather so I was surprised to find myself feeling down, old, and unloved. I pretty much decided it was going to be a shitty day and proceeded to make it worse! I considered baking myself a birthday cake, but instead I baked a batch of cookies. I took a pile of the warm, fresh cookies back to my bunk and planned to sulk by treating myself with a lazy day of reading. I was well into my sulk, not having talked to Tom or Andy for several hours, when one of the neighboring boats arrived unannounced.

From my bunk I heard them clomp up our boarding ladder and I thought it very brazen for them to come on board like that. When they came into the cockpit and sat down, Tom called for me to go up into the cockpit and talk with them. I was slightly annoyed with them for dropping by uninvited, but welcomed the opportunity to pull myself out of my sulk, so I chatted with them in a friendly manner. Soon two more dinghies arrived. Tom greeted them, helped them tie up their painters, and invited them on board. Then, I saw several more dinghies in the water heading toward our boat. Tom pulled out bottles of wine, wineglasses, and snacks he had been hiding in Andy's V-berth. The last dinghy to arrive brought the birthday cake. My wonderful husband, whom I thought had forgotten my birthday, had arranged a surprise party. He had invited all the boats in the anchorage and managed to catch me completely off guard! I felt wonderful and loved, yet very small when I realized how childish I had been acting. It was a wonderful birthday party, absolutely the *BEST!*

The following day we sailed to Farmers Cay. Andy caught six groupers off the stern of the boat. He cleaned them on the side of the dinghy where he was close to the water and could easily wash his knife and hands during the process. Unfortunately, one of the fillets slipped off the side of the dinghy and fell to the bottom. We heard him grumble about his error and when he told us what happened Tom said, "Well, jump in and get it. That's a good fillet down there and it makes no sense to waste it."

"You've got to be kidding. I'm not going to get wet for one fillet," Andy said.

"Well, I will," Tom said. "Hand me my mask, Mom."

Tom stripped and put on his swim mask. Just before he dove into the water we saw a large dark swish on the bottom. We watched a shark grab the fillet, shake it once, and eat it as quick as a blink.

"Wow," Tom said, "I'm glad I wasn't any faster. I could have lost my hand reaching for that fish."

LEAVING CHICKEN HARBOR

The next day we sailed to George Town on Great Exuma. We filled our fuel tank and considered buying water, but when we saw the color and condition of the water, we changed our minds. We could not imagine drinking water that was green and smelled weedy, and we did not want it contaminating our water tanks. Andy was the first to say, "Now I see what you mean about the importance of not using our boat water for showers. Yuck, that stuff would make us sick!"

The Exuma Chain had offered protection from the sea, but the following morning we sailed out of the pass into unprotected water. There are many stories about sailors who attempted to sail out of it only to find it so rough that they returned to George Town, sold their boats, and became farmers. Some referred to George Town as "chicken harbor", and

I could understand the basis of those stories as the waves in the pass were the most violent we had seen yet! We kept our engine on and crashed head-on into big greenies. It felt as if we were riding a mechanical horse. All we could do was to hang on and continue steering straight ahead. I think we were all a little frightened, but we were committed to continue forward. When we were finally through the pass, the waves changed to long rolling swells. I did not particularly like the ocean swells, but compared to the violent waves, they were preferable.

"DA BREAD SHE'S A BAKIN."

That night we anchored at Callobash Bay on the southern end of Long Island. It was without a doubt the worst anchorage we had ever experienced. The wind came from one direction while the ocean swells came from another, and both wrapped around that end of the island. The boat faced bow into the wind, and we took the swells on the beam. All night the boat rolled, making it impossible to sleep. I tried to lie flat on my back and spread my arms out to brace myself, but still I rolled from side to side. I finally positioned myself next to the bulkhead and built a wall of pillows and blankets on my other side, similar to what parents sometimes do to prevent babies from falling off an adult bed. There was no danger of my rolling off the bunk, but I could find no remedy for the continual back and forth sloshing of my intestines. As I sleeplessly fought the motion, I rested my eyes and tried to avoid listening to the dishes, pot and pans, and silverware in the drawers, slide monotonously back and forth.

We were tired, yet relieved, when we saw the first rays of light on the horizon, because it meant we could pull up our anchor and leave. I motored forward over the anchor as we had done many times before, while Tom manned the windlass, but the anchor refused to come up! We repeated the procedure several times, but each effort failed to bring it up. We were stuck. Finally, Tom put on his fins and mask and dove into the water to investigate the problem. As he suspected, our CQR anchor had wrapped itself around a large coral head in 16 feet of water. I steered the boat over the coral-head to provide slack in the heavy chain while Tom unwound it. It was a precarious procedure, but with repeated dives he was finally able to free it. "Nothing like a little swim to start the day out right," Tom said, feeling all refreshed from the cool water and excitement. I knew he was just as tired as I was, but he was determined to keep positive. I handed him a towel, knowing why I loved him so much.

We anchored the following night at the Bird Rock Lighthouse on Crooked Island. It rolled a little, but nothing like the night before. Andy and Tom loved snorkeling there because of the wide assortment of coral: fire coral, fan coral, staghorn, and elkhorn coral. Andy had the added excitement of spearing his first lobster which we shared as an *hors d'oeuvre* before dinner.

The following day, we sailed into Atwood Harbor on the northeast point of the Acklins. We walked two hot, humid miles to the small native village of Chester. We had become accustomed to being the only white faces around, but we became uncomfortable when surprised by three large, young, black men who blocked the path as we were about to return to the boat. They sat on their heels in the middle of the path obviously waiting for us to arrive.

"Mon, you all want sumpin to drink?" the largest of the three asked.

We had not prepared ourselves by carrying drinking water and we were thirsty, but saw nothing along the narrow path except tall grass and reeds that were over my head on both sides. The air was thick with humidity, and if there was any wind out on the water, not a flicker of it passed through the tall grass. We were hot and eager to get back to the boat, and did not feel good about being ambushed on that isolated path.

"Sounds good to me," said Tom, "but where would you get a cold drink out here?"

"Dat's easy mon. We's close to da bar," he said grinning and showing all his widely spaced white teeth. "Da bar, she's just over dar."

"Over where?" Tom asked, not seeing anything through the reeds where he was pointing. In spite of our uneasiness, we knew it was best to play along and show no fear. Nothing about the situation made any sense and we could not figure out what the young men were up to. They could see we had nothing of value with us. I wore no jewelry, we had no watches, and our clothing consisted of old shorts and tee shirts.

"Come on, follow me," he said. All three provided pearly white smiles while unfolding their long slender legs as they stood up from their squat. They began walking down another narrow path, a fork we hadn't noticed until then. We followed them, feeling vulnerable and stupid. Not only were we trapped and at their mercy, but we had left the boat wide open. Then it dawned on me. Were they supposed to keep us occupied while their buddies ransacked the boat? Or was there a more sinister plan? In spite of the heat, a shiver went down my spine.

We were surprised to see a small wooden shack only a few feet from the second path. Painted in large free-hand red letters was the word BAR. There were traces of dark green paint on some of the wooden boards, but most were bare and weathered to a silver-gray. The spokesman for the group disappeared around the back and reappeared from inside the shack while lifting the upper half of the front wall. Two long wooden poles were slipped into precut notches to support the side corners of the wall which became a sunroof for anyone standing in front. Inside, were two old refrigerators and a soda vending machine, both apparently run by a gasoline generator. He removed three frosty cold beer bottles from one of the refrigerators, one for each of them. "What you want — beer or soda?" he asked us.

"I'll have a beer," Tom said. Andy and I each asked for a soda. Tom paid him and we made small talk while we sipped our drinks. Conversation was not easy because we had a difficult time understanding them, but with concentration we grasped the general flow. We voiced our surprise at the little oasis hidden from sight and avoided mentioning anything that would make them aware of how suspicious we had been. The very existence of the bar made us wonder if there were other stores on the island that we had missed seeing. With new courage and confidence, we told them we would like to buy bread if it was available.

"Sure, mon, dat be no problem. My mama, she bake you some bread. She make good bread. When you want it?" he asked Tom.

"Don't you need to ask her if she will bake bread for us?" Tom asked.

"No! Dat be no problem. She do what I axeses her to do," he told us. "I brings you your bread tomorrow morning. You bees out on your boat in da morning?"

"Yes," Tom said. "We will be out on the boat in the morning."

Tom agreed to pay $10 for three loaves of bread. He paid for them in advance, thinking he would neither see the bread nor his money again. We thanked the young men for their hospitality, finished our drinks and walked back to the boat thinking we had just gotten out of a tight squeeze fairly cheaply.

The next morning while eating breakfast in the cockpit, a speedboat buzzed past us. A young man shouted, "Da bread, she's a bakin. Da bread, she's a bakin."

It took us a while to figure out what he was saying, but eventually we realized he was telling us the bread was in the oven. Apparently he didn't want us to think he would not follow through on his promise. We laughed at the ridiculousness of the situation. First, they pleasantly surprised us with the bar, then they spent their $10 profit on gasoline to tell us the bread was in the oven baking.

We used the day for snorkeling and diving. Tom speared two lobsters and a grouper. We were further delighted to find a bed of conch in a shallow river where we could pick them up while walking. We collected enough for dinner and added several fresh coconuts. Our skills at living off the water and land were improving, but still we were slow and clumsy at cleaning and preparing our finds. It took the rest of the day to get the conch cleaned and the coconuts cracked open. When we returned to the boat, there were three loaves of warm fresh bread lying on the side deck. They smelled wonderful. We had a feast that night, and I was able to make toast for breakfast and sandwiches for lunch the following day.

"DA PEOPLES HAVE COME."

The next several days were spent doing more motoring than sailing. They were unpleasant days with high seas and strong winds on the bow. Tom wrote in the ship log on January 24, "Upwind, upwind, upwind. I'm sick of it! It seems like I've been going up hill or upwind since I was born." We both remembered the advice about the "thorny path" from the cruisers we met at Beaufort, North Carolina, and we knew the business of going up-wind was exactly what they had been referring to.

It was a relief when we pulled into the anchorage at Abraham's Bay at Mayaguana. We took the dinghy to shore and wondered what strange new experiences to expect.

Not far from a dilapidated dock several expensive speedboats with powerful motors were tied to moorings. We tied our dinghy and walked up a short dirt path that brought us to a cement meeting-square covered by a wooden roof as protection from the relentless sun. Nearly a dozen men were seated on benches built around the inside of the square. Some smoked, some chewed on a long grass weed, and some listened while others talked. Since there were no walls, the soft breeze made it a cool and comfortable place to sit, meet friends, and chat.

A man beckoned us to join the group. He introduced himself as Henry and followed with a friendly third-degree. We sat with the men, sharing information about our travels and ourselves. Henry told us he was 68 years old and was born on a sailing ship. His grandmother reared him after his mother died when he was only eight years old. He had worked for the Erickson salt factory (now Morton Salt) on Curaçao when WWII broke out. Later, he took a job in Florida but "it wasn't so good for niggers in Florida then. I think it's better now, though." he said. He was married and fathered nine children: seven, he said, were "in marriage and two outside marriage." He didn't mention any granddaughters, but spoke proudly of his grandsons.

"Dem niggers is fast, man! De swim faster than Mr. Jack (jack fish). You knows what I mean? De is really fast. I don't know how de do it. Sometimes de stays down there tree minutes. I axks them, how come you don't die down der when you stays down so long? De says, 'What you mean old man?' I says, 'how you breathe? You think you is a fish'? De say, 'It's okay, old man, I bes just fine down there'." Henry shook his head, took another sip of red wine and a long drag on his third cigarette. "No sir, I just don't knows how de dus it."

As we sat on the bench and conversed we tried to make sense of the economics of that small village. For one thing, I was surprised to see I was the only woman sitting in the square with the men. "Where are all the women?" I asked.

"Home doin housework," Henry answered.

We noticed that the men were dressed in quality, American-style clothing, and even the younger ones wore clean, white brand-name slacks. The expensive clothing, the costly boats moored out in the harbor, and the lack of any visible means to support all of it did not add up. Tom's inquiries about work and jobs caused chuckling and innuendoes that we were not intended to understand. But we understood enough to suspect they got money for their part in some type of drug-smuggling operation. They were paid well to take risks, and they used their big powerful speedboats to keep their risks at minimum, and we decided it would be wise for us to learn no more. We excused ourselves and stood up with the intention of returning to the boat, but before we left Henry asked if we would like to return that evening for dinner.

"My wife, Alsada, she cooks you a good meal for only $3 a plate," he said.

Tom must have been able to read the excitement in my eyes at the prospect of not having to cook, so he did not even hesitate before he answered. "Sure, Henry, we would like that." Henry pointed out which of the buildings was his house, and we agreed upon a time for dinner before returning to the boat for an afternoon of maintenance and relaxation.

Tom changed both engine zincs and wrote in the log, "both all used up, but prop shaft zinc still OK." Zinc was a sacrificial metal that we attached to our engine, generator, and drive shaft to prevent electrolytic corrosion.

That evening, we dressed in clean clothes and went to shore for dinner at Henry's. We didn't see Henry when we arrived, and no one was sitting in the meeting-square, so we walked over to Henry's house. It was an unpainted wooden structure lit only by kerosene lamps. Alsada, a round woman wearing a tan cotton print dress a few shades lighter than her skin, seemed startled to see us standing at her door. She composed herself quickly, greeted us warmly, and pointed toward a table covered in red-checkered plastic and set with white plastic plates and triangularly folded paper napkins. The center of the table proudly displayed fresh wildflowers haphazardly stuffed into a water glass. She seated us, poured water, and stepped outside.

"Henry!" she shrilled. "Da peoples have come. Turn on da generator."

Henry appeared through the door. The lights came on, loud American music blared into the dining room, and we heard sizzling from the stove in the kitchen. Dinner consisted of fried fish, rice, a boiled white root, and cabbage salad. The best thing about the flavorless meal was that I didn't have to cook it. When we finished eating our dinner, Alsada indicated an interest in talking to me privately. It was a subtle request; she made a soft sound under her breath and motioned for me to go with her into the kitchen. I could not imagine what she wanted. When we got to her kitchen, she asked if we would be sailing to Providencialles. When I told her we would, she told me that one of her sons lived there, and she had neither seen nor heard from him in over a year. Neither she nor her son could read or write, which made communication tough. She wanted me to contact him, but she couldn't write his address or name. I asked her if Henry could write it for her.

"No," she said. "Henry, he ain't his father, so he don't care none about my son. My son was born by one of my udder husbands, so it only right dat he go live someplace else."

LADIES HITCHED A RIDE FOR LUNCH

It was early February when we arrived in Sapodilla Bay, Providencialles, Caicos, and the southeast trade winds blew hard. Just taking a dinghy ride to shore caused us to be sprayed by saltwater.

The Caicos Islands were an archipelago formed eons ago from volcanic rock similar to the Bahamas. The maximum height of each island was about 150 feet, making them difficult for sailboats to see from a distance. Soil was scarce, and what little there was of it, was poor, and supported very little vegetation. Food was available at the one and only grocery store, but it was expensive because everything was shipped in. Fresh milk, for instance, cost $7 a half gallon, but I was glad to have it at any price.

One day, two women cruisers and I decided to dress up and go into town for a ladies' lunch. We were told hitchhiking was the norm, so we stuck out our thumbs and within minutes had a lift to the town on the other side of the island. At the yacht club we had a tasty and relaxed lunch, drank wine, and talked about the things women talk about. We had a great time and never once did we mention engines, currents, tides, wind, or boat parts. We felt like women again for a few hours, and it was great! When it was time to return to the boat we stood out on the road to hitchhike back to Sapodilla Bay. It did not take long before we got a ride, but the car didn't go all the way to Sapodilla Bay. So, we got out and waited for a ride down the other road. We waited nearly half an hour and began to become concerned when a truck stopped and offered us a ride. We ungracefully crawled up into the back of the truck, but before we arrived at Sapodilla Bay, the truck turned off the main road onto a side road to the dump. When we saw where we were headed, we pounded on the back window of the truck. The driver stopped and told us he needed to go to the dump before he took us to Sapodilla Bay. We didn't know if we could trust him, but we did not feel we had a choice, so we stayed with him. How fortunate that the truck driver was as good as his word. He unloaded bags of trash at the dump, and then took us directly to Sapodilla Bay. We climbed out of the truck trying to keep our skirts from exposing our panties, and thanked him. That ride was followed by a wet dinghy ride back to our respective boats, a somewhat undignified ending to what was supposed to have been a luxurious afternoon. I thought about how the people back home would never have understood the risks we three women took that day just for the opportunity to go to lunch off the boat.

TRASH CAN BE SOMEONE ELSE'S TREASURE

I had not realized how many adjustments we had made since leaving Duluth, until I purposefully thought about them. Some things that seemed impossible early on, had become the norm over time, such as saving and recycling nearly everything because we never knew if, or when, we could buy replacements. Zip-lock bags, for instance, were washed, hung on the line to dry, and reused, and we became extra stingy with fresh water after seeing the polluted alternative. It was not unusual to see cruisers in that part of the world jump off the stern of their boat with a bottle of dish detergent in one hand to take a bath. We no longer gave it a second thought. I had even reached the point where I preferred salt-water bathing, having discovered that a little salt residue in my hair provided extra body, while fresh water left it feeling limp.

While the rationing we practiced was a huge change from our life in Minnesota, it was a small inconvenience compared to the problems we saw on a Haitian sailboat that had come to the Turks and Caicos Islands to glean from the local trash. The 30-foot wooden boat was remarkable for what it did not have. There was no motor, no electricity, no navigation equipment, no depth sounder, no galley, and no toilet. Even its canvas sails were weathered and torn. The four thin black men on board had muscles that glistened with perspiration as they worked in the hot glaring sun. Their shiny bodies were naked except for raggedy shorts held up by ropes. They were scavenging old bottles, plastic containers, and other items from the dump, and they carefully bundled their newly acquired treasures into burlap bags and stowed each bag below the decks of their sad little boat. Their mission was serious, and we never saw them smile or take a moment to rest. We observed them cooking their meals of rice, in a pan with a missing handle, over an open flame on the stern of their boat, yet I sensed a pride and dignity in those men.

We had talked about stopping in Haiti on the way to the Dominican Republic, but we heard it was not a very friendly port for cruisers like ourselves, and after seeing how poor those men were, we decided it might be better to avoid that country. The Turks and Caicos was a poor country by our standards, and I could not imagine how desperate the people of Haiti must be, if these men found profit gleaning from another poor country. When we last saw the Haitian boat, the men were frantically unloading the gunnysacks they had previously loaded, because the boat had sprung a leak, and they needed to find it before they sank. It seemed preposterous that they would go to sea in that rickety hull which barely floated in a calm harbor, and we wondered how it could possibly survive 50 miles of open sea. We wished we could have talked to them or helped them in some way, but that was impossible because of the language barrier and their unwillingness to take time away from their tasks.

DOMINICAN TEEN FEARED HIS DEATH WITHIN A YEAR

We entered Puerto Plata in the Dominican Republic in February. Despite the winter season, it was hot. Even the most leisurely walk into town produced a sweat. When I felt the sweat running down the center of my back I had to remind myself that it was only a few months ago that I complained of being cold, and of not being able to wear enough clothing to get warm. My mode of dress had changed dramatically since then, and I wore less and less each day, while still trying to stay within the confines of modesty in a devout Catholic country.

Most of the local women wore brightly colored, gathered skirts and peasant-type blouses. They were strong, barrel-shaped women and they carried huge loads on their heads. Large baskets, pots of water, and cloth bundles tied up in all four corners. Their bodies swayed under their loads as they marched down the dirt roads. After they passed us, we could see the white bottoms of their bare feet blinking rhythmically with each step.

The town was fascinating. It was old and only the main street was bricked while the others were made of hard, packed dirt. Most of the shops and storefronts were wooden structures with peeling paint. The only exceptions were the restaurants that were painted in cheery colors and decorated with potted plants. The church was a grand stone-and-brick structure in the center of town next to a small park, displaying a wide assortment of colorful flowers. Park benches had been strategically placed under shade trees, and offered an inviting rest stop after walking in the blazing sun.

Not far from town was a funicular (cable car) that took passengers to the top of the mountain. The ride offered a fantastic view of the harbor and surrounding areas, and the cool temperatures on top provided a welcome relief from the hot dusty town. We enjoyed strolling along the cobblestone paths through fern arches, vine patios, and flower gardens surrounded by lush green grass in the groomed Mountain Park. It was an oasis we had not expected to find in the Dominican Republic, and was as grand a park as we had seen anywhere.

Back in town, Andy made friends with Roberto, a boy his age, who begged us to take him with us when we left the Dominican Republic. Roberto promised to do any work we wanted him to do because he feared if he did not get out of the Dominican Republic soon that he would be dead within a year, due to the hazard of his job. Roberto made his living by diving for lobsters in water, sometimes as deep as a hundred feet, with no scuba gear. He and several other boys breathed from tubes that sent air to them from a compressor in a boat. If the tube was cut on coral, or if it got a kink in it, that boy would have to come shooting up to the surface to breathe and his lungs would burst, because there was no opportunity to depressurize by coming up slowly. Roberto told us many of his friends had already died. At only 19, he had already contemplated his death. We felt terrible for him, but knew we could not collect everyone we felt sorry for along our travels. So with the guilt of looking like rich, callous Americans, we told Roberto he could not come with us.

We checked out with officials before leaving the port of Puerto Plata, and that reinforced how desperate the Dominican Republicans were to leave their country. We could not have taken Roberto with us even if we had wanted to, because the police came on board and did a search before they allowed us to leave port. They opened every locker, cabinet, and cupboard large enough to be able to hide someone, and not until they were satisfied that there were no stowaways aboard, were we allowed to leave. Then they untied our lines and told us to depart immediately under their watchful eye. Puerto Rico apparently experienced so many illegal visitors from the Dominican Republic, that it adopted the practice of sending them back and charging the Dominican Republic government for their transport. As a result, Dominican officials were instructed to do their best to prevent their own people from leaving.

TOM'S ACCIDENT

It was an overnight passage to Samana, Dominican Republic. Andy and Tom did the early evening watch together while I slept. Soon after Andy went to bed, Tom thought he could sleep as well, so he woke me, and I stood watch alone for the rest of the night. It was a pleasant, clear night and I rather enjoyed my time alone on that particular evening watch. I appreciated the cool temperatures and the soft breeze that kissed my parched skin. The moon was a big, heavy ball that hung close to the horizon and lit a long silver steak in the water. Even the stars shimmered and sparkled on the ripples of the boat's wake, making the evening feel friendly and comforting. Toward morning, when the moon disappeared over the horizon, the seas began to build and the environment became less friendly. Soon, the seas were so high that the autopilot was unable to hold a steady course and I had to steer by hand. When I found myself almost falling asleep while standing behind the wheel, I woke Tom and told him I needed to get some sleep.

Before coming topside he wanted to make a pot of coffee, knowing it would be impossible for him to leave the wheel once I went to sleep. From the cockpit I saw him pick up the coffeepot in one hand and the can of coffee in the other, but before he could put the grounds into the pot, we were hit by a large rogue wave. The wave slammed into the boat, and as the wave rose, we rose with it and sort of spun off the top. Tom lost his balance and was thrown across the cabin toward the chart table. It all happened so fast that he automatically kept his grip on the coffee can and pot, leaving no hand free to brace himself or prevent his fall. He crashed into the back of the chart table chair, taking the full impact on his lower back. I saw him crumple to the sole of the boat and heard him cry out in pain like a wounded animal. I watched the horror of it, yet there was nothing I could have done to prevent it. When he hit the floor he was gray and pasty looking, and his forehead had broken out into a cold sweat. I locked the wheel and hoped it would hold for a short time while I tried to help Tom up to the sofa, but all attempts to move him caused him excruciating pain. He could not even straighten his legs. I was afraid he would go into shock and I didn't know what to do, but realized I had better not try to move him again. I left him on the floor, put a small pillow under his head, several pillows under his knees to support the legs that would not straighten, and wrapped a wool blanket around him. I yelled at Andy to wake up, and told him he needed to steer the boat. Andy stumbled out of his cabin not knowing what had happened, and looking a little seasick. His eyes grew large when he saw his dad lying on the floor, but before he could ask any questions I told him he needed to get up to the cockpit and steer the boat. He obediently stepped over his dad and went up the ladder. He unlocked the wheel and steered the course heading.

I dug out our first-aid kit and studied the medicines we had brought with us. We had pills for every kind of emergency, but I could not remember which were for which problem. Faced with the terrible consequences of giving Tom the wrong pill, I was petrified. I knew he needed to have something to dull the pain but I did not want to give him anything that might cause, or add to, any internal bleeding. Finally I settled on giving him a Tylenol with codeine.

Getting him to swallow the pill without moving his back or neck, while lying flat on the floor was no easy task. Fortunately, he was able to swallow it on his first attempt. Within minutes he was asleep, but I was not sure if that was a good or a bad thing. I worried that he might not be able to wake up once he went to sleep, but when I saw the pink color return to his face, I felt more confident that I had done the right thing. I listened to his breathing and was relieved to hear it was slow and steady.

I checked on Andy. He looked frightened but seemed to be doing a good job of steering and staying on course. "Did dad have a heart attack?" Andy asked when I came up into the cockpit.

"No, he fell and hurt himself," I told him. "I gave your dad a pain pill but I can't move him, so he will have to rest on the floor for now.'

I explained that I had to get some sleep and asked if he would be all right steering the boat for an hour or so. He said he could do it, and I had no choice but to trust him. I plopped down on the sofa next to where Tom was lying on the floor and fell asleep with my hand hanging over the edge, resting on his arm. I wanted to wake up if there was any change in his condition, but I also knew I had to get some sleep if I was going to be able to make any rational decisions. My last thought, seconds before drifting off to sleep was, thank goodness Andy was with us!

CAN'T SEND A WOMAN TO DO THE CAPTAINS JOB

"Mom, you'd better get up here. There's something ahead on the right," Andy shouted down to the cabin to wake me.

I sat up, surprised to see daylight and sunshine. Tom was still sleeping in the same position on the floor. I went up to the cockpit feeling somewhat refreshed. I was alarmed to see how close we were to land: steep red and golden cliffs. I had a hard time getting used to the ruggedness of that country after last experiencing the low flat islands of the Bahamas and the Turks and Caicos. Up ahead to starboard was something that looked like a long cement footbridge. I checked our position on the Sat Nav, comparing the coordinates to the chart. My calculations indicated that we were at the mouth of the Samana Harbor, but I didn't have much confidence in my charting accuracy, and was relieved when I found a photograph of the bridge in our cruising guide. Andy had done a good job by keeping us on course. We were positioned exactly where we needed to be.

"That's it, Andy. That's where we turn in," I told him.

We turned in toward the bridge and soon found ourselves blanketed from the wind by the hills. Andy took the sails down while I motored forward. When we entered the harbor, I circled until I found a space with 15 feet of water and ample swinging room for the boat. We anchored, and together we lowered the dinghy into the water using the main halyard as our muscle. Then I clipped the motor onto a three-part line attached to the mizzen boom, swung it out over the side of the boat, and lowered the motor to Andy, who waited for it in the dinghy. He guided the motor onto the transom of the dinghy, unclipped the three-part line, and tightened the motor-mounts. Tom had taught us well.

Tom was awake when I went back into the cabin. He wanted to know where we were, what was going on, and had a thousand other questions and concerns. Although the color had returned to his face he still had a great deal of pain in his lower back. With great effort he was able to get up onto the sofa where he planned to stay for the rest of the day. He said he wasn't hungry, but I encouraged him to drink fluids. Then Andy and I went in to shore to check in with the customs officials.

At that stage of our traveling, I spoke no Spanish, and the Dominican Republic is not only a Spanish-speaking country, it is also a Spanish-thinking country. None of the uniformed officials on the pier wanted to talk to Andy or me: I was a woman and Andy only a kid. They wanted to talk to "my captain," and they wanted him to bring the boat up to the pier so they could step on board. I tried to explain that my captain was injured and I could not get the boat up to the pier by myself, but they could not understand me, and made no attempt to try. They were angry and shunned me by dramatically turning their backs to me as I spoke.

I was so frustrated! There was current and surging water at the pier, not to mention long steel rods sticking out of it. It would have been a challenge for both Tom and me to get our boat up to it without damage. I knew I could not even consider attempting it by myself, so I followed the officials to the police station while carrying the boat briefcase that contained our boat papers, our passports, two hand pistols, and the ammunition for them. Judging from our check-in at Puerto Plata these were the items I knew they would want. I had hoped someone at the police station would understand some English.

One of the uniformed officials motioned for me to sit in the lobby. I sat and waited. When all the police left the station to check in another boat, I followed them back down to the pier. Still they ignored me. Finally, I found a cruiser who spoke some Spanish. I told her my dilemma and she translated the information to the policemen. When they finally understood that "my captain" was injured and unable to come in to shore, they changed their attitude, and became more accommodating. The woman interpreter explained that they thought "my captain" was trying to insult them by sending a woman in to meet with them. Once they understood, they got in our dinghy and went out to VONNIE-T. They were kind and apologetic when they saw Tom flat on his back, and unable to move.

For days, Tom lay on his back in pain, not knowing how serious his injuries were, and when blood started to show in his urine, we became even more worried. I checked our limited medical books but nothing of that nature was addressed in them. We discussed the possibility of going to one of the Dominican's medical facilities, but that seemed even scarier. Neither of us trusted their skills or their sanitation. We just had to hope that time and bed-rest would do the job. At least Samana Harbor was a comfortable place to rest. It was protected from ocean swells and had a soft sea breeze that made the temperatures bearable; it was quiet and the air was fresh and clean. After several days of lying in his bunk, Tom struggled to sit in the cockpit, and for several more days he sat viewing all that the harbor had to offer. In every direction was a panorama of great beauty: In one direction, green hills, in another, mountains, and in another direction, the jungle. That scenery changed hourly depending on the intensity and height of the sun.

Tom was confined to the boat for nearly a week while he rested and healed. Meanwhile, I rediscovered some of my lost leadership skills. Being forced to be in charge made me stronger, more determined, and more confident.

THE MONA PASSAGE - ANOTHER PASSAGE FROM HELL

Tom had never been able to do nothing, and when he had all the lying around that he could tolerate, he convinced himself that he was well enough to venture into shore. Getting on and off the boat, and in and out of the dinghy were difficult for him, but walking, standing, and sitting became a little easier and less painful each day. Still, I saw him wince with pain when he bent in certain ways. In spite of that he became itchy to do something, and he thought he would be able to handle land travel, so we took a bus trip to Santo Domingo on the other side of the island. The bus seats were comfortable for him, and the trip provided us with the opportunity to see much of the countryside. We saw sugarcane fields, rice paddies, and several vegetable stands selling little purple eggplants. We saw a lot of motorcycles piled high with goods being delivered someplace, and one had so many loaves of bread tied to it that it was impossible to see the person driving it. Another motorcyclist had a table and several chairs tied together and piled on his back. That was an amazing sight!

Toward the end of February, Tom claimed he felt better. I was skeptical about how much better he actually felt, but I recognized that he was eager to get moving. In the log he wrote "Departing Samana 0900, bound for Boqueron, Puerto Rico. ETA 2/23 at 1400. God willing!"

It was a rough passage with 10 and 12-foot seas and 25-knot winds. Items that had been stowed with no problem during previous passages often became "unstowed." Things not only slid around in their cabinets during the passage, but some actually flew out. Even the charts refused to stay on the chart table. We knew it was dangerous to leave things loose in the cabin to be flying around, so I dutifully went below to tidy things in spite of fighting seasickness. I dreaded going below, but that was preferable to the terror I felt every time Tom went topside to change sails. I constantly worried he would slip on the wet deck and take another nasty fall, especially when he was barefoot. Because of that concern I insisted he wear deck shoes. My insistence irritated him, and that, plus his lingering lower-back pain, caused him to become grumpy. He snapped and growled at me and complained that I should stop telling him what to do.

During sail changes he would shout, "Can't you see what needs to be done? You need to help by looking ahead at the next thing that's going to happen." At other times when I tried to anticipate how I could help him, he would shout, "Don't do anything until I tell you!"

I knew Tom was pushing himself to the edge, and that he still experienced pain. I was worried for his safety, tired of having him constantly correct me, plus I continued to battle seasickness. Our patience had worn thin and we were not having a good time! By nightfall we were in the center of the Mona Passage. We stopped talking to one another; we changed shifts like robots every two or three hours without exchanging a single word. Tom did all the navigating and charting. I slept upright piled in the corner of the cockpit while he was on watch. When he went below to rest or chart, I automatically stood watch, carefully staying on the same compass heading that he had been following. It was a long night!

At first light, we could faintly see a shadow of land ahead, and by late morning we were anchored in Boqueron, Puerto Rico. Neither of us wanted to talk about the previous night as we both knew we would regret anything we said prior to getting sleep. We silently ate breakfast, allowed ourselves short fresh-water boat showers, and went to bed.

After several hours of rest and talking on the radio with others who also had completed the Mona Passage trip, our passage didn't seem nearly as bad as what some of the other boats reported. Apparently it had been a difficult passage for everyone. One of the boats even lost its big Boston Whaler dinghy. The dinghy was too large to stow on deck so they tried to tow it, and of course it broke loose in the high seas. It was an expensive loss.

Instead of dwelling on the rough passage, we focused on looking forward to seeing Puerto Rico. The Boqueron anchorage was in front of the small town with several restaurants and small grocery stores. The U.S. National Park Service owns and maintains a campground with cement cabins on the sandy beach. For a small fee, U.S. citizens can rent the cabins on a weekly basis. There were a few Americans at the campground, but most of the cabins were empty. Apparently, the facility is a well-guarded secret because the last week of February should have been the height of the season. Joanne Meade, an American artist who came to the campground each year with her husband, could be seen on the beach early each morning with her easel and paints, capturing the essence of everyday life in Boqueron. She told us the occupancy was often less than half and that suited her "just fine."

We enjoyed the challenge of land travel in Puerto Rico by *por puesto*, which is a privately owned car whose owner follows a designated route, usually from one city or town to another. The *por puesto* driver would wait at a specific intersection until he had five paying passengers. Then he drove his route and allowed people to get on and off at various places along the way. We discovered that the Puerto Ricans did not live up to the negative stereotype we had. Instead, they were warm, friendly, family-oriented people. The typical family often consisted of three generations living together, and caring for one another.

We also rented a car for a several days and visited all the typical tourist spots: Old San Juan, El Yunque, the rain forest, and a coffee plantation. In Old San Juan we were besieged with hawkers who tried to coax us into their jewelry stores. They offered free drinks and flattery as enticement to "just step inside and take a look." Little did they know that this American woman who lived on a boat, had absolutely no use for expensive jewelry. At the tip of Old San Juan, which towered above the sea, we toured El Morro, a military and architectural marvel with incredibly thick walls. That evening we treated ourselves to dinner and a performance by the Areyto Folkloric Ballet at the restored convent, El Convento. Many of the buildings in Old San Juan had been restored, and characteristically had Spanish balconies, wide entrance halls, and interior patios that I found to be both lovely and practical.

At El Yunque we looked for the famous Puerto Rico parrot, one of the world's very rare birds, but we had no luck in sighting it. We did see many tropical plants, some with large waxy lily-like flowers, and the maguey plant, with it's thick spiky leaves that grow several feet high. We listened with fascination to the bamboo trees that made sounds like growling bears when the trunks rubbed together in the wind.

At the coffee plantation we learned that banana palms were planted between the rows of coffee trees to protect the valuable coffee beans from being prematurely blown down to the ground. The bananas were considered a "garbage fruit," meaning they were of little value in themselves.

There was a cock trainer at the plantation and we watched him during one of his training sessions. He taped a small bead over the sharp metal spur attached to the back of each cock's leg. The spurs served as vicious weapons during cockfights but by taping them during the practice session he was able to exercise his cocks and allow them to fight without endangering them. Raising fighting cocks and the sport of cock fighting was a lucrative business in Puerto Rico and the Dominican Republic. There apparently were no animal rights activists in either of those places.

We had many happy moments during our short land excursion around Puerto Rico, but we also had to face the sad moment when Andy would fly home. We dropped him off at the San Juan airport so he could return to school. We knew he was eager to get back to his buddies and a more comfortable environment, because his parting words were, "When I get home I'm going to McDonalds and order the biggest hamburger they have, and then I think I'll follow that up with a whole quart of milk." He was tired of the limited foods available on the boat, and yet I knew he would miss some of the adventure too.

When Tom and I returned to the boat it seemed so empty!

WATER PHOSPHORESCENCE

On the southwestern corner of Puerto Rico near La Pargura, we were greatly surprised by what appeared to be twinkling-lights deep down in the water. We did not know what to think! Could we possibly have stumbled upon some great discovery, and if so, what did it mean? We first saw the sparkles in the water when we returned to the boat after dark. There was a wide luminescent silver streak on the dinghy's prop wash that appeared to be an electric charge. As usual, I had to use the head as soon as we got back on board, and while still speculating about what we had seen I was further surprised when I saw the entire toilet bowl sparkle as I pumped it empty. The next day we learned it was a common phenomenon in that area called phosphorescence. It was only visible at night and in certain areas of the ocean where the water was extremely clean and just the right temperature for certain living organisms. Apparently any agitation of the water caused those particular organisms to light up like fireflies.

The clear water offered us something else as well. It was the first time we were able to see the barnacles that had attached themselves to the bottom of VONNIE-T. Our aging bottom-paint no longer resisted them. We were not accustomed to barnacles because there were none in the fresh water of the Great Lakes, but we had read about them and anticipated their growth. However, reading about them, and actually seeing them were two entirely different things. They had to be removed because they slowed the boat and placed an unnecessary burden on the engine.

In order to tackle the job, Tom rigged two secondary scuba regulators to thin hoses that he connected to an oil-less paint compressor. With the regulators in our mouths we were able to dive under the boat to scrape and scrub the barnacles off. The regulator and compressor made the job a lot easier, because we were able to breathe without having to carry cumbersome tanks on our backs. It was the same principle used by the boys in the Dominican Republic when they dove for lobsters, but there was not the same danger because we dove in only six feet of water and didn't need to decompress when we came to the surface. Still, it was an exhausting job and the razor-sharp barnacles cut our hands while schools of reef fish swarmed around us, eating the abundant food we scraped from the boat. Being in the center of schools of fish in a feeding frenzy took some getting used to, but I quickly learned I could keep them from coming too close simply by making small vocal sounds through my breathing tube.

A SUNBURNED ASS

With our clean-bottomed boat, we made several stops along the southern coast of Puerto Rico. One was at Isla Cayas de Muertos which meant "box of the dead" in Spanish. Based on its name, I wasn't sure I wanted to stop there, but when I saw the island I realized its name came from the fact that it was shaped like a large coffin, and not because of any special danger that it might pose.

The following day, we continued eastward to Salinas, Puerto Rico. Tom trailed a fishing line in the water and caught a barracuda and a wahoo. He threw the barracuda back, not wanting to risk ciguaterra fish poisoning, but we kept the wahoo knowing it was safe for consumption, and we ate that fish over the next several days. Out of necessity, my skill at preparing fish had begun to improve, and one of our favorite meals was stir-fried wahoo with fresh pineapple.

Before living on the boat, Tom and I had both jogged daily. He had been more serious than I, but I dutifully did my three miles each morning. In contrast, living on the boat required very little use of our legs and we looked forward to walking, and Puerto Rico offered many such opportunities.

One day, while walking through a lush, unpaved area of tall trees and brush, we came across a group of rag-tag boys who were carrying long skinny machetes that were obviously sharp and ready for use. I had no idea what thoughts crossed Tom's mind but I clearly envisioned the probability of being hacked to pieces and disappearing from the face of the earth. With the bravado of novice actors, we greeted them in a friendly manor, and they did likewise. Two of the boys chewed on mango pits, and when they smiled the strings from the fruit's yellow flesh hung visibly trapped in their front teeth. One boy asked if we were thirsty, and if so, would we like a water coconut.

"Sure," Tom said. I knew he didn't know what a water coconut was any more than I did, but was trying to go along with the flow of the moment. He was buying time and didn't want to show fear, so I followed his lead by saying nothing. Then, all of a sudden, we saw that same boy literally walk up the side of a coconut tree with his feet planted on one side. He gripped the trunk with his hands and allowed his machete to hang from a belt loop of his tattered shorts. When he reached a bunch of coconuts he shouted down to us.

"You people should stand back now."

He whacked at a clump of coconuts with his machete, and they plummeted to the ground. The other boys quickly gathered them up. With sharp whacks they sliced off the top of the thick green exterior exposing the three open eyes of each coconut before handing one to each of us. Soon, they each had one too, and were drinking the clear, watery liquid inside. Much to my amazement it tasted good and was refreshing. The smallest of the boys smacked his lips and proudly announced, "It tastes good and's good for us, too." We thanked them and resumed our walk, and I felt a little embarrassed by my earlier apprehension.

I thought about that experience again a few days later in Salinas while we walked into town for groceries. A woman with two small children stopped her car and offered us a ride. The children stared at us over the back of the front seat, and all we could see was their tight curly black-brown hair, their big, brown, curious eyes, and chubby little brown fingers gripping the seat. Neither she nor the children showed signs of fear, only curiosity. I found it wonderful and somewhat puzzling to meet people who were open and trusting of those who look so different from them. I had never met children who had not been indoctrinated with the "danger stranger" warnings, and I was saddened to realize how American children are taught at a very young age to distrust anyone they do not know.

The water coconuts were not the only new food item that we were introduced to in Puerto Rico. The island had an abundance of fresh fruit, and we appreciated all of it after having come through the arid Bahamaian Islands. We feasted daily on a wide variety of bananas; some had red skins, others were fat and short, and some were no larger than a human finger. All were good, and each type provided a unique taste and texture experience. A totally new fruit for us was the guanabana, similar in size to a cantaloupe, but it has a green pimpled skin with white flesh and large black seeds. The white flesh of the guanabana is chewy, sweet and delicious. All of the food items we had found so scarce in the Bahamas were readily available in Puerto Rico, and despite their weight, we gladly carried as many oranges, grapefruit, pineapples and papayas as we could back to the boat. With the abundance of fresh fruit and the fish Tom caught, we began eating well. We felt healthy and strong – so healthy and strong that we began feeling playful, and one day, while sailing off shore on a warm sunny day, we decided to go naked. The warm, dry air and gentle breeze made it an ideal day to do hand laundry as well, which normally was not one of my favorite chores, but doing it naked seemed both practical and rather fun. I washed and rinsed items of clothing while Tom hung them to dry on the lifelines around the cockpit. He loved the freedom of movement uninhibited by clothing. After all the laundry was hung he continued to prance about the deck wearing nothing but his white skin, allowing the gentle breeze to flutter past body parts that had previously been caressed only by *Fruit of the Loom*. He checked the sails, gazed at the skyline, put out a fishing line and enjoyed the feeling of being kissed by the air. When he finally stepped back into the cockpit and sat down he said, "Shoot! I got a sunburned ass." We both laughed while he struggled to find a soft spot to sit. "I guess I either need to get it more tanned, or keep it covered," he said, but paused only a second before saying, "I think I'll get it more tanned." I had to agree it felt great to be naked!

MARIJUANA VS TOMATO PLANTS

We were fully clothed when we arrived at the island of Culebra, where we met several long time cruisers. Bruce and Cathy Goble were coordinators for the Caribbean Maritime Mobile Radio Net, and because we had talked with them over the radio so many times, we felt like old friends in spite of never having met them in person. In ham radio jargon a face-to-face meeting is called "having an eyeball," so we had our first "eyeball" with them that day. They lived on their boat while operating a small marine store on land, and were in the process of building a home on the island.

We also met another couple we had heard many times on the weekly net. Shirley and Les Miller on ELEA. Les played the bagpipes and we soon knew when he was about to practice because we would see Shirley escape in the dinghy with their little dog. To us, at a distance of 100 yards, the music was entertaining, yet somewhat eerie and incongruent with the Caribbean. But we could easily understand how unbearable it would have been for Shirley to stay on the boat and listen at close range.

One of the other cruising boats had its laundry hanging out. Small clothing items hung on the lifelines around the boat like ours had, but we noticed the bed sheets were hung in a vertical position on the shrouds, allowing them to flap noisily as they dried. All that fabric flapping and snapping in the wind caused the boat to take on the appearance of a Chinese junk right out of a National Geographic documentary. This was better than an electric clothes-dryer, because the sheets were dry in a matter of minutes as the wind literally snapped the water out of them.

The next morning one of the cruisers announced over the VHF radio that she was willing to give haircuts on shore at 9am. The cost was $10, or its equivalent in canned goods. Her makeshift barbershop consisted of a folding stool set on the beach, and the area became the major social gathering of the day while we gathered around to wait our turn.

While we waited, one of the other cruisers entertained us with a story about his recent boarding by the Coast Guard. It seemed the Coast Guard thought he was growing a large marijuana plant on the stern of his boat.

"The officers were real serious fellows, and they came to investigate, all business-like. They wore bulletproof vests and boarded with their guns aimed right at me. I said, 'Hey fellows, you be real careful so you don't trip now. I don't want any of those guns going off accidentally.' They didn't say a word or make a single sound, just motioned for me to move back while they climbed aboard. Two of them kept their guns pointed at me while the other one went back to check my plant. You should've seen his face when he realized it was a big old, cherry tomato plant. I guess they assumed it was a marijuana plant. Then, they pointed the ends of their guns up so they were no longer aimed at me, and I showed them how I pollinated each blossom with a small paintbrush. I picked some too, so they could each taste one, but they were too embarrassed, I guess. They just left with no apology or anything. Nope, those guys just had no sense of humor."

We realized every person in the cruising community was eccentric in his or her own way. Zest for life was the common denominator and we enjoyed one another's company based solely on that. It did not matter if we were rich or poor, young or old, professional or blue collar, or had a large or small boat. It didn't matter if we played strange-sounding instruments, grew tomatoes, cut our own hair, or grew a beard. It was understood by all that our differences would be accepted and respected—and they were.

SUCKED THE RING OFF

From Culebra, it was a short day-sail to St. Thomas in the Virgin Islands. We looked forward to St. Thomas because we knew American food supplies, and a variety of boat items would be available. We also knew it was a dangerous port, made so by the hordes of tourists who swarmed into town from the five or six cruise ships in port on any given day. Tourists had money in their pockets, wore expensive jewelry, and left the island each evening in the cruise ships. Therefore, most tourists were not around long enough to press criminal charges when something happened to them. This was the perfect formula to attract thieves and scoundrels from all the neighboring islands, and St. Thomas was full of them. Even the forces of law and order were corrupt once one looked beneath the superficial tourism propaganda, but because the harbor was deep and fairly protected from bad weather, it was the perfect harbor for cruise ships and the tourists who arrived daily.

One cruiser told us of the time she was robbed when leaving the bank.

"I was hit on the head and pushed to the ground behind a bush. The robber took my money, and also wanted my gold wedding band. The ring was tight, however, and didn't slip off easily, so he put my finger in his mouth and began to suck it off. I gagged when I felt his teeth and warm wet mouth around my finger, but I lay still and pretended to have passed out, while I prayed that the ring would eventually slip off. I was really afraid that he would chop my finger off if it didn't."

Just the mere act of crossing the street in congested downtown Charlotte Amalie presents a danger because it is the only American territory where cars drive on the left side of the road. Many Americans and Canadians, tourists and cruisers alike, tend to forget and look in the wrong direction before stepping off the curb, often directly in front of cars. We learned that the reason for driving on the left side dated back to the early 1600s when Britain colonized the island. When the U.S. purchased the Virgin Islands in 1917, and attempted to change the driving to the right side of the road, it was chaotic because no one could train the donkeys and horses to change. The people were forced to go back to driving on the left. The saying we all needed to adopt before stepping off the curb to cross the street, was "Look right or die."

Cruisers, we learned, took care of one another and went out of their way to assist in any way possible. We met a couple who were keeping an eye on another couple's boat while they flew home to visit family. They anchored the two boats next to one another and checked on the empty boat every day. One night, they went to bed and awoke to find the empty boat was gone. They had not heard any unusual noises during that night, and blissfully slept through the theft. After the shock of discovering the boat was missing, they reported the theft over the ham radio and provided a description of the boat, knowing that it could not have gotten far in so few hours. Sure enough, cruisers who listened and participated on the ham radio spotted it on the island of Bequia. The police were notified and three men on board were arrested. The whole situation was taken care of before the owners returned, or even learned of the problem.

THE OCTOPUS DISAPPEARED BEFORE MY EYES

There are, of course, many positive aspects to the Virgin Islands as well. They have near-perfect year-round temperatures, and many beautiful and interesting sights. There are three main U. S. Virgin Islands: St. Thomas, St. Croix and St. John.

St. Thomas is 32 square miles and boasts a large protected harbor, a modern airport, and a major shopping area with goods from all over the world.

The island of St. Croix has two main towns, Frederiksted and Christiansted, and across the six-mile channel from Christiansted is the small Buck Island Reef with an underwater park, and marked underwater trails that lead to an assortment of coral formations and fish of every size, shape, and color.

The 20 square miles of St. John's Island are scalloped with coves, sand-covered beaches, several expensive resorts, and the historic Annaberg sugar plantation. There, sugar cane is grown symbolically, and not as a lucrative cash crop as it was in the days when it was harvested by slaves. Slavery is not a pleasant story, but the local people felt it was important to keep the visual reminders of the past alive.

Within a few hours' easy sailing is the British group of Virgin Islands. The main three islands are Tortola, Virgin Gorda and Anegada, but there are several smaller islands, each with its own native flavor. Our favorite of them was Virgin Gorda, especially the area called The Baths where we swam through and around artistically shaped natural rock formations. It was there that I saw my first octopus. I watched it change color, saw it squish itself into an unbelievably small crevice, and disappear. We had visited The Baths many times, and never tired of them. The natural beauty of the rock formations, the fish, coral, and toast-colored sandy bottom all added to our pleasure. The Baths were also special for me, because it was where I had learned to swim years ago by hanging on to a line tied off the stern of a boat. That was back in the days when we chartered. I never dreamed at that time the day would come when I would be able to swim with ease and comfort off the stern of our own boat.

Now with our own boat, many friends from Minnesota arrived in St. Thomas, and during that time we avoided doing boat work, and instead, we swam and played. One time, we treated ourselves to a restaurant barbecue held on the beach. We had several drinks at the hotel bar during happy hour while we waited for the barbecue to begin, and I discovered I rather liked a drink called a strawberry margarita. I had never been one to drink hard alcohol, but the strawberry margarita didn't taste like alcohol at all. It was so refreshing that I slurped down several more. Shortly after dark, a hotel employee rang a bell and invited us to follow him to the beach for dinner. There were 35 or 40 people following him down the steep cement road, and we all carried our drinks with us. I vaguely realized I was having difficulty keeping up with the group, but pushed the thought to the back my head. I walked on the outer edge of the road next to Tom and concentrated on putting one foot in front of the other. There were no lights along the path and it was difficult to see where we were going. The only light came from the stars, and even the moon would not be up for several hours. I knew I was feeling a little tipsy and realized that I should not lose sight of Tom. For a brief second I remember feeling airborne, and then I lost sight of everyone. At first I didn't know what had happened, but I later learned that I had stepped off the road and into a storm sewer. I didn't hurt myself, nor did I even spill my drink, but I needed help climbing out because the storm sewer was up to my armpits. Enough said about light little margaritas!

After our guests left, we pulled up to the fuel dock to replenish both fuel and water. While we waited our turn, another cruiser noticed a cracked swage fitting on our rigging. The fitting joined the stainless steel cable shrouds to the deck fitting that was bolted to the bulkheads. Upon further inspection, we realized there were several questionably unsafe fittings and we imagined the horror if we had lost our mast and sails at sea! The discovery was quite alarming because it meant our entire rigging was in jeopardy of falling down. We motored to a quiet cove and Tom began dismantling our stressed and cracked rigging. We had neither planned nor budgeted for that expense, but we were relieved to have discovered the cracks in time to prevent a potentially catastrophic, and even more expensive problem. The following day, Tom purchased Sta-Locks and put them on the bottom ends of six of the main mast shrouds before putting the rest of the rigging back together. We hoped this would prevent a terrible accident.

EVERYONE WAS NAKED

Once again we headed down the "thorny path," and by the first of May we arrived at the island of St. Martin, a tiny Caribbean island with the flavor of old Europe. The southern half of the island is a Dutch colony, while the northern half is French. We found the food shops on the French side a gastronomic treat, and we were able to purchase wonderful soft cheeses, pate, and baguettes at reasonable prices.

In the 17th century, the French and the Dutch fought over the island, only to be pushed off by the Spanish, but in 1648 the Spaniards left and soon the Dutch and French returned. After some struggle both country leaders sat down and negotiated an agreement called the "Mont des Accord" that divided the island. The island set a womderful example of international cohabitation between the two nations, agreeing to help each other in time of need, and today, that peaceful cohabitation continues. There is even a golf course that splits its greens and fairways between the two nations.

One of the less desirable things we became aware of on St. Martin is the prevalence of a tree called the Manchioneel. The tree is common on all the Caribbean islands and not unique to St. Martin. It is a graceful tree with silver gray bark and looks like the perfect shade tree or a place to take refuge during a quick tropical rain shower. In spite of its friendly appearance however, it drips a milky sap similar to poison ivy. We learned about the tree from the locals and were able to avoid any unpleasant experience with it.

We toured the island by riding the public bus and often rode from one end of the line to the other. As a courtesy to those who got on and off en route, we usually sat in the back so people did not need to climb over us. Often, we were the only white people on the bus. One day an elderly black lady struggled to get her bags of groceries off with her, so I assisted her by carrying them down the steps and placing them on the bench at the bus stop. A Rastafarian man with a full head of dreadlocks was seated nearby, but not only did he not offer any help to the woman, he recited a *sing-song* poem to criticize the help I gave her. "Da candy man don't look kindly on no help from no white woman……," he chanted. "Candy" supposedly referred to the supply of drugs that he sold to tourists.

Another day, while waiting at the telephone company on the Dutch side, we struck up a conversation with a young man from the *S.S. Norway*, a large cruise ship in port that day. He was the crew coordinator for the ship, which meant he hired and supervised all of the crew. Since the passengers were ashore, he invited us on board for a tour and lunch. We were amazed at the size of the ship, especially when we saw the behind-the-scenes areas. There were five dining rooms for the crew alone, each specializing in the ethnic foods of the crew, such as Filipino and Chinese. There was an upholstery shop where they constantly repaired furniture and draperies, and a seamstress shop where the uniforms of the crew were mended or altered, and the costumes of the performers maintained. Of course, there were many posh amenities for the paid passengers, including live theater, several dining rooms, swimming pools, exercise rooms, and dance halls. It was a virtual floating city and made little VONNIE-T appear very small and humble, by comparison.

The ship's doctor joined us for lunch. He complained that his job bored him. "There is seldom any real excitement" he said, "and it certainly isn't what I thought I'd be doing all those years when I studied and prepared for exams. I generally treat sunburn, hangovers, and seasickness." When the two young men discussed the issue of whether or not they were going to "go out that night," we did not understand what they were talking about, since we knew the ship went to sea each night. Finally, we caught on. They were talking about leaving their cabins to partake of the nightlife of discos, bars and restaurants onboard the ship. That was what they considered "going out."

One of the more memorable aspects of the French side of the island was our visit to Orient Bay, a quiet and peaceful anchorage in front of Club Orient, a naturalist resort. We had heard about the resort, and upon checking our charts, Tom saw it was deep enough for us to anchor. We brought our dinghy motor on board, tethered the dinghy to the stern of VONNIE-T, pulled up our anchor, and sailed to that side of the island. When we approached the harbor opening we saw there was shoaling water on both sides of the entrance, but calculated that if we stayed dead center we could easily go through. Tom lowered the sails and we powered through the opening. Perhaps a more accurate description would be to say we shot through the opening while being tossed in many directions. The dinghy tether held strong and we did not lose it, but we did lose the gas can that was in the dinghy. Once inside the bay, there was calm, clear blue water without so much as a ripple. We looked around for the gas can, but it was nowhere in sight, and we felt stupid for having lost it. Of course, there was the expense and inconvenience of replacing it, but of greater concern was that it was a pollutant.

We anchored in 15 feet and found we were the only boat in the anchorage. We checked out the beach with binoculars before going to shore. Sure enough, there were many people on the beach, all *a-la-natural*. "I think we should just snorkel into shore," Tom said, "instead of taking the dinghy in. That way we can just sort of blend in."

That was fine with me. I wrapped sunscreen, sunglasses, and money in a small towel and put them into a plastic zip-lock bag. I put on my fins, snorkel and mask and got into the water, leaving my swimsuit on board. Tom jumped in beside me and we began swimming toward shore. We swam to the far end of the beach, as opposed to swimming into the center of the busy part. Tom was concerned about getting slowly acclimated to this new environment. When we reached shore we got out of the water and removed our snorkel equipment. "I'll carry your fins for you," Tom said.

"You've never offered to carry any of my equipment before," I laughed. "Are you planning on doing some sort of fan dance with the extra swim fins?"

"Well, I'm just a little afraid I might embarrass myself, if you know what I mean," he said.

Before anything more could be said, another couple, also sans clothing, strolled by and struck up a conversation. Soon we found ourselves included in their social community. There were approximately 150 people of all ages on the beach. No one was a 'body beautiful', but then, no one was grotesque looking either. They were interesting people to talk to; all had substantial careers and normal lives back home. We enjoyed getting to know them and once we got used to everyone being nude, we found it was a free and comfortable feeling, and not a sensual or sexual situation. I have to admit I found it rather inconvenient when I went into the little local grocery store to purchase cans of fruit juice. I had no pockets for my change and I did not want to carry the cold cans in my arms next to my body, and I found it hysterical to see naked men and women in the store carrying purses.

One of the couples had a rental car and they invited us to join them for dinner in town that evening. We needed to wear clothes to go into town, and when our host met us on shore to help us drag the dinghy onto the sand, I almost asked him his name. I honestly did not recognize him with clothing on. Without clothes, he was a big hairy chest; with clothes, he had a face that I hadn't noticed before.

The dinner conversation was comfortable and relaxed and revolved around the local food. They all liked cracked conch, and were surprised when we said we knew how to prepare it. Tom said he would dive for conch tomorrow, and if he found some we would show them from start to finish how to prepare it.

Tom loved having a reason to dive and hunt, so early the next morning he was in the water on his quest for conch. In less than an hour he had several nice large conchs, and he invited the group out to our boat for conch-cleaning lessons. All six people with whom we went to dinner the previous night, were interested in seeing the process and they eagerly swam to our boat to watch the lesson.

My supplies consisted of a bucket of fresh salt water, a cutting board, a very sharp knife, and a meat hammer, all of which I set up on the stern of the boat where there was ample room to work. While I demonstrated, Tom videotaped the process and explained for the audience and the camera what I was doing during each step. After the cleaning demonstration I showed them how to cook them, and everyone enjoyed eating the demonstration sample.

We had a good time with the people and we stayed at the anchorage for several days enjoying their company. I loved their down-to-earth attitudes, and when it came time for us to leave, it was almost sad. One woman gave me a big warm hug, bare breast to bare breast, and wished us "Good luck with your travels." Then she stepped back and said something that puzzled me. She said, "I envy you so much." When I told Tom about her remark, he sat up extra tall and smiled proudly. I was dumbfounded to learn he interpreted it as a compliment to his anatomy. Incredible!

THE AROMATIC SCENT OF ROASTED MARSHMALLOWS

St. Barthelemy, usually referred to as St. Barts, is another of the French islands in the Caribbean that we really liked. In general, we found it to be quieter and more laid back than St. Martin, but one morning while anchored in a peaceful and protected harbor, we awoke to the horrible screeching of a peacock. It seemed incongruous that such a majestic-looking bird would be making such a terrible noise in such a serene place.

A few days later we set sail with a course setting of 190 degrees for Saba, a Dutch island that could easily be seen from St. Barts. Since I could see the island with the naked eye, it appeared deceptively close and I anticipated a lazy, comfortable sail. We enjoyed steady 15-knot winds and moved along at 6 knots, with only the roller-furling jib.

When the sun was high in the sky I became certain that I smelled roasted marshmallows, but since we were many miles off shore and had no marshmallows aboard, the mere notion was preposterous. Then we noticed large black curls of something falling from the air onto the deck of the boat. The curls were feather light, and when we tried to pick them up they disintegrated into greasy soot. Behind us, on one end of St. Barts, we saw a large patch of black smoke drifting toward us and then it dawned on me; we were witnessing what the local people referred to as "black snow." They were burning sugar cane fields to

The town built on the top of Saba Island is called Bottom because it's built on the bottom of an extinct volcano.

make the harvest easier. What we did not realize until then, was that the burning sugar cane gave off the wonderful sweet odor of roasted marshmallows, enough to cause our mouths to water.

The short sail to Saba Island seemed to take forever. Our log and instruments each indicated a distance gain, but it seemed as if we were getting no closer. The island is a small mountain formed from an extinct volcano, and because it stuck up so high it was visible for 40 miles on clear days, making it appear to be closer than it actually was.

When we were still 20 miles away, we watched soft, fluffy clouds forming at the top of Saba's highest peak. The clouds were created as the sea breeze slid up toward the peak. As it raised higher, it cooled and condensed, thus forming clouds. When each cloud became heavy with moisture, it dropped rain, and after the cloud emptied, it moved off into the atmosphere while others gathered moisture, repeating the process. We had never before so clearly witnessed the cycle of rain, and seeing it occur repeatedly was fascinating!

Our hypnotic watching of the clouds was broken when we noticed an orange fishing boat that seemed to fit the description of one that had been reported by Saba radio, as "missing" and "overdue." All morning we heard Saba's radio request for any craft in the vicinity to be "on the lookout for an orange fishing boat with two motors and two persons on board." Just how many orange fishing boats could there be? When we spotted it we changed our course heading with the intent of offering assistance. We assumed they had run out of fuel and needed a tow into port, but before we were able to get near, they sped away to pull in more fishing nets. They were clearly in no danger and seemed oblivious of our heading in their direction, and apparently also unaware of anyone looking for them. They were simply fishing.

We called Saba radio to report what we saw, and at the same time we inquired about anchoring in their harbor. We learned there was no natural harbor, only a man-made pier with a long dock and a seawall, but we were invited to tie up to the seawall.

Saba radio must have informed the port authorities of our pending arrival and requested that a place be reserved for us. They also arranged for a taxi to wait at the pier for our arrival. Our driver, Topo, was an excellent tour guide and he told us there were only 1,000 people living on Saba. Half were black and the other half white. Everyone seemed to know everyone else, and all were friendly toward one another regardless of skin color.

Topo, one of the black people on the island, was married and had "three normal children." He told us that others who marry on the island were not always so lucky when it came to having normal children, because first cousins are allowed to marry, and they often do. With such a small pool of potential marriage partners and an obvious awareness of the problems with inbreeding, we were surprised to learn there were only three interracial marriages on the island.

The narrow cement road that led from the pier wound in a tight hairpin curve up the steep side of the mountain-island, and looked more like a ski run than a road. The airport on Saba was another amazing site and special permits to land there were issued to only the most experienced pilots. The runway, built in 1963, is a mere 1,580-feet-long. At the end is a sheer drop leading directly into the sea. Airplanes could stop in that short distance only when landing under ideal conditions and with great skill. Locals sold T-shirts with the saying, "I survived my landing at the Saba Airport."

Topo took us to all four towns: Bottom, English Quarter (sometimes also called St. John's), Hell's Gate, and Windwardside. Bottom is actually the highest town, but earned its name because it is situated on the floor (the bottom) of an extinct volcano. Unlike elsewhere in the Caribbean, the Saba homes were neatly painted, had red tile roofs, and were surrounded by small, well-tended gardens.

When we passed a small grocery store at one of the relatively few straight areas in the road, I asked how often supplies were delivered to the island. "They come every week by boat," Topo said.

I am sure I would have answered that same question by saying "we only get supplies once a week." Instead, Topo very positively said "every week."

He eagerly told us about Saba's youth: "Those wanting to go to college do so at the Dutch government's expense. They attend college either in Holland or on one of the Caribbean islands. It's their choice, and the best part is, everything is paid for, even room and board."

At first glance the island looked peaceful and Topo described Norman Rockwell-like villages, but I wondered what life was like on a daily basis with so few people and all of them knowing each other's business. In spite of Topo's charm and positive attitude, I did not get the impression that everything was rosy. Seeing the mental hospital where the unfortunate byproducts of inbreeding spent their days, suggested there was a layer of hurt and despair that a first time visitor might not see.

The wind direction had changed by the time we returned to the boat, allowing a nasty surge to enter the harbor. It was unsafe for our boat to remain tied to the seawall. Our fenders were not heavy enough to protect the boat from the unforgiving cement pier, so we were encouraged to motor around to the west side of the island to an area called the Ladder Landing. It was very deep there, much too deep to anchor, but there were moorings available, so we tied up. We had a comfortable night on the mooring, and marveled at how far we were able to see into the clear water, where it was said more than 120 species of fish lived.

MY FLAG INSULTED THE NEW GOVERNMENT

Since we were going to spend the evening on board, I dug out the portable sewing machine and made several more country courtesy flags. I had purchased the sewing machine, an old Viking model, before we left Minneapolis because it was heavy enough to do temporary sail repairs and delicate enough to sew other things. With the sewing machine, an assortment of colored nylon ripcord scraps, and a flag book with colored photographs for each country's flag, I was able to make all our courtesy flags. While proper flag etiquette was important, purchasing each country's flag would have been expensive.

We raised the country courtesy flag on our starboard spreader directly under the orange "Q" (quarantine) flag as we entered a new country. Many years ago the "Q" flag literally meant the crew was quarantined until a doctor came onboard to check for yellow fever, or other infectious diseases. Until that had been done the crew was not allowed off the boat; only the captain could set foot on shore. Today, however, the "Q" flag is taken down immediately after the paperwork has been completed with the customs officials and the emigration office.

Early the following morning we left Saba with several new courtesy flags made for the next countries we planned on visiting. It felt great to be a little ahead of my work for a change. We had barely raised the sails up and established our desired heading when Tom pulled in a 15-pound yellowfin tuna. He cleaned it and cut it into meal-size pieces, bagged the individual pieces in plastic ziplock bags, and laid the bags directly on the refrigerator cold plate. By chilling the fish first it saved the freezer from losing its cold. I saved one piece and cooked it for fresh tuna sandwiches for lunch that day.

It was a warm sunny day and an easy sail. By 5pm we were anchored off the northwest coast of St. Christopher Island (St. Kitts). Unfortunately, the harbor had a lot of surge and VONNIE-T rolled from side to side like a sick whale. I had not felt seasick all day, but I began feeling queasy shortly after we had the anchor down.

With great difficulty Tom got the dinghy in the water. I swung the mizzen boom out over the side of the boat and lowered the motor to him by using a three-part line. He received the motor while bobbing up and down in the dinghy, and secured it to the dinghy transom. I handed him the plastic pouch with our boat papers, and watched him motor toward shore for the purpose of checking in with customs and emigration. He struggled to reach the pier cleat where he secured the dinghy tether, then reversed the dinghy and threw the small stern anchor out. After tightening the anchor line to prevent the dinghy from getting caught under, or smashed against the pier, he made a giant leap up onto the pier with the boat documents in one hand. I watched him from the boat with mixed feelings. I admired his agility in jumping up on that dock in spite of the surging water, but still I worried that he might fall and re-injure himself. At first I was relieved that I did not have to go with him and thought that the worst thing about staying behind would be worrying about him, but that was not true at all. It was far from a picnic being on the boat. As VONNIE-T continued to roll from side to side I felt myself get sicker and sicker. I hoped Tom would be able to check in quickly and get back to the boat so we could move to a more comfortable anchorage. Meanwhile, I attempted to ignore my nausea by doing something productive, so while Tom was on shore I hoisted the courtesy flag I had made for St. Kitts and our orange "Q" flag, by scooting my rear-end along the rolling deck until I got to the shroud with the flag tether. Then I slid back to the cockpit where I waited for Tom to return. It seemed like he was gone forever, and when he returned he yelled at me, "Get that flag down!"

He shoved a very different-looking flag towards me. "They've just had a change in government," he said, "They have a new flag now, and were insulted by the one you made. They insisted that I buy that one," he said, gesturing toward the flag he had just thrust into my hands. "They yelled and acted as if I had intended to insult them. What an act! I didn't really catch on until they charged me $35 for that piece of stenciled crap they call their new flag."

While he was still ranting and raving I lowered my homemade flag and the "Q" flag. I replaced both flags with the new flag and raised it to the starboard spreader. The new flag was made of cheap, loosely woven cotton, and even the stenciling had been done poorly, as the lines were smudged and fuzzy. The poor stenciling job did not really matter though, because I knew the sun would fade the cotton fabric within a few days. The sun was also harsh on the flags I made out of nylon ripcord, but at least they lasted several months.

The next morning we both went ashore. The wind had changed and the surge was not as strong. I got my reciprocal ham radio license, and we had our two-meter radio repaired. That afternoon we moved the boat to a quiet little bay a few hours from the main town. We snorkeled and swam in crystal-clear water and could hardly believe our good fortune when we swam over a large conch bed. Tom dove and picked them off the ocean floor, two at a time, and handed them to me to swim them back to the dinghy. He was surprised to discover he was free-diving in 35 feet of water, because when he dove he saw the dinghy anchor hanging straight down to the bottom, and the anchor line was 35 feet. He remembered when he had difficulty diving 15 feet, and that didn't seem so very long ago. I made Conch St. Jacques for dinner that evening, and it was a feast.

THE OWNERS OF THE NEVIS RESORT WERE FROM DULUTH

A few days later we were at Nevis, a sister island to St. Kitts. We had read about an old health resort there where hot sulfur springs were reported to have cured all types of ailments. The resort was no longer in operation, but we had heard that wealthy people from all over the world used to come to bathe in the restorative waters. It was only a short distance from the main town, so we walked over to see it. It was a ruin now, only a shell of a building, but the bathing cubicles still stood and there were about six inches of warm sulfur water still flowing over the brick floors.

As we walked the grounds we commented on how picturesque a herd of local goats was. The young girl with the animals corrected us softly by saying, "sheep."

Somehow, we did not understand what she said and when we again called them goats, she said, "sheep."

"Sheep?" we finally asked.

"Yes," she said, "sheep. All the tourists think they're goats, but they're sheep."

"But they don't have thick wooly hair like sheep." I said.

"Of course not," she explained. "They're Caribbean sheep. Caribbean sheep have long silky hair. You can always tell the difference by how they carry their tails," she informed us. "Goats carry their tails up, while sheep carry their tails down."

Obviously we knew nothing about sheep, or goats.

We toured more of the island by way of our usual mode of transportation, the public bus. In Georgetown, we got off the bus at the entrance of an enticing tropical resort called the Nisbet Plantation. The grounds were bursting with colorful bougainvillea that climbed freely on anything in its path, and large flamboyant trees displayed large red-orange flowers. All of that kaleidoscopic growth, with no evidence of people puzzled us. We finally found the owner, George Barnum. Apparently we had arrived on one of the rare days when there were no tourists, but that did not seem to present a problem. We were welcomed and encouraged to stay for lunch.

It was pleasant to have the opportunity to talk with an American, and during the course of the conversation we were surprised to learn that he and his wife Elizabeth were from Duluth, Minnesota, our homeport! It was strange to discuss places and people we knew in common, yet we had never met or even heard of the Barnums before that day. We marveled at the coincidental meeting.

MILLION DOLLAR BOATS & THE BEAUTY & THE BEAST CONTEST

The morning we set sail for Antigua was a day of lumpy seas and rainsqualls. It made for a cold and uncomfortable sail, but the most frightening part was watching downspouts all around us. They were long funnel-shaped clouds that reached into the ocean and sucked up water (on land, downspouts are called tornadoes). We knew they had the power to pick us up out of the water and drop us many miles away, and realized how easily we could become victims. Yet there was nothing we could do to protect ourselves. Our only choice was to continue on our course and hope one wouldn't reach us. Once again we were lucky, and the worst thing I can say about the day is that we were cold, wet, and uncomfortable.

When we arrived at Antigua, we anchored and checked in at English Harbour. I called J.R., a ham radio contact who had befriended us on the radio, from one of the pay telephones near the customs office, and arranged to meet him the next day to secure my reciprocal ham radio license for Antigua. He graciously invited us to his home to meet his wife, see his "ham shack", and attend the local ham-radio club meeting that met at his home that evening.

A few days later, Herman Saul, one of my ham instructors from Minnesota came with his wife to spend "Sail Week" with us. "Sail Week" was a popular regatta with lots of partying and festivities. The week began with an evening barbeque high up on Shirley Heights, where we were serenaded by a local steel band. The musicians were in a dark corner of the room, and their dark skin and equally dark clothing caused them to appear invisible, while they played, and we danced to the joyful music.

Early the next day, the regatta began with million-dollar boats run by skippers who flew in to meet their crew and take command of their costly status symbols. Some of the cruisers entered their boats thinking that their sailing skills might in some way compensate for the additional weight a cruising boat typically carries, but not us. It is one thing to race an expensive toy, but quite another to race your home. There is risk when boats are trying to maneuver in such a close space. We did watch the race, however, and we were horrified to see one boat's bow anchor get hooked and pull down another boat's entire rigging. It was a terrible thing to witness, but it further confirmed our decision to watch, and not race.

After the regatta, there were other contests, all of them involving lots of beer drinking, laughing, and general "whooping it up." Tom especially liked the Beauty and the Beast contest where the beauties all bared their breasts. The entire event was a lot of fun.

When we tired of the loud noise, we pulled up our anchor and found a quiet anchorage away from English Harbor. Swimming and snorkeling were on our agenda every day and we managed to become

An Antiguan man walking down the street, carrying his useful machete and other items on his head.

tired from all the fun, so one warm afternoon Herman and Tom decided to take naps, while we women relaxed in the cockpit with books. It was one of those peaceful days when there did not seem any reason to be alert, but for some unknown reason we women both glanced toward a soft noise in the water. Our eyes fell upon a naked man who was floating on his back, with a very large erection. It was difficult to believe what I had actually seen! In a flash, he rolled over, dove down into the water, and swam away.

Later that afternoon, Tom went spear fishing out near the harbor entrance and he noticed a young couple attempting to swim to shore. He brought the dinghy over to them and offered a ride which they gladly accepted. Tom learned that they were newly-weds who had walked out to the point so they could be alone and do some nude sunbathing. But they were interrupted by "a strange man who came out, got naked and lay down near them." The young couple was so frightened by him they decided to try to swim all the way back. Neither of them were strong swimmers, and if Tom had not happened along, the end of the story might have been tragic.

Before we went to bed that night I dug out the pair of rat traps that I had stowed away, and set them in the cockpit. We all rested a lot easier knowing that if anyone stepped into the boat while we slept, they would be in for a big surprise.

A SLIPPER LOBSTER

After the Sauls left, we planned to have a few days of total relaxation without fancy meals or the pressures of entertaining non-boat people 24 hours each day. We pulled up our anchor and headed to a small, seldom-used cove where none of the Sail Week activities would take place. En route we spoke on the radio with Ted and Elinor on the sailing yacht CANOPUS, and learned they were heading to the same anchorage. Elinor was a marvelous cook, and it was she who had given me the recipe for Conch St. Jacque. She and Ted were kind and interesting people, and in spite of our original plan to have time alone, we looked forward to seeing them. The sail to the new anchorage had been surprisingly rough, but because it was such a short distance I had not bothered to mention on the radio how high the seas were.

"LaVonne, you didn't tell us it was lumpy out there," Ted said when he saw us. I had to smile at myself. It wasn't so very long ago when I could not get over how the old-time cruisers seemed to either minimize bad weather or not bother to mention it. I never dreamt I would reach that point.

Soon after both boats anchored deep inside the bay where the water was calm, all four of us went swimming. Of course Tom and Ted immediately headed off toward the coral heads with their spears, ready to hunt for lobsters or some other tasty morsel for our dinners. Tom spied some prehistoric-looking thing crawling on the bottom that Ted called a slipper lobster.

"Is it good to eat?" Tom asked.

"As far as I know it tastes just like any other lobster," Ted said, so Tom dove back down and speared it. It looked prehistoric to me too, but I checked our book and it indeed was listed as edible. Elinor and Ted picked up a couple of conchs and we combined our catch for a feast on board our boat.

DOMINICA

A few days later we sailed to the island of Dominica, an independent island that is unpopular with most cruisers, for good reason. We might have skipped it completely, except we wanted to visit our friends, Barbara and Ken Egertson, who lived there during Ken's work/exchange assignment sponsored by the Agricultural Extension Service at the University of Minnesota. Barbara and Ken had been our neighbors in Minnesota and our children had grown up together, so it was a stop we really wanted to make.

En route, Tom studied the chart and found no anchorage that looked particularly comfortable or safe, because the entire shoreline was exposed to open sea. There was an area in front of a hotel where the water depth appeared to be reasonable, and our chart indicated it might be an acceptable anchorage, so we headed toward it.

As we made our approach, we were overrun by a dozen or more boys, each in some rickety type of craft and all wanting to "help us tie-up" for money. They seemed to appear from nowhere and the numbers continued to grow. Two considerably older fellows, perhaps 20 to 30 years old, were highly practiced at the game of extortion. One claimed he worked for the hotel, the other claimed it was "against the law for us to tie-up by ourselves." Both threatened to cut our lines if we did so.

Tom was angry about the threat, and felt frustrated and vulnerable. The "boys" greatly outnumbered us and could easily have taken over our boat if they had wanted to. As the tension mounted, I become concerned that the situation could erupt in a flash into uncontrollable violence. Nonetheless, Tom refused to be intimidated, and we anchored as we always did. When the anchor was set, Tom got in our dinghy and took our stern line in to shore and tied it to a rung on a wall, in accord with our guidebook's suggestion. The harassment continued the whole time he rowed to shore. I called on the two-meter radio to ask ham radio people on the island what the rules were for anchoring, and explained what was happening to us. A woman ham, with whom I had been having conversations for several days, immediately became concerned and called the Coast Guard. Within minutes the Coast Guard cutter Melville launched an Avon to provide us assistance. The "boys" magically melted into the shoreline at the mere sight of the Coast Guard boat.

After that, Tom was reluctant to leave the boat for very long, wondering if or when the gang might return. We did go to the Egertsons' house for breakfast the next morning, and we made a short trip to the farmer's market, truly the best in the whole Caribbean. But he worried the entire time and said he would not leave the boat unattended in that anchorage again. When Barbara invited us to their home for dinner the next night, he declined, but Barbara was one step ahead of him.

"Well, that's simple," she said, "we'll just bring dinner to you." It was the perfect solution. We ate one of Barbara's delicious home-cooked meals on our boat. They enjoyed an evening on the boat and we enjoyed their company, without having to worry about our security.

THE 61-INCH WAHOO

Our visit to Dominica was short and a few days later we set sail for Martinique, another of the French Islands. As usual, Tom trailed a fishing line, and on that day he hit the jackpot. He caught a big Wahoo. Not only was it one of our favorite fish, it was also the largest fish Tom had ever caught. It provided a marvelous fight and when Tom actually landed it, he could not have been more impressed by its size. Once the creature was on board, however, we didn't know what to do with it. It was too large to take below into the galley, and the seas were too rough for Tom to try to clean it up on deck. The only option left was to slide it into the cockpit where we could at least keep it in the shade, and that was where it lay for the rest of the day. We photographed it, measured it from tip to tail, and wrote the vital statistics in the log: Wahoo, 61 inches long.

We arrived in Martinique at dusk. By the time we anchored it was dark, but then we had to butcher and clean that fish. The task took place in the cockpit and made a terrible mess that also had to be cleaned before we could begin dinner or think about going to bed. We chilled the packed pieces in the refrigerator, and the next day we found a business with a commercial freezer, where we made arrangements to have it flash-frozen.

Later that day, we visited the museum where items were on display from the tragic 1902 Mount Pelee volcanic eruption. It was awesome to see boxes of steel nails fused together from the heat while still intact in their original box, and to see dinner plates where the food was petrified and perfectly preserved. Apparently, only one man survived the ordeal because he had been jailed in a deep dungeon where the gases and ash couldn't reach him.

THE PÂTÉ THAT TURNED OUT TO BE DOG FOOD

When we got back to the anchorage, those of us who had traveled together by bus to visit the museum decided to get together on our boat for a potluck dinner. Cruisers often do potluck meals that are usually held on the boat with the largest cockpit. Topics of discussions usually center on boat maintenance and/or where to find needed supplies. Since we were on a French island, the topic that evening fell to the delicious foods we were finding in the local stores and markets. We all agreed that the French baguettes were wonderful! There was a bakery near the dinghy dock that baked them fresh every two hours, and the sign on the front of the shop announced when the next hot batch would be ready. Of course, we did not need to read the sign because the wonderful aroma floating across the water told us what we needed to know.

One Canadian cruiser raved about the fantastic canned pâté he found in one of the grocery stores. The French cruiser replied, "that's strange, because pate is usually fresh. I

Photo by Michelle Houston of VONNIE-T at anchor near Puerto La Cruz, Venezuela.

 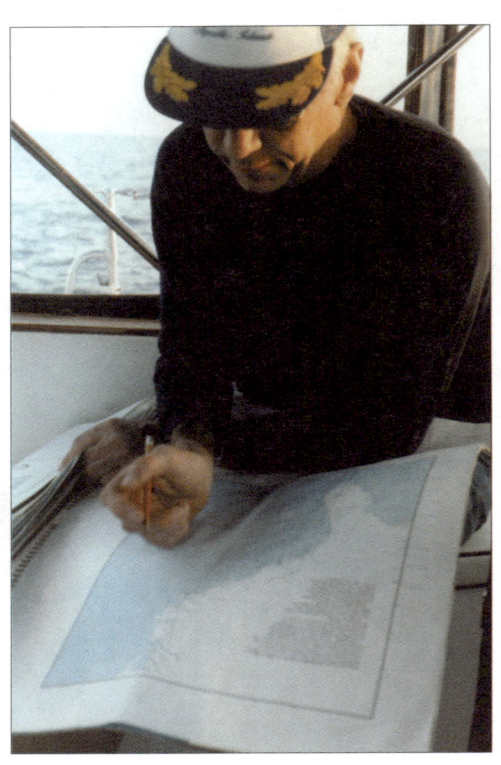

Above: Tom at the helm when the autopilot didn't work. Right: Tom studied the details of all the pertinent charts. Below: VONNIE-T pulling at her anchor in a choppy harbor.

Right: Seagulls often enjoyed perching on our high Spreaders. Below: Photo taken in New Caledonia by Dr. Robert DeMalet, the new owner of VONNIE-T.

Above: Tom is sitting at the Navigation table opposite the galley and next to the main salon. Left: The starboard interior of the main salon. Below: One of two heads; this is the starboard stern.

OPPOSITE PAGE Top: From left to right is Loran C; radar; VHF Radio and Sat Nav. Middle: The teak dining table was mounted to the mast in the center and could seat eight when the extra leaf was put up. Bottom: The galley had a built in microwave, a gimbaled oven and stove, plus a refrigerator and small freezer that opened from the top.

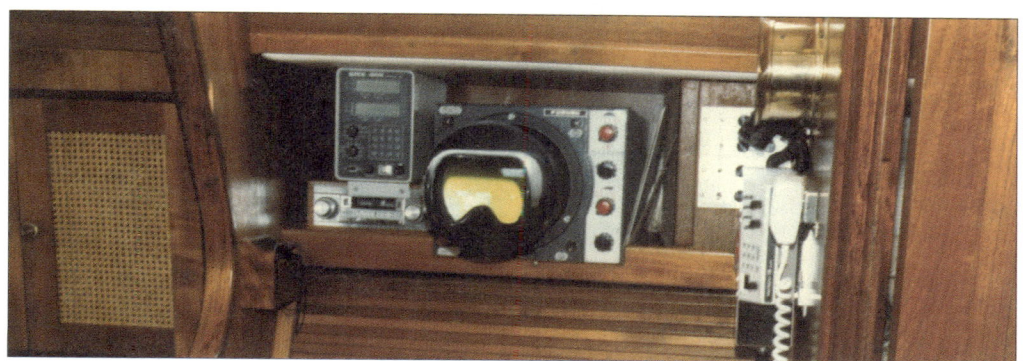

OPPOSITE PAGE: VONNIE-T sailing downwind using only a genoa and mizzen sail.

Above: By using our electric anchor windlass, I was able to hoist Tom up the mast to do repairs while he sat in a bosun's chair shackled to the main halyard. Below: Tom and I enjoyed the privacy and beauty of the Dismal Swamp estuary while varnishing the teak.

OPPOSITE PAGE: Living on the boat required very little use of our legs therefore we looked forward to an opportunity to walk and check out lighthouses like this one in Puerto Rico.

Above and Below: Two views of Virgin Gorda, which is one of the ten British Virgin Islands.

Left: While in the Los Aves Islands Tom brought up all the lobster we could eat. Above: Freshly caught Jack fish. Below: When we had the luxury of filling an air tank Tom loved to dive and hunt for dinner with his spear gun.

Above: Both these sea creatures, crab and squid, became fine dinner fare on VONNIE-T. Right: Son, Clark said he felt like a rag doll while being pulled through the water when he speared this 46" wahoo in Fiji. Below: Son, Andy caught this wahoo with a fishing line.

Left: El Salto Angel (Angel's Falls) is the highest waterfalls in the world and is hidden in the Gran Sabana (an area locally known as Guayana) near Canaima, Venezuela.

Above: Wild parrots and macaws are prevalent in the mountains around Camp Canaima, a three million-acre national park established in 1962.

Above: Trinadad may be the only place in the world where Hindus and Muslims are friends, and we were honored to be invited to attend a Hindu wedding by our Muslim Ham Radio Friend while visiting Trinadad.

Below: The bride wore three different dresses: a red one, a yellow one and a white one. Right: The broad shouldered six-footer groom is shown here wearing his bright pink wedding dress.

Left: Woman in Chili selling fresh fish along the waterfront. Above: These live crabs were tied in a bunch to prevent them from crawling away before they could be sold at the market in Manaus, Brazil. Below: At low tide these vendor's boats sat on the mud at the mouth of the Amazon River in front of Belem, Brazil.

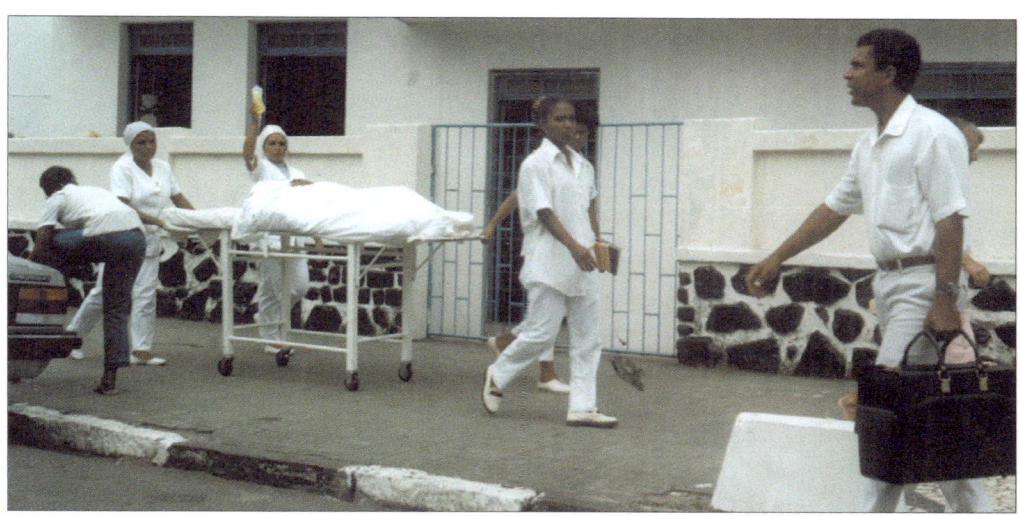

Above: In Recife, Brazil we were amazed to see two nurses escorting a patient on a rolling hospital bed across a busy street, apparently to another section of the hospital. Right: It was common to see caskets sold in the corner shops of the local hospitals in Northern Brazil. Below: Fortaleza, Brazil water front.

Above: Rio de Janeiro has miles and miles of beautiful sandy beaches. The large modern city has all the amenities and cultural opportunities for comfortable living and it pulses with life and excitement.

Left: The cable car for Sugar Loaf.

Right: Another view of Rio from the top of Sugar Loaf.

OPPOSITE PAGE Top : The walled-in city of Cartagena, Colombia, called Cuidad Viejo (old city), still operates as a commercial and residential community much as it did when it was first built. The bricks used to form the streets are the original ballast from cargo ships that sailed there from Glasco, England.
Bottom: The harbor at Cartagena, Colombia is huge, almost a sea, but has shallow areas requiring deep-drafted sailboat to follow the channel markers.

Above: One way to help cope with the Colombian heat is by indulging in fruit smoothies at any of the many fruit stands along the harbor front.
Right: To get on and off the boat in the Cartagena harbor Tom drilled two holes in one end of the old fender board and tied a short rope through each hole. Then he slid the plank to the pier and secured our end to the stanchions off the stern of our boat.

Above: North of Panama on the Caribbean side of the canal is a group of nearly 100 small islands called the San Blas islands. Below: This San Blas Island family is standing in front of their living hut dressed in typical daily attire.

OPPOSITE PAGE Top: The men were able to speak a little English and manned the open boats that were unstable dug-out tree logs. The women spoke no English. Bottom: The men wore shorts and t-shirts. The women wore brightly colored multicolored skirts gathered at the waist, and puffy short-sleeved blouses with mola designs on the front and back. They tied their thick black hair back with long red scarves.

21

Above: Iguazu Falls, the largest waterfalls in the world, is impressive not only by its power and size, but also by the development of the viewing grounds all around it. Each holds a Kodak-moment. Below: VONNIE-T had already successfully transited the Saint Lawrence Seaway, the Welland Canal and the Erie Canal, and is shown here (lower right of photo) in the Panama Canal sharing a lock with a large ship.

Above: In preparation to cross the Pacific, we stocked up on many provisions that included a whole stalk of bananas, a pile of green oranges, flats of eggs, a large bag of potatoes, squash, carrots, onions, and lots of fruit. Below: After filling all of our tanks, we put on extra fuel and water in jerry cans on deck.

Left: All yachts are required to have a registered Ecuadorian guide on board when visiting the Galapagos. Guilillermo, was our guide. Below: The Galapagos offered both land and snorkeling experiences.

OPPOSITE PAGE Top left: Baby frigate bird. Top right: Crab. Bottom: Prior to refrigeration, old schooner ships used to keep large Galapagos tortoises in the ships hold as live food. Today it is illegal to do them any harm as there are so few alive in the world today.

Above Left: Darwin used the Galapagos finch to help explain his theory of evolution. Above Right: Frigate Birds are wide-winged black birds the size of a goose. They are masters of the air in that they are able to pluck an unsuspecting fish from the water without ever sitting on the the surface or getting wet.
Below: The Galapagos Islands are rugged and made from volcanic rock formations.

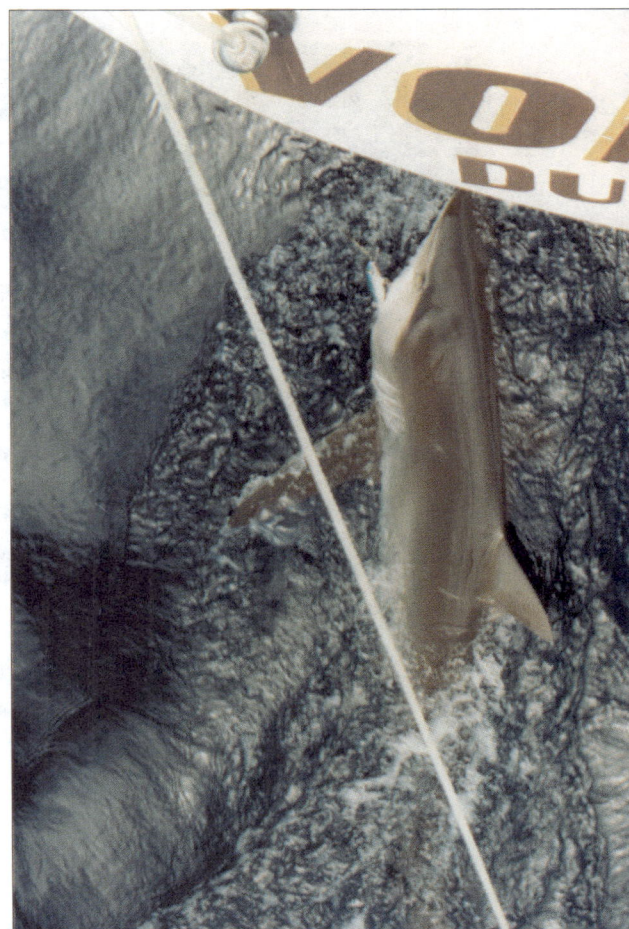

Top: A Galapagos land iguana. Above: We were greeted by kind, gentle faced sea lions with round, black eyes as we entered the Galapagos Islands. Right: Both, Tom and this shark were tired after a 45 minute fight, then Tom reached down into the sharks mouth and ripped out his Rapala lure.

OPPOSITE PAGE Top: In Western Samoa the buildings were called Fales, as shown here. They are open-walled structures with a cement floor and covered by either a thatch or tin roof. Bottom: A family of ten was the total population of Suvorov, one of the Northern Cook Islands. They lived primarily on fish and the few goods the supply ship brought them twice a year.

Right: Evenings, in the French islands of Tahiti and Moorea, we watched the outrigger canoes practice their racing skills. Below: We arrived at Bora Bora in time to witness and participate in Féte, a national holiday.

Above: In Western Somoa, we were invited to join the instructors of the Piula Theological College for Sunday dinner after their church service. While everyone else appeared to be comfortable, we found it extremely difficult to sit cross-legged on woven mats, especially after learning it was an insult to point ones toes. Below: In preparation for a feast, these Tongans prepared a cooking pit, sharpened green saplings, and strung raw chickens and pigs on them.

Above: While it was exhilarating to see so much food available in the Tahitian grocery stores, we found it to be both expensive and somewhat startling. *Right:* Western Samoans often brought gifts of fresh fruit when they rowed out to visit us in the anchorage. *Below:* Because we honored this Western Samoan woodcarver with our visit he put on a clean lava-lava, killed a chicken to serve us lunch, and proudly showed us his current project, a hand carved kava bowl with 14 legs.

There are few things that are better in life than the serenity of a quiet harbor with good holding.

don't ever remember seeing it in a tin." Upon further investigation, it was discovered that the Canadian had been eating dog food. Everyone had a good laugh, but we all realized how easily any of us could have made that same error, as few of us could read French.

THE YOUNG AND THE RESTLESS

St. Lucia was our next island stop. Over the past several months I had been in radio contact with several hams there. We looked forward to meeting them and seeing the island. When they learned we would be arriving in Rodney Bay, several of them were at the harbor to greet us.

Joe took me to the ham-radio licensing office the next day so I could acquire my reciprocal license, and later he took us to his home to "see his shack" (the room where he had his ham radio). We met his wife, who was also a ham radio operator, and together they showed us their honeybee operation, which was in a small building in back of their house. They gave us a large jar of their homemade honey.

Johnny, a young single ham, took us up to the top of the mountain to see the two-meter repeater station that he had helped build. He showed us around the downtown area and pointed out highlights. He was especially proud of their fire engine that had been donated by the Canadian government. Tom and I wondered why our government donated only money instead of American-made products that a country may need, like the used Canadian fire engine. Every time that fire engine was used, the island people received a good feeling about Canada, while money could never provide the same positive public relations.

Another interesting ham radio operator we met ran a small television station out of a building no bigger than a single car garage. He used only five watts of power and stole the programs off the satellite, paying no royalties or fees. He sold advertising spots to the local merchants and simply dubbed in the local island advertising. When he learned that many of the cruisers enjoyed watching one of the daytime soaps called *"The Young and The Restless,"* he directed his antennas toward Rodney Bay during the half-hour it was aired. Imagine a whole anchorage of boats eating lunch, and watching a U.S. soap opera, without commercials, in the southern Caribbean. It did not seem possible.

Rodney Bay was so protected and quiet that, providing you had all the required parts on board, it was an ideal place to get caught up on boat repairs. One of the cruisers on a boat anchored next to us accidentally dropped a boat part into the water. He watched it fall and thought he could dive down to retrieve it in spite of the murkiness of the water. He planned to go hand over hand down his anchor chain, and when he reached the bottom, feel around with his hand and retrieve the lost object. We watched him jump into the water with his fins on, knowing he would be going down that chain just as fast as he could. We figured he would need to take several dives before he actually found it, but when he came up he was laughing loudly and announced that the ocean gods could keep anything they wanted down there. He told us visibility was so bad that the only way he knew when he got to the bottom was when his forehead went right into mushy muck, residue from boat heads. He got out of the water and headed directly into shore to purchase a hot, soapy shower.

Tom was able to get a lot of boat maintenance done at Rodney Bay, and he became a happier man as his clipboard "to do" list became shorter. While Tom finished some of his chores, I took the public bus, (really a beat-up van), into the Castries open food market to purchase fresh fruit and vegetables. I took two canvas boat bags and a nylon backpack with me and filled all three. I was used to carrying the heavy bags by then and had learned how to balance the weight so I could wear the backpack and carry a canvas bag on each shoulder with no problem. I walked back to the bus stop with my full sacks and waited for the next bus. When my bus came I sat next to a handsome young black man, put the canvas bags at my feet, and the backpack in my lap. I had become a beast of burden, but I did not feel conspicuous since many of the native women carried just as much. They even carried large bundles or baskets of produce on their heads, but I had not yet reached that level of proficiency. The young man next to me graciously moved his feet in an attempt to accommodate my more than fair share of the floor space. Then he said, "I know just how you must feel."

I gave him a puzzled look. He wasn't carrying anything so I didn't understand what he meant.

Then he said, "I used to be married to a Swedish woman and we lived in Sweden. I was always the only black in the crowd. I guess I just couldn't take it anymore." Then, I realized what he meant. I was the only white person on that bus but until that very moment, I had not been aware of it. I was amazed to realize how comfortable I had become with our new way of life.

THE WINCH HANDLE

There were still several hours of daylight left after I got back from the Castries, so we pulled up our anchor and left Rodney Bay. We sailed past the majestic Pitons and anchored for the night near an area reported to have once had an elephant.

According to the story, the elephant had discovered that boats had food on them and would walk out into the water, reach down with its trunk until it found the anchors and pull the boats to shore where it could get that food. Of course, the people on board the boat were not about to challenge an elephant, so the elephant was able to help itself to whatever it wanted. We didn't see the elephant, but the story lived on among the cruisers and I found myself scanning the shoreline wondering if we would spot him, or he, us.

We stopped at several more islands as we traveled south down the thorny path, anchoring for a few days, and then moving on. Among our stops were St. Vincent, Bequia, and a whole group of islands in the Grenadines called Petit Nevis, Mustique, Mayero, Togagos and Petit St. Vincent. Each had its own special flavor and offered unique experiences.

At St. Vincent we met a vendor who sold simple flutes made of bamboo. The air-holes had been crudely burned into them with a hot metal rod, but the vendor played the flute with ease. They cost only two dollars, and we were amazed at the incredibly beautiful music they produced. Tom bought one, thinking it would be an enjoyable pastime while sitting on watch in the cockpit, but when we got back to the boat and he tried to play it he discovered his flute didn't sound nearly as good as the one the vendor had been playing. In fact, he hardly got any sound to come out at all. He was convinced that he had purchased a dud and went back to the vendor, insisting upon trading his flute for the very one that the vendor had been playing only to become totally embarrassed when he discovered that he could not make that one sound very good either. The vendor found us so humorous that he not only gave Tom playing instructions, he gave me a flute free of charge.

Friends on another boat had a much less humorous experience. When they were in St. Vincent they met a native who offered to sell them a boat winch-handle. Our friends marveled at how similar it was to theirs, but declined to purchase it since they already had one. Of course, when they returned to their boat, they discovered that their winch-handle was missing. So they returned to shore, found the man, and told him they just realized they did indeed need a new winch-handle. The arrogant little thief had the audacity to raise the price but there was nothing our friends could do. They paid the asking price, knowing they were purchasing their own equipment.

BEQUIA, THE SISTER ISLAND

Nearly every time we were about to enter a harbor and when the depth meter registered 20 to 25 feet, Tom caught a fish. It seemed it often happened at a bad time, such as when we were near rocks, and/or it was time to take the sails down in preparation to enter the harbor. Each time, I found myself annoyed with Tom for not bringing in his fishing line sooner. Tom was delighted, and almost never felt there was an inappropriate time to catch a good-eating fish. When there was a fish on the other end of his line he looked like a kid on a new pair of roller skates. He would leap to the side-deck, grab the pole from its cradle, and rock his entire body back as he set the hook. Mostly he caught albacore tuna which we either ate that night or gave to other boaters. Sometimes he caught barracuda, and he would toss those back.

As we were about to enter Bequia, his line screamed as it sped off the reel at an incredible speed. We knew something big was on his hook. Tom stood on the aft deck clutching the rod with both hands. He reeled it in when he could, but allowed the line to run free when the fish dove. It was a matter of losing line or losing the fish. The fish seemed tireless as it frantically dove, tugged, and struggled in an effort to free itself. It did everything with the exception of surfacing, so we had no idea what it was. Finally after a long struggle, Tom said he believed the fish was tired since it had stopped fighting so he started bringing it in. Were we ever surprised when he reeled in the head of a tuna. The head alone might have weighted three pounds, and we didn't even want to think about what had eaten the body off a head of that size!

There were several aspects of Bequia that we liked. It had a protected harbor with the perfect anchoring depth, and the water was so clean that Tom was able to snorkel and sometimes spear lobsters in time for dinner. He also appreciated being able to purchase more fishing line, weights, and Rapala lures in one of the few sports stores in the Caribbean. I liked Bequia because there was a small restaurant that specialized in American pizza, and apparently a lot of the other "yachties" liked that too, because it became a hangout.

It was there that we met an elderly Canadian gentleman who had recently purchased a large section of land fronting the cove where we were anchored. He had a young trophy wife, and was building their dream retirement home on the property. During the building process he discovered ancient broken crockery buried on his land, so the time devoted to building slowed while he excavated his own private ruin. It aroused the hidden archeologist in Tom, and we were invited to stay and help dig. We helped for a few days, but we knew if we stayed longer, we would get stuck there and start to put down roots. We also observed the wife's distaste for her husband. She made no secret of her plan to find a way to take his money and live comfortably someplace else after he died. We moved on.

AN OLD WHALE-BUTCHERING SITE

At Petit Nevis, we visited an old whale butchering site. Whaling was still legal, but had not been practiced there for several years. The stones and rocks at the site still reeked of whale oil. It was a musty, heavy odor, and after having smelled it once I would never mistake it for anything else. Whaling is, of course, a brutal and dangerous practice. When I saw the small open boats the whalers used to chase the whales, I could not help but marvel at the men's courage. They would stand on the bow and spear a whale when it came to the surface to breathe, with a spear attached to miles of rope tied to the boat. Then the speared whale would take the boat on an ocean sleigh-ride. If the spear was not placed where it was fatal for the whale, it could certainly be fatal for the men. If and when the whale died, the men sewed the whales' mouth shut to prevent it from taking in water and sinking while they towed it back to their island, which could be many miles away.

Our next stop, Mustique, was one of the most ostentatious islands in the Caribbean: Both Mick Jagger and Princess Margaret have summer homes there. These homes are mansions with groomed lawns, security guards, and tropical gardens. Missing were the dirt roads lined with plastic bags and empty soda cans that were prevalent on the other Caribbean islands.

We happened to be anchored at Mustique during a time when a delivery ship was bringing gasoline to the island. The deep-draft ship had to anchor quite a distance offshore. A crewman from the ship came to each boat in the anchorage in a small runabout and handed us a printed flyer that explained the fuel-delivery process, and requested that we not smoke or light any matches during the next hour. After all the flyers were distributed, we watched in fascination as the runabout carried the nozzle of a long black hose up to a tank on the shore. The hose floated on top of the water all the way back to the ship and carried the gasoline into the tank on shore.

THE UNITED STATES BOMBED GRENADA

We visited several of the Grenadine islands: Mayero, Tobago, Petit St. Vincent and Petit Martinique. We went ashore on each, met the local people, and swam. Life was good!

Each day, Tom speared lobsters and fresh fish which we ate for dinner, and I had become more confident in the water, even though I had not developed the skills to hunt. At least I snorkeled with ease, and I loved swimming into large schools of reef fish and watching them part around me. I was amazed at the fish's sense of radar. No matter how hard I tried, there was absolutely no way for me to get close enough to a fish to touch one.

One day, when I saw a conch on the ocean floor in only six feet of water, I decided I would try to dive down to retrieve it. I took a deep breath and dove as hard as I could, but could not get my rear end to break the surface of the water. I tried diving repeatedly and each time I came floating up to the surface. It was a good thing that conch move slowly, because it took me nearly a dozen tries. When I finally succeeded, I came up to the surface exhausted, elated, and a little embarrassed to find Tom treading water nearby, watching. He was clapping his hands and laughing at the amount of work I had made out of retrieving one poor conch.

On Petit Martinique, we found it interesting that over half the population of 800 had the same last name. They were all Batelles, and all related. They did fishing and boat building for a living. They lived simple, modest lives, and we found their interest in politics a surprise. They especially wanted to know what the situation was on the island of Grenada, where they had come from, having fled for their lives. They were disappointed to learn we had not been there yet, and they hinted that perhaps it would be better if we did not do so. With effort, Tom and I recalled something about our American military having gone into Grenada during President Reagan's term. From what we could remember, the invasion had something to do with freeing American medical students. The story the Batelle families told us was very different from the stories Tom and I remembered from the American newspapers.

When we left the Grenadine Islands we stopped at Carricou to check into customs for Grenada. I had been in ham radio contact for some time with Tony, J39CM, who lived on Grenada, and we looked forward to having an "eye ball" with him. Tony had gone to England for his education and was a well-spoken, interesting man. When we arrived in Grenada, he met us and took us on a tour of the island. He showed us a quiet, blue harbor called Quarantine Harbor, and we walked through the bustling downtown and market areas, breathing in the sweet fragrance from the impressive red flamboyant trees, as well as the other tropical trees and plants. We got to see bananas being packed for shipment and learned that each stalk had a blue plastic bag placed over it during its growing period to prevent bugs from leaving marks on the peel. We also toured the nutmeg factory. Grenada

View of St. Georges Harbor, Grenada in the Caribbean.

is the world's largest producer of nutmeg and mace. The factory, a dusty place with nutmeg powder hanging heavy in the air, would never meet OSHA air quality standards in the United States, but it was a fascinating place, and I never realized that those two spices came from the same plant. Mace was from the red membrane that surrounded the actual nut of the nutmeg.

Tony made sure we saw all the positive aspects of Grenada before he told us the truth about the military events on the island. "It's not at all the way your American press reported it," he said. "Your president did the right thing, but the press was not told about it ahead of time. They got their noses out of joint because they had not been informed in advance, so they reported the whole thing badly. Your president had to keep it a secret because the attack needed the element of surprise in order to be successful," he said.

Tony said he knew the press reported that American troops were called in to free U.S. medical students, but it was something even more than that. "We had a tyrant and his thugs running the island, and they had plans to march right up through the whole Caribbean and take over one island at a time. Cuba was backing the project, and provided both the funding and manpower to build our big airstrip. They, in turn, received their funding from Russia. On the heels of the Cuban crisis they needed an airstrip large enough to accommodate military fighter planes. The thugs had everyone on the island fearing for their lives, and they had our president locked up.

One day, with all the innocence of young children, the grade school children united and marched into the president's courtyard. They sang and chanted a request to have our president released. They were sweet children, hundreds of them all in their little navy blue skirts and slacks and white shirts or blouses, innocent and harmless, just expressing themselves." Tony could hardly go on with his story. Tears ran down his face. Finally he said, "They were fired upon and literally mowed down—slaughtered, all of them. It was terrible! There were piles of little bodies. They shoveled the children's bodies up with road grader equipment, tossed them into boats and dumped them in the ocean. Anyone who got in the thugs' way, was killed.

In the middle of the night, I was dragged from my bed and placed in an underground dungeon." He showed us the dungeon, unlocked the steel door covering the steps and invited us to go down in it. We went down only a few steps, enough to see that it was damp, dark and filthy—and that's what it looked like with the trap door open. I can't imagine what it would have been like to be locked in it for days, as Tony was, with no idea of what was to happen next. He told us how many steps there were and where every blemish was in all four walls, the ceiling and the floor, but he couldn't bring himself to go down in it. Apparently, the reason he had been arrested was because he was a ham radio operator. The thugs who took power didn't want any news of what was happening to get to the outside world,—not while they were disposing of children's bodies.

For three days the entire island was under house arrest. If anyone was seen out of their home, they were shot on sight, and of course, the families couldn't even acknowledge their

Woman working at the Grenada nutmeg factory, where both nutmeg and mace are produced.

missing children. Some families lost several children. Not only did they have to grieve for their losses silently, but many also went without water and food for three days, because most of the homes on the island didn't have refrigeration or running water. Typically, the families would gather what they needed each day, one day at a time.

"On the third day I could hear bombing and a lot of gunfire while I was in the dungeon. Then everything got quiet for a while. Pretty soon I heard voices, and people opened the dungeon door. I walked up those steps not knowing what would happen next. Then I saw a garden hose. I walked over to it, took off my filthy pajamas and hosed myself down. I stood there naked, clean for the first time in days and alive. Later, my wife and I were able to put all the pieces together, and we're very grateful to you Americans!"

Tony and his wife invited us to dinner that evening at their home. We heard the story again from the wife's viewpoint. She told us she was frantic when she had been locked in her house, not knowing all that time if her husband was dead or alive. She saved pictures and newspaper clippings from the entire event. She kept saying, "It's not true, the way your American press reported it. If your troops hadn't come when they did, a lot more of us would be dead, and many of the Caribbean islands would be under Cuban control by now. Your president did it just right. He did a surprise attack, and he stuck around just long enough to appoint temporary leadership, then he pulled the troops out."

NO GUNS

Learning about the military happenings on Grenada first hand from Tony and his wife, gave me chills. Tom and I dug deep into our memories, trying to remember how the American press had portrayed the incident. That was the first time I ever even questioned the accuracy of how our American press reported world events. I had always naively believed that Americans were kept well informed, and that the information we were given was accurate and completely unbiased. Yet, here was a situation we knew had not been reported objectively or accurately. Tony's words kept ringing in my ears, "the press got their noses out of joint because your president hadn't notified them before the invasion." Tony had a great deal of respect for our president and acknowledged that not only was the element of surprise important, but he also was pleased that the American military power got in, did what they needed to do, and then got out. The problem was that the whole thing was done and over with before the press even knew what had happened, so they took a critical position, rather than a supportive one.

We stayed in Grenada several weeks, anchoring in many different harbors, the last being Prickly Bay. We went ashore daily to purchase supplies and I was quite surprised when one of the fruit vendors asked, "Are you mixed?" Since I had become such a regular customer she felt comfortable asking. Her question prompted me to look at how differently Tom and I tanned. His skin tanned with a light pink or a slight copper look to it, while mine was a dark muddy brown. Even my feet were the color of walnuts.

We left the comfort of the English-speaking islands and sailed to Margarita, an island belonging to Venezuela. Unlike the British islands where everyone spoke English, or the French islands where many of the officials spoke English, in Margarita everyone spoke Spanish. We learned on the radio from other cruisers of a husband and wife team on the island who made a business of assisting boats with their check-in process, and helping with the language problem. The wife was Venezuelan and the husband American, and for a fee they would take our boat papers and walk them through the entry process for us. For another fee, we could use their address to have our mail forwarded.

Before arriving in Margarita, Tom and I had talked about the encumbrance our two handguns had become, and with the added challenge of a language barrier, we wished we did not have them at all. Having guns on board and having to check them in and out of each country, was a nuisance. We were required to check them in at the port of entry, and then had to return to that port to retrieve them. They had become more than just an inconvenience, because sometimes we were forced to make our departure from a port that did not provide the most desirable angle to the wind for the next crossing. We talked and talked about it, and finally decided to stop admitting to having guns on board. We knew there was a risk involved with that decision, and we weighed the pros and cons against the risk we took each time we left from a port not to our liking. We decided the risk of not telling, was a risk worth taking.

After living on the boat for nearly a year, I had became familiar with many small hiding places, and I was fairly confidant I would be able to hide the guns so they would never be found. There was a sliver of space between the headliner on the ceiling of the aft cabin and the deck of the boat. Our headliners were attached with velcro and could be removed easily if you knew how to do it, yet they stuck up firmly and could support a small amount of weight. Tom hid his loaded gun in the headliner over his bunk. It had never been fired, but it was accessible.

There was also a triangular space behind each of the built-in drawers in our back cabin where the flat backs of each drawer met with the curved hull of the boat. I put my gun and ammo boxes in thick socks and put them behind my sock-and-underwear drawer. If anyone tried to remove the drawer, it would simply look like my underwear was falling out.

Once we made that decision and checked in at Margarita Island we never spoke of those guns again, not to friends, and not to officials. As far as we were concerned we simply did not have guns on board!

MY LEAVE OF ABSENCE WAS UP

The anchorage in front of the small business office on Margarita Island was far from ideal. There was no dinghy dock and there was a considerable surge that caused wet feet, and sometimes, soaked clothes, when we went ashore. Getting wet in this warm climate wasn't really the worst thing, but because it was saltwater, whatever got wet dried with a white, crusty look. Having become a pair of "old salts" had taken on a new meaning.

We were impressed with how the Venezuelans seemed to take every opportunity to make a small need into a business. The fact that there was no dinghy dock was seen as a business opportunity for Jimmy, a rotund, bald Venezuelan. He waited until he saw a dinghy heading to shore, then walked out into the surf and gallantly scooped the ladies up into his arms and carried them to land. He always gave me a big gold-toothed grin, said something in Spanish, and a kiss on the cheek before he set me gracefully on the sandy shore. Tom, of course, was left standing in the surf until Jimmy returned to take the dinghy painter. Jimmy tied all the dinghies together on a mooring until we each returned for them. He had the valet parking business for dinghies.

He was on the job early each morning and late into the evening if there were any dinghies still on the mooring. Because he was so reliable, we were all surprised when one morning he wasn't on shore. No one remembered having seen him that morning. Even the couple who ran the check-in service did not know where Jimmy was, but when they opened the office that morning they found a strange brown thing sitting on the desk. It was about two inches long and nearly an inch in diameter. It was firm but was soft too. They couldn't imagine what it was until one of them recognized the fingernail on one end. It was a human thumb! Later, we learned that Jimmy had been sitting in an aluminum, folding lawn chair on the beach and as he leaned back his thumb got caught in one of the hinged joints. Apparently the weight of his body caused the entire thumb to be severed, and the act of placing his severed thumb on the desk was his way of explaining what had happened. We all knew he would not be around until both the stump of his thumb and his ego had time to heal.

In spite of the language barrier, Margarita offered many new creature comforts for us. There were modern stores on the island, and some were even multi-storied. We could buy almost anything if we could learn how to ask for it, and there was even a modern hospital where one of the cruisers delivered her first baby. The couple stayed on their boat until the first contractions began, which of course were in the middle of the night. So, in the dead of the night they rowed to shore, tied up their own dinghy, and walked up to the road to hail a taxi to the hospital. The next afternoon they returned to their boat with the baby. I admired that young mother's stamina and bravery.

We exercised bravery in a different manner. We flew to Caracas on a Venezuelan airplane while we waited for our mail. Airfare within the country was incredibly cheap, and we decided to make it a one-day excursion to get my ham radio reciprocal license. Our friends John and Mary, from the sailboat FIA, flew with us to get their licenses as well, making the day seem like a party, or a mini-vacation from the boat.

We returned after dark that same evening. There was a sweet fragrance from flower blossoms in the moist warm air, and no one was ready to put such a fine day to rest, so we sat together in our cockpit enjoying a nightcap. "Oh look, there's another boat just like ours," John said. "It looks like he's heading out tonight." We all watched passively while sipping our drinks. Then John said, "That *is our* boat!"

Sure enough, it was FIA slowly drifting through the anchorage. We assumed the anchor was dragging. Tom leapt in the dinghy and started the motor, and John was right after him. They shot off in the direction of FIA while Mary and I stayed on VONNIE-T. It was difficult to see in the dark, but when we could no longer hear the dinghy motors we assumed they were on board FIA getting her safely re-anchored. Not until much later did we learn that the boat had not dragged its anchor. Someone dove off the boat when Tom and John approached in the dinghies. The anchor had been brought up and someone had been attempting to hoist the sails — someone who had no idea how to do it because the sheets had been threaded inside the shrouds instead of outside. What might have happened had we not been sitting in the cockpit, just then?

The next morning, John and Mary reported the incident to the proper authorities while we picked up our mail. In and among all the wonderful letters from home were two very disturbing letters. Both were addressed to me.

One was from the Charlottetown Coast Guard in response to my letter of complaint concerning our harrowing experience when trying to enter Wood Harbor.

The letter said they checked the tape recording and found that I had not specifically said the words "This is an emergency." Therefore, the Coast Guard accepted no responsibility. Reading that letter made my blood boil, but I knew there was nothing more I could do. My only satisfaction was in knowing that in spite of the polite letter denying any wrongdoing, I was fairly certain that the man on duty that evening found himself having to answer some rather difficult questions from his superiors. If, as a result of my letter, he was more careful and considerate of the next boat call he received, my letter served its purpose.

The second letter was from the University of Minnesota. Its intent was to remind me that my one-year leave of absence was expiring, and that they expected me back to work on the first working day following that date. I could hardly believe a full year had slipped away. Early in the trip, when I was bone-achingly cold, fearful, and seasick nearly everyday, I would have given anything to get off the boat and return to my teaching duties. But everything was different now. We were in the warm tropics and I had become comfortable and considerably less fearful. We had learned so many things together since we had left Minnesota a year ago. We had finally found peace with our dependence on one another, and discarded our neurotic compulsion of having to accomplish something each day. I was not nearly as frightened anymore, and I could not remember the last time I was seasick. Did I really *want* to go back to work?

Tom assured me that this was a decision I needed to make without his influence. Still, I knew what he hoped I would decide.

I did not sleep well that night. I tossed and turned in my bunk, mentally arguing with myself. I rehashed all the miserable aspects of boat life: the constant need to ration water and then never feeling clean, living on the edge of fear, being seasick (which added to my feeling of uselessness because I could function during those times no better than if I had the flu), and never being in charge of anything. I still had not adjusted to the reality of not being the boss — the one to make decisions and having others follow my directions.

Perhaps, worst of all was having lost my freedom to come and go at will. We had only one dinghy and it was the equivalent of the family car. We needed to share it. That meant when Tom decided to go ashore I needed to drop whatever I was doing if I wanted to go with him, otherwise I would have been trapped on the boat until he returned. I never felt as if I could take the dinghy to shore by myself because I seldom could get the motor started by myself. It was just one more thing that made me feel completely inadequate.

I weighed all those negatives against the positives, the most obvious of which were the many places we had been, and people we had met. We had visited nearly all of the exotic Caribbean islands, and we not only met extremely interesting people but we actually touched, and in some ways, tasted a portion of their culture. Imagine having had the opportunity to hear the history of Grenada firsthand from people who had lived through it. And how many people could say they transited the St. Lawrence Seaway, the Welland Canal, the Intracoastal Waterway, and the Dismal Swamp Canal? I also had to remember that when we started on our adventure I could barely swim, but now I thought nothing of swimming across an entire anchorage to greet an incoming boat or visit friends on another sailboat. I loved snorkeling and seeing all the colorful fish and the coral in the water. And now, I could even dive down to get a conch, and that was a major accomplishment for me.

Another aspect of our cruising life that I liked was our togetherness. Early on, the strain of living together 24 hours of each day in close quarters was a problem, but now after a year's time, we had worked though the lumps and I actually enjoyed our time together. By morning I was exhausted, but I knew what I wanted to do. I wanted to continue cruising. I could not be this close to South America and not see it.

Together, Tom and I were like a seasoned stew with each of us contributing different ingredients to create a tasty blend. We had learned how to balance one another's moods, fears, and daily needs, and I knew the stew in our pot was finally ready. We would continue.

I wrote my letter of resignation and took it to the telegraph office. A Spanish-speaking person collected a fee based on the words in the letter, and then she typed and sent it to the University of Minnesota. I never saw the final copy before it was sent, and to this day, I have no idea what my letter of resignation looked like when it was placed in my personnel file.

CHAPTER FIVE

South America Calls

EXPERIENCING VENEZUELA

It was a short sail from Margarita Island to the Cumana Marina on the mainland of Venezuela, and after finally coming to grips with the decision to continue cruising, I found myself excited to see as much of Venezuela as possible. The Cumana Marina offered electrical hook-ups, floating docks, and access to fresh water. All these amenities at bargain prices contributed to an overall good feeling, and the marina quickly became our new home.

Our arrival was planned to coincide with the season in the Caribbean when hurricanes roam from early August until early December, but seldom, if ever, touch South America. Few of the boats in the marina were local Venezuelan boats; nearly all were cruisers like us waiting out the season south of the storm path.

With the ease of stepping on and off the boat at will, friendships flourished, and the newly formed social networks facilitated the sharing of supplies, charts, and both accurate and inaccurate information. There were always rumors about thefts, the locations of the best deals, and the local politics. As a whole, however, our lives were light and easy, and seldom were the negative rumors taken seriously.

One day the young couple who had given birth to their baby on Margarita Island showed up on our dock. Their boat was still on Margarita but they had flown to Cumana to pick up boat parts, and they asked if they could spend the night with us before returning to Margarita the next day. We were surprised, but happy to see them and their healthy baby, and we welcomed them aboard without a second thought, putting them and the baby up for the night in our main salon and V-berth. While a request of that nature would have been considered a big imposition if we had been living in a house, it was not on a boat. I loved the expectation among cruising people that there would always be a helping hand if one was needed.

With all the camaraderie in the marina, small groups of "yachties" often rode the public bus together into town for lunch or dinner. I was a little surprised at how many lacked the confidence to travel into town by themselves. Perhaps they lacked our adventuresome spirit. Perhaps they may have believed some of the rumors about thefts, or maybe they were simply reluctant to deal with the challenge of the language barrier. Whatever the reason, most seemed to feel more comfortable in a group. Overall, the first impression of the group was a motley sight in salt-stained shoes, ragged cut-off shorts and disheveled hair. Upon closer inspection it got worse; nearly all the men and many of the women had semi-permanent engine grease under their fingernails from working on their boat engines. Tom had finally shaved his beard and no longer looked like a skunk, with a white steak down the center of his chin.

One of the more unsavory-looking characters in the group was Franco, a young single-handed sailor from Italy. He and his boat looked as if they had been assembled from a salvaged wreck, but he was friendly, had a keen mind, and a great sense of humor.

"What was all the commotion we heard coming from your boat last night?" one of the men asked him.

"You mean just after dark?" he responded, with a sly grin.

"Yeah, it sort of sounded like a gun shot, followed by what even I knew, was swearing, although I don't know a single word of Italian. I almost came over to see if you needed help, but when all the scuffling simmered down I decided you must have gotten whatever it was, under control."

All eyes were on Franco and our curiosity was piqued. I was not sure if he enjoyed the attention or was embarrassed by it. He delayed answering while running his fingers through his oily brown hair. He pulled a pack of cigarettes from the pocket of his shirt that had only one button holding it together, and slowly lit his cigarette. Finally he said, "It's those damn rats. When I saw one of 'em waltzing across my bunk last night just as big as you please, I just lost it. I grabbed my pistol and shot one. They're smart bastards. I've set plenty a traps but they just lick up all the peanut butter without even tripping 'em. And then for dessert they chew up the wires of my electronics." He took a deep drag on his cigarette and continued, "'Course, I shot a hole in the bottom of my boat, but one of 'em is dead."

"You actually shot a hole in your boat?"

"Yep, I did," nodding his head and almost looking proud of it. "'Course I had to get humpin' then to get that little indiscretion plugged up before she sunk. Now, that'll give you all sumpthen to cluck about, won't it?"

We all laughed and loved him for his unpretentious manner. He appeared completely free from worry. I think we all had some paternal feelings toward him, and I suspect those feelings somehow allowed us to feel braver than any of us really were. His youth and inexperience helped us feel a little less vulnerable as we each explored the unknown of our own adventures.

Despite the unsavory appearance of our group, restaurants welcomed us because we ordered lots of food and paid in cash. My favorite restaurant made Caesar salads at the table the old fashioned way by rubbing the inside of a large wooden bowl with fresh garlic and cracking in a raw egg. The practice is not allowed in the United States because of sanitation concerns with raw eggs, but the resulting salads were scrumptious and we never became ill from them. Tom's favorite was the rotisserie-roasted chicken. These were "walking around" chickens which meant they had extra texture and flavor, but I was not particularly fond of them because they were basted with so much butter.

By late October we were checking the post office each day in anticipation of receiving our absentee ballots and a big pile of news from home. Each day we stood before the post office clerk with our boat name printed on a piece of paper. She took the paper and disappeared into the back room where we could see racks and racks of mail, but each day she would return and hand us back our piece of paper. "No" was her only word for us. One day out of sheer desperation we insisted on going back to look for our mail ourselves. Before we left the U.S.A. we left several large envelopes marked with bright yellow tape in each of the four corners. As soon as we walked along the mail rack I spied one of our envelopes.

"That's ours," I said to Tom.

"Are you sure?" he asked while reaching up to grasp it .

Sure enough, it was ours. Then we realized the problem of having a boat name beginning with the letter "V". Spanish speakers pronounce "V" and "B" similarly. Our mail had been filed under the "Bs". Unfortunately, the ballots had not been mailed out early enough to allow for this error or the slow Venezuelan mail, so they reached us a week after the election. What a bummer!

I was motivated to do something very American on Thanksgiving. I coordinated a menu with my favorite restaurant manager, and together we agreed upon a fee that would be prepaid by each boat wishing to attend. The restaurant was able to duplicate everything a typical Thanksgiving feast would have with the exception of the cranberries. We tried but never came up with a Venezuelan substitute for cranberries. Despite the missing cranberries, it was a great event. The turkey, stuffing, mashed potatoes, sweet potatoes, and even the pumpkin pie were delicious. Thirty boaters participated in that Thanksgiving feast, predominantly Americans but we also had Canadians, Germans, French, and even a few English to help us celebrate that very American day.

That month of November was a happy time for me. All the woes from the previous cold-weather sailing days were far behind us. We had no health problems and no money problems, since nearly everything in Venezuela was inexpensive. Perhaps the most enjoyable aspect of all was that we had no problems with each other. We enjoyed our time together and we settled into a pattern of working and playing together. We had become each other's best friend.

As with all good things in life, however, there is usually a small downside and our newly expanded social life was no exception. With so many friends in close proximity, we lacked privacy. When we hired 15 year-old Tony Lugo to give us private Spanish lessons we had go below, close the hatches, and turn on the air-conditioning as a means of discouraging people from popping in and interrupting the lesson. It was difficult for me to grasp the grammar and the proper form of the verbs, but I quickly picked up on many of the nouns. I was especially amazed to learn that the word for peanut was *moni*. Until I learned that word I thought the children we saw downtown calling out "moni, moni, moni" were begging for money. Instead, they were selling peanuts, peanuts, peanuts!

Each day we learned new things. Some we picked up on quickly while others took longer and sometimes were a struggle. For example, it had taken us nearly a year to learn how to relax and not take life so seriously, yet we had not completely shed our strong work ethic. We attempted to split the day in half using the cool mornings to accomplish small tasks and the warm afternoons to socialize and explore the town. But our plan had a major flaw, as it did not fit the culture. Businesses were closed for siesta during the heat of the afternoon, and the only people visible in the town between 1pm to 3pm were sweaty, sunburned *gringos*. Reluctantly, we began our town excursions in the morning, and learned to rest or do projects on the boat in the afternoon.

Doing our town chores in the morning was especially important on days when we purchased meat. We needed to arrive at the market early, shortly after the animal had been slaughtered, because the carcass would hang on a hook with no refrigeration until all of it was purchased. Of course the flies appreciated fresh hanging meat. After telling the butcher how many kilos I wanted, he would hack off the approximate amount with a big knife. There was no extra charge for the flies and no mention of a particular cut of meat. Two kilos were two kilos, and it didn't matter if they came from the front, back or middle of the animal. The one exception was the tenderloin, called *"lomito."* It was slightly more expensive than the other hacked-off meat.

The market, which was an unpainted cement building, bustled with people each morning, and housed a variety of smells and sounds. Added to the crowded aisles were young boys pushing makeshift wheelbarrows, the Venezuelan version of shopping carts, and offering their hauling services for the equivalent of seven cents. It would have been fun to hire one of them, but we didn't dare. By not having a car, we couldn't take the chance of buying more than we could carry and we knew that danger existed if we began to fill up a wheelbarrow. So we put all our purchases in the boat bags that we each carried on our shoulders. Our shopping formula was simple. When our bags became heavy, we stopped buying. Even so, the walk back to the boat with our filled bags was a physical workout.

With the exception of eggs most of our purchases weren't fragile. Venezuelan eggs were brown and they were placed in a loose paper sack with feathers and other debris still attached. My facial expression when I first saw them caused the vendor to struggle in an attempt to explain how they would stay fresh and safe for weeks without refrigeration if I did not wash off the natural protective coating. I was not inclined to believe her, but nonetheless I purchased a dozen and tested her theory over the next week's time. I left the eggs on the countertop without refrigeration until they were either gone or rotten. Each morning when I cracked open a new pair of eggs, I expected them to have gone bad, but that never happened. So, on my next trip to the market I brought one of the hard-covered plastic cases designed to hold raw eggs and requested that she fill it. She pushed a long strand of black hair back into the bun on top of her head and gave me a broad, broken-tooth smile. I knew she remembered me from the previous week, and I was surprised at how gratifying that small acknowledgement was. Perhaps she appreciated my attempt to talk to her in my pigeon Spanish, or she might have simply appreciated getting my business. Whatever it was, I enjoyed connecting with her and was pleased at my attempts at becoming more "native" each day.

One day I began thinking more about Franco's rats and decided to make screens for the hatches and portholes that we liked to leave open at night. We already had become fastidious about removing all trash from the boat immediately after each meal, but I thought screens might be useful, too. So, as one of my afternoon projects, I made screens that attached with Velcro.

We were able to purchase anything we wanted because the American dollar was strong. Often our trips to the market had more to do with practicing our Spanish than with actually needing anything, but, like most Americans, we loved a bargain and seized the opportunity to do boat upgrades that we might not have been able to afford elsewhere. One project was to have the interior of the boat reupholstered, because both the fabric and the labor were extremely reasonable. We considered having it done in leather, and even mentioned it to our friends, but before we made any commitments, a couple we had never met before, stopped by our boat.

"Hi, are you the people who are thinking about having your boat reupholstered in leather?" they asked.

I was not sure I liked having total strangers know our business while they peered into our boat. I probably had a look of disgust on my face because the woman finally said, "Dear, we haven't even introduced ourselves yet."

"My name is Jim and this is my wife Doris," the man said. "Our boat is just across from yours and down the dock a little ways, and when we heard you were considering leather we just thought you might like to see what leather is really like before you commit to it."

"What Jim is trying to say," Doris said, "is that if you're available we'd like you to join us for cocktails tonight at about 6pm and we'll show you our leather interior."

I thought that was rather sweet and my attitude about them improved dramatically. While accepting their invitation I asked if there was anything we could bring with us.

"Sure," Doris said. "Bring a pair of towels," and with those confusing parting words, they walked away.

By 6 o'clock I was almost sure we had not heard her correctly and I felt silly going to their boat with towels in my arms, but once we got on board and sat on their lovely gray leather cushions, the mystery became clear. While the leather looked great, it was uncomfortable to sit on in shorts, especially in the hot humid conditions of Venezuela. We were soon happily sitting on our towels.

Doris said, "We really liked the leather up in New Jersey, and it was O.K. most of the way down the coast, but once we got past the Bahamas, we hated it. I hope you don't mind us butting in like we did, but I just couldn't let anyone else make the same mistake we did."

I found myself liking Doris more every minute. She was a practical, down-to-earth woman. We had a pleasant evening with them and learned Jim was a retired urologist and that Doris had been his nurse. Tom told him about his accident in the Dominican Republic. He told him he still felt some pain, but he hadn't had any blood in his urine for a long time. "You're lucky you didn't let those doctors start cutting on you," Jim said. "It sounds like you ruptured a kidney and time was exactly what was needed to heal."

We went back to our boat feeling really good about two things. We could stop worrying about Tom's injury, and we knew they saved us from making a big mistake concerning our reupholstering project.

A few days later we visited a *tapaceria* and picked out maroon automotive-grade velour for our cushions. Negotiating the price, the date it was to be finished, the size of the cording, number of covered buttons, and thickness of the cushions was an English-Spanish challenge, yet Tom loved every step of the negotiation. We were so impressed with the finished cushions that we ordered new exterior cushions as well. Later, we gave our old exterior cushions to a group of fishermen we met at the fuel dock where diesel was a mere five cents a gallon for fishermen. The yacht price was seven cents, but we were treated like fishing pals.

While waiting out the hurricane season, we did land trips. On one trip we rented a car with John and Mary from FIA. The rugged mountainous countryside was majestic, and I found the many small shrines along the narrow mountain roads sobering. Each shrine was placed where people had been killed in car accidents. Most were of whitewashed cement, about two feet tall and housed a small religious statue, a lit candle and plastic flowers. Often there were photographs of the deceased (usually young teenagers) but occasionally there was a picture of an entire family. It left a heavy feeling in my heart to see the faces of strangers who had lost their lives on the road, but it made me appreciate the rocks and small pieces of red cloth that the truck drivers placed in the road to alert fellow travelers of a danger ahead. These dangers consisted of complete road washouts, fallen trees, or boulders that blocked the road. Without the warnings, a car could easily plunge off the side of the narrow mountain roads. Roads in the Venezuelan countryside had no guardrails or government highway patrol signs to assist motorists. Each motorist was responsible for himself.

Each day we traveled and saw new parts of Venezuela. At the Guri Dam we learned it was the second largest hydroelectric project in the world. When we visited the C.V.G

Ferrominera Orinoco iron ore mine, we learned that at the present rate of 20 million metric tons mined per year, Venezuela has reserves for the next 100 years. We also visited Minerven, a gold mine established in 1970 and nationalized in 1974, and learned that it, too, was in full operation and extremely lucrative.

We visited the city of Maracaibo, bound on one side by Lake Maracaibo and on the other by a desert laden with riches. When oil was discovered there in 1917, the colonial city boomed and became the second largest in the country. The Venezuelan petroleum industry, the second largest in the world, was originally jointly owned and operated by the American and Dutch companies, Lagoven and Maraven. The Venezuelan government later nationalized their production.

There were several ironies about Lake Maracaibo, but the most striking was seeing the American houses built on stilts next to the Dutch houses, that were built low to the ground. It would be difficult to find a stranger looking community! This unusual housing practice was based on the fact that the ground was sinking several inches each year because of the great volume of oil being sucked from beneath the earth. Of course, as the land sunk, the lake became higher than the land. Since the Dutch are masters at dike building, they simply built a large dike around the lake, and because they trusted their dikes, they built their houses on the ground.

Near one of the mining towns we had a difficult time finding rooms for the night. At several of the hotel/motel type of establishments, we were told they were full. *No hay* (There are none) is precisely what they said, but it made no sense to us. There were none of the obvious signs indicating they were fully booked. The parking lots were empty and there was not a person in sight. We didn't know what to think and could only conclude they didn't want to rent rooms to Americans. Finally, we found a pathetic looking place with two available rooms. By then we did not even mind the run-down appearance; we were just happy to have found a place willing to accept us.

Each room had a tile floor, whitewashed walls badly in need of paint, and two single beds with thin mattresses slung over saggy metal springs. There was one all-purpose sheet per bed. A bare light bulb hung from an open ceiling rafter and was the only modern amenity in the room. The common bathroom was located across the empty tile courtyard, and consisted of one toilet room and one shower room that needed to be shared by all the hotel guests. We did not see that as a problem however, since only the four of us seemed to be there.

After checking in, we walked down the street to stretch our legs and explore the tiny town. We found no restaurants, and dinner that night consisted of tacos from a street vendor's cart. Nothing seemed to be happening in the town, so we returned to our rooms for an early night's rest. In the middle of the night when I awoke to use the toilet, I was amazed to find the courtyard filled with sleeping bodies; all were men, all were dirty, and most were snoring loudly. I nearly tripped over them as I threaded my way around the raggedy mattresses and hoped none would grab at my legs as I passed by. I made it to the bathroom and back safely, and was tempted to wake Tom and tell him what I had just seen, but he was sleeping soundly and I decided to wait until morning. Imagine my surprise to find the men gone before we even got out of bed the next morning. We learned they were miners and that they returned after dark each night to rent a mattress on the floor. Apparently it was the same situation at all the other hotels.

I could hardly wait to tell Mary and John of my experience during the night, but they had their own story to share. A family of bats lived in their room and the only way they could get any rest was by leaving the light on all night.

During another trip to a city called Ciudad Bolivar, Tom learned they had an active horse race track. He could hardly wait to see it and wanted to place some bets. The track wasn't much to look at - a lumpy dirt oval with no grooming, but the excitement of the spectators was far from disappointing. We placed bets with our limited Spanish skills and had a great afternoon in spite of not winning.

The next morning we flew on *Aeroeotuy*, a small Venezuelan airline out of Ciudad Bolivar to Camp Canaima, a 3 million-acre national park established in 1962. In the park is the hidden *El Salto Angel (Angel's Falls)*, the highest waterfalls in the world. The falls were named after Jimmy Angel who, with his wife, was killed in their quest to survey the area. (See Color Photo Insert, page 12.)

For years they explored the virgin terrain in their own home-made lightweight aircraft, constantly seeking the falls that could be heard, but had never been seen by man. The falls were finally located in a place called the Gran Sabana, an area locally known as

Tom and LaVonne wearing backpacks and boarding a small Venezuelan Aerotoy airplane in the Grand Sabana.

Guayana. The entire area is dominated by flat-topped mountains known as tepuis. Some of the tepuis rise thousands of feet in the air and are, to this day, mostly unexplored.

Our plane stopped at a few of the already explored and populated places, landing on bumpy, grassy runways. At one stop the pilots unloaded supplies at a mission school. The children, padre, and nuns all stood along the runway to greet us and wave us off after the supplies had been unloaded. They were Indian children, with dark skin and ruddy cheeks, and they stared at Tom and me with big black eyes and amazed expressions. We may have been the first white people they had ever seen.

At noon, the airplane landed again and bumped along another grassy field. There was no visible sign of civilization and no announcement concerning the purpose of the stop. We were stumped and concerned when both pilots left the plane and began walking across the field, while the other passengers silently climbed out and sat with their backs against the airplane tires on the shady side of the plane.

"Hey, what's going on?" Tom shouted to the pilots.

They turned around and said, "We're going to lunch. You're welcome to come with us if you want."

Since we were hungry, we broke into a trot to catch up with them. Just across the field was a beat-up flatbed truck with keys left in the ignition. The pilots got in and started up the engine while Tom and I crawled into the back. It had big tires and I had to step onto the wheel axle before I could kneel onto the top of the tire and crawl onto the flatbed, and doing it in a skirt did not make it any easier. But if I wanted lunch, that was what I had to

LaVonne with the children from a mission school located on top of a Venezuelan mountain tepuis.

do. I hung on to something while the truck bounced over the hard turf until arriving at a cement house that seemed to appear out of nowhere. The front door consisted of a piece of white cloth, perhaps an old sheet. On a rock next to the entrance was a bucket of water, a bar of soap, and thin towel. We washed our hands before entering the house, and I mused at the efficiency of it all. The sun had warmed the water and the thin towel would quickly dry itself and even be disinfected on the sun-heated rock, and the cloth covering the doorway kept the sun and bugs out of the house. Without knocking, we entered the house by pushing the fabric aside. We sat at a long wooden table on the long wooden bench seats. Soon, bowls of food were placed before us and we ate in silence. I have no idea what we ate; it was hot and tasted good. When we finished eating, the pilots told us what we were expected to pay for our share, and that was that. Thirty minutes later we were back at the airplane, and lifting off.

At another town we picked up three women from a mining camp. The woman who sat next to me fingered a rosary and whimpered with fear as the plane lifted off the ground. She spoke no English and did not seem to understand my limited Spanish, but she accepted my comfort when I put my arm around her. Slowly, I realized she spoke only her native Indian language. When Tom turned around and saw my arm around the woman, he laughed out loud.

"What's so funny?" I asked.

"The pilot just told me you have your arm around a prostitute," he chuckled.

I hadn't realized that, and it made sense after Tom pointed it out, but I didn't care. I felt sorry for her. Her clothes were little more than rags and she was frightened to death of flying on that rickety little plane which didn't even have seat belts. If anything, I feared she might have known something we didn't, but at that moment, ignorance was bliss.

At Camp Canima we took several river trips led by the local Indians. The rivers were strong and swift, and I was glad when the boat captains insisted we each wear a life vest. I was equally glad when I saw back-up motors in each of our canoes, which were hollowed-out 20-foot logs called *curias*.

The sun seemed extra bright up that high where there was no pollution to deffuse it, and the brilliance reflected off the water. By midday the humidity was nearly unbearable, and the Indians stopped the curias at the side of the river. We walked to a small lake that was fed by a waterfall, and we took a refreshing swim while our dinner was prepared for us. The Indian men did the cooking by placing whole chickens on wooden sticks over an open fire, and while the men cooked, one of the Indian women taught us how to shoot a blow dart. Traditionally, the Indians used blow darts for hunting and for protection, and she demonstrated how she could shoot the dart with force for several yards. She made the skill look easy, but after several attempts my dart barely tumbled out of the dart gun and then landed at my feet.

During one of our excursions we were taken to the cabin of a 74-year-old hermit named Mr. Laime. His crudely built two-room cabin housed hundreds, maybe thousands

Mountain hermit, Mr. Laime, found Jimmy Angle's airplane and is mapping the unexplored areas of Canaima.

of books. He claimed to be the man who found Jimmy Angel's airplane 18 years after its crash, and he, like Jimmy Angel, devoted most of his life to mapping the area and writing letters to help promote Angel Falls to be listed as the Eighth Wonder of the World. We saw some old photos of Mr. Laime and Jimmy Angel when both were young, and Tom noticed that although Mr. Laime wore glasses in the photos, he wasn't wearing them now. When Tom asked about this, Mr. Laime chuckled.

"You've got a sharp eye there, young man," he said. "Yep, I used to wear glasses, but I just got tired of 'em. I'd been nearsighted most of my life and one day I just decided I was sick of wearing glasses, so I started exercising my eye muscles to correct the problem. Today I read whatever I want to, and I don't wear glasses for any of it."

We enjoyed visiting with Mr. Laime even though we suspected the entire hermit set-up might be a tourist trap. We anticipated a request for money or some form of donation, but to our surprise, no request came forth. He let our guides know when he was tired of talking with us by returning to the large, unfinished map spread out on a table. As we walked away, our guides told us he sometimes requested that they bring people by for a visit just because he liked speaking English once in a while.

GUESTS ARRIVED OUR SECOND YEAR

We stayed in Venezuela for the duration of the hurricane season, and relied heavily on historical weather patterns, as shown in the Pilot Charts, to help us determine when the hurricane season would end that year. When Tom deemed the appropriate time had arrived for our departure, I cooked several meals and put them in microwave dishes in the refrigerator. I knew I would not be capable of cooking anything resembling a whole meal if seasick, but I'd be able to pop pre-prepared meals into the microwave.

Like brave little soldiers we left the protection of the Cumana Marina and set sail for St. Croix, one of the Virgin Islands. It was our first attempt to sail nonstop for three days and nights. I had my usual apprehensions, but my anxiety was for naught because it was an uneventful passage. Nonetheless, neither of us got much sleep and we were exhausted when we reached St. Croix.

We had tentatively planned to attend the SSCA party hosted by Cathy and Bruce Goble on Culebra, but we suffered from sleep deprivation and decided not to make the extra one-day sail. That may have been the only time in my life when I admitted to needing rest more than I needed sociability.

A few days later, when fully rested, we sailed to St. Thomas, where Sara and Andy were due to arrive at the airport with their college roommates for Christmas break. This time, they brought no false expectations of unlimited hot running water or American fast food. Instead, they brought realistic goals of getting lots of sunshine, fresh fish, and tropical experiences, expectations we could deliver with ease. Much to our amazement, they seemed to appreciate going to bed early so they could get up early and not miss any of the daylight hours. What a nice change that was!

Our days were spent playing in the water, laughing, swimming, and fishing for dinner. On a lark one day, Tom borrowed a windsurfer from one of the neighboring boats, just to try it out. He tied a long line on it to prevent it from getting too far away, and he, Andy, and Andy's roommate, Jim, all tried to ride it. They fell in every possible dramatic way, and sometimes they were laughing so hard, they scarcely had the strength to get up on the board. What a show they put on!

It was a great two weeks, and we were sad to see them leave, but we were not given much of a chance to miss them because we welcomed friends from Minnesota from the same incoming airplane that Andy and Jim were scheduled to fly out on. We put a lot of

Minnesota guests were able to walk across the street from the St. Thomas airport and board our dinghy.

effort into showing each of our guests a unique experience, which began with our anchoring directly in front of the St. Thomas airport. When they de-planed and picked up their luggage, they did not have to face finding a taxi or taking a long bus ride into town. Instead they simply walked across the street, stuck their white toes in the sand, and got into our dinghy. Imagine coming from sub-zero weather carrying down jackets, and walking barefoot in warm saltwater within minutes of landing. We knew it was a wonderful way for them to begin a great vacation.

Most of our snowbird friends from Minnesota had not considered visiting us during our first year on the boat, but I guess after having survived that year we had proven ourselves, and were deemed safe. By then we were also fairly knowledgeable about the islands and that also made it a lot easier for us to take our visitors to all the best snorkeling spots.

Hand-feeding the stingrays at Caneel Bay on St. John's was a unique highlight. They were wild creatures, but had learned that people usually had food for them, so we never had to look far for them. Instead, they found us and swam with great speed directly toward us. Then they slid their bodies up and down ours in search of a hand with food in it. They felt like firm foam rubber, but every inch was filled with muscle. Of course we always included a swim at The Baths on Virgin Gorda, and no matter how often we went, none of us ever tired of The Baths. It was such a special area that even our non-swimming friends put on life vests and snorkeled there. Our guests and I enjoyed watching the marine life in action under the water, while Tom loved the primeval notion of catching fresh fish or seafood for our main meal each day. With his daily catch, and the availability of almost anything else we wanted at St. Thomas, meal planning was easy, regardless of the size group we had to feed. Even the problem of washing sheets and towels after each guest left was simplified, because there was a laundry available at the St. Thomas marina.

TOM SAT IN OLIVER NORTH'S CHAIR

While we enjoyed having the company, when the last couple left we were ready for time alone, and we soon left the hustle and bustle of the Virgin Islands behind. Once again we headed south, working our way back down the Caribbean chain that had become familiar the previous year, and we stopped at several of our favorite islands. It was comfortable to return to familiar harbors and pleasant to have local friends at many of them, but something was missing that second time around. Going back the second time just wasn't as exciting as the first time; the "wow" was missing.

In an effort to get some of the "wow" back into our daily lives, we went out of our way to visit new harbors and new islands. The first of those was Montserrat, with a population of 11,000, predominantly descended from slaves owned by the original Irish families. I thought it ironic that they chose to maintain the identity of their slave owners by keeping Irish names. It seemed more than a little strange to see dark-skinned people with the last names of O'Brien and O'Reilly, instead of the freckled, blue-eyed, redheads that one might have expected to have those names. Our passports were even stamped with a green shamrock to further maintain the Irish identity of the island.

We enjoyed the quiet rural feeling of the island and took the opportunity to exercise our weakened boat legs by walking part way up a volcanic mountain in an area called Soufriere Hills. The farther we walked, the stronger the sulfur odor became, and soon our pleasant walk became a revolting endeavor. When we could tolerate the stench no more, we turned around and walked back through the town. While passing one of the larger buildings, we investigated what sounded to be the hum of machinery at work, and found fifty or more young women spinnning and weaving what they called "natural sea cotton." The cotton was a creamy color and they made no effort to dye it, as it was beautiful in its natural form. Both the spinning and weaving were done on large, old-fashioned pieces of equipment that may have dated back to the beginning of the Industrial Revolution in our own country. I was mesmerized, almost in a hypnotic trance, watching the yarn twist, the spools spin, and the shuttles slide back and forth across the warp.

Several days later we sailed back to Granada and anchored in St. George's Harbor in front of Angela and Ray Smith's home which was perched high up the hill. Angela held an official position with the British Embassy, and one night they included us when they hosted a dinner party. We found ourselves seated next to some very important people. Next to me was the English Ambassador to the Island.

After dinner, in proper English form, we were invited to move to the veranda where it was cool and the men could smoke, if they desired. Tom sat in a big, wooden rocker while taking in the beauty and serenity of the lighted waterfront, from that height. The view was spectacular. The parallel boats tugged gently at their anchor lines, the twinkling lights reflected in the sea, and the wind rippled on the water's surface, creating a feast for the eye and a gift for the soul.

"That's the very chair where Oliver North sat when he was here," the English ambassador told Tom while sipping her after-dinner cognac.

"It is?" Tom responded in surprise. "When was he here?"

"Oh, he was here shortly before the war," she said. "I thought him a rather strange chap, though. What do you Americans think of him?"

Somehow, Tom managed to change the subject because neither of us knew enough about the war in Grenada, or Oliver North, to speak knowledgeably. The conversation quickly moved to our travels and Tom told her we were planning to visit Trinidad next. She and others nearby expressed a unified horror.

"That's a terrible place, very dangerous," one said. "You shouldn't even think about going there! You'll surely get robbed, or maybe something worse."

Another said, "Not long ago there was something in the paper about a cruiser who had been murdered right in his bunk while at anchor at Trinidad. They're really terribly uncivilized people down there!"

I won't say their remarks fell on deaf ears, because they certainly increased my apprehension. Still, we did not let their warnings alter our plans. We had been in radio contact with Fred on PROWESS, the cruiser who grew his own tomato plants. He was in Trinidad at that time and had only positive things to say about the island. So later that week, we bravely set sail and headed for Trinidad.

TRINIDAD

We did not like the idea of sailing at night but even more, disliked the idea of arriving at a new port at night. It was easier and safer to navigate narrow passageways and harbor entrances with full daylight, so we opted to sail the open sea at night so we could arrive at Trinidad in the morning light.

Fred met us at the pier. He helped us tie up, showed us where to check in with Customs and Immigration, led us downtown to the appropriate office to get my reciprocal ham radio license, and told us where we could find a bank to obtain local currency. By midday we had completed all our business and we returned to the boat for naps.

The next morning I checked into the ham radio nets with my new reciprocal call sign, and within days several local hams befriended us. Clearly the most gracious of the lot was Mohammed Yasen Ali (9Y4BG), who preferred to be called Ali. He invited us to his home where we met his wife and beautiful daughters who, much to our surprise, were not kept hidden under a Muslim wrap. The family was warm and friendly. They took us sightseeing, included us in family gatherings, and even invited us stay in their home. We declined, but I thought the offer was extremely generous. Ali and his family took us to see the sinking tar pit/lake where sailors, back in Columbus' day, harvested tar to caulk the bottoms of their wooden boats. We saw mangroves, where thousands of scarlet ibis' returned to their nests each evening, just before dusk. We were even invited to attend a Hindu wedding, and what an experience that was.

The bride's dress was a bright yellow lace formal with an elaborately beaded headpiece that covered her face. She was seated on a floor mat in the center of an open walled room when we arrived, and we watched the bride's mother symbolically present her with a bitter and unpalatable herb that she was expected to eat. Then an attendant painted the bride's toenails.

Off to the side of the wedding hall a group of musicians were getting ready for the festivities to follow. I was amazed to see one musican busily tuning his drum by heating the skin over an open fire. Both activities took place simultaneously in separate sections of the room, with no explanation for those of us who needed it. My interest in the ceremony had begun to fade when a large black car arrived and an immense person wearing a bright pink floor-length dress, stepped out into the middle of the wedding party. I was somewhat surprised to see such a huge woman, but more surprised to learn that was the groom. The bright pink dress struck me as completely incongruent for a six-footer with broad shoulders, but everyone else seemed nonplussed. He was led to a floor mat next to the bride and several men immediately began attending to him. The attendants were in such a tight huddle we were unable to observe the ceremonies each performed.

With all the attention on the groom, I had not realized that the bride had disappeared, until we saw her return to her mat wearing a jeweled red dress. It was made of lace and layers of mesh netting, and was even more bejeweled than the yellow dress. (See Color Photo Insert, page 13.)

After several hours of sitting on hard, folding chairs and not understanding the rituals, Ali told us it was our turn to eat. We were led to an outdoor faucet where we washed our hands in cold water with the bar of soap presented to us by a young girl. She offered a thin damp terrycloth towel for drying and led us to a long table with bench seating. A fresh banana leaf was placed on the table in front of us, and an assortment of food was deposited directly onto the leaf. All the food was vegetarian, and some was spicy, but no two foods tasted alike. We ate it with our fingers. That, too, was symbolic as it was a practice done only at weddings and other traditional festivities. On a daily basis, everyone in Trinidad used flatware.

Ali suggested we leave shortly after we had eaten. Apparently Hindu weddings went on for three days, and people came and went as they pleased the entire time. It is worth noting that Ali was Muslim, yet we attended a Hindu wedding as his guest. Trinidad may be the only place in the world where the Hindus and Muslims maintain close friendships. Historically, the East Indians, both Hindu and Muslims, were brought to Trinidad as indentured servants to replace black slaves after slavery had been abolished. The blacks were given government jobs, and they still hold nearly all the government jobs on the island, while the East Indians operate most of the businesses. Because there is such a small percentage of East Indians on the island, they tend to develop friendships, regardless of religion.

We were interested in the business and politics of Trinidad. For one thing, the exchange rate was strange. We paid a heavy penalty to exchange our dollars into the Trinidad money at the bank, but learned we could get a much better exchange rate with the Indian business owners who needed American dollars to purchase their inventory. We exchanged a large sum of money in this manner with the owner of an appliance store simply by writing him a personal check. It was a huge risk, because we needed to wait several days for the check to clear our bank before he gave us our money, and we would have had no legal recourse if the owner had decided not to pay us. We took the risk, and it worked out well.

People in Trinidad were, for the most part, financially comfortable, but like any city there was also poverty. One morning we saw a ragged, wrinkled shell of a man who was eating noodles out of a garbage can outside a restaurant. His long bony fingers picked up each strand of spaghetti, and after examining it and removing the debris he sucked it into his mouth, like a straw. It was common also to see children who should have been in school selling lottery tickets on the street.

We had several warm and touching experiences in Trinidad. One was on the public bus when the only empty seat left was across the isle from where I sat. A large woman with three young children got on the bus and sat down. She put her parcels on the floor at her feet and the two youngest children in her lap. The oldest toddler was left standing next to her and began looking around for an empty lap and immediately spied mine. His big black eyes looked up at me, questioning the availability of my lap, and as soon as I smiled at him, up he climbed. His chubby little arm reached up to touch my straight hair, which was very different from his tight black curls, but once his curiosity had been satisfied he thrust a thumb into his mouth, dropped his heavy little head on my chest and went soundly to sleep. He had such an innocence and trust to be able to go to sleep, without a peep, in the lap of a stranger. On another bus ride, a proud young mother asked if I would like to hold her baby who was a mere five days old. I was the one who was apprehensive about holding a stranger's newborn, while the mother instinctively trusted me.

All our experiences in Trinidad were top-notch. We never felt threatened or unsafe; in fact, quite the opposite was true. We had built several strong and lasting friendships that would remain in our memories for years, and those made it difficult to say goodbye and move on. When we told our new island friends we were heading back to Venezuela, they warned us to be very careful.

"There may be some good ones, but most of them are really bad and they'll take you for all you're worth. So, just be careful, that's all – just be really careful because you can't trust them." I thought it interesting that their warnings were so similar to what our friends in Grenada had said about them. Since we had already been to Venezuela, we checked out of Trinadad and set sail with no apprehension.

"NO VOOM," I TOLD THE AIRLINE OFFICIAL

Carefully we motored out of Trinidad harbor to clear the small outer islands before putting up the sails. Tom kicked the engine throttle up, but instead of going faster, the engine overheated. Perplexed, he dove over the side to investigate and discovered that the bottom of the boat had become a reef of barnacles. We could not continue in that condition, so we turned around and dropped anchor in a small bay.

It was a protected little bay, and we snuggled up close to a heavily wooded shore where there were a few other boats. At the far end of the bay was a small military base and we thought it best to keep our distance from it. But our effort to not encroach on them certainly was not reciprocated because early the next morning we were awakened by a bugle call followed by a male voice echoing over the water on a loud speaker:

"Wakey, wakey, rise and shine.

The sun is up and looking fine.

You've had sleep, now let me have mine.

Wakey, wakey, rise and shine."

I could hardly believe grown, uniformed men would sing/song that ditty with any degree of pride, but apparently the routine is a strong British tradition. We ate breakfast in the cockpit, still smiling at the words, and to top off the morning's amusement, wild monkeys fought and scampered in the trees next to us, making incredibly loud screeching sounds. We watched them run and jump from branch to branch and wondered what the fuss was all about.

We soon tired of all the monkey business and after breakfast we dove under the boat to scrub and scrape the barnacles, slime, and seaweed from it. Our splashing and thrashing in the water apparently aroused the curiosity of the captain on one of the Trinidad sailboats anchored near us, and when he realized we were cleaning the bottom of our own boat he expressed his surprise. "I usually hire that to be done," he told us. "There are plenty of young boys willing to do that for a small fee, you know."

"Yes, I know," said Tom. "Problem is, how do you know how good a job they've done when they're finished?"

Either he approved of Tom's answer and/or he felt we might be interesting company, because the next time we came to the surface gasping for air he invited us to come to their boat for dinner that evening. We readily accepted, and over dinner we learned our hosts were native to Trinidad and "planned to go cruising as soon as the boat was ready." He fired jillions of questions, and we soon realized he would never go cruising because he was afraid to pull up the anchor and leave port. For him, the *plan* to go cruising was his adventure – not the actual *cruising*. He must have been very concerned about security because he even had metal bars on his hatches so no one could break into the boat while he and his wife slept. I doubt that he ever left Trinidad, but we left the next morning. I sure would not miss being awakened by a bugle call and a silly "wakey wakey" ditty, but I did hate to leave the monkeys. They were such rascals, and I'd become rather fond of them.

We had an easy sail back to Venezuela with steady winds the entire time. When we arrived at the Cumana Marina it felt as if we had returned home. We knew where to check in and whom to see. We knew where to catch the bus, where to go for dinner, where to shop, and where to schedule the boat for a haul-out. We desperately needed a new bottom-paint-job, and scheduled it right away.

The haul-out facility consisted of a set of rails that ran down into the brown murky water from a small runoff river. The boat cradle slid down the track while we motored into the center of it. After the divers threaded and attached wide braided straps under the boat, the cradle was pulled up onto land and the boat sat snugly in the straps. It was awesome to be on a big heavy boat while it swung freely, high in the air over dry land. The yardmen put a tall ladder up to the side of the boat so we could get on and off, but it was like crawling down the side of a two-story building. Many of our friends slept on their boat during haulouts, but not me, thank you very much. I had no intention of crawling up and down that ladder in the middle of the night in my nightgown each time I needed a toilet. Besides, the boatyard toilets were disgusting beyond belief. They were small, square, unpainted cement structures with barely enough room for one's knees when seated, and there was no toilet paper; we were expected to bring our own. In the corner next to the toilet was a used paint pail filled with everyone's soiled toilet paper.

Apparently the toilets became plugged when paper was flushed, so Venezuelans customarily deposited the used paper into a pail or bucket. It was a disgusting and unsanitary practice, and one of the major reasons we rented a hotel room while our boat was in dry dock.

We had added many things to the boat since we left Duluth, causing it to sit lower and lower in the water. We almost looked like an over-laden drug- running boat, so to make it look spiffy once again, we had the yard paint a new boat stripe about three inches higher than the old one. Each additional task added days to the time the boat was on land and we were grateful for the comfort of our hotel.

One of the pleasures we allowed ourselves while waiting was going to the movies. They were American-made movies with Spanish subtitles. We thought it might be a good way for us to learn more Spanish because we could hear the English and read the subtitles, but we discovered the subtitles were not always accurate. There were times when we would laugh at something, only to discover we were the only people laughing in the theater.

When the haul-out was completed, we made arrangements to return home for a family visit. There were many things we needed to attend to back in the States, not the least of which was attempting to get the autopilot repaired, once and for all. Tom carefully removed it from the boat and placed it in a padded boat bag. At the airport, he attended to our luggage while I cradled the autopilot, much as I might a sleeping child. Unfortunately, it looked like a bomb to the airport personnel, who stopped me from boarding the plane and requested that I remove it from my bag. Their jaws dropped when they saw wires hanging from the bottom of the autopilot, and with fear in their eyes I saw a renewed determination to keep me off the plane. They spoke so fast and with so much agitation, that I could not understand what they were saying. The only word I understood was "voom," and all I could say back was "no voom. Tango una barko de vela" (I have a sail boat). I showed them our boat papers, and for some unknown reason I guess they finally believed me, because suddenly they allowed me to get on the plane with the autopilot. Perhaps I didn't fit the description of a political terrorist about to commit suicide.

NAKED AS A JAYBIRD

The flight went well and the officials in the Miami airport ignored the autopilot completely. In some ways it felt as if we were still in Venezuela because of all the Spanish that was spoken at the airport. We transferred planes to Minnesota, and upon our arrival found ourselves immediately caught up in a whirlwind of activity. There were relatives and friends to be visited, dental and medical check-ups to be scheduled, boat equipment to be ordered, clothing to be purchased, repairs to be made, and many business details needing our attention. We also accepted an invitation to give a slide presentation at the monthly meeting of The Ham Radio Club, and when I learned my high school class reunion was taking place during our visit, we attended that, too. It seemed we were busy from the moment we opened our eyes each morning until we fell into bed very late each night. On the boat we were accustomed to getting up with the sun and going to bed shortly after the sundown, so the late social activities quickly took their toll on us. In spite of having a great time, we soon felt weary, and when we were tired we both tended to overlook details.

One night while visiting Tom's mother, his brother Mike, and sister in law Bobby Jo, we offered to show the video we had taken of our travels. The small detail we overlooked was the section of film taken at the clothing-optional beach at St. Martin. At that section of the video neither of us offered explanatory comments. I think we figured it wouldn't offend either Mike or Bobby Jo, and because his mother's eyesight was so poor she wouldn't notice that we weren't wearing clothing, but we could not have been more wrong!

"Those people aren't wearing any clothes," his mom stated clearly.

"Well, Ma, it's a clothing-optional beach," Tom said, somewhat defensively, surprised that her eyesight was not as bad as we had all thought.

"My land!" she said, never taking her eyes off the screen and leaning forward in her chair to get a better look. "Oh, my goodness, is that you, LaVonne?" she asked in total disbelief. "Are you naked, too?"

I guessed it was a rhetorical question because she did not seem to expect an answer. Instead, she continued mumbling, "Lordy, Lordy, Lordy, what's this world coming to?" Then she stopped and said, "Tom, you had your clothes on, didn't you!" It was more of a statement than a question.

"Sure, Ma," said Mike. "Just because he was behind the camera doesn't mean he wasn't naked as a Jaybird."

Her lips pursed, she flashed Mike a glare, but quickly the eyes softened and the rigidity of her body dispersed and she slouched back into her chair. She could never remain angry with "her boys." This matter would clearly never be spoken of again.

It was great seeing everyone and knowing that family support was always there. Being "home" also offered us the opportunity to eat American food, buy clothing that fit, find our way around easily, and enjoy a clean environment. Still, something seemed wrong. We no longer fit in as comfortably as we once had. Our experiences made us see and feel differently about things. I couldn't quite say what was different about us, but it was *something*.

When the time came for us to leave Minnesota, we were both ready and eager to get back to the boat. We looked forward to our more relaxed way of life. We boarded the plane with a sense of relief and excitement, heavily laden with all our new "stuff."

ZIGGY AND HIS NEW VOMAN

As the plane circled Caracas airport we saw thousands of shacks made from sheets of tin, cardboard, and tarpaper perched on nearby hills. Large numbers of people lived in those ram-shackled "barrios" where there were no streets or sidewalks, and no electricity, water, or plumbing. I could not begin to imagine what daily life must be like there.

I was still pondering that mass of humanity during our walk, after checking into our hotel. It was late afternoon and people were just beginning to come out on the streets following their afternoon siesta, when I noticed a handsome young boy walk toward me with a big, contagious smile on his face. I smiled back and said, "Buenas tardes." I was pleased at the opportunity to practice my Spanish again and was caught completely off-guard when he reached out and grabbed the thin, gold chain at my neck. I had forgotten I was wearing it, but instinctively grabbed for it when I felt it cut into my skin. It was an automatic reflex, not to prevent him from taking it but to protect myself from being choked. I felt it sliding from his hand, and when he realized it wasn't going to be an easy snatch, he ran like a gazelle into the crowd.

When Tom caught up to me he asked, "What did the kid have to say"?

The whole incident had taken place so fast that Tom was not even aware of what had happened. I was relieved that I was not hurt, but angry with myself for forgetting to remove the necklace before returning to Venezuela. We had made a point of not wearing jewelry during any part of our travels, not necessarily because we were afraid of losing it, but because we did not want to flaunt any signs of wealth. Our straight teeth and tall strong bodies were already signs of affluence, and by contrast that boy probably lived in one of those dilapidated hovels on the hill, and may not even have had food that day. What a desperate future he had.

We experienced another theft several days later while riding down an escalator. I was standing in front of Tom when a young man in front of me dropped a pack of postcards at the bottom. When he bent over to pick them up, he caused quite a commotion because he was blocking the bottom of the moving stairs. It appeared as if people were going to be piling on top of one another, and we prepared to step around him by putting our hands on the side rails. Meanwhile, the person standing behind Tom picked his pockets clean, and Tom never felt a thing. By the time he realized he had been pick-pocketed, there was no one around. The entire theft was smooth as silk.

In contrast to those two thefts, there were many positive experiences in Caracas. We enjoyed the ambience on the sidewalks at night when people set up checker and backgammon games. Sometimes they were friendly games between old friends and other times, they were betting games where someone paid to play and bet against their opponent. The vendors also came out at night and spread their goods on blankets on both sides of the street, requiring pedestrians to carefully step over and around them. Just about everything one could think of was for sale: artwork, trinkets, watches, jewelry, blankets, household goods, luggage, handbags, flowers, clothing, and food.

Another positive experience was an encounter with a well-dressed woman we met at the Caracas airport, while waiting for our luggage. She lived in Cumana and held some prestigious government position there. When she learned our boat was in the Cumana Marina she invited us to her birthday party, gave us the date and said she would send her chauffeur for us at 8pm on the night of the party. We were flattered to have been invited to a Venezuelan home, and in anticipation of being out late that night we took afternoon naps. Decked out in our best clothing, we walked to the marina gate where we were to be picked up. We made sure we were there a few minutes early, and sat on boulders to wait. We talked with many of the other cruisers as they came and went, and enjoyed the teasing and whistles we received for being so dressed up.

One of the cruisers we talked to was Ziggy, the German we had met in Florida with the "bumble-bee machine" on the bow of his boat. We had not seen him since we shared a dock with him in Fort Lauderdale.

"How's Gertrude?" Tom asked.

"Ahg, she's alright, I guess," said Ziggy. "We're not married any more you know, but she vas a great voman."

"Well, she sure impressed the hell out of me," Tom said, while remembering how she scolded those vulgar kids that night. "What happened?"

"Ahg, vell.....she vent back to Germany to visit her mama and papa and I stayed here on da boat.....and viel she vas gone I sorta had a Venezuelan girl staying vith me on da boat. You knows vat I mean? Vell, Gertrude sorta figured it out ven she got back. She got real pissed and divorced me. You know vat she did at the divorce? She valked right up to me in front of the judge and slapped me hard across da face and said, 'I still love you, you son of a bitch.' Ya, she did that. She vas a good strong voman, not veek like these Venezuelan girls. Now I gots a Venezuelan girlfriend, but it's not much good. She's lazy and just vants me to buy her tings all da time. I already bought her a house and I'm tryin to learn some Spanish from her, but I'm jus learnin girl Spanish. Naw, it's not going to vork out much longer."

After Ziggy left we realized how late it had become. We began to think we had misunderstood about the party and nearly returned to the boat, but just then the chauffeur showed up and drove us to the home of our hostess. Surrounding the yard was a six-foot security wall with pieces of jagged glass cemented at the top and armed guards walked the perimeter of the grounds. Our hostess welcomed us and ushered us into a lovely living room where we were given drinks, then left alone to explore the house and gardens while she greeted other arriving guests. By midnight the house was packed, food began to appear, and a band began to play. The party was only just beginning by the time we were ready to go home, but the chauffeur did not take us back to the boat until the sun rose. We were exhausted, both by the late night and the effort of trying all night to speak and understand Spanish.

We slept most of the next day, but then found it difficult to put ourselves to bed at a reasonable hour that night. It took days before we were back on our schedule. The party made us aware again of the differences in cultures, and we decided to take a land trip into Brazil to experience that culture, also.

FOR AN AMERICAN, I WAS CONSIDERED NICE

We arranged to put the boat up on land in one of the new boat yards in Puerto la Cruz for a few months while we traveled on land. We thought it was a good idea to let the fiberglass have an opportunity to dry out, especially some of the blisters we'd begun to notice on the bottom. The yard had an armed guard on duty at all times, and the office managers assured us the boat would be safe.

With adventure in our souls, we took the local bus and headed to Cuidad Bolivar. En route the bus stopped in many small towns to drop off and pick up passengers, and in one town we needed to transfer buses. While the driver loaded and unloaded the luggage, vendors stood under the bus windows hawking their wares. Mostly they sold food and soda that passengers purchased through the open windows. After consuming their purchases, the containers and wrappers were dropped on the floor, in the aisles, under the seats or tossed out the same window they were purchased through. The need to keep the countryside and the bus litter-free seemed to be unknown to them.

By contrast, we were pleasantly surprised at the cleanliness of the second bus at our transfer point. We were amazed when the assistant driver came down the aisle with a plastic bag indicating that we were to put our trash in it. "Wow," I thought, "there really were some Venezuelans who were concerned about sanitation and the environment." It warmed my heart to see people bending down under their seats to pick up the litter they had just tossed there. People dutifully placed their trash into the bag as the assistant worked his way down the aisle, and when he had collected all the trash, the driver opened the front door, and the assistant tossed the entire bag out onto the side of the road. We could hardly believe our eyes! Apparently the driver wanted a clean bus but had no concern for the appearance of the countryside itself.

In Cuidad Bolivar we transferred from our bus and boarded an airplane headed for Santa Elena, a small mining town located on the Venezuelan-Brazilian border. I was fortunate to have been assigned a seat next to a woman who spoke some English and appreciative of her patience with my limited Spanish. I learned that she planned to visit relatives in Santa Elena, and she told me many things about the town including where we would be able to rent a room for the night. Before parting she said, "For an American, you are very nice." I knew she thought she was paying me a compliment.

DANGEROUS BRIDGES

The room she recommended was nothing more than a cement cubicle with one naked dusty light bulb and two twin beds. I don't even want to think about how many other people may have slept on those sheets since they had last been washed. We avoided spending time in the room by exploring the town and purchasing the next day's bus tickets to cross into Brazil. We saw a shack of an office where miners sold their gold nuggets and diamonds. The broker-buyer who had to sit alone all day waiting for a miner to come in, was happy to have us to talk to, and from him we learned that both diamonds and gold were found in the same streams that ran down from the mountains. We purchased a few small gold nuggets (at $15 each), and he threw in a few industrial diamonds. They were practically worthless to him, but they meant a lot to me.

Left: One of several bridges that our bus crossed on our way to Boa Vista in Northern Brazil.

Top: Our fellow bus passengers watching our bus drivers negotiate their way across the bridge.

The next morning we boarded our bus and headed across the border to Boa Vista, Brazil. The size and comfort of the bus was a pleasant surprise. It was air-conditioned and had two drivers, who alternated. Both young men looked handsome in their uniforms: bright fuchsia colored shirts and black slacks. I had every reason to anticipate the day would be relaxing and worry-free. I readied myself to do nothing more stressful than observe the jungle as it flew past my window, but as soon as we crossed the border I learned how false that expectation was. When we came to the first dilapidated wooden bridge on the dirt road, the bus stopped and all passengers were requested to get out and walk across it. The bridge was a complete disaster; it had no railings, was missing a number of planks, and had holes large enough for a person to fall through. Below the bridge was a river with rocks and fast moving water. Tom and I walked across the bridge with the other passengers, each of us carefully picking our way across. After we were all safely across, the bus followed at a snail's pace. One driver walked ahead to guide it around the largest holes while the other drove, and we listened as the bridge groaned under the weight. I wondered how they determined who would be the unlucky one to do the driving across that bridge. I might have turned back at that point had that option been available, or if I had known what was yet to come, because that was only the first of many such bridges. Each looked as disastrous as the previous one, and I marveled when we successfully traversed each of them.

THE MISSING AIRPLANE TICKETS

Midday we stopped at a makeshift restaurant where we were able to purchase soda, tacos, and a plate of rice and beans. Out in back were two open-pit bathrooms (a hole in the ground surrounded by tall sugar canes lashed together) – one for the men, the other for the women. My memory of Venezuelan bathrooms was not so bad compared to the ones I had seen at that point in Brazil. At least Venezuelan toilets flushed – holes in the ground did not.

When we arrived in Boa Vista we donned our backpacks and walked until we found a cheap hotel. It was not much of a town and we woke early the next morning and boarded another bus headed for Manaus. It was a long, hot, dusty ride and we didn't arrive in Manaus until well after dark. We were sweaty, tired, and in need of a shower, but we collected our backpacks and walked until we found a hotel. We checked in, brushed our teeth, and went right to sleep.

The next morning Tom awoke first and nudged me. "I think you should take your shower and then we should get out of here," he said. "Don't get upset and don't look out of the window because it looks into a filthy elevator shaft. Just get up and let's get going."

The place was squalid. Even in daylight the cockroaches brazenly scampered about the room. I didn't even want to think about how many had run across us as we slept.

Manaus is a city surrounded by the jungle and the Amazon River. Every street stirred with human activity, and had some type of market where people squatted to sell their goods: meat, fruit, baskets, china dinnerware. fish, or live crabs tied in bunches to prevent them from crawling away. (See Color Photo Insert, page 14.) The sounds of hawkers and the haggling of customers melded into an unpleasant decibel level, making it impossible to hear any individual conversation, while odors of fish, rotting meat, and body perspiration hung in the hot, humid air.

We purchased airline tickets to fly to Belem on the Atlantic coast at the mouth of the Amazon. Tom put the tickets in a small nylon daypack that he carried on his shoulder, and because we had time to kill before heading out to the airport, we walked around and watched the circus of vendors. As it neared the time to head to the airport, Tom reached into his daypack to double-check our departure time and discovered the tickets were gone! Someone had slit the bottom of his bag allowing the tickets to fall out.

We rushed back to the place where we purchased the tickets, and they told us that this kind of thing happens all the time. They kindly reissued tickets with a warning to keep a better lookout for thieves who use razor blades on purses, bags and luggage. We were lucky that time as our tickets were replaced at no charge, but we knew we would need to be more careful during the rest of our land travel in Brazil.

WALKING WITH THONGS ON THEIR HANDS

When we sailed, Tom and I had to be constantly concerned with the tide, especially when we were tied to a pier or dock, but also when we were at anchor. Never, however, did we have to deal with changes as extreme as the boats on the Amazon River. At high tide the vendors' boats bounced gently in the water while they were tied to the quay, but several hours later those same boats were tipped on their sides in mud flats. We were told the river was very wide, still we thought we could see land on the other side. But we were wrong. What we saw was an island in the center of the river – an island about the size of Switzerland. (See Color Photo Insert, Page 14.)

We continued traveling by bus in a southerly direction along the East Coast and were struck by the extreme poverty. It was at its worst among the indigenous people of the north where they lived in dirt-floored, open huts, with grass roofs. They were small-boned people with dark leathery skin, and they looked like they had adult heads on bodies of undeveloped children. We saw many deformities, particularly clubfeet, and it was not uncommon to see people wearing rubber thongs on their hands in order to walk on their hands with their deformed feet swinging in the air. In one town, we saw a young man selling artwork that he had drawn with his one operational limb—a foot. There were beggars every place we looked, women holding infants or toddlers, but also old men and deformed people of all ages. All were unkempt, sad, and sickly looking. We saw the locals toss small useless coins in their direction, sometimes worth no more than a fraction of a cent. We decided not to give them money; instead we gave them food in the form of packaged milk, formula, or fresh fruit. We figured they would benefit directly from the food, but we were never sure where, or to whom their few coins might go.

Land travel in the northern part of Brazil is not for sissies, and yet there was something rich and wonderful about it. To get the full flavor of the country, we rode the crowded city buses where we saw many poor people hang onto the outside bar of the bus and stand on the lower step. They would drop off when the ticket taker approached them because they were unable to pay the bus fare. We learned that most of the people in the northern part of Brazil had never attended school, and they seemed completely unaware of the need for even the most basic sanitation practices. The city buses seemed little more than cylinders of metal, bouncing along on a set of tires stirring, up dust. One day. while I sat on the aisle seat and Tom sat next to the open window, he got a spray of something wet in his face. It was puzzling because there was nothing but dry dusty air billowing through the open bus windows. When it happened the second time we noticed a mother assisting her child while he vomited out the window. The mother and sick child were out of Tom's line of vision, but I could easily see them from my seat. So for the rest of the trip I watched them with the concentration of an eagle, and every time the boy leaned his head out the window I'd quickly elbow Tom, which was his signal to immediately close the window. Sometimes he barely got the window up in time before the splash of vomit hit it. For the next several hours we had our choice of looking at vomit or wearing it; needless to say, we chose to look at it. When the bus pulled into a rest stop I found myself glaring at the mother when she purchased a god-awful looking pile of beans and rice for her son to eat. I knew exactly where I would see those beans again. They looked disgusting in the first place and I did not even want to think about what they would look like later on our window.

THREE SETS OF MONEY

At each rest stop there was some sort of toilet facility, and I learned to cope with them. Often a woman stood at the door selling squares of toilet paper (there was never toilet paper available inside). The charge for paper was a Cruzario bill worth about 3 cents, but it looked very impressive with the number 25,000,000,000 on it. It was a bill from their third oldest currency, printed several months earlier, and I soon realized the importance of keeping a supply of them in my pocket.

It was 1991, and inflation was rampant in Brazil. The government added to the problem by frequently printing new sets of money. Every day we operated with three separate sets: old Cruzerios, Cruzados, and NCZs. It was very confusing! Thank goodness Tom was able to keep them straight because I was not able to do so. Sometimes a bill with six sets of zeros on it was worth only pennies, while a bill with a single number had a high value. I was content to keep only the most worthless money in my pocket; I needed only enough to allow myself entrance to the toilets. Tom kept the other two sets. In his left pocket he kept Cruzados, which was the middle currency; in his right pocket he kept NCZs, the highest value of money. The exchange rate changed dramatically each day making it prudent for us to exchange money often. There was no point in exchanging larger amounts because it could lose value overnight. A $100 supply of Brazilian money one day was often worth only $90 days later.

DENTAL FLOSS BIKINIS

We witnessed Brazil's first democratic presidential election. There were 20 or more presidential candidates in the primary election, with Lula and Collar competing in the final election. Collar won, and would be the one to face the problem of trying to slow the national inflation.

While we walked the street in the heat of the day from yet another bus stop looking for a cheap, clean hotel and struggling under the weight of our backpacks, I realized I was content. Not only did I not mind walking several miles with 50 pounds on my back, I actually enjoyed it, and I liked the challenge of hunting for accommodations in each new town. I had even grown accustomed to seeing the poverty and lack of sanitation around us and took a perverse satisfaction in learning how to manage each toilet situation. The best part was I did not feel seasick. On land I felt strong and ready to meet each new challenge. I felt in control of myself!

In Recife we chuckled in ghoulish humor when we saw caskets sold in shops on the corner of the local hospital. We were amazed to see two nurses escort a patient on a rolling hospital bed across a busy street, apparently to another section of the hospital. One nurse held up a bottle of liquid that fed the patient intravenously, while they waited at a traffic light. (See Color Photo Insert, Page 15.)

In Victoria we visited the English Department at the City University. The students found the opportunity to speak English a luxury, and three sweet girls leapt at the chance by volun-

Brazilian University students showed us the highlights of their city because they wanted to practice their English.

teering to show us around their city. While they practiced their English, we practiced our limited Portuguese. We were aware of the similar spelling of many nouns in Spanish and Portuguese, but the pronunciation was very different, so words we should have been able to recognize we didn't even know when we heard them spoken. The Portuguese language has a melodic lilt. Words are spoken with a lot of *gh* and *shaa* sounds. The girls took us all around their city and even showed us cocoa trees. As a thank you, we bought dinner for them and their husbands that evening.

Just when we had become accustomed to the Third World nature of Brazil, we arrived in Rio de Janeiro, where we were impressed by the sophistication of the city. Gone were the small, underdeveloped dark people of the north; in Rio the people looked European. They were larger, strong, and healthy looking, and some were blond and blue eyed. Rio is a modern progressive city with all the amenities, cultural opportunities, and possibilities for comfortable living. (See Color Photo Insert, pages 16 & 17.) The miles and miles of beaches in Rio hosted some of the most beautiful bodies we had ever seen, and I thought Tom's white eyeballs were at risk of sunburn, with all the ogling he did at the 'dental-floss' bikinis. From the back, each bronzed goddess looked naked; the thong of the swimsuit literally disappeared exposing firm, little, tan butts. From the front, three miniscule patches of fabric were visible on the women, and one on the men. I speculated how many swimsuits the manufacturer was able to make from a yard of fabric!

In spite of my ungoddess-like body, I loved Rio! The city pulsed with life and excitement. We were fortunate to find an inexpensive room only one block from the ocean in an area called Leblon, and by then we didn't even mind the cockroaches. We had become accustomed to them. Well, that isn't exactly accurate; it is more accurate to say I had learned to tolerate them by making sure our suitcases were zipped tight each night. I could accept living with them during our land trip, but I did not want to bring them back to the boat.

After two months of land-travel we discovered we needed to add pages to our passports, and found that to be an easy process at an American Embassy in Brazil. Soon it was time to return to the boat, and it was also time to talk about all the sensitive topics that we avoided discussing on the boat. On the boat we knew we had to keep peace because our lives depended upon each another, but on land we had the luxury of having open and frank discussions. I was able to tell Tom how much stronger I felt on land, how I felt more in control of myself, and how good it felt not to be constantly fighting seasickness, but the issue of whether or not we would cross the Pacific still hung unanswered.

THE BREAK-IN

We saw happiness fall off the faces of workers when they saw us enter the boatyard. Such puzzling behavior was confusing and alarming. The absolutely worst thing we could think of was that our boat had fallen off its cradle, but we knew that had not happened because we could see VONNIET-T standing exactly where we left her. As we continued to walk across the yard toward the office, we could feel their eyes following our every move. The tension in the air clearly said something was wrong. Tom's pace changed to long deliberate strides – a sort of I'm-in-control-of-myself type of gait, and I scurried along behind him. When we reached the office he knocked once, stepped up onto the single cement block that served as a step, and entered without waiting for a response. I followed right on his heels.

"Ah," the yard manager said with false bravado, while quickly pulling down his t-shirt that had been rolled up to cool his fat, round tummy. "So you have returned. How was your trip?"

"It was fine," Tom said. "How were things here?"

"Well, yes, ahem — not so good, actually," he stammered. "We had a little problem." Slowly and painfully he explained that our boat had been broken into. He told us they immediately notified the police and that everyone hoped the police would be able to get our things back — that is, after we told them what was missing. "The police," we were told, "probably would have found your things right away, but they didn't know what to look for because they didn't know what the thieves had taken."

We almost felt it was our fault for being away. The long and short of it was we needed to go through the boat and make a list of the missing items.

While we received the unhappy news, the worker bees in the yard placed a ladder up onto the side of our boat. Everyone in the yard knew we would want to get on board right away. Tom went up first. He slid the hatch back, complete with its broken clasp, and opened the portholes to let fresh air in and the stale heat out. I had already prepared myself to expect a messed-up cabin, assuming the thieves would have rummaged through things rapidly leaving behind chaos, but I was totally unprepared for having to deal with white fingerprint powder on everything! Much of the interior surface was covered with a thick layer of the stuff, even the burgundy velour seats. I couldn't vacuum it because the batteries on our hand vacuum were dead from sitting uncharged for so many months, and wiping it up was futile. The powder had a greasy feel, yet it was so fine that it seemed to float from one place to another. I felt we had been more violated by the police than by the thieves.

With a lot of effort we got the boat cleaned over the next couple of days and we tried to take inventory of the missing items but found it surprisingly difficult. Sometimes we didn't realize something was gone until we reached for it and it wasn't in its usual place. The yard agreed to purchase replacements for us or pay the equivalent in cash for everything that had been taken, so it was important that we try to identify exactly what was missing. The yard manager made every effort to appease us with the hope we would not speak negatively about them with the other cruisers. They recognized the power of the radio network among "yachties" and did not want us to promote a boycott of their yard. We were surprised to discover our list of missing items wasn't as long as we thought it would be: a VCR, a small TV, and some other small items. None of the equipment essential to sailing had been taken. Through the whole process, the yard was so kind and accommodating that we found ourselves promoting the yard in spite of the break-in, because we knew no American yard would have done that. We also knew the yard had increased its security and the chance of anything like that happening again was remote.

CHILDREN UNIFORMED AND ARMED

Boats were not meant to be up on land and it felt good to have VONNIE-T back in the water. We anchored near Puerto La Cruz in a small anchorage with good protection from the surge. Being at anchor where the boat could swing freely to capture a nice breeze through the cabin, was a nice change from the Cumana Marina.

It was there that we met Linda and Dave on REBECCA. Their boat was aluminum and

Woman cruisers went out for lunch and shopping in Puerto La Cruz, Venezuela on Tuesdays.

built specifically for Dave so he could handle it in spite of his withered arm. We were impressed with his quick mind and careful planning. They had been cruisers much longer than we had, and spent most of that season at that anchorage. Linda told us Tuesdays were considered ladies day, which meant that all the women went to town together for a day of shopping and lunch. A lot of useful information was shared within the group, including which store got a fresh batch of peanut butter and where we could purchase a whole deboned chicken stuffed with apricots or prunes. All week I looked forward to the one day when I could dress up and talk about things completely unrelated to the mechanics of the boat.

There was discord and unrest in Venezuela. Student demonstrations had become commonplace, and the military was often called in to break them up. Seldom, however did the politics of the country affect those of us who lived out on the water, and frankly, the mood of the demonstrations we had witnessed never felt particularly hostile. It seemed to us that most of the demonstrations were merely a show for benefit of the press.

One Tuesday a student demonstration was scheduled on the same day the women planned to meet in Puerto LaCruz for lunch and shopping. The demonstration was not a secret and we all knew about it, but we ignored it as we had the others. We should have known there was something different that day because the shop owners were in the process of closing up and barricading their doors and windows when we stepped off the bus. We were not able to shop, but the restaurant remained open, and we proceeded to have lunch and ignore the potential unrest. We spent the extra time laughing, talking and drinking more wine than we should have. At the designated time when we each needed to return to our boats at separate anchorages, we walked to our respective bus stops as we did every Tuesday, but the normal disorder of the streets was missing. Instead, we were ordered by military guards to line up in perfect queues while we waited for our buses. When each bus arrived only the number of riders who could be accommodated with a seat were allowed on board. A military guard with a machine gun was posted at each door. Theoretically, they were there to protect the passengers, not harm them. But they were mere boys; most were too young to shave and I was more afraid of one tripping over his shoelaces and setting off his automatic gun accidentally than I was of any student demonstrators. I had seen the poverty and slums from which these boys had been recruited, and I suspected they had been provided little training. Their lace-up leather boots did not fit properly, and I wondered if they were accustomed to wearing shoes at all, let alone big clumsy army boots. Luckily, there was no accident while Linda and I were on the bus, and the guards smiled and tipped their hats to us as we got off. Days later we heard about incidents reporting that people had been killed that day.

FRESH OYSTERS

The unrest had been highly dramatized in the American news media, and when our son, Clark, and his buddy Glen scheduled a flight to meet us, Clark's travel agent had been reluctant to book the flights. They came anyway, but not without some difficulty. I suppose two young men traveling with duffel bags and long, metal, spear guns instead of the typical tourist luggage, made them appear suspicious. Their bags were searched and they were interrogated at the airports at both ends. It was not the most ideal way to begin a vacation, but any anxieties they had enroute were completely forgotten once they were safely on the boat.

Clark immediately tossed his duffel bag into the V-berth and pulled out his diving gear. With spears in hand, he and Tom dove into the water to hunt for dinner – not that there wasn't enough food on board, but because it was just one of their favorite things to do.

While they hunted I was left to entertain Glen, who was experiencing an ocean for the first time. I noted a look of subtle panic in him at the thought of climbing down the boat ladder and actually getting into the water. I knew he was attempting to muster up his courage, and since Clark and Tom were already in the water, he was willing to try it, also. I guided him through his first snorkeling lesson:

"Blow out through your nose when you first put your face in the water. That will create a tight seal around your mask and prevent water from leaking in. Stretch out on your stomach and breath slowly through the snorkel. Bend your knees slightly and make long graceful sweeps with the fins. Try to relax and enjoy what you see around you."

Watching Glen adjust to the ocean environment brought back memories of how I felt that first time. It was nice to see that same excitement in him that I had once felt. I had become so accustomed to the water by then that I had forgotten what it was like to see all those things for the first time. It was a joy to see sea life again through his virgin eyes, sort of like seeing Christmas through a child's eyes.

Each day we anchored and swam in a new location and one day we anchored near a boat called BANDITTE with Bente and Ole on board. Ole earned his living by writing articles for a cruising magazine in Denmark. We could hear him clacking away in his cockpit on a small manual typewriter, and while he wrote Bente did a lioness's share of the boat chores. They appeared to be a good team, and they lived more simply than any boater we had previously met. When we took the dinghy over to say hello and introduce ourselves, they told us the other side of the boat was the preferable side for us to visit them because the side we were on was used for their "boo bucket."

"Your what?" I asked, not grasping the jest of the conversation at all.

"Our 'boo bucket'," Bente said in casual manner.

I still didn't understand and finally Clark had to tell me, "The bucket they use for their head, Mom."

"Oh," was the only response I could utter.

They lived off the sea as much as possible and told us about a nearby reef where we could get all the oysters we could eat. Ole whetted our interest and desire to harvest the oysters, so we invited them to sail with us and show us the exact spot. Ole was delighted.

Son, Clark, with Bente and Ole from BANDITTE shown here eating raw oysters with fresh limes.

He showed us exactly where to anchor, and for the better part of that day we collected oysters by cutting them off of a sheer reef wall with heavy diver's knives. After gathering plenty, and when everyone was exhausted and waterlogged, they showed us how to eat raw oysters with salt and fresh lime juice. It was a great afternoon.

The next day we went back and anchored in front of Puerto La Cruze. Clark noticed there were young women near his age on one of the neighboring boats. Much like a male peacock trying to attract the female, he dove into the water with a big splash. I could hardly believe my eyes, and then in a loud voice I heard him say, "Mom, would you mind tossing down the shampoo? I think I'll wash my hair."

I didn't understand what was happening until I heard him say to the two lovely young ladies looking down in the water at him, "Oh, hi. Are you vacationing on a boat, too?" As corny as the whole scene was, it worked. He wasted no time at all in arranging dinner dates for that night.

All too soon Clark's vacation was over and we arranged with "Clunker," a German retiree living in Venezuela, to take the boys to the airport. Clunker drove an old beater that appropriately matched the name of his taxi service, but he was reliable and we knew we could count on him to be at the boat at whatever time we required, even though it was the middle of the night.

We didn't have a chance to feel too blue when Clark and Glen left, because we immediately got word that Andy and our dentist friends, Mark and Michelle would be arriving shortly. We took a bus to meet them at the Caracas airport and took the opportunity to take some side trips on the way back to the boat.

We stopped at Merida, an Andean village 5,000 feet above sea level, rode the Teleferica (cable-car) up to the top of Pico Bolivar, and swam in one of nature's self-made spas high in the Andes.

THE ENGINE RECEIVED A NAUTICAL ENEMA

Once we were back on the boat, we sailed to a different anchorage each day. Tom and Andy fished with a troll line behind the boat and caught several fish. As soon as the anchor was down, we all went in the water. Some of us went sightseeing while Tom and Andy hunted with spear guns. Between the two modes of fishing we had more fish than I had space for in the refrigerator or freezer, and we were able to give fish away to other boaters in the anchorage. I was faced with trying to make fish taste different each night. We had Spanish mackeral, yellowtail snapper, grouper, and wahoo. I found I could stir-fry wahoo because it had a firm texture and large flakes of meat, and it also held up well in fish chowder, while some of the mushier fish could only be fried lightly, baked or poached.

With people vacationing on board, we vacationed as well, which meant we did not do any boat maintenance, and used our time to swim, fish, explore, and play. We had nearly perfect sailing winds of 15 to 25 knots out of the east and lots of sunshine. After breakfast each morning, we would pull up our anchor, sail for a few hours, then put the anchor down in a new anchorage by midday. One day we had a change in wind direction and we sailed with 8 – 10 foot seas and a 30-knot following sea. It was not a pleasant sail! Following seas were the absolutely worst for making me feel seasick, but a greater concern was when the engine nearly didn't start just when we needed it before entering the Los Roques.

Tom had to coax it to turn over by removing the injectors, and then he turned the engine over with a battery and pumped water out of the exhaust manifold and piston chambers. He explained, "Our engine was below the waterline and the exhaust was just barely above the waterline. That's OK under normal conditions because there is a loop in the exhaust line to keep the water out, but with a following sea the water managed to back up into the exhaust manifold and the poor engine got a nautical enema."

Luckily, Tom knew how to flush what needed to be flushed, and we hoped the saltwater hadn't been in the engine long enough to do any serious damage.

LOBSTER HEAVEN

Eventually Mark and Michelle's vacation time came to an end and they flew home, but Andy decided to take another quarter off from school. While he was with us, we met up with friends Neil and Scarlet on LEBENHO. Neil was just as big a fishing nut as Andy and

Tom, so we decided to sail in tandem to the Los Aves Islands, a group of remote islands just north of Caracas. Both Tom and Neil had become excellent snorkelers. They could each free-dive to 20 feet or more without the use of a tank, and they enjoyed hunting the coral reefs together.

When we arrived at the Los Aves Islands, Tom stood on the bow and directed my steering with hand signals through the maze of coral heads. Carefully we threaded our way around large heads of brain coral, through crevices of swishing fans of fan coral, and we motored past other kinds of coral we'd never seen before. LEBENHO followed closely behind us deep into the interior of the reef until we found an area wide enough to allow swing room for both boats to anchor. In no more than 10 feet of water we dropped the anchor, and Tom dove overboard to make certain it was firmly planted in the sand. With our six-foot draft we had only four extra feet of water under us. Tom surfaced laughing like a lunatic and babbling about lobster being all over waiting to be picked up. As soon as the sails were down and stowed, we were all in the water to check out the sights. Sure enough, there were lots of lobsters and in a very short time the guys had speared all we could eat. The next day when Andy, Neil, and Tom went hunting they became much more selective. They took no female lobsters, (the ones with the small pinchers on their hind legs) especially those with eggs. Still, they brought up more lobsters than we could eat in one night. Again we gorged ourselves, and I put some in the refrigerator. By the third day we did not want to taste another lobster for a long time. We had had our fill of the rich delicacy, and their hunt reverted to finding grouper, a mild, tasty fish. (See Color Photo Insert, page 10.)

SHIPS LOG TOM'S ENTRY: APRIL 14, 1990
Los Aves de Barlovento: 12°N Latitude, 67°W Longitude.

"Wow, today I saw something that possibly no other human being has ever seen. I watched a female lobster plant embryo. This fine lady was in the birthing process and instantly I knew I was in for a view of one of nature's wonders. The male Spiny Lobster has ten legs, each with a toenail-like pointed foot. The female also has ten legs, but the rear pair is equipped with a small pincer for birthing. My lady lobster friend was busily taking eggs from an opening in her body, dipping them in semen that had previously been deposited on her carapace by a male, and then planting the new embryo under her tail. It was so fascinating that I took a dozen or so trips to the surface for air, returning to the birthing depth, in wonderment. The process was going rapidly and she was planting embryo at the rate of about one per second using each of her hind legs alternately. She probably saw me, but wasn't threatened as I stayed out of her "zone". I understand that the full process involves thousands of embryos, and it occurs only once a year. So, what are the odds of me being in the right place at the right time? Thousands of new baby lobsters sounds like a lot, but at first they are very small and once they are on their own they are called zooplankton. Lots of critters in the sea eat zooplankton, so hopefully, if a few survive, the species will flourish.

A SOBERING STORY ABOUT A SHARK BITE

We were surprised when a boat flying a Venezuelan flag anchored near us. Neither of us had ever met the people on board, but it didn't take long for us to all get acquainted. The captain was a retired Mexican doctor who had a Venezuelan girlfriend with him. He spoke both Spanish and English, but was eager to be in the company of English-speaking people. When he spied our American flags, he quickly became the third boat in our private little group out in the middle of nowhere. Our attempt to befriend his girlfriend failed, however, because our Spanish was too limited and her English was nonexistent. As a result, she kept to herself while the rest of us socialized. I felt sorry for her because I remembered how lonely and useless I felt during our first year on the boat, yet there did not seem to be anything we could do to help her.

The doctor did not seem the least concerned about her and had lots of interesting stories he gladly shared with us. One story was about a shark attack on a couple who dove and hunted just like us. "The husband did all the hunting," he told us. "He took each fish off his spear and threaded it onto the stringer for his wife to hold. She swam behind him with the stringer until they returned to their dinghy together. Unfortunately, the fish on the stringer floated next to her leg while she swam, and one time a shark lunged out and took a bite of the fish she was carrying. I don't think the shark meant to bite her leg. Her leg just happened to be in the way of the fish, but the long and short of it was that the flesh on most of one leg had been ripped away. Shark's teeth go in every direction, you know, and they do an excellent job of tearing anything they put their teeth into." I shivered while listening to the story. He went on to tell us how he treated her, what unsightly scars it left, and how she almost died from the infection. Infection is apparently the biggest problem with a shark bite.

THE MAN WHO WOULDN'T EAT "VEGETERRIBLES"

Without a care in the world, the occupants of our three boats played each day in our own private Garden of Eden, but then a sobering thing happened. A dinghy with a motor on it washed across the reef, and we could see it bobbing against coral. I know we all dreaded the possibility of finding dead bodies, but with mixed emotions we went to investigate it. Much to everyone's relief, no one was in it at all, dead or alive. It was an empty dinghy in perfect condition and seemed to have appeared like manna from heaven.

Over the radio the next morning, I asked if anyone had lost a dinghy and motor, but nothing had been reported missing. The announcement was made three days in a row and when no one claimed it, we divided up the find as equitably as possible. The doctor took the dinghy and our old motor, we took the new 15 HP motor, and the doctor gave LEBEN-

HO cash. Everyone was happy with the arrangement.

We stayed at that anchorage, a virtual water playland of wonderment and excitement, until we began to run out of supplies. First, we ran out of propane cooking gas and had to begin cooking everything in the microwave. Next, we ran out of dinghy fuel, but that was not a big problem because we could either swim or row the boat for the short distances that we needed it. When our food supplies began to get low it was more of an annoyance than a major concern because we certainly had an abundance of seafood, though there was not much in the way of side dishes left in the boat larder. But when our water supply got low, the situation worsened, so with great reluctance we left to re-provision.

We sailed to Bonaire, one of the Dutch ABC islands in The Netherland Antilles. The water around the island was warm and crystal clear, making it inviting for diving, and there was also no shortage of tourists to patronize the scuba resort, in spite of its cost and lack of amenities. The island people wanted to maintain a laid-back quiet tourist trade. One night each week the resort showed a movie for its guests and anyone else who wanted to attend the outdoor movie. It was great! All the tourists we met were happy with their meager accommodations. They loved the simplicity of life on the island and the beauty of what they saw in the water each day.

Tom and Andy seemed to be the only sourpusses on the island. They were unhappy because there was no hunting allowed in the ocean around Bonaire. The resort business knew it had to preserve its natural resources, and the only hunting allowed was done with a camera. We weren't even allowed to anchor near the islands because of concern that anchors might injure the coral, so we were tied up to a pier in their marina next to a small European boat. After a brief conversation with our neighbors they invited us to join them at the Green Parrot for lunch.

"They make a really great half-pound hamburger there," he said enticing us to join them, "and they don't serve any of those yellow and green things." Andy's eyes grew large when he heard the word "hamburger." It had been a long time since any of us had had red meat.

"Yellow and green things?" Tom asked. "What are you talking about? I don't understand."

"You know," he said, "those vegeterrible things. I don't eat anything that's yellow or green! Stick to the browns and tans. That's what I say."

We all laughed and agreed to go with them for lunch. I was interested to hear about their passage across the Atlantic and was especially eager to talk to them about the foods they took with them, because they were both large people and obviously interested in food.

They were in perfect agreement. "You must take all the comfort foods you can possibly put on your boat before any major crossing. Don't worry about the things you think you should have with you 'cause you won't eat 'em anyway. Just take lots of the stuff you like to eat cause that's what you're going to eat."

THE ROGUE WAVE

Andy had to get back to school before the next quarter began and when we returned after taking him to the small Bonaire airport, the boat seemed painfully empty. I washed his bedding and towels, and could see Tom's moist eyes look toward his empty V-berth.

We left the marina the next morning and headed to a small anchorage. We were surprised to see a 35-foot sailboat floating freely while the owners dove deep into the water around it. They had only snorkel equipment, no diving equipment or tanks, so they surfaced often for air. After getting our sails down and anchoring securely we swam over to meet them to see what they were doing.

"Hi," they said. "We're looking for our anchor. We'd love to have your help."

"Sure," we responded. "How did you lose your anchor?"

"Well, we were just sitting in the cockpit eating our breakfast and we saw a huge rogue wave coming in at us. I can't even imagine how high that wave was. It was way over our mast though, I can tell you that," the captain said. "Anyway, I knew right away that this wave would have pushed us right up onto the shore, so I cut the anchor line and we motored right at it, heading out to sea. Then it took an hour or more before this anchorage settled down enough for us to return and look for our anchor. I hated to cut the line on it, but there just wasn't enough time to try and pull it up. We just had to go as soon as we saw it. Anyway, I'm not sure what we're going to do if we can't find it. I don't really have a reliable spare."

We had read about waves like that and were grateful that we had never experienced one at anchor, but we were happy to be able to help them and get our minds off of our empty boat. We tethered their boat next to ours with several fenders between us, and I tended both sailboats while the three of them searched the newly sifted ocean floor for the missing anchor. The couple was excited and relieved when the anchor was finally located.

THEY GOT STUCK AT THE SALTWATER LAKE

The Netherland Antillies is made up of three islands often referred to as the ABC islands, with each letter representing one of the island names: Aruba, Bonaire and Curaço.

At Curaço, we anchored at the Sarifundy Marina where there were many live-aboard cruisers, most having been anchored in the same spot for years. We could only imagine how reef-like and barnacled the bottoms of their boats must have been. We could understood why they stayed, though, because it was a very comfortable anchorage, perhaps the most comfortable we had experienced. The water was perfectly still, with total protection from ocean surge, making it more like a saltwater lake than an ocean.

The marina had a large, wooden dinghy dock low to the water, making it easy to climb up onto the dock. It was wide enough to accommodate several dinghies at any given time and had no sharp objects sticking out to puncture the rubber sides. Another bonus was bus service within walking distance. Perhaps most impressive was a refrigerator stocked with beer. Boaters were asked to deposit money in a small-cardboard box each time they helped themselves to a beverage. To see that kind of trust was exceptional!

Downtown Willemstad, a short bus ride away, was highly civilized and oozed with Dutch charm. It was divided into two parts: Punda and Otrabanda, and connected by a floating pedestrian bridge named the Queen Emma. A large open market operated daily along the water canals. As protection from the sun each vendor covered his stand with a different-colored fabric that was also used as an enticement to purchase items from their stand. For example; "Get the best-tasting tomatoes here under the red awning." Even if we didn't purchase tomatoes that day the idea was planted in our minds that the red awning vendor had the best-tasting tomatoes.

The purchase that excited us the most was the Dutch varnish Epiphane. We had learned about it from other cruisers at one of the Seven Seas Cruiser's meetings, and we used it whenever we could find it. It was superior to any of the other varnishes in that it held up much longer under the harsh sun and saltwater environment. It wasn't easy to find, and when we did it usually cost a little more than other brands, but we did not mind the added expense.

The quiet anchorage offered a marvelous opportunity to get a lot of work done. I put several coats of fresh varnish on all our exterior teak, while Tom attacked several jobs on his list. First, he removed the water heater that hogged engine room space and cleaned and painted both engines. He installed the new, low-power autohelm, and together we waterproofed the bimini. It was marvelous to have a quiet anchorage to get all those tasks accomplished and we could understand how the other cruisers had become sort of stuck there. Curaço was friendly, colorful, clean, and neat, and there was little motivation to leave.

A SEA SLEIGH RIDE

If we had not been in ham radio contact with Jim and Carolyn Schafer on MORNING TIDE, whom we first met in St. Thomas, we may not have moved on so quickly either, but they whetted our appetites to see Colombia. Carolyn was the cruiser who had been mugged outside the bank on St. Thomas and had her wedding rings sucked off her finger by the thug. If she said Colombia was safe, I believed her. Everyone else spoke about Colombia with great apprehension, but not them. They had only good things to say about the country, and they especially liked the city of Cartegena.

The one caution they had was about a malaria epidemic rampant in Panama and the San Blas Islands. So just before leaving Curraco, we visited a Dutch doctor to stock up on malaria prevention medication. The malaria we heard about was a cloroquine-resistant strain, and the doctor told us the World Health Organization recommended that we protect ourselves by taking Fansidar before we entered the San Blas islands off the coast of Panama. He didn't think we would need it for Colombia but encouraged us to purchase the pills and begin taking them one week before entering the San Blas islands.

"Take one pill a week," he instructed, "and begin by taking your first pill one week prior to when you will be in a malaria area. These pills should protect you against all strains of malaria, including the chloroquine-resistant type."

We left his office feeling secure in the knowledge that we had once again acted responsibly. The next day we stocked the boat with fresh food, filled our water, gas and propane tanks, and headed toward Cartegena, Colombia.

When we checked out of the country, the official said, "You sure you want to go to Colombia? You know, you look like nice people, so I'm gonna tell you. I see people leave here for Colombia all the time and they never come back. Do you know what I'm saying? There are a lot of things that just happen out on the ocean in the drug-running business and we just never hear from a lot of those people again. Are you sure you want to go to Colombia?"

We thanked him, completed our checkout, and headed out to sea. We discounted the Colombia narco and pirate stories and were pleased to see there was no bad weather forecast anywhere near us. That first night we enjoyed cool, crisp temperatures and the clutter of stars in the sky. We also enjoyed going downwind for a change; Tom had all our sails up, including the big 150% genoa headsail, and we flew along at 7 knots. On the second day the winds picked up, but it was still a comfortable downwind ride, and our new autopilot did a fine job of steering a compass course of 287 degrees. We wanted to stay far off the coast of Colombia, far away from the strong current of the Rio Madgalena River near Cartagena. When the winds continued to build, Tom dropped the mainsail and rolled in the genoa. He raised the staysail and poled it out on the leeward side. We expected the winds to diminish, but instead they continued to build. It began to feel as if we were riding a toboggan down a very wet mountain, and soon we wished we had had less sail up. We especially wished we did not have the whisker-pole up, but it was too late for wishing and too dangerous for Tom to be up on deck to try to take it down, so we disconnected the autopilot and took turns hand steering. We could not take a chance of having the autopilot not correct rapidly enough and cause us to broach. (Broaching is getting sideways in the trough of a big wave and then having the mast knocked into the water).

The winds continued to build until they reached gale force, 35 to 45 knots, and the seas were 15 to 20 feet on our stern. Hand steering became difficult and required our total concentration. We knew we were sailing down the backs of each wave much too fast, nearly out of control, making helm duty frightening. One wrong move and we could easily get knocked down, and if that happened and we took water into the cabin, the boat would surely sink.

We closed all the hatches and clipped ourselves to the cockpit with safety harnesses. If we were knocked down, we would have all we could do to prevent the boat from filling with water, and we needed to make sure neither of us got washed overboard. We took turns wrenching at the helm by putting our full body weight into the steering wheel. One moment we were at dizzying heights on the crest of a wave and the next moment we were nearly smothered deep in a watery trough. Such demanding helm duty could only be done for about 20 minutes at a time, and I soon found my muscles achy and shaky from fatigue. Steering drained us both mentally and physically, so much so that when it was our turn to rest we each lay on the floor of the cockpit and fell sound asleep. One time when Tom finished his watch and turned the wheel over to me, he was so tired that he began snoring in an upright position within seconds of having sat down. He was completely exhausted and running on nothing but raw nerves, but in less than three minutes he jumped up and said, "OK, it's my turn."

The pressure and responsibility on each of us was enormous. Just one wrong move or turn of the wheel could easily have been fatal. If the sea had swallowed us up, no one would ever have known what happened to us, but I suspect everyone would have assumed we had met our demise as a result of pirates or drug runners. Instead, we were on a very wet sleigh ride, and I doubted that any drug runners would have been crazy enough to be out in those conditions.

Over the next six hours we traded off doing wheel duty at 20-minute intervals. When we finally neared the mouth of the Cartegena harbor, the wind began to let up. By then we were completely exhausted but the favorable change in conditions was so uplifting that fatigue seemed a small matter. I was so happy to see the harbor entrance that I did not even think about the possibility of the engine not starting due to the following seas we had just endured, but Tom worried about it without mentioning it to me.

The harbor was huge, almost a sea all by itself. We checked our charts, changed course, took down the staysail and whisker pole, and put up our mainsail. There were several shallow areas requiring that we stay alert and follow the channel markers, as we steered for Club Nautico on MORNING TIDE'S recommendation. As we neared the docking area, Tom turned on the engine to ease our docking, and he was greatly relieved when it turned over with no problems.

"I was pretty worried that it wouldn't start," he said, "but I guess we sailed down those waves so fast that the water wasn't able to enter the exhaust system."

We were greeted at the dock by three local men and a senorita who helped us stern tie to their pier with about 10 other boats; four were American, one from El Salvador, and the others from Colombia. In the spirit of friendliness, they brought us cold beers as a welcoming gift. Everything about the harbor looked beautiful to me on that sunlit Monday morning, and we were happy to be there. It happened to be a Colombian holiday, which meant most of the town was closed, but that was O.K. with us. We needed rest before beginning the check-in process, and we could easily wait a day before we began exploration of our new surroundings.

We needed to figure out a way of getting on and off the boat while it was stern tied. We noticed several of the other boats had a wooden plank running from their boat to the pier, and Tom dug out the old fender board that he still had stowed under the bunk in the side cabin. He drilled two holes in one end and tied a short rope through each hole. Then he slid the plank to the pier and secured our end to the stanchions off the stern of our boat. (See Color Photo Insert, page 19.)

"That should do it," he said as he stood up and proudly examined his work.

I could only think, "My God, am I going to have to walk on that?"

There was a lot of boat activity in the harbor, including taxi boats, and they all created water movement that in turn caused the plank to sway up and down. I was petrified at the prospects of having to walk on that plank with nothing to hang on to for added balance.

After introductions and drinking our beer, we washed the salt off the boat with the fresh water hoses at the dock and went below for much-needed showers and naps. Even the noise of outboard motors and the rock-and-roll activity of the water didn't keep us awake, and as far as the board was concerned, I knew I'd learn to walk that plank after I'd had a full night's sleep.

CHAPTER SIX

A World Awaits Through the Canal

SEARCHING FOR THE FLAPPER VALVE

Before seeing Colombia, I had always surmised it was a backward Third World country, but after seeing it firsthand and reading a little of its history, my view changed. Colombia is an old and politically seasoned country with a long, interesting history, but not backward, ignorant, or undeveloped.

I was eager to explore the city of Cartagena further, but Tom, being far more pragmatic, insisted that we first address the problem of our exhaust system. He was adamant about wanting to prevent water from entering the engine again, should we be in following seas. So we walked and walked, checking every shop in the city we thought might carry flapper valves, and in the process we found ourselves talking to many Colombians and seeing a lot of the city. It wasn't the part of the city I was most interested in seeing; nevertheless, we quickly became familiar with every corner of the working part of the city.

We learned how to use the local bus system to go to the areas we couldn't reach on foot. On one occasion an *ejecutiveo* bus stopped for us. The fare was posted at the door, and it cost two and half times more than the regular bus, so we motioned for it to go on without us. While we waited for the regular bus Tom did the exchange-rate calculations to determine our equivalent cost of the bus we had motioned to go on. We were embarrassed to realize we rejected a ride that cost 25 cents in order to wait for a 10-cent ride.

After developing a better understanding of the Colombian money, we realized our exchange rate made everything extremely inexpensive, so much so that we occasionally even took a taxi. During one of our taxi rides, we got into a small fender-bender-type of accident with another taxi. After the impact, my first thought was one of relief that no one was injured, but that was quickly followed by a thought of dread. I fully expected that we would find ourselves in the middle of an escalating fight between the drivers, and I could tell Tom must have had similar thoughts, because when our eyes met they seemed to say, "Be ready for just about anything." We sat quietly frozen in the back seat and spoke not a word. Both drivers stepped out to inspect the damage and then the least expected thing happened. Our driver returned to his taxi, stepped in and we drove away. He did not even seem upset. Instead, he began talking to us in fairly good English. When he grasped for an English word, we were sometimes able to supply the Spanish word. So with our limited Spanish and his limited English, we were able to converse with him. He was interested in finding out who we were, where we were from and, what we were doing in Colombia. I think he thought we were Canadians, because when he learned we were Americans, he laughed, and asked, "Aren't you Americans supposed to be afraid to be here?"

We knew he was right. The U.S. State Department had issued a suggestion that all American travel in Colombia be postponed due to the potential for danger. It was a little embarrassing to be sitting in the back of his taxi and having to acknowledge that. We found the people kind and rather gentle, not like what we had read in the press. Since we were not rich, not involved in politics, and were in no way involved with the drug trade, we felt perfectly safe. However, when we ate out in restaurants at night, we noticed large extended families, often with a conspicuous absence of middle-aged men. Neither of us spoke of it, but one couldn't help wonder where the men in those families were. Had they been murdered, as the press would lead us to believe?

THE MISSING DURUM

While still trying to sort through the mixed messages about the country, we made friends with a handsome Colombian man on one of the boats in the marina. He was a single-hander and seemed rather lonely, and since we were eager to show off the new cockpit table Tom had just built, we invited him to join us for a spaghetti dinner. We looked forward to an interesting evening with local conversation and perhaps an opportunity to better understand the area's politics. Imagine our surprise when we learned the Vice President's brother was sitting at our dinner table! Over a glass of wine he told us he "was a rich man because he was invisible and could safely go about with his life" —unlike his prestigious brother who constantly lived "in fear of his life."

My sauce was delicious but I was embarrassed when it came time to serve the pasta. For some reason it had become mushy, and I thought I had gotten so interested in the conversation that I'd overcooked it. I apologized as I served.

"Is this Colombian pasta?" he asked me.

"Yes, I just bought it today," I told him.

"That's the problem," he said. "Colombian pasta doesn't have durum in its flour and it will never have the firm texture that pasta in your country has." We had expected to learn something about the politics of Colombia that night, but I never expected to receive a lesson on the chemical make-up of pasta from a male Colombian.

GUNS POINTED AT US

By afternoon the following day, our search for a valve finally paid off, and we were elated to find a threaded, three-inch, bronze, flapper-type check-valve. It was designed to swing open under normal conditions and let the exhaust out, but gravity would swing it shut when seawater tried to enter from the stern. The only problem was that the valve required hookup with a three-inch hose, and the only adapter from thread to hose that could be found was made of aluminum. Tom was aware of the potential problems of electrolytic corrosion between dissimilar metals, but that was all that was available and he really did not know how rapidly the corrosion would take place. If it took years, it really wouldn't matter because we did not plan to live on the boat for years. He installed the flapper valve and was very pleased with the results.

The summer weather in Cartagena was the same everyday; hot and sunny. The thermometer seemed almost stuck at 100 degrees Fahrenheit. Many wealthy Colombians have summer apartments or flats on the waterfront, and with the valve finally installed we decided to ride slowly around the harbor in our dinghy just to see what there was to see. We noticed a large, attractive residential area and motored past it slowly, but were met with armed gunmen who shooed us away. Later we learned from the Vice President's brother that it was the President's summerhouse. Further down the harbor we motored past an old, anchored battleship, but once again military personal pointed guns at us and motioned for us to leave.

We decided there must be safer ways for us to handle the heat. One was to indulge in smoothies at any number of the fruit stands along the harbor front. Colombia had wonderful fruits. (See Color Photo Insert, page 19.) Many of them were new to us and came from the tropical interior. Women often sold fruit from large baskets that they carried on their heads, and we could hear them soliciting for trade long before we could see them. All the local fruit was tasty, and at 20 cents a smoothie, Tom sometimes ordered two for himself. He also liked the local Aquila beer and began carrying cases of it back to the boat. It wasn't pasteurized, which meant he occasionally got a bad bottle, but for the most part he liked the flavor and at 10 cents for a 10-ounce bottle, it was a great bargain.

One day we visited an old Franciscan Catholic Church that had been turned into a museum. It housed an assortment of grotesque torture racks which had been used during the Inquisition, and we saw the little window where people had been encouraged to leave anonymous tips about suspected infidels. A neighbor or relative would slip the name of someone they did not like into the window and that person would be brought in and tortured until they confessed to being a witch or having done other heretical crimes. History acknowledges the cruelty and unjustness of the Inquisition, yet in its day it was practiced in the name of God, and no one challenged it.

THE PARTY

The ham radio community kept us in contact with other English-speaking people every place we went, and Colombia was no exception. One evening we were invited to a party hosted by Americans who lived in Cartegena. One of the people I had been in regular contact with over the past several months agreed to pick us up at the marina and drive us to the apartment complex where the party was to be held. We were informed that nearly everyone at the party would be American and would speak English, but we were not told what these Americans were doing in Colombia. We wondered if there was an American company there that we were not aware of. Or we thought they might have some government positions at an embassy. It even crossed my mind that they may be involved with the war on drugs.

It turned out they were missionaries out to destroy the very core of Colombian family life. First, it was the Catholics who forced the people to accept their religion and denounce all the cultural rituals that had worked for thousands of years, and now these Protestants were trying to reform the Catholics. We were shocked and angered by the arrogance of the missionary philosophy. What did those missionaries think happened to the family when one member became converted to a faith different from the other family members? Of course they became a splintered family. I have no idea why we didn't voice our opinion, but we did not, and instead made every attempt to avoid being rude and left just as soon as it was gracefully possible to do so.

SEEING OTHER PARTS OF COLOMBIA

The more we mingled with the local people, the more fascinated we became with the country, and when ham radio friends Erik and Lucy Fog invited us to visit them at their country home outside of Bogota, we readily accepted. Lucy was a Colombian who married a man from Denmark, and we had no fear of either of them being missionaries.

Our only concern was leaving the boat unattended, because shortly after arriving at Cartegena, we experienced a storm and had seen first-hand the ravages of what happened when wind and waves whistled down the long fetch of that harbor. The buildup of waves broke lines and pulverized boats that were tied to the pier. We had been awakened in the middle of the night when that storm blew in. Since we were on board, we were able to release our dock lines, pull in our walking plank, and motor away from the pier. We hovered out away from the dock and the other boats until the storm was over, and then we anchored there for the rest of the night to allow time for the wave action to settle down. Several other live-aboard cruisers had done the same thing. During the height of the storm, it was pitch-black out and the only time we could see what was happening was when lightning lit the sky, but we were able to hear the destructive sounds of boats as they smashed against the pier, and each other. During one brilliant bolt of lightning, we saw the bow of one unattended boat "hole" the side of the boat next to it. The wave action caused the beating to continue all night until the lifelines and stanchions were ripped off the deck. We heard the shrouds as they snapped and twanged into the air. The final blow came when the mast plummeted down in pieces, spearing a hole through the deck of the boat that had begun all the damage. Listening to the devastation and being unable to prevent any of it was terrible, but seeing the full extent of the damage the next morning was worse.

Witnessing that storm before our land trip provided valuable information on how we could best protect our boat in our absence. We put an anchor out off the bow and tied the stern of our boat to the pier with a light sacrificial line, one that would break easily if there were strong winds or waves. If a storm blew up while we were gone causing the line to break, VONNIE-T would swing out away from the pier and hang on its anchor. That way VONNIE-T would be safe and cause no damage to neighboring boats. LEBENHO, with Neil and Scarlett, was tied to the same pier and they promised to bring our boat's stern back to the pier when it was safe to do so. If they had not been there to keep an eye on VONNIE-T, we may not have considered going.

First, we took a bus ride to Bucaramanga through an area that looks like our Grand Canyon, which was breathtaking in both a beautiful and frightening way. Often there was no shoulder on the road and it appeared that we could easily fall off the side of the mountain. The sleepy village of Bucaramanga was primarily a pleasant resort town, also full of a lot of young people, mostly backpackers. Later, we flew to Bogota, transferring planes in Cali, the well-known city of drug barons. The Cali airport was as good as any we had ever seen. Apparently a lot of private money had gone into its design and embellishments, because it was artistic, modern, and comfortable.

We found Bogota to be a wonderful surprise, too. It was modern and clean. I'm not sure how I expected it to look, but I did not think it would be a spotlessly clean version of any large city in the United States. It bustled with the kinds of activities we would expect to find in the United States. We found a moderately priced hotel and after checking in we walked up and down the tree-lined boulevards, looking at the shops and observing the people.

When we learned there was a big gold museum near our hotel and that it boasted of having over 36,000 artifacts of pre-Colombian gold on display, we decided to visit it. Pre-Columbian refers to the time period before Columbus discovered the Americas, and was the period when the Indians valued gold pieces for their cultural significance, not for the monetary value. When the Spanish conquistador, Hernando Cortez, first came to the Americas, the Emperor Montezuma gave him a whole room full of gold, as a good faith gesture, but it is reported that he was soon sorry for having done so.

Montezuma said to Cortez, "If I had known that you Christians would fight over my gold, I would not have given it to you, as I am a man of peace and harmony. I am amazed at your blindness and insanity, that you destroy these well-wrought objects and make sticks of them and that you – although friends – fight among yourselves over such a vile and petty thing. You would be wiser to be in your own country, so far from here, and where there are – you say – so many wise and cultured men, than to come here to fight in a land that is not yours and where we live happy." (Text: Carl Heinrik Langebaek, Pre-Columbian GOLD)

The gold ornaments on display were delicately designed, very different from our modern gold jewelry that is smooth and thick in appearance. The ornate detail of each piece was achieved by what is referred to as the Lost Wax method, in which the wax melts when the hot gold is poured into the mold. It's mind-boggling to realize that the Indian people knew and exercised this skill during pre-Columbian times.

We had a good night's sleep and the next morning we met up with Erik and Lucy Fog. We visited with them for a short time at their Bogota apartment which was large and decorated nicely. It covered an entire floor and would be considered lavish by anyone's standards. Erik got his car from the underground garage, and we rode with them to their farm. I tried to show off a little with my command of a few Spanish words and said something about their *granja*, the word in my Spanish dictionary for farm, but I was quickly corrected.

"We don't have a *granja*," Erick said. "A *granja* is a large farm that makes money. We have a *finca*. It's just a hobby farm."

When we arrived at the *finca*, the *campesino* family, who lived and worked the farm for the Fogs, met us. They were a young couple with one small child. I think the child was a girl but she was so shy that she never left the back of her mother's knees long enough for us to get a look at her. The *campesinos* cooked our food, served our meals, built a fire in the fireplace, served brandy after dinner, turned down our beds, milked the cows, and did all the other unseen work as though it was their pleasure to have the honor to serve us. They did all this for a minimum wage and the right to live in their own quarters on the farm. They seemed happy, and we never sensed a feeling of discontent, but we wondered how they could not resent the obvious gap of rich and poor, or the haves and have nots.

In the morning we walked through the tall green grass while a big breakfast of eggs and fresh ham was being cooked for us. It was easy to understand why people referred to the area as the place of eternal spring. It felt like any spring day in Minnesota. The morning and evening temperatures were cool year round, while the afternoon temperatures were warm and comfortable. The air was moist and smelled of tender green grass, and I breathed it deep into my lungs. Its essence made me homesick.

At the airport on the way back to the boat, we looked for an English language newspaper

A hobby farm (finca) in the rural area of Bogota, Colombia where the weather is always spring.

and found a Florida Union-Tribune. It was two days old, but that was current enough for us, so Tom bought it. Sharing the paper was never a problem with us. Tom begins with the front page and reads each section from front to back while I begin with the family or travel sections and read the other sections as Tom finishes with them. It has worked well for us for years. On that day I started with the travel section and was really excited when I saw there was a full article on Colombia. The young man who wrote the article claimed to have been in the very same cities we had just left, but he described them entirely differently. The more I read, the more disgruntled I became.

The headline read: *"Colombia is Still a Dangerous Place To Travel."*

"It may be years before you'll want to consider making Colombia a place to visit. The tension can be felt all around," he wrote. *"If you're in a restaurant and the waiter drops a tray of dishes you'll find yourself hiding under your table next to all the other patrons in the restaurant and you'll know you are in Colombia. At night you lay out your running shoes and a set of get away clothes then you push a dresser or chair in front of your bedroom door before you can feel secure enough to attempt getting a night's rest."*

We did not feel any of the tension he wrote about. Quite the contrary, the atmosphere in the restaurants was pleasant and cheerful. There was the usual noise when dishes and silverware were dropped or cleared from tables but no one exhibited a case of the jitters, from thinking the noise was from anything but the dishes. In our hotel room there was no sign of furniture having been slid across the room to block the door by any previous guests, and I doubted that the author of the article had ever been in Colombia. He claimed to have visited the same cities we had just been to, yet he did not describe any of the things we had seen or experienced.

The more I thought about it, the more annoyed I became. That was not credible journalism, and Americans had the right to get accurate information from their newspaper. Instead, it was a rehash of old fears based upon misinformation with no redeeming values. It hurt tourism in Colombia, cheated Americans of the opportunity to see and visit an interesting country, and provided no support for the courageous leaders of the country who were willing, at great risks to themselves, to stamp out the drug czars. The only one who benefited from the article was the author who obviously got paid for having written it, and I believed that was not fair. It motivated me to write a letter to the editor. I hoped that because I was an American writing from Colombia, with Colombian postage, the editor would give my letter a little notice, and acknowledge its credibility. Of course, I never received a reply, and I have no idea to this day if my letter appeared on the editorial page because it was months before we ever saw another Florida Union-Tribune.

An article of interest that we read in the local Colombian papers reported that the drug czar, Pablo Escobar, had offered to pay off the entire national debt of Columbia, amounting to some $20 billion dollars if he could have "peace with the government". We could not help wondering how much of that $20 billion would have come from the youth of America.

KUNAS AND MOLAS

North of Panama on the Caribbean side of the canal are the San Blas Islands. Each of the nearly 100 islands in the cluster is small, sometimes less than a mile across, and most are ringed with white sand and clear blue water. (See Color Photo Insert, page 20.) They are considered to be a part of Panama but are individually owned by extended families of Kuna Indians who have lived and farmed coconuts on them for thousands of years.

As we entered the San Blas group, we saw canoes sliding along the horizon, and I admired the courage the canoeists had to venture out into the open sea in what I deemed un-seaworthy craft. By comparison, our boat was a Sherman tank with full protection from the elements. We had sophisticated radar, state-of-the-art navigational equipment, high freeboards to prevent swamping from the waves, and comfortable living quarters. Their little boats had none of that, making them vulnerable to the wrath of the ocean and weather changes.

Our only vulnerability was our unfamiliarity with the islands and their navigational hazards. Even our sophisticated equipment could not compensate for our lack of local knowledge, and we needed to pay close attention and "read" the water.

Tom stood on the bow and kept a keen eye ahead so he could direct me around coral heads. The water was amazingly clear, making his duty fairly easy. When he spied a smallish island with a white sandy beach, we sailed toward it to investigate it as a possible anchorage for the night. As we neared the tiny island, we were delighted to find the waves had flattened and the water was calm and protected from ocean swells.

Tom directed me to head the boat up into the wind while he dropped our sails and then we motored the rest of the way toward the beach until he found the place he wanted to anchor. When our depth-meter indicated we were in 15 feet of water, he dropped the anchor and allowed a few moments for it settle into the bottom before motioning for me to put the boat in reverse, a procedure referred to as backing down on the anchor. Another hand-motion indicated I should put it back into neutral while he peered into the water to see how snug the anchor chain remained. We repeated those same steps again while he looked at a stationary point on land. If we stayed in the same place while backing down on the anchor the second time we felt reasonably sure our anchor was securely set. We began the routine of folding and covering our sails, but before we could finish the job, several canoes were bouncing along side.

The canoes were nothing more than dug out tree logs. They were crudely carved and appeared to be extremely unstable, and covered in some type of tar pitch that made long black streaks along our white fiberglass each time they bumped against it. The canoes were primitive entities worthy of a museum, and the canoeists were *National Geographic* material. (See Color Photo Insert, page 21.) No one was over five feet tall. They had dark skin, jet-black hair and eyes that looked like two pieces of charcoal. The men were dressed much as we were, with shorts and t-shirts, but the women wore brightly colored mismatched prints. Their skirts were pieces of multicolored fabric gathered around the waist, their puffy short-sleeved blouses had mola designs on the front and back, and they tied their thick black hair back with long red scarves. The men controlled the canoes while the women laid an assortment of molas on the side deck of our boat for my inspection in the hope that I would purchase them. What an amazing sight!

Not a word was spoken. All communication was done with the eyes and hand motions. In any other setting I might have been frightened by the presence of so many canoes and people swarming upon us, but the quietness of the scene calmed me and I felt no alarm.

Each mola is an 18-inch cloth square consisting of three or four layers of solid colored fabric. Crude designs were cut into the top layers, which were stitched back to allow the colorful designs of the under-layers to peek through the top layers. All the stitch-work had been done by hand and must have required many hours and thousands of tiny delicate stitches. The cost for each mola was $4, truly a bargain for such a labor-intensive pieces of work, yet I couldn't buy them all and I did not want to buy from one canoe and not the others. Overwhelmed by the situation, Tom suggested that I buy one mola from each canoe, so I unearthed some of our one-dollar bills and selected several molas. They seemed to understand that I was going to buy one, and only one, from each canoe and once I made a purchase from a canoe, they began to leave as silently as they had appeared, slipping across the horizon to wherever they had come from.

The next day we went ashore and met the family who lived on the island where we were anchored. They greeted us warmly. (See Color Photo Insert, page 20.) Most of the conversation was with the men, especially the older men who had learned English during the days when they worked on the Panama Canal. The oldest man was particularly proud of his gold tooth which he displayed with every smile.

"I got this when I worked for the Americans on the canal," he told us.

Seldom did the women speak, but when they did, they spoke in their Indian language. They proudly showed us the interior of their home, which consisted of two thatched huts. One was a cooking hut, the other a sleeping hut.

The cooking hut was a large open room with a sand floor that was swept with palm fronds. There were four long log benches placed in a square, where family members apparently sat facing one another while they ate and held discussions. I was surprised at how dark it was inside. The only light came from the daylight at the door and the small crevices between the fronds of thatched roof. It took a few minutes before my eyes adjusted from the contrasting brilliance of sun and glistening water. I noticed there was a fireplace built into the far corner of the room, and upon closer inspection I saw the cooking grate was made from fresh-cut green tree branches, with their one and only pot hanging on it. The concept of a wooden grill was difficult to imagine, but there it was. When the green branches became charred they were replaced with freshly cut ones.

The men fished and hunted while the women gathered roots, vegetables and herbs that went into their stew pot. Next to the fireplace, there was a large sack of rice that they brought with them from the mainland. Scooped-out coconut shells were used as bowls, and they must have drunk their meals from them because I saw nothing that resembled a spoon or fork.

The other hut was where the entire extended family slept, each person in his or her own hammock. During sleeping hours the hammocks were strung out across the room from one wall to the other. In the morning they were unhooked from one wall and hung on the other, thus making a large open space on the sand-floored room where the women could stretch out fabric and supplies when they made molas.

With great pride, they showed us their two water-wells that were nothing more than foot-wide holes dug down into the sand. There was no cement or protection around the holes to prevent sand or anything from falling down into them. Both wells contained fresh water but only one was used for drinking; the other was used for washing. They offered us the use of the wells if we needed fresh water but cautioned that we needed to respect the designated use of each one. We were deeply touched by their generosity to share such a precious commodity as fresh water with us and we thanked them but explained that we would not need to use their water because we carried an ample supply on our boat.

Tom gave the men some of his fishing gear, knowing we would be able to replace it when we got to the Panama mainland. They thanked us for these gifts and encouraged us to remain anchored in front of their small island.

On that particular day the men planned to collect and harvest coconuts. They invited us to come on shore to watch. I think they enjoyed having the opportunity to show off, knowing we would be impressed to see them walk up the sides of each tree. They worked in pairs. The man up in the tree whacked each coconut off with a sharp machete while the man on the ground caught it and placed it on a large cloth on the ground. When the cloth was full, the four corners were tied into a knot and the bundle was carried to their canoe. Each bundle was a huge bulging thing, and it didn't take long before the canoes were full and piled high above the rims. Somehow the men squeezed their thin bodies into the canoes and paddled off someplace to sell the coconuts. They returned in empty canoes just before sunset.

While the men were gone, we avoided going on shore out of respect of how the women might feel with strangers while their men were gone. Tom spent the day diving for fish but he found very few, and those he did see were so small that he did not even spear them. The area was pretty much depleted, and there was even evidence that someone had cleaned out and killed an entire reef by using poisons such as laundry bleach. The only big thing he saw in the water was a very large shark. The shark didn't bother him, but because it was so very large Tom got out of the water and decided he'd had enough hunting for the day.

I used the day on board to sew courtesy flags for the next two countries: Panama and Ecuador. Then I baked cookies and cooked something from our freezer for dinner.

The next morning, Tom dove with the men from the island. They fished on the side that was open to the sea, where there were larger fish, but even those were small by our standards. While the men fished, the women sat on their heels in the sand and sewed molas. Every adult member worked or contributed something to the group and even the children did what they could. Tom kept one small fish from his catch for our dinner and gave the others to the men for their stew pot. We knew it was going to be a thin stew for all those people, so I sent in several canned items that I thought could be added to their pot.

Each day our trust with the Kuna people grew, and slowly we developed a relationship with each of the family members. The makeshift canoes and women from the neighboring islands still visited us regularly, and they spoke to us gently with their eyes. We knew they all worked hard, lived at a subsistence level, did not steal, and had no welfare. Because we were in their waters, we felt it was our duty to continue our policy of purchasing a single mola from each canoe that approached us. To avoid jealousy or turf problems with our island family, I purchased extra molas from them and continued giving them canned food and sometimes shampoo or soap. Then one day, with smiles, the island family presented me with a mola. It had a sailboat on it and they would accept no money in return. I was so deeply touched that I felt my eyes moisten.

Something even more emotional happened several days later when a woman with two small children paddled her canoe over to our boat. There was no apparent husband, and they looked a lot worse off than most of the others. I guessed both children were under the age of five. The boy looked fairly healthy, well fed and groomed, but the girl looked poorly nourished and neglected. I bought two molas from them and gave the children homemade oatmeal cookies while telling the mother how pretty her little girl was. I figured the boy was treated well enough and that the little girl could benefit by a few positive remarks on her behalf. I saw the mother talk to the girl and assumed she was conveying my compliment to her, but I could not have been more mistaken. Instead, she was making preparations to give the girl to me because the next words to me were, "Quiere usted?" (Do you want her?) As she asked the question she lifted the little girl up to the side deck of our boat and I had to quickly respond, "No es posible." (It isn't possible for me to take your child) I selfishly could think only of how complicated our lives would have become if we suddenly acquired a child with no passport or legal documents, not to mention the added responsibility of caring for a young child. Even today I think about that poor child and wonder whatever became of her. I melt with the guilt for not showing her more compassion.

HUNTING WITH CLOROX KILLS REEFS

Because the gold-toothed man spoke English, the others would send him out to ask us for things. One time he paddled out in his canoe, knocked on the side of our boat and asked if we had any medicine-shampoo for head lice. That's how we learned the entire family had head lice. We didn't have any of the head-lice shampoo on board, but I added it to our shopping list for when we got to Panama. On another day he asked if we had any Clorox bleach, and I nearly snapped his head off.

"Why do you want that?" I challenged.

"My wife wants to wash clothes," he answered sheepishly as he backed away from me.

"Oh," I said. "Yes, I have Clorox for laundry. I was afraid you wanted it to go fishing."

As I handed him the Clorox, I remember him looking at me as if I'd lost my mind. I know he wondered how I could possibly think he could go fishing with Clorox. He was too innocent to even understand how someone had already destroyed the reef off the end of his island by pouring Clorox down holes to force the larger fish, octopus and lobsters, to come out of their hiding places. We knew it might take years before that reef would have the opportunity to heal itself; meanwhile he didn't even know there was a problem.

The sixteen-year-old boy paddled out to the boat daily for English lessons. At first he wanted to copy words from our dictionary, thinking that was the way he could begin to learn English. But since I had several English-Spanish children's workbooks on board that I had studied from, I began using them to prepare lessons for him. He was a dedicated student, and he never missed a day, but sometimes he wanted to lounge or recline while he read, or worked on some of the lessons. Before I had learned about the head lice, I didn't care if he lounged in the cockpit, but once I learned about it, I did not want his head to touch anything on the boat, especially soft surfaces such as our cushions or pillows. So, as soon as I began to see him slump I would tap my pencil and say, "If you're going to be in school, you need to sit up straight." He would smile and sit right up. I think he thought it was fun, and I felt like a strict old school marm.

TOO MUCH PREVENTION

We took our first Fansidar pill to protect us from malaria on a Sunday night, and on the following Sunday we each took our second. That night I awoke in the middle of the night sick and shivering with chills. My entire body was freezing, and even my teeth were chattering. I woke Tom and he put every blanket we had on me. I was still freezing and finally he just lay right on top of me and wrapped his arms around me to try to get me warm. As suddenly as the chills appeared, they disappeared, and I broke out in a sweat. Off came all the blankets and even the sheet. My temperature soared and the rest of the night and the following days were consumed in the alternating states of chills and sweats. Each episode diminished somewhat and became less extreme, but as we neared the third Sunday we faced the question of whether I dared to take another Fansidar pill. Clearly, I had a severe reaction to it, similar to having had a case of malaria.

Through the ham radio I was able to get medical advice, and we received the alarming news that some people had died from a similar Fansidar reaction. The doctor asked if we had any antihistamines on board. He recommended that I take an antihistamine and discontinue taking the Fansidar. I thought our medicine chest had everything we could ever possibly want in it, but there were no antihistamines. I just had to hope for the best and since I had already survived the worst of it, I assumed I would make it. I followed the doctor's advice and discontinued taking the Fansidar, deciding I would just have to take my chances on not getting malaria. Meanwhile, Tom was told he should continue taking it since he did not get a reaction. On the third Sunday he took his third pill and that night he experienced similar chills and sweats. His were not as violent as mine probably because his large body could absorb more than mine, but that was the last Fansidar pill either of us took.

It was frightening to think our sophisticated and scientific medical world could make such an erroneous recommendation, and somewhat humorous to realize we were recuperating in front of an island where the people had lived medicine free for hundreds of years. It was a rich and rewarding time for us – a time when we could cherish the simple things that life offers each of us: kindness to our fellow human beings, and the pleasure of sharing and being together.

MAIL ORDER BRIDE

When we became well and strong again, we bid farewell and set sail toward the Panama Canal. We stopped before reaching the canal in order to meet a ham radio acquaintance, who was a cruiser before he built his home on Panama's north shore. His house was accessible only by boat. We talked to him that morning, and he invited us to anchor out in front of his place and take the dinghy to shore. I was always a little surprised when I met someone in person for the first time after knowing them on the radio. Somehow the person never looked the way I thought they would and this particular "eye ball" meeting was even more dramatic than most.

I had no preconceived notions or special expectations about his house, yet I was surprised. It was the most unique house that I had ever seen. It was more like an elaborate tree house with large open rooms that faced the ocean. The bathroom outhouse may have been the one and only room with four walls; the others had only partial walls. He had built everything himself, and powered the house as if it were a boat, with a gas-driven generator for lights, refrigeration, radio, TV, etc. He was a handsome young man with curly blond hair, soft blue eyes, and a quiet disposition. Without question he was a bright man, talented and knowledgeable in a variety of areas He seemed to enjoy receiving the company of those of us who lived on boats, but shunned all other contacts. When he had decided it was time for him to "take a wife," he placed an ad in a bride mail-order catalogue in the Philippines. After interviewing several by mail, he flew over to meet them and made his selection. During our visit she was pregnant with their first child. I sensed they lived in cooperative harmony, fulfilling their contractual agreement, but I saw none of the signs of love or excitement that I would have expected of a couple expecting their first baby.

We spent only one night in front of their home, then sailed the short distance to Colon (sometimes called Cristobal), Panama the next morning, where we looked forward to beginning the process of getting permission to go through the Panama Canal.

THE MISSING YACHT

On the way we saw a boat named NORDSTJARMAN that we recognized as one that had been reported on the ham radio net as missing. We sailed closer, unsure of what we should do. If the boat had been stolen, our lives might be in danger if we approached it. If, however, the owners were aboard, they may not even have known family members had been trying to reach them. As we got closer we could see there was a couple on board: a man and a woman, neither of whom looked like boat hijackers. We decided to take the risk, and anchored near them. We lowered the dinghy into the water and motored over.

"Hello, is your name Jill?" I asked with a cautioned friendliness while trying to get a feeling about the woman.

"Why, yes," she said. "How did you know?"

She seemed genuinely surprised by my knowing her name so I told her there had been a search announced on the radio for her and the boat. "Apparently, a family member has been concerned for your safety, and they are very eager for you to contact them," I said.

She explained that they had only a small single-side band radio on board with just the emergency Channel 16 on it, so we invited them over to our boat to use our radio. Apparently Jill's daughters had not heard from her for some time and they were concerned for her safety and wanted to know her whereabouts. We felt good about the encounter and our ability to assist. We also made a mental note to ourselves to do a better job of keeping our own family informed of our whereabouts.

WE WERE ROBBED

Arriving at Colon after spending time in the San Blas Islands was a big adjustment for us. The canal was the main jumping-off point for those who plan to cross to the Pacific, but we were surprised when a reporter from the *Cruising World* magazine approached us and asked if that was our intention. We were not used to having anyone interested in our travels, even our family. But as a result of that interview, our pictures and a short article about us appeared in the January 1991 issue.

After living the simple life with the Kuna Indians, we found the bureaucratic demands of Colon annoying. To make matters worse, we knew it was not a Panamanian bureaucracy that required all the rules; it was the Americans who taught the Panamanians what to do and how to do it. For instance, all boats, regardless of how common or standard their hull size, had to be "ad measured". Of course there is a substantial fee for "ad measurements" and even if you can present the officials with detailed drawings of your boat, you cannot get out of the "ad measurement" or the fees that accompany it. The same wizards insist that a canal pilot take charge of your boat during the canal transit – never mind that the captain of his own boat knows how to handle his own vessel in tight quarters a lot better than someone who has never been on it before. Another requirement we didn't like was the need to have four line handlers on board. It didn't matter that Tom and I had already successfully transited locks all through the Saint Lawrence Seaway, the Welland Canal, and the Erie Canal. There was no room for exceptions to any of these rules or requirements.

The officials at the "ad measurement" office willingly provided us with a list of young Panamanian men (mostly hoodlums was our understanding) eager to serve as line handlers for a fee and anything they could manage to steal from the boat during the transit. The reports we heard over the ham radio about this were not pleasant, and as a result, cruisers took it upon themselves to line handle for one another. The cruisers preferred to take the public bus back and forth to assist total strangers on another boat rather than hire anyone on the standard list, and everyone was more comfortable with that arrangement.

Never before had we experienced such a war-torn city as Colon. It was only two months after the Americans removed Noriega from power, and witnessing the real thing was considerably different from seeing war on the television news. The bullet holes in the sides of buildings were real, as were the broken windows. Glass and trash lay in the street waiting for no one to sweep it up, while thugs ruled the town. In Noriega's day, thugs were shown no mercy. If caught, they were shot, unlike the American version of "full due process" which in some way, freed them from serious risk.

At the marina restaurant, we struck up a conversation with a man who we learned was the last American to be hired as a canal pilot. He was fascinating, and we enjoyed hearing him tell about the recent history of the canal. We told him we would be going through the canal soon and asked if he could be assigned to go with us, but we learned he took only large ships through. Of course, we then inquired about going through with him on a ship, just to see the difference; he smiled and said he'd consider it. He cautioned us to stay off the streets for our own safety. "If you need to go someplace, be sure to take a taxi, and feel free to give me a call if there is anything I can do to help you. By the way, my name is Rod," he said, handing us his card.

Tom has never been one to take a message of caution with any degree of seriousness, and true to form he ignored Rod's well-intended caution as well. After all, he felt we had been in many of the "tougher places" in South America and we had no serious problems in those places. When we needed to go to a grocery store we put our empty boat bags on our backs and began walking as we always did. The streets looked deserted, causing me to have grave reservations, but once we actually started walking I didn't feel as if we were in any danger. When it started to rain, we ducked into a small alcove and sat on a bench under an overhang to wait for it to stop. Panama, we learned, has many short bursts of heavy rain, and it is best to just wait them out as they seldom last more than a few minutes. We noticed two young men loitering about nearby but ignored them, thinking they too, were waiting for the rain to stop. We sat close together with the empty cloth bags between us. We hardly noticed when one of the young men walked over near us, but quick as a flash he grabbed the bags and galloped down the street like a young gazelle. I felt the bags slide out from under my hand but could not command my hand to grab them tight enough to hold onto them. Of course the young thief was nearly a block away before it even registered that we had been robbed. Our thief must have been very disappointed to discover the bags were empty, but we were pretty bummed about having lost them too.

When the rain stopped, we found a taxi and took it to the grocery store. We knew this was a case of closing the chicken coop door after the chickens were already out, but we did not want to risk our personal safety, and even Tom realized how vulnerable we were in Colon. The grocery store looked like it might be Fort Knox, with two armed guards standing in front, and I found it rather difficult to think about the items on my lost grocery list when there were men with automatic machine guns at the cash register. With much anxiety, we finished our grocery shopping, returned to the boat, and immediately began making arrangements to transit the canal. There was no point in hanging around Colon because there was nothing more we desired to see.

We paid for our official "ad measuring" and, based on the results, our toll was then calculated for the Panama Canal Net Tonnage for our vessel. We were required to hire, and pay, a Panamanian officer who would serve as captain of our boat during the transit, and we needed to meet a list of other requirements before we were allowed to transit the canal. The list included:

1. Four serviceable mooring lines not less than 100 feet long,
2. Four linehandlers in addition to the master,
3. An anchor,
4. Adequate fendering,
5. The vessel must be able to maintain a speed of five knots under its own power.

We easily met all the requirements, but declined to hire line handlers from their list. Instead, we located other cruisers who said they would do it for the same fee the Panamanians would have received. Once everything was arranged, we needed to make a cash deposit with the Agents Accounts Branch to cover all the tolls, pilotage, wharfage, ad measurement and any other charges levied against our vessel by the Panama Canal Commission.

The Panama Canal is 40 miles long, connecting deep water in the Atlantic to deep water in the Pacific. It was cut through at one of the narrowest places and at one of the lowest saddles of the long isthmus that joins North and South America. The original elevation was 312 feet above sea level, where it crosses the Continental Divide in the rugged mountain range, and it takes approximately nine hours for an average ship to transit it and to be raised and lowered 54 feet in a continuous flight of steps. (See Color Photo Insert, page 22.)

"WATCH OUT FOR THE ALLIGATORS!"

The morning of our scheduled transit the weather could not have been better. The sun was out and the sky was clear. It was the perfect day to photograph every step of the process. Everyone was on board at the designated time, with the two other cruisers who were serving as additional line handlers, and the assigned Panamanian canal pilot – a total of five people. We motored over to the holding pen and waited instructions with nearly a dozen other boats. While we waited, we became acquainted with our pilot and decided he was an O.K. chap, especially after he pointed out the failed cut where the French first began the canal. "A lot of people died making this canal," he said. "It's too bad the French had to waste so many extra lives on that false cut. They just didn't study it very well before they began. There's a really good book about the canal, called *The Path Between The Seas*".

At last we were instructed to enter the first lock, and since VONNIE-T was one of the larger boats going through the canal in that pod we were placed against the lock wall, with two smaller boats tethered to our port side. There were several other rows of three boats tethered together in front of us, and several more rows tethered in a similar fashion behind us. After all the boats were in place within the lock, the door was closed behind us and the chamber began to flood. There is always turbulence from the rush of water entering a lock, but this was much more than what we had experienced in the St. Lawrence Seaway or any of the other locks we had gone through. The water flooded into the lock with tremendous force, and we were propelled to the new level so rapidly that it required attentiveness from each line handler so they could continually tighten the dock lines between our boat and the lock wall. When we reached the new level, the front of the lock opened. All the tether lines between the boats were released, and we each motored to the next lock where the entire process was repeated. Several more locks were handled in the same fashion until we reached Gatún Lake, a 163-square-mile man-made lake and one of the largest artificial bodies of water in the world. Most of the boats prepared to anchor in the lake for the night, but we didn't join them. Instead we motored over to the Pedro Miguel Yacht Club where we had arranged for a slip. Our line handlers were able to catch a bus back to Colon where their boat was waiting for them, and it was there that our Panamanian captain bid us farewell.

The yacht club was different from all other marinas we had experienced. To begin with, the slip it assigned us was so shallow that our keel bounced and ground into the mud. We had to winch the boat over to the dock knowing all the paint on the bottom of the keel would be worn off as it plowed sideways through the mud. We welcomed any and all water motion at that time as it helped lift our boat and allowed it to gently bounce over the mud grooves that we already carved. Gradually, we managed to pull ourselves closer and closer to the dock, and finally with lots of huffing, puffing, grunting and grinding on the winch and the dock lines, we got ourselves close enough to be able to step off the boat without the use of a walking plank. Our neighbors sympathized, having gone through the same experience themselves. Part of their greeting included providing us with local tips; the most alarming was the casualness with which they pointed out the alligators who were sunning themselves on the logs next to our dock. "They are only about three feet long and there haven't been any reports of injuries from them," one of the "yachties" told us as she introduced herself. "Still, you ought to be aware of them and try to keep your distance."

Until she pointed them out I hadn't even seen them, but sure enough, they were stretched out on the rocks sunning themselves, amazingly well camouflaged. If one had not picked up its head and moved, I might not have seen it at all.

Once we became used to seeing them there and got used to feeling the boat bump up and down once in a while on the soft muddy bottom, we rather liked the place. We especially liked sitting in the cockpit watching the world go by in both directions in the nearby lock. We found the people and the rest of the yacht club facilities to be friendly. After dinner on most weekends we met the others in the clubhouse to watch world news on an American television station. On Fridays, everyone was invited to participate in a potluck dinner that often turned out to be a feast of sorts, with delicious assortments of food representing many different countries. Life was really very good for us at the yacht club, and Wednesday was the only night we stayed on our own boats with our hatches closed. That was the night when the spraying machines came into the yacht club grounds and fogged for mosquitoes. The process stunk and left a heavy mist of poisonous gas hanging in the air. We all hated the fumes, knowing they were unhealthy, but to my knowledge no one ever complained because we appreciated being protected from malaria.

LEFT ALONE IN PANAMA

Just when we were settling into the yacht club routine, Tom received news that his mother was having surgery for colon cancer. His brother, Mike, indicated that it did not look good for her, so we thought it best that Tom get home to see her as soon a possible. He flew out the next day, leaving me to fend for myself in Panama.

At first I felt almost abandoned. I had never been on my own in a strange country before and I hate to admit how frightened and helpless I felt. I had myself a good cry that first night and awoke the next morning with a strong resolve to make the most of it. If I was good at anything, it was giving myself pep talks when I needed them. I told myself I was presented with a great opportunity to do some of the sewing projects that I had neither the time nor the supplies on board to do. I guess I believed myself because I jumped right into several projects.

My first project was to make some kind of bedspread or covering for our bunk in the stern cabin. I wanted to improve on its normal rumpled appearance. That very morning I took the bus downtown to Panama City where it was a lot safer than Colon and I purchased fabric and supplies. I was surprised to discover it was fun, and I was rather proud of myself. I was able to practice my Spanish, negotiate my own money, and make it back to the boat all by myself. I made a similar trip on following days and soon learned that it was important to take an umbrella because it poured buckets on me every day at one o'clock regardless of sunshine and clear skies in the morning. The rain lasted approximately 20 minutes, and when the sun came out the air felt hot and sticky. Over the next several days I completed many sewing projects and even began sanding and varnishing the exterior teak. Before I even realized it I had made friends with several women. One was a

Panamanian, while the others were American wives or girlfriends who had lived in the American Canal Zone for many years. I was amazed to learn that none of the American women had learned Spanish while they lived there. Apparently they had not felt a need for Spanish while living in the American Zone because all shopping and services were provided for them within the English-speaking sector. But now that the Zone no longer existed, these woman were all too happy to pick me up when they needed to go shopping in Panama City so I could help them communicate with the Panamanians. How ironic, I thought, to have them depend on me — I, who had felt so incompetent only a few days earlier; I, who had depended on Tom to do all the money transactions in the past; and I, who spoke grammatically incorrect Spanish with an extremely limited vocabulary. I was delighted for the company, the transportation, and the respect they showed me. With them, I was able to visit other parts of their country too, parts I would not have been able to see any other way.

One day, my Panamanian friend drove me out to the country to spend an afternoon at her parent's home. The air was clean and the countryside was green and lush as a result of lots of sunshine, warm temperatures, and the daily dousing of rain. What a treat that day was for me, and what a pleasure it was to meet and talk with her parents. "All Panamanians appreciate you Americans," her father said. "You've done many good things for our country, but now you're going to turn the canal over to us and I don't think that's a very good thing."

"Why isn't that a good thing?" I asked. "I thought the Panama people wanted control of the canal."

"Panama politicians want control of the canal, but the people — they aren't so sure. You know it takes a lot of maintenance to keep that canal running and maintenance is often put off here in Panama. It's not a concept common to our thinking. I predict our politicians will make a mess of it, and you Americans will have to come back to clean it up. You Americans are clever people, but sometimes you're not so smart. This thing with the canal that you are going to do, this is not so smart."

On the way back to the boat we passed an area the size of several football fields filled with appliances: refrigerators, stoves, washing machines, clothes dryers, and dishwashers. The sun bounced off the sea of white enamel and I was not sure if my eyes were deceiving me. "That's exactly what you think it is," my friend said when she observed my puzzled look. "It's a sea of appliances. Each time a new family came to The Zone they were guaranteed a new set of appliances, so the old ones from the former family were moved out here. Each item is numbered and organized in perfect military order and left to rust and deteriorate in its spot. I understand that even the landscaping from former families was removed so the new family could do their own landscaping. Of course a lot of that will change now that The Zone is officially closing."

On another day she took me to the area where Noriega was reported to have had his bunker. It was a pile of rubble from the bombs American fliers dropped in an attempt to kill him. About a mile away there was a similar pile of rubble where more bombs had been dropped. Apparently there had been reports that Noriega was hiding in an apartment complex there, and what was once a large apartment complex with hundreds of low-income families (mostly women and children) existed no more. All those people were dead and Noriega was still alive and hiding someplace.

"All those people were killed?" I asked in horror.

"Yes, but no one really cares because they were all poor people. They were just blights on our society anyway, so it wasn't really any big deal."

Good God, I could hardly believe my ears! How could she be so calloused about the lives of innocent people? Just because the Panamanian people didn't value the lives of their poor, it did not give our American military the right to kill them. What a botched-up job! I wondered if our American press ever got wind of what really happened, and if so I wondered how it had been reported. I was ready to bet anything the bombings and killings that took place in Panama had not been reported accurately back home.

SCALING UP AND DOWN THE SIDE OF A GREEK SHIP

Rod, the American canal pilot that Tom and I met in Colon, stopped by the boat to see me too. Sometimes he brought one of his many girlfriends with him, and sometimes he came alone with his unread mail. It was no secret that his real love was the Canal; he was completely content to sit in our cockpit, read his mail and watch the ships go past as they entered and exited the lock while I sewed or worked on some project. One evening when he did not have to work, he invited me to join him and one of his girlfriends for a dinner out. She was a nurse, and when she learned how old our emergency medical kit was, she agreed to come aboard the next day and update our supplies. It was a great evening and after dinner the three of us went to see the movie "Pretty Woman."

"Do you still want to go through the canal on a ship?" he casually asked. "If you do, I'm taking a Greek ship through tomorrow night and I know this captain. He wouldn't object if I brought a visitor." Of course I jumped at the opportunity. In preparation I tried to take a nap that afternoon knowing I would be awake through the entire night, but try as I may, I could not sleep. I was just too excited!

At 7pm an official canal car was sent for me. The driver took me to the office where I met Rod and Raphel, the other captain who would go on the transit. Large ships required two captains to transit the locks, one for each side of the ship. I was able to watch the entire check-in procedure and was amazed at all the details the captains had to know about the ship before they took it through the canal: overall tonnage, length, width, cargo, crew and even the height of the bridge. It was a science and all the formulas had to fit. After the paper work was complete, we boarded what they called a tender. To me it looked more like a beat up old tugboat. It had a flat open deck with heavy rubber fenders around it. There was no seating available, just a metal bar to hold onto while standing on the chipped, painted metal deck. The boat sped out into the Pacific, pounding across the tops of waves at full throttle, and as much as I wanted to ask him to slow down I didn't. Instead, with clenched teeth and a sweaty white-knuckled grip on the bar, I bent my knees to cushion each successive thud and made every effort to look unfazed. Relief is the only word I can think of to describe my feelings when we began to slow down as we approached the large Greek freighter that was anchored and waiting our arrival.

"We're going to bounce up against the ship when we get there," Rod told me. "There'll be a Jacob's ladder hanging down on the side of the ship. You will need to grab it and begin climbing as fast as you can toward the top. Don't stop or look down along the way. Raphel and I will be right behind you, and you need to go all the way to the top."

Good God, what had I gotten myself into? I had no idea I would be scaling up the side of a ship that looked more like a huge city building. When the tender bounced against the side of the ship, I nearly fell from the impact. I looked up and there I saw a rope ladder with narrow wooden steps swinging out toward me as the ship rolled toward our tender. I was too frightened not to do just as I was told, so I grabbed the ladder and started climbing as fast as I could. Sometimes it swung out away from the ship and I felt myself sort of flying in midair, and the next moment I was slammed up against the side of the ship. I kept climbing and looked up to see how much farther I had to go. Way up high I saw a small light shining down on us. It was like climbing up the side of a 15-story building; only this building was swaying from side to side out in the pitch-black night of the Pacific Ocean. When I reached the top I saw a short Asian man with a flashlight. He offered his child-sized hand to assist me as I stepped up and over the railing and onto the ship. Not a word was spoken. (I assumed he didn't speak English.) Rod and Raphel were right behind me and he escorted the three of us to the bridge where I met the Greek ship captain.

The captain shook my hand, and in broken English offered me orange juice and told me exactly where he wanted me to sit. It was not a suggestion; it was an order. Clearly, I was supposed to stay in that chair and let the captains get to their work. Rod took the starboard side of the bridge and Raphel took the port side. The huge anchors groaned and clanked as they were pulled up, and the ship began to move slowly towards the first lock. Rod gave the helmsman practice orders, asking him to turn the ship two degrees in one direction and then two degrees in another direction. When the helmsman over-steered Rod demanded, "Don't ever, ever over steer. Do just as I tell you. If I tell you two degrees I mean only two degrees. Anything more could wipe out the entire lock!" His insistence on the preciseness seemed a little overbearing to me at the time. I must admit that I wondered if it wasn't an act for my benefit, but as we entered the first lock I saw how little space there was between the ship and the walls of the lock and I realized how important his practice instructions had been. There was scarcely a foot between the ship and the walls of the lock. I couldn't get over how small the locks appeared while looking down on them from the ship's bridge compared to how large they seemed when looking up at them from the deck of our sailboat. We never even saw the tops of a lock from VONNIE-

T's deck.

Between locks it was totally black and the helmsman steered by radar and compass headings, but when we were in the lock everything was brightly lit. Each was exciting because of the importance of entering it at the right angle and speed. During the long dark passages between locks, the captains relaxed and made small talk. Raphel was married and had several small children. He hated his job because he never got to see his kids. "I'm working all the time while they're sleeping and when I get home in the morning I'm bushed and have to sleep while they're up and about. The whole thing stinks! What keeps you at this job, old man?" he asked Rod.

"I like the work," Rod said.

"Yea, but I'll bet you could retire and earn as much as you do now," he said. "You've been here a long time."

"I've considered retiring," Rod said, "and you're right. I'd actually earn about the same as now, but then what would I be? I'd be an ex-canal pilot!"

His words hung in the air....

We finished transiting the entire canal by the time the sun began peeking over the horizon. It had been an interesting evening, but as tired as I was and as ready as I was to get some sleep, I dreaded getting off the ship because I knew I would have to crawl back down the same Jacobs ladder that I crawled up on. As soon as the anchors were down on the Colon side of the canal, we were escorted to the ladder. Rod went down first, I went second, and Raphel followed me. I just kept going down and did not look down until my foot reached no more rungs. I heard Rod say jump and I did, trusting there would be something under me. There was. The tender took us to shore where there was a car and chauffeur waiting for us. The three of us climbed into the back seat. I was in the middle and after only a few words, both Rod and Raphel were sound asleep and snoring with their mouths hanging open. I put my head back, just to rest my eyes and listen to their snoring, but I must have fallen asleep, as well, because the next think I knew we had pulled up to the marina where VONNIE-T was waiting. The driver woke me and I remember mumbling something that resembled goodbye, thanks, and I'll see you, while I stumbled out of the car over Rod's legs. I walked past the alligators and fell onto my bunk without even bothering to wash my face or brush my teeth.

A few days later, when the condition of Tom's mother had improved dramatically, he returned to the boat. I wished he had been on the transit with me, but I shared all I could with him so he could enjoy it vicariously. I was glad he was back, and we were both eager to move on.

On the day we departed, we untied our lines and turned on our engine knowing we would have to slug our way out of the mud ditch we had settled into over the past several weeks. The noise startled the alligators, and we saw them scamper into the water. We had traveled only 50 feet from the dock when our engine quit. Tom knew immediately what had happened just by the sound. He'd become astute and in-tune with every sound on our boat.

"You'd better get my bathing suit," he said.

What a strange request! I wondered if I had heard him right but when I saw him begin to get undressed, I knew I had.

"We've got a line caught in the prop," he said. "I'll have to go down and free it, so don't turn on the engine or anything while I'm down there."

I looked down at the muddy water and thought about the alligators there and could not imagine how he was going to free a line from our prop with no visibility. He wouldn't be able to see the hand in front of his face in that brown goop; he'd have to feel everything with his hands. That meant the alligators could not see anything either, and I did not even want to think about the likelihood of him sticking his hand on an alligator while he was groping around for the prop. Yuck!

Into the water he went. Up he came gasping for breath. Down he went again. I stood on the stern, my heart pounding as I watched for him. Up he came gulping for air, and down he went again. Each time he surfaced I felt relief, but that relief was short lived because he'd dive back down as soon as he filled his lungs with fresh air. Finally, he came up and asked that I lower the ladder for him. He climbed up onto the stern, took a shower from our sun-shower bag to wash the mud off, and went below to get dressed.

When he came back to the cockpit he said, "OK, you can start the engine now. Hopefully there won't be any more stray ropes or lines in the area." Slowly we motored toward the last of the locks and entered the Pacific Ocean.

THE FISH ARE DIFFERENT!

On the Pacific side of the Panama Canal is a group of islands called Islas De Las Perlas. We anchored among them in one of the many little coves that first evening after leaving the canal, and in doing so we rediscovered our joy of being alone with one another. We had almost forgotten how pleasant it could be for just the two of us to be at anchor with no other boats nearby. We marveled at the fullness of the moon and commented appreciatively at the brilliance of the stars. How quickly we had forgotten how majestic the stars could look without competition from city lights.

While we reveled at these natural wonders, we also worried about our anchor. It hadn't seated itself into the ocean floor as well as we would have liked, and an added cause for worry was the fact that we had not practiced our anchoring skills for a long time. Of real concern too, was the 13-foot tide that was scheduled for that night.

We liked to feed out a 5-to-1 scope of chain, which meant we would put out a length of chain that was five times the depth of the water at the bow of the boat. We carried 200 feet of chain on our anchor and after that it was rope. If our calculations were wrong and we didn't allow for enough chain or rope, the anchor could pull out and the boat would become loose and float freely at high tide. If we over-estimated and put out too much anchor chain or rope, the boat could be in a different type of danger by floating too close to the island at low tide and becoming grounded. In crowded anchorages it was not unusual to hear about boats bumping into each other during periods of full moon and high tides. Fortunately, there were no neighboring boats to be concerned about that night.

Neither of us slept well however. We both got up several times during the night to check on our position relative to the island, but with the friendly smile of the rising sun and the beckoning call of crystal clear water all around us, Tom awoke in high spirits. He could hardly wait to go over the side and go hunting.

"I'm coming back with fresh fish for dinner tonight," he announced while suiting himself up against the cold water temperatures of the Pacific. I smiled when I saw him struggle into his red, skin-tight wetsuit thinking he looked amazingly similar to the figure on the label of the deviled ham cans stashed in the boat larder. (See Color Photo Insert, page 10.) With his big flippers, round goggles and snorkel hanging on his tall, lean body, he made quite an imposing figure. He jumped feet first into the water, his flippers making an impressive splash. I didn't expect to see him back at the boat for at least a half-hour, but instead he was back to the surface in only a few minutes, laughing hysterically.

"All the fish are different," he said. "I don't know any of these fish. I knew all of them on the Caribbean side, but over here they're all different! I don't know which ones are safe to eat and which are risks for ciguatera poisoning."

We both remembered the warnings we'd received from the SSCA members about avoiding ciguatera poisoning. After learning about it I wrote to the University of Puerto Rico where they were doing research on ciguatera. We learned that the disease was found primarily in reef fish and in fish that fed on reef fish between the latitudes of 20 degrees north and 20 degrees south. Ciguatera is cumulative in both the fish and in humans, which means when the larger fish eats the smaller fish the larger fish will have more of it in its system than the smaller fish. Ironically, it doesn't seem to affect the fish in any way, but when people get enough of it, it affects the nervous system. It made for interesting reading and caused us to be very cautious about which fish we ate.

"There's lots of abalone down there. If you think you know how to cook 'em, maybe we should just have that tonight," Tom suggested from the water.

"Hmm, I don't know — maybe," I said, "just a moment, let me check." Neither of us had ever even seen an abalone before. Tom only recognized it from pictures, and he treaded water eager for a new type of hunt, while he waited for my answer. I went below and pulled out my cooking bible, *The Joy of Cooking* that had its own special place in a corner of the galley. "O.K.," I said. "There are directions here for them so lets give 'em a try."

In no time at all Tom gathered a pile of abalone in the dinghy. He cleaned them by prying the shells open with a knife and carefully placing each morsel of meat into a clean bucket of salt water. Then he tossed the shells back into the ocean. That night I sautéed them lightly in a pan with a little butter and garlic salt. We were amazed at how that big pile had shrunk down to barely enough for the two of us, but they tasted excellent.

We moved to a better anchorage that night and struck up a conversation with Gerda and Dieter, a German couple on another boat anchored nearby. Their joy of the Las Perlas islands was almost infectious, and they told us they had been hanging around the area for several months. "It's pretty nice, you know. Whenever we need new supplies we just head over to Balboa in Panama and stock up for several more weeks. It's perfect really," they said.

While they praised the Las Perlas, I felt it was rather perfect to have run across them, and we took the opportunity to tap their wealth of knowledge. During the course of our conversation Tom received a valuable crash course on the edible fish on that side of the canal.

ALMOST A PILE OF FIBERGLASS SPLINTERS

We thanked them for their information and set sail for Ecuador the next morning. It began as a gentle sail with perfect winds. That afternoon I made several contacts via ham radio and was pleasantly surprised to find myself talking with Eric, our wonderful host in Bogata. I thanked him again for his and Lucy's hospitality and told him we were on our way to Ecuador.

"Will you be anywhere near Salinas, Ecuador?" Eric asked.

"Yes, our charts indicate there is a marina in Salinas and that's where we plan to anchor," I answered.

"Then I must put you in contact with one of my Danish ham friends who lives there with his Ecuadorian wife. We have a Danish Net that meets every Sunday morning and I'll tell him about you next Sunday," he said.

"That would be great," I said.

After I got off the radio, I took a short nap before preparing dinner. After dinner Tom went below to sleep while I stayed on watch. Toward morning we switched positions again, so I slept while Tom was on watch. There wasn't much of anything to do while on watch. A watch is just that – a time to watch: for debris in the water, for ships or other boats in our path, for changes in wind direction, for sails that may need attention, or anything else that might be a problem or not operating as it should.

On that particular morning everything was calm and peaceful. The entry in our log indicated we were at 1 degree north latitude (60 miles north of the equator) by 81 degrees longitude (4860 nautical miles west of the Greenwich England Meridian), steering a magnetic course of 142 degrees and making 5.9 knots. The wind was steady at 15 knots, there was no barometric change, and the clouds in the sky were fluffy white. Tom had the full main up with no reefs in it, and our large 150% Genoa was loosely sheeted and billowed off the port side. With the Genoa sail out that far it was a little difficult to see the horizon on that quarter of the boat, but we were used to ducking down to peer under it periodically to scan for oncoming traffic. It always seemed like a silly exercise because there was never anything there; nonetheless, we both knew it was what we should do.

While I slept that morning, Tom sat in the cockpit quietly working a crossword puzzle. He apparently got so involved with the puzzle that he became complacent in his watch duties and forgot to check under the Genoa sail, nor did he bother to turn on the radar to check for the possibility of oncoming boat traffic. Suddenly, I heard him shout, "LaVonne, on deck now NOW!" I was jarred out of a sound sleep, startled, and confused. I had no idea what was happening. I bolted out of my bunk and ran to the cockpit totally naked.

"Turn on the engine," he demanded while simultaneously cranking in the Genoa sheet and turning the wheel as hard as he could.

Then, I heard the problem! The deep thump, thump, thump of very large engines could be heard off our port bow. I didn't have to see the ship to know that it was big and dangerously close. Under full power and with sails flapping uselessly from having become starved of wind we made a sharp starboard turn and motored under full throttle away from the treacherous pounding sound. We "hobby-horsed" across the ship's bow wake not a minute too soon. Fortunately our engine was strong enough to overcome the eddy that forms around a large vessel as it plows through the water. Not until we were out of danger was I aware of how fast my heart was pounding, and I looked up to see what the people were doing on the bridge of that ship during our narrow escape. I had completely forgotten that I was still naked! I just wanted to glare into the faces of the people who steered that close to us. Everyone knew sailboats had the right of way and I was furious to think that a ship of that size would so blatantly ignore that basic rule of the sea. Imagine my surprise when I discovered that the ship's bridge was empty with no one on watch – absolutely no one! If we had not moved out of the way in time that ship would have plowed right through us without even knowing they had hit and sunk us. VONNIE-T would have been reduced to a pile of fiberglass splinters floating in the water and no one would have known what had happened to us.

When we were safely off the stern of the ship, Tom humbly set a new course heading and reset the sails. He felt bad for not maintaining a better watch, but we both knew it could have happened to either of us and we treated it as a good lesson to keep better watches from that point forward. He suggested I try to get back to sleep, but that was impossible. I could not have been more wide-awake had I drunk an entire pot of coffee. We were both keyed up for the rest of the day, and periodically we heard phantom *thumps* from an engine. Each time, we carefully looked around, but there were no other vessels to be seen and nothing on the radar. Still, the *bang-thump, bang-thump, bang*-thump seemed so real, and we both heard it. Finally we realized there really was a *bang-thump* sound and it was coming from us – from someplace under the boat. We tried not to overreact just because of the near-encounter with the ship, but try as we may we could think of no logical reason for a thumping sound to be coming from the bottom of our boat. Absolutely nothing came to mind and when the thumping grew louder, we decided to turn back. Tom would have to dive under the boat to check it out, and we didn't want to do that out in the deep ocean, nor did we want to go into Colombia's western shore. Not only did we not have charts for the western shore, but we had never heard of any boats stopping there, and we assumed there must be some good reason for that. I knew Tom was concerned about the thumping sounds because I had never known him to turn back for anything. But back we went, all the way to the Las Perlas Islands.

THE SACRIFICIAL ZINC

We anchored at one of the outermost islands and as soon as the anchor was set, Tom dove into the water. Within minutes he came up with a broken sacrificial zinc in his hand. Before we had put the boat back into the water after our last haulout, we placed a donut-shaped zinc on our propeller shaft to prevent, or slow down the process of electrolysis from eating and pitting our bronze propeller and through-hull fittings. Using zinc as a sacrificial metal on boats in a saltwater environment is common practice, but when it started to fall apart it made the most worrisome noise. Our zinc had become loose on one side, allowing it to rotate freely around the shaft, and each rotation caused it to slam against the shaft. Eventually, it would have probably fallen off, but we were glad that it was a simple problem and happy to have the opportunity to replace it. The next morning we started that leg of the trip again.

A VERY LONG FISHING NET

Once again we had ideal conditions. We had steady 15-knot winds and our sails were full, but the boat no longer sliced through the water like it typically did, and once again the situation made no sense. We were completely stumped by our loss of speed. Getting across the equator seemed to present a series of problems for us, enough so that I was almost becoming superstitious about it. We should have been moving along at six-knots, but instead we barely moved. While puzzling over it, we heard a small motorboat off to our starboard side. The motor gradually got louder and then we noticed it was heading directly toward us. When it got closer we noticed a man standing and swinging his arms up and down while shouting something at us. We could not imagine what he was trying to tell us, and because we were not far off the west coast of Colombia, we were somewhat apprehensive. He seemed to be telling us to lower our sails. Typically, before we lower our sails we turn on our engine so we have some maneuverability, but he nearly had a fit when he saw we were going to turn it on. We didn't know what to think, but we decided to comply with his wish. I released the Genoa sheet while Tom cranked it in, then he lowered the mainsail. As soon as we had all the sails down and we were dead in the water, we saw a long fish net float to the surface behind us. Apparently we had been dragging it for some time and that was why we weren't going very fast. How big the net was and long we had been dragging it is something we will never know. We couldn't even see the fishing boat with the naked eye. Once the net was free the man was happy. He waved us off and his little boat tender zoomed off across the choppy water.

Tom raised and trimmed our sails and off we went, zipping along like we should have been doing all along. "If we were puzzled about having slowed down," Tom chuckled, "just think how puzzled that fishing boat must have been when we started dragging them in some direction they had no intention of going. I would have enjoyed hearing that conversation."

ECUADOR

I began to wonder if anything about the passage would go smoothly. It was November 11, or at least I thought it was November 11. It was getting more and more difficult to keep track of the days and dates. Having so few responsibilities, I felt like my brain was turning to mush. We relied on our satellite navigation system to help us with the dates as well as our navigation and when it began to provide fickle and unreliable data it was both frustrating and worrisome. It was a poor time for it to act up because we had learned from other boaters that both the Cabo light and the Isla La Plata lights were out. If ever there was a time when we needed accurate navigational data, it would be while going around those points.

Tom was faced with all the responsibility. He pulled out the instruction book for the Sat Nav and carefully went through each step to reprogram it. Still, the tension on board was electric as we rounded each of those unlit critical points. It was a great relief when we cleared both points with no major incident, and by 3:30 the next afternoon we were moored safely in front of the Salinas Yacht Club in Ecuador.

There was another cruiser anchored there among all the local boats. It was a little, red-hulled sailboat appropriately called STRAWBERRY. The young couple on board was darling but financially strapped, and as a result they could shed very little information about the amenities of the yacht club. They lived on beans, rice, and whatever fish they were able to catch. What they were eager to do, however, was exchange paperback books. The policy was to trade books by the inch of thickness, as books in English were becoming a prized item. The other thing we learned from them was to put all newly acquired books in a plastic bag and spray them with roach killer before bringing them aboard. The practice eliminated bringing cockroaches, or their eggs that may be in the bindings waiting to hatch.

Salinas was a resort town, but to our amazement there was almost no one around. We were told the people would come in a week or two, but the assumption that the town could go from empty to full within a couple of weeks seemed preposterous. Buildings and shops stretched along the shoreline, but there were only two paved streets, each designated for one-way traffic in opposite directions. The secondary streets that ran past rows of empty cement condos looked more like dusty, potholed alleys, and the condos owned by wealthy Ecuadorian families who came to Salinas for their summer holidays, stood empty.

The town was a disappointment, but the yacht club made up for it. It was carpeted, tastefully decorated, and had a full, changing menu each evening at reasonable prices. I was ecstatic about eating there and not having to cook for a while, and we were pleasantly surprised by the quality of the food and the skill with which it was presented. Each evening we hoped to meet and develop a relationship with some of the members of the club, the "socios," but we were disappointed in our quest. The affluent Ecuadorians who ate at the yacht club wanted nothing to do with us. They were not blatantly rude; they just made it a point to ignore us. They would exchange pleasantries or answer our questions, but then they would walk away never extending an invitation to join them at their table as we hoped. We were welcome to eat meals at their club but not welcome to participate in their social groups. We were "transient" boat people and they were clearly not interested in us.

In contrast was the genuine friendly attitude of the laborers who worked at the club for the equivalent of $35 dollars a week. Those happy-go-lucky worker-bees cooked the food, waited on the tables, and maintained the grounds. Some who held the title of "marineros" maintained the expensive marine toys of the rich members.

The yacht club made its boatlift available to us, and Tom arranged for a haulout early one morning. He hired a couple of men to help him, and together they were able to scrape the bottom of our boat, get a fresh coat of bottom paint on it, and put it back in the water all within two days. It was great getting the job done so quickly and Tom learned a lot of local practical information from the men who worked with him. They told him how to use their local bus, how to go to the next town to buy groceries at the open food market, and which bus we would need to take in order to go to Guyaquil.

When Tom told them we wanted to do some land travel in Ecuador but were concerned about leaving the boat, they had a suggestion for that as well. "What you really worried about, captain?" the head marinero asked. "You worried about theft? You worried about a storm? What you worried about?"

"I would worry about both of those things," Tom answered.

"I got an idea for you," he said. "You put out all your anchors so that no storm gonna bother your boat, anyway we don't get storms this time of year. That only leaves the problem of theft and in the daytime there be no problem with that because I'm here and can see if the boat be O.K. At night that be a different story. Things can happen in the night. How about you pay one of my marineros to sleep on the boat each night. That way no one for sure gonna rob your boat at night."

"I don't like the idea of anyone inside the boat," Tom said. "I'd want to have the boat locked up."

"*Si*," he said while scratching his armpit and thinking the problem through. "I think that be right, too. How about he sleeps *on* the boat but not *in* the boat?"

"Do you mean have someone sleep in the cockpit?" Tom asked.

"*Si*, is that what the center open part is called, a cockpit?" He asked.

"That might work," Tom said, "but would anyone be willing to do that?"

"Sure, my head man would be willing to do that if you paid him just the same as what he earns here in the daytime," he said.

So Tom brought the headman out to the boat for a look around. We showed him how to zip the cockpit enclosure for warmth or unzip it for fresh air, and we showed him where he would sleep. We put several blankets, a pillow, a jug of drinking water, a six-pack of soda and

The Ecuadorian "marinero" who slept in our cockpit while we land traveled in South America.

some snack foods in the cockpit for him. We agreed to pay him the equivalent of $70 for two months, plus a bonus of an extra month's pay if there was no harm done to the boat upon our return. It was a risk. We had a lot of money tied up in the boat, no insurance, and fairly fresh memories of the break-in we'd had in Venezuela. But we didn't want to become slaves to the boat. So off we went on another land trip.

We took a bus to Guyaquil. In route we were able to see a lot of the countryside. One of the most appalling sights was seeing large trucks suck up water up from small rivers and streams and transport it back to the little towns where the local people brought empty jugs and containers to be filled. Even small children were adept at carrying containers of water on their heads, which told me it was a common practice, but I had seen the lack of clarity in those streams and I shuddered at the thought of the bacteria and organisms that lived in that water. It essentially does not rain in that area, and the streams came from the distant mountains. I supposed that the people had learned to boil the water, but still I wondered if it could be boiled enough to make it safe enough to drink or cook with.

From Guyaquil we took an airplane to Quito, some 9,300 feet above sea level. I felt a dull headache when we first arrived, and at first we could only walk very slowly. After a good night's rest, however, we were as good as new, and we struck out to find the Ministereo of Defensa where we filed our permits to visit the Galapagos Islands. Officials were happy to process our papers but expressed surprise that we were filing for the permits in their office as opposed to our American Embassy. We told them we had friends who filed through the American Embassy a year ago and they still had not received their permits, so we decided to come and do it in person at their office. We could not have done it without having some Spanish skills because all the questions had to be answered in Spanish. After completing those forms we were directed to the office of The Parque Nacional (The National Parks Service) where we needed to file a second application. That was the first time we had ever heard about the need for two permits. No wonder most of the yachts that applied never got permission. Even after doing all the paper work in person, we learned it would take three months for everything to be processed and cleared, and then were told we could pick up our permits on the first of the Galapagos Islands when we checked in at San Christobal.

Mark and Michelle wanted to see the Galapagos too, so we called and told them when they would be able to meet us. Meanwhile, we did land travel. We spent several weeks in Quito and during that time we took incredibly inexpensive Spanish lessons and kept our eyes on the pavement during our walks to avoid falling into some of the huge holes in the city sidewalks.

We left Quito by bus and visited many rural towns, villages, and small cities. In Otavalo, a village populated entirely by the Otavalo Indians, everyone wore navy wool capes over snowy white clothing. Their white dresses, slacks and shirts made a striking contrast against their dark skin, and although they presented a rather handsome image, they did look rather inappropriately dressed as they toiled in their gardens or fields. They were hard working people with alert deep-set eyes, and everyone, even the men, wore their hair in a thick, black braid down the middle of their backs.

In another town, the women sat in the town square where they knited and sold sweaters made of untreated llama wool that still smelled of natural lanolin. Their needles clacked along like a small train – *clickity, clack, clickity, clack*, and I was amazed to see them talk and barter the price without dropping a stitch or losing the rhythmic momentum of their needles. The sweaters were a handsome bargain, and we bought several as Christmas gifts for our Minnesota family members. The sticker shock came when we took them to the post office to mail them. Due to the weight of the lanolin it cost more for postage than the original cost of the sweaters.

PERU AND CHILI

We bussed our way south to the Peruvian border and then crossed on foot wearing our backpacks, as we learned that flights within a South American country were relatively inexpensive, but flying from one country to another was very costly, so we waited until we were inside Peru before flying to Lima.

I felt safe doing land travel in South America with Tom at my side; I even found it exciting, but when Tom brought up the possibility of crossing the Pacific Ocean, the mere thought of that big unforgiving ocean was cause to make me whimper inside. I told him I simply did not want to do it, and he dropped the subject.

Each day we took a new bus for one day's ride. When we got off the bus we'd walk until we found a cheap room for the night, and the next day we'd repeat the routine heading a little further south each day. In Pucon, Chili, Tom signed up with an organized tour to hike up the mountain to the top of the active volcano. Each person on the tour was given a half of a lemon wrapped in cheesecloth. They were encouraged to rub it under their nose and breath in the scent with the idea that the lemon was more pleasant to smell than the strong sulfur odor from the volcano. Unfortunately, Tom wasn't able to go on the tour because the tour guides couldn't find crampons large enough for his feet. Crampons are spike-like devices worn over shoes to help them grip the ice. Everyone was required to wear them on the mountain, but the tour guides could not find a single set in the entire town large enough.

The farther we traveled south, the colder the temperatures became and soon we were layering ourselves with wool sweaters and jackets. The ocean temperatures must have been cold, too, but the Humboldt Current carried with it an assortment of delicious fish that were served at small ma-and-pa restaurants. At Port De Mont it was often the wives and daughters of the fishermen who ran the restaurants, each seating no more than six or eight customers at any given time. We not only dined well in Chile, we also wined well because of the country's smooth delicate wines, my favorite being from the Undurraga vineyards.

Over the Christmas holidays we took a ferry to Chiloway Island. At that point we'd done our share of econo-style traveling, but that was the first time we'd ever shared accommodations with horses. No one else seemed to think anything of the fact that there were a couple dozen horses on the ferry. The appearance of the island was interesting from the moment we pulled into the port. Apparently, the residents had to contend with a ferociously high tide because the houses on the lower part of the island were on tall stilts. The local graveyard was on one of the highest sections on the island and consisted of little cement houses where the dead were placed in vaults.

That evening we met a Canadian couple at dinner, and we leapt at the invitation to share a table with them, elated for the opportunity to speak English. Together we commiserated on how exhausting it was to be constantly trying to communicate in a foreign language. We shared with them our frustration at trying to find out when the ships would resume traveling to the southern tip of Chile to Tierra Del Fuego. The Canadians faced the same frustrations, and we came to the conclusion that there was no definite date. Apparently it depended upon the weather, as it would be dangerous to take a ship into the iceberg-laden channels too soon. Judging from the nightly temperatures, it could have been months before there was improvement in the weather. For weeks we'd been living in layers of our warmest clothing: winter jackets, sweaters, jeans, gloves, and wool hats. I didn't do well with the cold and the damp, and often the best part of the day for me was sitting in front of a fireplace at night with a bottle of Chilean wine.

CHILEAN/ARGENTINA LAKE DISTRICT

When the boat schedule was finally announced we learned the first trip wouldn't be until January 7. We couldn't wait that long and decided instead to take the bus/boat trip through the lake-district on into Argentina. We met an American family — Pam, Jim and their daughter Maya on that trip. Both parents were teachers at the American (English-speaking) school in Bolivia. "We can't afford to see the world the way you are," they said, "so we accept teaching assignments at different places every couple of years. That's our way of seeing the world." Eleven year-old Maya attended school in whatever portion of the

Active and inactive volcanoes can be seen in the lake-district between southern Chili and Argentina.

world they were teaching.

They had reservations at a rather expensive hotel in Barilochi, Argentina, and asked us where we planned to stay. We told them we didn't have reservations and that we planned to find whatever we could when we arrived. They decided to see what accommodations we were able to find before they checked into their expensive hotel, and when we found a nice place for a lot less money, they changed their plans and joined us.

That afternoon Tom and I went to the market and bought fresh lettuce, cucumbers, and tomatoes, to make a salad. We were prepared with a flexible plastic bowl in my backpack for the purpose of mixing salads. We also bought a large loaf of bread, some cheese, fruit and a couple bottles of wine. That was dinner. We had knives, forks and plastic plates with us too, and we invited our new acquaintances to join us for our little feast. Soon their vacation was over and they had to return to their jobs, but before parting company they invited us to stop and spend a couple of days with them at their home in Bolivia. We thanked them and agreed to do it.

We continued traveling in Argentina, finding it to be a sophisticated and European-type of country, not at all what I had expected, and very different from the rest of South America that we'd seen. Tom and I were humbly dressed in Buenos Aries, compared to the local businessmen who wore suits and the women in heels and tailored dresses. Many of the communities were made up of German families who had come during and after WWII and even their homes looked like solid European dwellings of brick and flagstone.

We visited Iguazu Falls, the largest waterfalls in the world, and were greatly impressed not only by the power and size of the falls, but also by the development of the viewing grounds all around it. (See Color Photo Insert, page 22.) There were miles and miles of walking paths that led through lush greenery and colorful flower gardens, all of them with Kodak-moment views of the falls. Not far from the falls was the Mission of Asuncion, a notable ruin with an elaborate history which Hollywood used during the making of a movie about it, entitled "The Mission". The heat and humidity were nearly unbearable and we stopped often for something to drink. Tom loved the local custom of placing his chilled beer bottle in a Styrofoam container. At one place I ordered iced tea and was told they only had hot tea, so I ordered hot tea and a tall glass of ice. When our waiter watched me pour my hot tea into the glass over the ice he could hardly believe his eyes. How, I wondered, could a country with such intense heat not know about iced tea?

From Argentina we took a bus into Uruguay and Paraguay. Both were interesting but the temperatures were even hotter. The backs of our shirts were soaked under our backpacks, so much so that the backpacks had begun to have an odor. What a contrast to southern Chile where we were freezing.

One afternoon during a short burst of rain we ducked into a coffee shop. We ordered sandwiches and waited for the rain to stop. When it did and we stepped outside, we were amazed to see that the entire street had already dried. The heat from the street dried the rain as fast as it had fallen, with the exception of one rectangular square where a car had been parked. That area had been kept cool under the shade of the car, and when it drove away that was the only wet area on the entire street.

BOLIVIA

When we arrived in Santa Cruz, Bolivia, we looked up friends Pam, Jim and Maya who taught at the American school. They offered us their guestroom, and wanted to hear all about the rest of our travels. In the morning, they left early for work but arranged for their maid to make us an American breakfast of fruit, eggs, toast and coffee. It was a welcomed treat, and in an effort not to be a burden Tom returned our dishes to the kitchen when we finished eating. That evening Pam asked us to please refrain from bussing our own dishes in the future. The maid had interpreted Tom's help as an indication that she had not done her job quickly enough, so instead of being helpful we had insulted her.

The next day after breakfast we took a bus to LaPaz, Bolivia, which was 12,000 feet above sea level. It was a large bus but it didn't have a toilet on it, and after only a few hours I wished that I hadn't had any coffee that morning. I tried to ignore my full bladder thinking that we'd stop soon, but we didn't. The bus just bounced along the rutted dirt road. Finally, I could hardly stand it and I asked Tom to inquire about how much longer it would be before we stopped. He came back and said there was no plan to stop the bus for two hours. I knew I wasn't going to be able to last much longer. My bladder was about to burst.

"Please tell him I have to stop," I pleaded.

Tom went forward and in his broken Spanish convinced the driver that it was an emergency, and he needed to stop. In the middle of nowhere the driver pulled over to the side

A Bolivian mother walking up a dirt packed trail carrying a load on her back in a La Paz market.

of the muddy road and opened the door. There wasn't even a shrub or a bush for privacy, but I was in too much pain to care. I stepped off the bus, took a few steps along the side, unbuckling my jeans, squatted and relieved myself on the already muddy road. What a relief. It was nearly exotic! While I continued splashing a puddle around my feet the rest of the people on the bus came to urinate as well. There we all were: total strangers urinating in unison. Next to me was a round woman who wore layers of skirts and a black bolero hat, on the other side was a skinny man in baggy brown wool pants and a tattered suit-jacket and matching wool knitted cap with earflaps. When I finished I pulled up my pants and walked back to the door of the bus passing dozens of others who were still blissfully urinating. All those people needed a bathroom break, but it took a *gringo* to ask the driver to stop.

When we arrived in La Paz we checked into a hotel at the top of a hill overlooking an open market. After locking our backpacks in our room we took a walk into the downtown area to find a restaurant for dinner. When I mentioned to our waitress that I wanted something light because I had an altitude headache she recommended that I order coca tea. It was made from the same coca leaves that cocaine is made from, but it apparently was not narcotic at that stage. She brought the tea right away and by the time our food arrived my headache was greatly reduced.

It was dark by the time we left the restaurant to return to our hotel, and when we were about half way up the hill, the entire city had a blackout. It was a dark moonless night and the only light visible was from shopkeeper's flashlights. We were concerned that it could be an opportunity to be mugged. We held hands to avoid becoming separated as we walked upward toward our hotel, and we avoided talking, thinking our best protection was in not exposing ourselves as foreigners as we walked. We got lost a couple of times in the narrow, winding streets, but finally we came upon our hotel. The hotel manager was standing in the front door waiting for us with a candle. He escorted us to our rooms and lit our one and only candle. There was barely enough light to find the bed let alone try to read or do anything else, so we turned in early.

Early the next morning we were awakened by the noise from the active street market below our window. All forms of fresh produce were sold out of large sacks or boxes in the section near our hotel, while other areas of the market sold other things. One section was for clothing, another was for musical instruments, and another was identified as the Witches Market, where they sold items such as dried sheep fetuses for people to bury under one corner of their house as a good luck measure. All the items sold at the Witches Market were for good luck, not for casting evil spells on people. After seeing the Witches Market and thinking about my experience on the bus when I needed a toilet so badly, along with all the other experiences we'd had since leaving Minnesota, I realized I was willing to put up with almost anything to keep traveling. As much as it frightened me, I knew I was going to cross the Pacific Ocean with Tom. I knew he wanted to go badly, and I would never let him go alone.

RETURN TO ECUADOR

We hardly recognized Salinas when we got back. What had seemed like a ghost town was buzzing with people. We were pleased to find our boat was safe and in good shape when we returned. I had the impression the man who slept on the boat rather enjoyed his prestigious post because he kept the exterior washed and somewhat polished. Tom paid him the amount they had agreed on and then he gave him some extra, just for good will. The man seemed pleased and we, of course, were nothing short of grateful.

We met the Danish ham radio operator that Eric Fog told us to look up. The Danish couple was in Salinas at their winter home. They had a shrimp farm in the area that was run and managed by hired men most of the time. But because it was a huge investment, the couple liked to check on it periodically. They were kind to us and invited us to their home. When they learned we were about to cross the Pacific Ocean, the conversation moved toward the issue of our health at sea. We told them we had been inoculated for quite a few diseases and had full physical exams prior to having left our home in Minnesota. "But what do you do about amoeba?" she asked. "Do you carry amoeba medication with you?"

"No," I answered. "I don't even know what amoeba's are." We learned they were some form of parasite common to the area, and that the local people "got cleaned out" once a year by taking some pill. Everyone who could afford the pill did the annual cleansing ritual, but then she cautioned, "It should only be done where you have access to a doctor or a hospital in case there are complications."

I didn't even want to ask what those complications might be, and I wondered what all those poor people who drank and cooked with water from the small streams did about their amoeba's. I knew they could not afford pills or doctors, and I guessed they all had amoeba's.

Before leaving Ecuador, our new friends drove us to the next town so we could stock up on provisions for the boat. Their car made it possible for us to buy bulky things like a full stalk of bananas (for 50 cents), flats of eggs, a large bag of potatoes, squash, carrots, onions, and lots of fruit. (See Color Photo Insert, page 23.) I also stocked up on toilet paper, paper towels, and several large bottles of shampoo which I discovered worked better than dish detergent as a salt-water body wash. All the items were cheap in Ecuador, and since I didn't know when or where I would be able to buy them again, I stuffed the boat with all it could hold.

We hung the banana stalk on the mizzenmast and cushioned the oranges in a string hammock next to them. The flats of eggs were placed in the side cabin, snuggled between plastic containers filled with fresh produce. Since the eggs had never been washed or refrigerated (there was still grime and feathers on some of them), they would keep for several weeks without refrigeration.

I also bought four small plastic dishpans, a bag of potting soil, and leaf lettuce seeds. We already had a roll of plastic screening on board, and with those few items I set up two small lettuce gardens, one on each side of the cockpit, next to the main hatch. (See Appendix A for directions on Growing Leaf Lettuce On Board)

We did not want to put the local tap water on our boat, so we found a place that sold five-gallon bottles of mineral water at 10 cents a gallon and decided that was the water we would use. We couldn't take the round glass bottles to our boat so we bought 10 five-gallon plastic jugs and washed them out with bleach water; took them to the water store, and transferred the bottled water to the jugs. After filling all the jugs, we put them in the trunk and back seat of a taxi, and with the taxi axle dragging close to the street, we returned to the marina where our dinghy waited for us. There we transferred the full jugs to our dinghy and motored out to the boat. Tom lifted each one while I held the funnel in the water fill hole on the side of our boat. We made five such trips until our 200-gallon tank was filled. It took us all day to accomplish but it was worth it knowing we had clean safe water on board before we made our crossing.

Last, but certainly not least, we put together an emergency overboard bag. In a large canvas bag we placed fishing equipment, hand-held navigation equipment, a flashlight, sun screen, chap stick, toothpaste and brushes, two longsleeve white shirts, wide brimmed hats, a can opener, two sets of flatware, two plastic plates, bowls, and cups, and waterproof matches. To the drawstring I attached a list of items that I would grab and put in the bag at the last minute: canned food, bottled water, the EPIRB, and wool blankets. The plan was that while I gathered and filled the man-overboard bag, Tom would launch the life raft and our dinghy and motor. There would be only two reasons we would ever abandon the boat. One was if we were sinking, the other was if we were on fire. That was our plan but we hoped we would never have to exercise it.

Tom made one last trip to shore by himself. He had been thinking about the dedication and kindness the workers had shown us, and when he learned they had no sick policy it bothered him. When one of them was ill and unable to work, he lost pay for each day he missed. Tom didn't think that was fair for those already earning so little, and he wanted to contribute seed money to begin a sick fund. So he found the head "marinero" and made a $100 donation towards the workers' first Health Fund. His generosity was such a surprise that word of it spread quickly. From the far corners of the yacht club, workers gathered around, shook his hand and offered a big *Gracias*.

PART THREE
The South Pacific

CHAPTER SEVEN

The Galapagos & Crossing the South Pacific

"GEEZ, YOU'RE BLEEDING ALL OVER MY DECK"

As usual, Tom put out a fishing line shortly after we left port. Often in the past I had been irritated when he did that, as we usually still had plenty of fish in the freezer. But this time we had no fish on board, because we had emptied the freezer before leaving on our three months of land travel, and I actually welcomed his fishing. Mark and Michelle would be joining us in the Galapagos and that meant I would be feeding four people, and from a practical point of view, fresh fish would be a welcome addition to the meat we recently added to our small freezer.

There had been no action on his line for many hours, when all of a sudden the fishing reel began screaming. *Zeeeeeeeeg!* The line went out and out and out while Tom leapt out of the cockpit and grabbed the fishing pole from its mount. Even before he reached the pole he began shouting commands. "Get the engine on and turn upwind," he ordered.

I locked the wheel, went below, and turned the ignition key. As soon as I was back in the cockpit I turned the boat up into the wind. Meanwhile, Tom stood on the stern of the boat without the security of wearing a lifeline, and fought whatever was on the other end of his fishing line.

"I don't know what I've got on the end of this line, but it's the biggest God damn thing this pole has ever seen!" he said while playing the line the best he could.

When the fish dove deep it took yards and yards of line, and when it came closer to the surface, Tom reeled in as much line as he could. The excitement was explosive, and I worried about Tom on the stern all by himself. I knew he would risk anything to land that fish.

"Stop watching me and concentrate on what you are doing. You've got to keep the boat upwind and slow it down," he demanded. "I can't handle this thing at this speed."

I tried to concentrate on allowing the sails to luff a little, but not allow the boat to go completely through the wind. It wasn't easy. Each time I would let the sails lose their wind, there was the risk of having gone too far, and not being able to recapture it without getting ourselves in irons. We'd been through this many times, and I hated the routine. I knew we would be screaming at one another before he got that fish on board. Not only that, but I did not seem to have the amount of power I needed to bring us back downwind. I sensed something was wrong, but that this was not the time to mention it.

Usually the fishing fiasco was over within a few minutes, but not this time. This was a big, strong fish, and Tom fought it for 45 minutes before he even saw its outline in the water. What had begun as a thrill and a lot of fun, had turned into a chore, and I could see by his posture how fatigued he had become. Finally, the fish tired too, and Tom was able to reel in nearly all the line and bring it close to the boat.

"Good God," he shouted. "I've got a shark on the line and it's seven feet long! Now, what am I going to do?"

I didn't know what he was going to do, either, but I did know that I did not want it on board.

"Why don't you just cut the line?" I suggested. "If we're not going to eat it we sure don't need a shark flopping around on deck, not with the saw blades they have for teeth." Seldom did he agree with me when it came to anything concerning fish, but he did that time.

"Well, he's not going to take my nice Rapala lure with him, that's for sure," he stated stubbornly. Before I could even respond, he had the gaff hook in his hand, and hoisted the shark's head out of the water so that it lay on the transom, with only its tail hanging in the water. "Put the boat on course and lock the wheel," he ordered, "and then get a pliers and my leather gloves. I'm going to try to get my lure out of his mouth before I throw him back." (See Color Photo Insert, page 27.)

That is exactly what he did. To my horror, I saw him reach into the shark's mouth between all those rows of uneven teeth and rip out the lure, before allowing the creature to slip back into the ocean. With rod and the rescued lure in his hand, he slowly stepped back into the cockpit completely exhausted, but pleased with himself for having saved his fishing equipment.

I was relieved that he was OK but really upset with him for having taken, what I felt was a stupid risk! Imagine taking a chance of getting your hand gored by a shark over a fishing lure. Stupid, stupid, stupid!

"The hooks are pretty bent up, but I can straighten them out," he said.

I was too angry with him with him to respond.

"I had to," he explained, after hearing my silence. "I don't know when or where I'll be able to buy line, or get lures again."

"Well, we may have bigger problems than a shortage of fishing equipment," I snapped. "I couldn't get much power out of the engine while I was trying to keep it into the wind.

Sometimes, I wasn't sure if I would have enough power to bring the boat back at all."

He wanted to drop the subject; he was tired and needed to rest. He went below, got a soda, a pencil, and a fresh crossword puzzle. When he returned to his place in the cockpit it was understood that he did not want to discuss the shark, the engine, or anything that was controversial or unpleasant. He wanted nothing more challenging than which word might fit in which square on the paper in front of him.

The next couple of days were pleasantly uneventful. The winds were steady, the seas only slightly lumpy, and there were no storms to set our nerves on edge. The loud silence between us had mellowed to a soft accepting silence. We enjoyed each other's presence, slept in shifts, read, wrote, or worked crossword puzzles during our time on watch. Any words of anger that had been spoken over the shark incident were long forgotten, and three days later we arrived at San Christobal, the first of the Galapagos Islands. This was the island where our cruising permits were supposed to be waiting for us.

Tom lowered our sails outside the harbor where we were greeted by sea lions. They swam along both sides of the boat as we motored through the harbor entrance. They lifted their large whiskered snouts out of the water and barked as they escorted us into the harbor. Each had a kind, gentle face, with big, round, black eyes that watched Tom's every move. (See Color Photo Insert, page 27.) They curiously watched him drop the anchor, pump up the dinghy, and lower the dinghy into the water. When Tom stood in the dinghy as I lowered the motor to him, they watched that too, but they no longer barked. They simply watched. Not until we finished getting the dingy motor on did we realize the seals had disappeared. Where they went we had no idea; they were simply gone.

With boat papers in hand, we took the dinghy into shore to check in with customs and pick up our cruising permits. The officials behind the desk were young, handsome, and charming. They flashed their white teeth and greeted us with an excitement in their eyes that told us not many boat captains actually entered their office. Piles of papers were stacked on desks, spilling off the tops of cabinets, and falling out of the filing cabinet drawers. Thus, it was no surprise to us when they said they were unable to locate our cruising permits. We asked them to look again, but in that jumbled mess I doubted that anything could be found.

We returned to the boat not knowing what to do. Mark and Michelle were scheduled to fly in and meet us within the next few days, and they fully expected to see the Galapagos Islands. We wanted to see them too! The more we thought about it, the more upset we became. We had done everything right: we had filed with the Ministerio de Defensa, and with the Parque Nacional. Heck, those papers were someplace in that office. Just when we had a good angry steam going, two of the young officials who were now off duty came out to visit us on the boat. We invited them on board because we did not feel we had any other choice, and offered them something to drink. "Would you like coffee or a soda?" I offered.

They looked at each another and smiled sheepishly. Then one of them asked, "Do you have beer?"

So that's what they had come for. "We have a little beer," Tom answered "Would you like a beer?"

Their faces lit up in anticipation. In the relaxed atmosphere of beer drinking, we brought up the problem of our missing permits. "Could we help you look for our papers tomorrow?" Tom asked.

With their hands still happily clasped around their beer cans they agreed to let us help them look for our permits in the morning. While they enjoyed their beers, we made an effort to keep the atmosphere cordial by struggling to hold a conversation with our limited Spanish. When I had to search for a word, I looked it up on the English side of our dictionary. Then I showed them the Spanish equivalent and asked them to pronounce it for us, but neither of them wanted to look at the printed word in the dictionary. It puzzled me at first, but then it dawned on me. They could not read, and that was why the papers were piled everywhere. They did not know how to file them.

That evening, while we sat in the cockpit and admired the stars, we heard an unusual splash near our dinghy. Tom shined the flashlight down to see what it was, and there, sitting in the dinghy was a huge sea lion! It could easily have weighed 300 pounds.

"Are you going to allow it to sit there?" I asked.

"As far as I'm concerned, he can sit anyplace he likes. Did you see the size of him?" Tom asked. "Unless you would like to shoo him out of there. I only hope he doesn't leave any little surprises for me to clean up in the morning," Tom added, with a chuckle.

"I hope he doesn't decide to come up into the boat," I said. You don't think he could get up here, do you?"

"I don't think so, but I would never have guessed he'd get into the dinghy either, so what the hell do I know?" I put the hatch boards in that night, (something I seldom did), and we went to bed knowing the seal could not get inside the boat ,even if he did get into the cockpit. After having been at sea for two nights, and sleeping only short intervals in shifts, we needed an uninterrupted night's sleep, especially if we were going to take on the task of finding our papers in that messy office the next day.

A sea lion sat in our dinghy next to our boat in the Galapagos Islands.

Fortunately, the seal lion was gone the next morning, and he left no "surprise" for Tom to clean up. We were also fortunate with the paper maze. Our permits were near the top of a stack, having recently arrived, and we found them much more easily than expected. The young men seemed equally relieved that we had found them, and I sensed they really did aim to accommodate us, they just didn't know how.

It was only a one-day sail to Santa Cruz where we were to meet Mark and Michelle, but it was a long day, mostly because the wind was light and we had to motor. For some reason we could not get speed over two knots. That did not make sense because our engine was fully capable of going 6 or even 6½ knots. Tom checked the oil and a few other things. Everything seemed OK, but of course a speed of two knots was not OK. Could it be possible that we needed a new transmission? Ugh, what a thought in someplace as primitive as the Galapagos Islands.

It was dusk when we arrived at Santa Cruz, and well after the hours when we could check in, so we anchored for the night with plans to check in with the officials first thing the next morning. We were surprised to see two other cruising boats anchored in the harbor and wondered how they had secured their permits. One flew a German flag, the other flew a French flag. Ordinarily we would have attempted to greet them in some manner, but that night we were tired, hungry, and salty, and we made no effort to contact either boat. Instead, we took baths off the stern of the boat, and while I started dinner Tom wrote in the ship's log, studied the charts, and tried to decide how we could get our transmission either repaired or replaced.

We had not bothered to put clothing on after our baths, and because we were both naked, it added to our panic when we heard people climbing on board, uninvited. Tom grabbed a pair of shorts and I quickly wrapped myself in my still damp towel as we scurried to the cockpit in time to see three uniformed men stepping up onto the side of our boat.

"What is the meaning of this?" Tom demanded, in his most authoritative Spanish.

"We come see permits," one young man said in his best English while pointing to his eye (the universal signal to indicate he wanted to see something). "You no have permits, you then pay us."

"You want to see our permits?" Tom asked in amazement. "I'll show you our permits, but I talk to only you," Tom said, poking his index finger into the chest of the spokesman for the group, "and you stand there and go no further," he said, using his best authoritative tone. Tom told me to get our permits while he stood his ground, and he prevented the three men from advancing. "You two, get off my boat." he shouted. "I only talk to one man, not three."

The other two men returned to their official boat. "No get mad, *Señor*, if you no got permit you can pay us in dollars or whiskey. That be no problem. It be done all the time," the spokesman stated, with a lot less conviction.

"I have permits," Tom said, and he waved the permits in the official's face. "See, I have permits and I'll bring them into your office in the morning."

"You have permits?" he asked in amazement. "You need two permits, not just one."

"Yes, I have two permits, one from the Ministerio de Defensa and one from the Parque

Nacional. Now, get off my boat. You will see the permits in the morning."

They seemed really surprised that their little game of extortion had not worked. Apparently it had worked for them in the past, and since we were the largest of the three boats anchored in the harbor that night, they tried it on us. We were the most likely to have money and/or whiskey on board.

The next morning, we checked with the other two boats to see if they had a similar visit from the officials. Neither had, and when we officially checked in we reported the incident to the captain in charge. We were able to identify the spokesman for the group, but not the other two men who had been with him, because it had been dark. The Captain apologized for his men and assured us he would find out who the other two were, and would take care of the matter.

Tom asked if there was a mechanic on the island and briefly explained our transmission problems. No, there was no mechanic but we could stay as long as we wanted while we waited for one to be sent from the mainland, if that was what we needed to do.

"If you decide to take your boat to any of the other anchorages you will need to have an Ecuadorian guide, but here in this anchorage you can stay as long as you need to," he said.

It wasn't as if the engine did not work at all, it merely propelled us very slowly. Since we were a sailboat, not a powerboat, we decided to think on it for a while with the hope that some solution might come to us. Meanwhile, we decided to move forward with our plans to see the wonders of the Galapagos.

We visited the National Parks office to hire a guide. Just outside the office we met a young man named Guillermo, an Ecuadorian who told us he was a registered guide. He seemed friendly, had some command of English, and was willing to go with us on our sailboat for a week. We negotiated a price with him before the three of us entered the office.

First, the office manager did not believe we had secured both sets of permits, but after poring over the documents we brought with us, there was no question about that. Then they tried to tell us we could only visit the islands on one of their official boats. We knew that wasn't true, and was only another form of extortion. They charged a lot for their boat experiences and we'd heard they were bug-infested, damp, and uncomfortable. Anyway, we would never leave our boat unattended in that harbor. We knew it would be stripped clean within a day of our leaving port.

Just when I thought we had them willing to cave in, they discovered one more loophole. They showed us how our papers were only for Tom and me, and they became very upset when they learned we had guests arriving at the airport that afternoon. Our guests, they figured, would have to take one of their official boats.

But having Guillermo sitting next to us, and so obviously wanting the job, put additional pressure on the park officials. Finally, and with great reluctance on their part, we got the permission we needed.

We returned to the boat to get it ready for our guests. I moved everything that had been stored in the V-berth to the side cabin, put clean bedding on the bunk where they would sleep, cleaned the forward head, and tidied the galley and main salon. Tom washed and waxed the exterior of the boat and I polished the stainless steel stanchions. When we finished, we bathed in the water behind the boat. After bathing, I stood on the swim ladder with my feet still in the water while I shampooed my hair. Apparently my painted toenails looked like some tasty morsel to a puffer fish that swam past, because it bit a chunk of flesh off of my little toe, and it hurt like hell! I let out a scream and scampered up onto the boat.

Did Tom act concerned about me? No! Did he even inquire about what had happened? No! Instead, he said, "Geez, look what you're doing. You're bleeding all over my clean deck!"

ROMANCING FRIGATE BIRDS

Mark and Michelle's airplane arrived on time. They each had one small piece of soft-sided luggage, and a third bag full of goodies for us: home-baked chocolate-chip cookies, canned nuts, candies, fresh crunchy snacks, mint tea, packages of dry yeast, more lettuce seeds, alfalfa spout seeds, horseradish sauce, an assortment of boat parts that Tom had ordered, some clothes that I ordered out of the L.L. Bean catalogue, and a large bundle of mail. They also brought two small, battery-operated fans to help keep the V-berth cool. Not only did they know how to pack light for themselves, they also knew what things we might need. They came each year bearing gifts like a pair of Santa Clause with the items we had not had access to for a long time.

Guillermo agreed to meet us at the dock early the next morning all packed and ready to go. We were a crowded, happy, cozy little group. Tom and I had our cabin in the stern, Mark and Michelle had the V-berth, and Guillermo slept in the main cabin. The three of them shared the forward head, and we had a private head in the stern.

We had a wonderful time visiting anchorages on different islands. We swam with penguins, marine iguanas, tortoises, sea lions, and sharks. The penguins were little fellows, not more than a foot tall, and they swam past us like small torpedoes. The iguanas, which were somewhat cumbersome on land, were fantastically fast in the water, but the most amazing of all, were the sea lions. They didn't ignore us as the other animals did; they actually played with us in the water. They swam to within arm's reach and stared at us with their big puppy-dog eyes. They especially loved playing with Tom, as he would twist and dive to attract their attention. Then they would mimic his twisting and turning, and wait to see what he did next, so they could repeat that antic, too. All was great fun until one of us got a little to close to a female, or a youngster. When that happened, the bull, the dominant male of the group who might have weighed 700 pounds, would charge at us. He never bit or touched us, but let us know that he could do some harm if we overstepped our bounds.

I was able to get very close to this sleeping baby sea lion.

The blue-footed boobies were fascinating, too. These large duck-like birds, with bright periwinkle-blue webbed feet appeared colorful when alone, and when there were many of them together, they looked as if all had just stepped out of a bucket of paint.

Another fascinating bird was the frigate, a large, wide-winged black creature about the size of a goose, but unlike the goose, this one was the master of the air. It had the remarkable skill to dive to the surface of the water without ever sitting on it or getting wet, and then plucking an unsuspecting fish up into its beak. (See Color Photo Insert, page 26.) We happened to be there during the frigate's mating season and we were able to see several males sitting on the nests they built. After building the nest, the males blew up a large red sack in the front of their neck and shamelessly solicited the females who circled above them. They cooed solicitously to the females and puffed their large red sacks until it looked like it was paper thin and appeared as if it might burst. The females continued circling above. When one made her selection of mate, she descended to the nest, and the two seemed to hug each another in wrapped wings. It was a beautiful sight, and they were not the least bit bothered by our being there.

Without Guillermo, we might not have found that spot. He was a knowledgeable guide, and we enjoyed having him aboard. He led us on long island walks, and before each walk Guillermo always reminded us to bring sunscreen, hats, and wear good walking shoes, because the Islands were volcanic and it would be easy to get scraped feet on any number of rock formations. This was our first exposure to volcanic rock, and while it looked heavy and unforgiving, we were amazed at how lightweight it actually was. Tom, like a skinny Charles Atlas, picked up a large boulder and held it above his head for a photo op.

At one anchorage, Mark, Michelle, Guillermo and I went snorkeling while Tom stayed on board to do some bookwork and puzzle over our transmission problem. There was a dealer in Florida who might be able to find a transmission for our motor, but even if we could get it sent to us, we did not know how we would manage to install it. We would probably have to cut a hole in the floor of the cockpit to get at it. Prospects did not look good.

Meanwhile, we swimmers were not paying very close attention to the changing tide and soon found ourselves a lot farther from the boat than we should have been. When we began swimming toward the boat, we got no place fast. In fact, no matter how fast I swam, I could barely stay in the same place. Going on shore was not an option because the entire rim around the island was covered with very sharp coral. We would have been cut badly if we tried to go across it. We called to Tom, hoping he would come and get us in the dinghy, but he was below decks and oblivious to our plight. Mark was the strongest swimmer, so he put all his effort into swimming back to the boat to get the dinghy. Meanwhile, the rest of us hung on to a section of coral so we would not get pushed further and further out to sea while we waited for Mark to return with the dinghy. Hanging on to that coral and knowing that we could not swim back to the boat was a frightening and sobering experience. The tide had changed so quietly that none of us noticed until it was almost too late. I made a note to myself to never let that happen again, as we all happily climbed into the dinghy that Mark had brought back for us.

Most afternoons, Mark and Tom went spear fishing for the evening meal. We had plenty of food stowed aboard by then, but there was some masculine satisfaction in bringing back fresh fish. They were usually successful, but sometimes they did not have much time in the water because the sharks would arrive and begin acting aggressively.

The vacation time spent with Mark and Michelle was wonderful, and ended all too soon, and when we returned to the main harbor we were surprised by Guillermo's eagerness to get to shore. We assumed he would have dinner with us, and go to shore in the morning when we took Mark and Michelle in to catch their plane, because all week he had made it known that he really enjoyed his experience on a "private yacht." But no, he stuffed his few belongings into his backpack and insisted that we pay him immediately and take him to shore. It was rather puzzling behavior. The next morning, when it was time for my ham radio schedule, I looked for the extra watches we kept in the chart table. I could more easily keep track of the Greenwich Mean Time and Minnesota time by keeping one set on each of those times. Both of them were missing. Even the extra batteries we put on board were gone, and we could only assume that Guillermo had taken them. How disappointing, after we had trusted him, and how sad for him to have compromised himself over the theft of a few cheap watches.

DECISION TIME

When only Tom and I were left on the boat we had to deal with the problems at hand. The biggest was the transmission. It was clear that we were not going to be able to have it repaired there. Nor did it seem practical to have one sent in to us because that meant first finding a match to our engine, then facing the cost and logistics of having it sent. Even if we accomplished all that, we still would have to find a way to install it when, and if it arrived. That left two options. One was to return to Ecuador mainland, the other was to cross the Pacific with the engine as it was.

"We're not going to be able to use the engine anyway," Tom rationalized, "because we won't have enough fuel. We're going to be crossing the largest expanse of water in the world and we can only do it under sail power. The only time we will even be able to use the engine is going in and out of ports," he stated, while trying to convince both himself, and me.

With that mindset, we decided to cross the Pacific in our present condition. Still, there were a few things we needed to attend to. We needed fresh provisions, we needed to replenish our water and fuel, and we needed to do laundry. Purchasing fresh fruits and vegetables was easy, and we even purchased some fresh beef. Getting fuel was no problem, either. The government officials brought fuel out to us in a large barrel, and willingly sold and siphoned it into our tanks.

Water was a big problem, however. The local water was so green that I did not even want to wash the sheets in it, let alone consider putting it in our tanks. Before I could begin worrying about a solution, the sky gods decided to be good to us. That night, it rained! Rain in the Galapagos was a rare and precious gift, but it rained really hard. Hard enough to wash all the salt off our decks, hard enough for us to collect water for our tanks, and hard enough for me to wash all our sheets and towels on the side deck.

So with clean bedding, 250 gallons of water in our tanks, 175 gallons of fuel below decks, and an additional 25 gallons in containers topside, a well-stocked larder, and a sick engine, we began our sail across the South Pacific with the intent of being in New Zealand sometime before the next hurricane season began.

CROSSING THE LARGEST SECTION OF OCEAN IN THE WORLD

Crossing the South Pacific was nothing like I expected. For months I had worried about it being a hair-raiser, but instead it was a slow easy sail, enjoyable in every sense. The winds were steady, and we sliced through the water at such an even pace that Tom had no need to adjust the sails. In fact, during those first few days he had little reason to leave the cockpit, until one of us noticed the sheets were showing signs of fraying where they were threaded through the blocks. After discovering that none too soon, he made small adjustments to them each day, even if the wind conditions did not require it.

The sea was calm, consisting of wide, rolling waves instead of the violent, sharp-edged ones that I had found so jarring. The liquid hills swelled up from the ocean floor allowing the boat to slide gracefully up one side and down the other. I likened it to a motion similar to being on a swing: *up and doooowwwwn, up and doooowwwwn.*

Our routine became lazy; we sat in our preferred spots in the cockpit, and neither of us bothered to wear clothing during the day when the temperatures were warm. I spent my time reading, writing letters, cooking, baking, tending my two small gardens, and making radio contacts. Tom busied himself with navigating, working crossword puzzles, playing his harmonica, and sometimes strumming his guitar. Unfortunately, he sang when he played the guitar, and while I would be the first to list his many fine attributes, I would never include his singing on the list.

We shared watches during the day when we were both awake, and we took turns during the night, while one of us slept. Seldom did we speak more than a few words to each other, not because we were not on speaking terms, but because there just was not much to say. Our silence was comfortable, and in many ways we never felt emotionally closer. A thin line on the horizon indicated where the ocean stopped and the sky began, and that was the only visual item of interest beyond the confines of the boat. There was nothing else as far as the eye could see; still, neither of us felt lonely or isolated. Instead, we had a feeling of calm, and we became somewhat mesmerized from the rhythmic *swooooosh, swoooooosh* of the water, as it was pushed away from the path of the boat.

WE SLEPT IN SHIFTS

Late in the afternoon Tom took a gallon of water from our tank into our sun-shower and hung it on the stern of the boat, to be heated by the sun. When the sun was still warm in the cockpit, we each took mini-showers. After our showers, he turned on the generator to charge the batteries in preparation of running the nightlights, and to allow me the use of the microwave so I could prepare our evening meal. To think how I chuckled when I first saw the built-in microwave before we bought the boat. It seemed like such a foolish luxury and poor use of space at the time, but it was not long before I realized how handy it was.

Preparing food in a boat galley is a much bigger challenge than in a home kitchen. Every movement on a boat requires forethought because nothing stays where it has been set down, and it would be suicide to set down a sharp knife without securing it. Still, I took pride in preparing meals that were balanced, tasty, and nutritious. We had either fish or some type of meat with each meal, a vegetable or potato, and a small fresh salad from my topside garden. Sometimes our salad was no more than one lettuce leaf each with alfalfa sprouts, chopped fruit and a few nuts with dressing, but even that was a luxury out in the middle of an ocean. Many of the cruisers we talked to on the radio had no refrigeration and had to rely on canned vegetables, rice, and pressure-cooked dry beans.

During this passage, we ate early each evening to take advantage of the daylight, and after I cleaned and washed the dishes, I would take an early evening nap. I missed having a glass of wine with dinner, and I know Tom missed having a beer before dinner, but we had long ago made it a rule never to drink alcohol when underway. For short passages involving only a couple of days and nights, the sacrifice didn't seem monumental, but when faced with a long passage like crossing the Pacific Ocean, we found it more difficult.

After dinner, I slept until 10 or 11 p.m. before Tom woke me for my shift on watch; then he would sleep until sometime before dawn, when I woke him. It was a good arrangement for us because I was able to take another morning nap before I made my radio contacts, and Tom had a fairly long stretch of uninterrupted sleep each night. Since he did all our navigation, which required working with numbers, I felt it was more important for him to have that uninterrupted sleep, than it was for me. Besides, I had begun to rather enjoy my time alone at night, and I was able to sleep during daylight if I felt a need, whereas Tom wasn't able to sleep after the sun was up. When I awoke from my morning nap, he had fresh coffee ready, the ham radio all tuned, and our position report ready for me to read to the net coordinator.

GOOSHY BANANAS

Typically after my radio check-in, I made breakfast. Then I mixed a batch of leavened bread, or baked banana bread from the over-ripe bananas that were falling off the stock hanging from the mizzenmast boom. When we bought and hung that stalk, we had no idea the bananas would all ripen at once. We thought they would ripen gradually and we would be able to pick a few ripe ones each day, but that was not how it worked, and we now had ripe bananas falling off and making a gooshy mess when they hit the deck. There were so many of them that we'd begun to ask one another, "Did you eat your obligatory half dozen bananas today?"

I made a lot of banana bread and that could be mixed and baked right away, but we still needed leavened bread and that needed time to rise and a warm place to sit and allow the yeast to work. The perfect temperature for the rising bread was in the engine compartment. The challenge was in managing to prop the bowl so the rising bread would not dump over the engine. I solved the problem by placing the bowl in a large string bag and tethering the bag to the piping over the engine block. It worked perfectly. Sometimes, as a special treat I'd make cinnamon rolls with the leavened bread dough, but we used it predominantly for toast or sandwiches.

THE BIG DIPPER WAS UPSIDE DOWN

Life on board was both simple and good, and we began to appreciate small subtleties each day. A piece of trash floating in the water caught our interest and we speculated as to how it got there. The shapes of the clouds were noteworthy; and so were the shadows on the deck. Even the rich grain of the teak all around the cockpit added interest to our day. Night watches had their own special dazzle. Often there was phosphorescence that made the water around the boat appear white and frothy, or the moon artistically painted its long silver path across the miles of black liquid. It was a joy to see billions of twinkling stars away from the competition of city lights, and to notice how different each constellation looked in the Southern Hemisphere. The Big Dipper no longer looked like a dipper. In the Southern Hemisphere, it was upside down and looked like a big question mark. Occasionally, there was the added interest of seeing the lights of another boat or ship far across the horizon, but that was rare. Days and nights consisted of listening to the rhythm of the water pushing past our hull, the creaking of the rigging, and the wind gliding off the face of each sail. The sounds were continuous and reassuring.

WHY WOULD A NAKED MAN NEED SHOES?

There was virtually no excitement on board until the day Tom prepared to hoist the mizzen sail and began removing the sail cover. Two very large brownish-blackish, beetle-shaped cockroaches plunged onto the deck. Apparently they had slipped aboard with our stalk of bananas and had been living in the sail cover. It would be difficult to say who was more surprised, because when they hit the deck they scurried at lightning speed in opposite directions. Tom let out a yell and began jabbing at them with the boat hook. "LaVonne, bring me a shoe," he shouted.

"A shoe?" I asked, not understanding why a naked man would want a shoe.

"Yes, a shoe, and hurry it up!" He demanded.

I dug a pair of his shoes from the depth of his clothes locker and carried them up to the cockpit in time to see him prancing around and jabbing the boat hook onto the deck. *Bang! Plunk! Bang* went the boat hook.

"There are two really big cockroaches up here and we've got to kill them or get them overboard before they get below decks," he shouted.

We each took a shoe and swatted at the scurrying invaders. They were slick, ugly, and fast! Finally, Tom killed one with a loud clump of the shoe. I remained in hot pursuit of the other when it turned and scampered toward the stern. Instead of killing it I flipped it off the boat. Hopefully, some fish had a feast.

"Those were such big roaches they actually scared me," Tom admitted, before he hoisted the mizzen sail.

As I put the shoes away, I noticed the little peach fuzz on my arms was still raised. A few days later, I noticed a different type of cockroach run across the top of the refrigerator. It was much smaller, light brown, and almost fine and delicate in its appearance. I squashed it and hoped I would not see another one,—but no such luck. More and more kept appearing, especially at night. I opened all the food lockers and did a good search. I thought I had been so careful when we put provisions on board, but I realized that I had left the pasta and rice in their original boxes. There must have been eggs in and under the flaps just waiting to hatch, and hatch they did. I washed the food lockers with bleach water, removed anything that was in a box and put it into plastic zip lock bags or glass bottles, and tossed all the cardboard boxes overboard. Then I opened several roach traps and placed them in the food lockers, and each night, as part of my watch duties, I kept an eagle eye for them seconds after I turned on a light. I wanted to kill all of them before they began to multiply. For two years we had had a bug-free boat and I hated knowing we had them on board now.

More pleasant excitement came a few days later when we came upon a school of porpoises. They played in our wake for several minutes before heading off to wherever porpoises go. On another day, a small, beat-up bird landed on our deck. Where it came from is a complete puzzle, but I doubt that it could have survived much longer had it not been able to land and rest when it did. It had many loose feathers that stuck out in an assortment of directions not conducive to flight, and it was too tired to eat, drink, or be bothered by us. It hid behind our dorade box (an air vent) where it was out of our sight and protected from the wind, and when I checked the next morning it was gone.

That same day we saw a small sailboat on the horizon. We radioed to it but got no response, so we adjusted our course heading a little in order to get closer to it. Then we saw it was STRAWBERRY, the little sailboat that we'd met in Salinas. We could hardly believe our eyes. Imagine meeting up with a boat that we knew, way out in the middle of the largest ocean in the world. They did not have a radio on board so we couldn't talk to them, but it was great to see some other sign of humanity and we waved joyfully at each other as we sailed past.

I had already tossed the bug-infested cardboard overboard knowing that it would disintegrate easily in the salt water, but we still had all our other trash on board, and it had begun to present a problem. We had to make some decisions about what to do with it and finally decided to put anything overboard that the sea could decompose, and keep those things that the saltwater could not digest. That meant all food-scraps and paper went into the ocean. We broke a hole into the bottom of glass bottles so they would sink and could begin the process of becoming sand. All plastic and aluminum was flattened and kept on board. We continued to be extremely frugal with water, using only 35 gallons a week, and that included our mini-showers and the half-cup that I dripped daily onto the lettuce garden and alfalfa sprouts. One of the ways we conserved was to wipe the dishes and pots with a single sheet of paper toweling before running a soapy sponge over them, and then they were each carefully rinsed with a very small amount of water. We didn't conserve our drinking water and instead drank as much as we wanted, knowing it was crucial to avoid becoming dehydrated.

A FISHING LURE MADE FROM A SCREWDRIVER HANDLE

On the ninth day into the passage, we overheard a radio conversation between two sailboats and recognized one of the voices as Scarlet, on the sailboat LEBENHO. We were delighted to learn they were only a hundred miles from us, and I had to smile while we listened to her scold the captain of the other boat for not wearing a safety harness when he was topside doing sail changes. Only Scarlet, I thought to myself, would take it upon herself to do that. The captain she talked to was named David. We had never met him, but learned he was a single-hander on the AFRIGAN QUEEN, (not African), Afrigan. He was soft-spoken and sounded somewhat appreciative of his scolding, and we looked forward to the day when we would meet him. When they finished their conversation, we broke in and made contact. Tom, of course, could hardly wait to ask Neil how his fishing was going.

"Hi Tom, is that you?" Neil asked.

"Yea, it's me, old buddy. Have you been having any luck fishing?"

"Well, I've lost all my lures and now I'm fishing with a make-shift lure made from a yellow, plastic screwdriver handle." Neil admitted. "How about you? Have you been having any luck?"

Tom told him the shark story and bragged about how he saved his lure. He told him about the bird that came on deck, our position, our wind conditions and how successful my little lettuce garden was. It was all rather exciting and we established a time and frequency to meet with them on the air again the next day.

That night during my watch, something cold and wet hit me on the chest with a *thump!* I woke, startled and rattled, realizing that I had been derelict in my duties by falling asleep when I should have been awake and alert. Whatever it was that hit me, bounced off my chest before it fell to the floor of the cockpit, when it woke me. It was still there and made soft *flip-flop* sounds. Quickly, I grabbed the flashlight from a nearby niche behind me. What a surprise to see it was a flying fish helplessly flopping this way and that. I shined the flashlight across the upper deck and saw several more, all gasping for air and probably wondering how they found themselves on something as hard as the deck. While chastising myself for having fallen asleep, I picked up the one from the cockpit floor and tossed it back into the ocean. The others had to wait until morning, because one of our safety rules was that neither of us was allowed up on deck without both of us being awake.

Each day droned on in much the same manner, except that I did a better job of staying awake at night.

SHIPS LOG, TOM'S ENTRY
April 11, 1991, 7°S Latitude, 115°W Longetitude

This day finds us half way between the Galapagos and Marquesas Islands. We left the Galapagos 10 days ago, on this 3,050-nautical-mile passage. We are now further from land than at any other place in the world.

It is an easy passage, sunny and warm, with the 15-to 18-knot trade winds on our starboard quarter. We haven't seen another vessel for five days. We are alone on this very big ocean without fear, nor the "boat fever" that makes others yearn to get onto dry land.

We are naked; our privately warm world only calls for clothing after sunset. Our bodies are well tanned and in pretty good shape for a couple of 50-somethings.

I am sitting in the cockpit, watching the water with the same fascination that some find watching an open fire. I am also fishing, but little attention is required. The line is rigged to sound a *bzzz* when a fish is hooked. I am also steering, but that too is attentionless, since the autopilot maintains the heading that was given to it hours ago. I am also navigating, but that only requires going below every couple of hours to check our coordinates on the satellite navigator, and make the appropriate entry into the log. Now, my mind roams from thoughts of potential boat problems, to family, to wondering about what lies ahead in the Marquesas.

I look over at LaVonne and think Gawd, aren't we lucky. She is busy reading a book, but I notice that she occasionally looks around to verify that all is well,

and maybe sneak a look at her dishpan garden with rows of lettuce growing at different levels of maturity. She tends to it dutifully, and it provides us with a small, daily ration of fresh lettuce. I love that woman.

We kept a daily radio schedule with LEBENHO and AFRIGAN QUEEN, and the private fishing contest between Tom, Neil, and David inspired much interest among the three boats. When no one caught any fish we talked about how many miles we'd made the previous day; what we had for dinner, lunch, or breakfast; what books we were reading; or any other piece of trivia we could think of just to keep the conversation going.

For practical entertainment, we chased a small rain squall when we saw one on the horizon, with the hope of catching water for our tank. But the cloud was always empty by the time we reached it, and we got excited over nothing.

On the fifteenth day we heard a MAYDAY from s/y CACADU, one of the Europa 92 boats. They reported losing a man overboard at 1600 GMT at South 4 degrees 57 seconds, West 100 degrees, 28 seconds. They had been looking for him for several hours and were in the process of arranging a search with several other boats from the fleet, but we knew the likelihood of them finding him was remote. It was always difficult to learn about someone drowning at sea. At the same time, it served as a reminder not to become overly complacent about our own safety precautions. To take his mind off the drowning, Tom busied himself with several boat maintenance projects. He repaired the fuel lift-pump for the generator, checked the oil for both the engine and the generator, and checked the water level. He also made a list of repairs that we would need to do when we got to port, such as: varnish exterior teak, repair grommet on second reef of main sail, reinforce zippers on cockpit enclosure, check air leak in generator, do something about broken mast track slides on the mainsail, and replace number #1 house battery.

On the nineteenth day we began seeing birds. After 21 days and over 3,000 miles, we sighted four tall islands appearing on the horizon. What a memorable dawn it was!

CHAPTER EIGHT

Enjoying Life in Polynesia

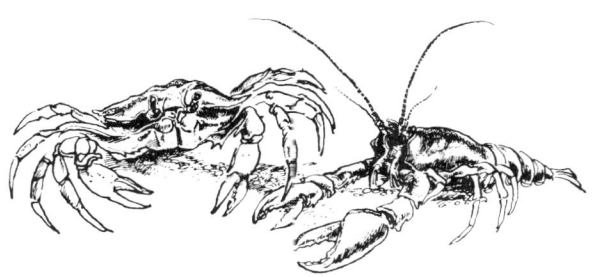

HARBOR ROCK N' ROLL

With excitement and anxiety that had been foreign to us for three weeks, we began our approach to the first set of five archipelagos in the French Marquesas. It was a little frightening to be close to land after being away from it for so long, and the closer we got, the more apprehensive we became. We stayed alert when we were near boat traffic, and watched the water for potential hazards such as fishing traps or coral heads, while we searched for the entrance to the harbor.

We entered the harbor at Hiva Oa and anchored in front of its main town, Atuona, a small, picturesque harbor surrounded on three sides with steep hills of lush green foliage that hung from tall, jagged, black, rocky slopes. There were about 20 local boats moored in the harbor, and a four-foot swell rolled in from the open sea.

Unlike the soft, gentle swells at sea, those in the harbor were confused and violent as they hit the shore, and bounced back. We had just crossed the largest expanse of ocean in the world, and I didn't get seasick once during the entire passage, but the water action in that harbor caused me to feel sick. All I wanted to do was pull up the anchor and leave. The waves made it difficult to lower the dinghy into the water and tricky to get the motor lowered and secured onto it, but somehow, as always, Tom managed to accomplish the seemingly impossible.

We gathered up our boat papers, stepped into the pitching dinghy, and headed toward shore, but not before we gasped with surprise at the sight of the long-necked barnacles that were attached to the entire length of our boat near the waterline. We headed to shore, dreading the task of scraping them off. But we would have to deal with them later. We tied the dinghy near a small boat ramp which was slippery with seaweed, and we nearly fell before getting up onto land.

WE LOOKED LIKE DRUNKEN SAILORS

Walking was a joke, too, and I'm sure we looked like we were drunk. Getting re-acquainted with our feet and legs on solid ground took effort. Just putting one foot in front of the other without tipping over required concentration. The ground seemed to move, and we soon found ourselves panting and short of breath from the slight exertion and the uphill walk to the port captain's office. Luckily, all our papers were in order, and the check-in process went smoothly, so we were able to return to our boat quickly and get out of that harbor.

In the challenging roll of the swells we brought the dinghy motor back on board, belayed the painter to the stern, and allowed the dinghy to trail behind us. I turned on the engine so Tom could use the winch to pull up the anchor, and we motored at two knots, using our sick engine to pull our barnacle-infested hull to the flat, quiet anchorage of Tahuata. What a relief it was to have just the slight boat motion once again.

THE POISONOUS FISH

As soon as we were anchored, Tom dove on it to make sure the hook was set, and of course, since he was already wet, he decided to go spear fishing. We should have begun the job of removing the barnacles, but we put it off for another day. While he explored our new underwater world, I tidied the interior of the boat, planned dinner, and baked a batch of cookies. The local people were curious about us and several came by the boat in outrigger canoes, smiling and gawking. One brazen young man actually grabbed onto the side of the boat and said something to me. Since I spoke no French, I had no idea what he said, but I offered him a fresh, warm cookie. He accepted it and asked with sign language if it was to be eaten. He tasted it suspiciously, and I think he was surprised to discover he liked the little brown disc.

I was wearing a bathing suit at the time, and I knelt on the side of the boat during our exchange. When he finished eating his cookie he reached out with one hand and stroked my bare leg. His touch so completely surprised me that I jumped back and shook my finger at him, as I might a small child. I wanted to make sure he knew that touching was not a polite thing to do. He just grinned, sat back in his canoe, and paddled off. Maybe he couldn't resist finding out what white skin felt like, although by then I was fairly brown.

While this was happening, Tom was in the water pulling the dinghy along with him until he saw a fish or a hole he wanted to dive on, and then he dropped the dinghy anchor and would go after whatever prize captured his fancy. He had just speared what he thought was a nice-sized fish for dinner, but when he came up to put the fish in the dinghy, a native boy was in a canoe next to him and motioned for Tom to put the fish back in the water. At first, Tom thought the boy was unhappy about his fishing in their harbor, but then the boy made a motion across his neck indicating that that particular fish was deadly or poisonous, so reluctantly, and with the boy's encouragement, Tom returned the fish to the water. A little later, when Tom speared a few other fish, Tom showed them to the same boy. The boy smiled and nodded his approval. Apparently, they were safe to eat, and when he brought them back to the boat he said,

"I'll be damned."

"What are you talking about," I asked.

"Do you remember seeing those long-necked barnacles on the side of the boat?" he asked.

"How could I forget those?"

"Well, they're gone," he said. "I think I remember reading someplace that they attach themselves to fast-moving objects. Apparently, now that we aren't moving any more, they lost interest in us and left to seek something that's moving."

That was fine with us! We couldn't have been happier to find we didn't have to scrape them off.

THE CAR ON THE CANOE

The next day we went on shore to try to rebuild some strength in our legs and to see what the little village looked like. Everyone we passed — and I mean every single person - smiled at us, and many stopped to give us fruit from their trees. They gave us *pompemouse* (a very large, thick-skinned grapefruit), mangos, papayas, and bananas. I wasn't sure I'd be able to choke down another banana, but these were small, finger bananas, and they had a whole, new exciting flavor. We graciously accepted all the fruit because we could see the villagers had an ample amount still on their trees.

Both the men and the woman wore long, colorfully printed cloth they called *pareos*. The women tied the fabric around them up under their armpits, while the men tied it around their waists, leaving their chests bare. Many of the men were heavily tattooed with

Above: This Marquesan man is showing us the beginning of his necklace tattoo, all he could afford.

Left: Heavily tattooed Marquesan holding a conch horn and displaying a war challenge with his tongue.

blue ink, but the tattoos were nothing like those seen in the United States. Their didn't display names, hearts, or eagles; instead, they were repetitive designs that formed armbands, ankle bracelets and necklaces. A few of the women had tattooed ankle bracelets, but mostly it was the men who wore the tattoos, and not all of the elaborate necklaces were complete. We learned the high cost of having a tattoo meant they were done and paid for one section at a time, and sometimes it took years before a necklace was completed.

Most of the social life of that little village revolved around the church, and the pride the people took in keeping that building maintained was obvious. Every night there was some church function with singing and socializing. By contrast, there did not appear to be any pride in repairing their dilapidated houses.

The peaceful little harbor was perfect for Tom to do several maintenance tasks. One was checking our transmission oil. He found it was low, so he changed the oil and filters, and much to our surprise, our engine no longer ran at two knots. Instead, it ran perfectly once again. Apparently, when he checked the oil in the Galapagos there was so much boat motion from waves and the prop spinning freely, that the oil slopped up on the dipstick, indicating there was more oil than there actually was. We shuddered to think how close we came to making major transmission repairs when there was never anything wrong that a little more oil wouldn't have solved. What a relief!

Then one morning the sleepy little village seemed all aflutter. We couldn't imagine the cause of the excitement, but then we saw a supply ship pull into the harbor. There was no pier, so the men went out in canoes, then paddled each load toward shore, while the women and children waded out into the crashing surf to remove the cargo by placing it on their heads and car-

A car is being lowered with ropes to two canoes because this Marquesan Village had no pier.

rying it ashore. Everyone was busy and did their part. Even the smallest of children carried what they could.

Just when we thought we'd seen most of the show, we got the grand finale. Two large outrigger canoes came out to the ship once more, but this time several boards had been placed between them to form a platform. Then we saw the ship's crane lift a car up and gently place it on the platform between the two canoes. We could hardly believe our eyes! Apparently, there was already a driver sitting in the car because when the canoes neared the shore, the car drove off the platform onto the sandy shore between sets of waves. It was like a theater-in-the-round; cheers resonated from every angle of the harbor. The natives all along the shoreline shouted and clapped their hands, and the crew aboard the supply ship whistled and shouted their approval, as well.

SHIPS LOG, TOM'S ENTRY;
UaPou, 10°S Latitude 141°W Longitude, 25 May 1991

I was snorkeling along a rocky shoreline, looking for edible critters, preferably lobster, but probably grouper.

The visibility was excellent, well over 100 feet. I looked over my shoulder and saw a huge pair of wings gently "flying" through the water. It was a big manta ray. Its head looked like a Darth Vader helmet with its downward curving sides that he used to funnel little critters into his mouth. Its wing span was about 12 feet. He must have seen me and was curiously approaching. I knew about mantas, but had never seen one in the wild. They are not meat eaters and are generally friendly. Nonetheless, I got a little edgy as he approached, but I wanted to see it up close, and possibly pet it. When he was about 15 feet away, I panicked. He was a hell of a lot bigger than I was. I scrambled up the rocks as fast as I could, and breathed relief. I sat on the rocks and watched him turn and head up the shoreline with his big, undulating wings powering his way. Now, I was mad at myself for not staying for an eyeball with this magnificent, harmless creature.

FRENCH TV

Most of the Marquesas' harbors were coves that offered only limited or partial protection from the sea. None of them had a pier or dinghy dock, making it difficult for us to land our dinghy. I think Tom rather enjoyed the challenge, but I dreaded it. The plan was for me to jump out of the dinghy at just the right moment with the painter in my hand, and run as fast as I could toward shore, pulling the dinghy up onto shore with me. Meanwhile, Tom's job was to stand up in the dinghy and tilt the motor up so the propeller wouldn't get damaged on the coral or sand.

Each time we faced a new landing through the roaring, gurgling surf, I was knotted with fear. Our efforts seldom went smoothly, and I hated being wet up to my crotch with salt water. Worse yet, if I didn't do it correctly, the dinghy, with Tom and the motor, could be flipped over and slammed onto shore. It was never our finest moment together, but once we got on shore, the episode was usually put behind us, and we made it a point to enjoy the experience. Of course, during the entire time we walked on shore, my saltwater-soaked underwear acted like sandpaper where the elastic dug into my skin, and made it difficult not to think about the task of reversing the process when it was time to return to the boat.

On one island, soon after landing our dinghy, we met a handsome woman wearing a bright yellow *pareo,* with a matching fresh flower tucked behind one ear in her jet-black hair. As we passed her, she said something to us in French, and we motioned that we didn't understand. She turned to us and asked, "English?"

"Yes," we said. "We speak English."

"My Roger" (pronounced Rojay) "he talk English," she said, and motioned for us to follow her.

We followed her to a three-sided shelter made from long, thin tree trunks and topped by a bright red tin roof. The cement floor was covered with mats woven from some type of leaf. Next to the only bed was a functioning television. A pile of children lying on their stomachs, were lined up on the bed with their heads propped up by their hands, and various lengths of bare feet and legs swayed in the air. They were watching something similar to the French version of "Dallas", but when we appeared, their interest in the television was lost. They scrambled off the bed and focused their big brown eyes on us. One of the children scurried down a path into the jungle, and returned a few moments later with a tall, strong-looking man carrying a machete.

"Hello," he said, shaking our hands. "I'm Roger, and I see you have already met my wife Dora and our children." He introduced each of the children. Dora soon poured fruit drinks for everyone and served them in scooped-out coconut shells. "This sure is a surprise," Tom said to Roger. "I would never have believed there would be television here."

"Yes. The French government wants to keep as many people as possible on the islands, so they've made it possible for us to have television. Of course, I need to cut a lot more copra (coconuts) now in order to pay for all the electricity that the television uses, but I guess that makes both the government and Dora happy. She likes it because now she knows where our children are. They're right here, watching TV instead of getting into trouble someplace, and the government likes it, too, because they get a lot more copra from me."

He demonstrated how he split the outer husks of each coconut by holding it firmly in both hands and slamming it down onto a sharp stake, that looked like a huge screwdriver embedded upright in the ground. He opened the husk with one strong slam. No wonder his arms and hands were strong! He pulled the coconut from the husk, drained the milk into a jar and cracked the coconut open on the same stake. Then, we followed him to a small electrical machine that looked almost like a juicer, except it had sharp curved blades. He turned the machine on and placed the coconut up against the blades. Presto! The blades gouged out the tender coconut, allowing shredded pieces to fall into the catch pan below.

"That's how it's done," Roger said. "Copra"

"Whew," Tom said. "That is some machine!"

Out of earshot of Roger, Tom said to me, "Do you realize how dangerous that thing is? It would slice up a hand in no time flat." I hadn't paid much attention to the copra machine. I was still trying to figure out what trouble the children could possibly get into on the island. On the screen was a man wearing a tuxedo, and a woman wearing a low-cut evening gown with a diamond necklace and earrings. Each of them held a long-stemmed wineglass, and they were discussing something of great seriousness. By contrast, Roger and Dora were wearing cotton *pareos* without a single seam and drank fruit juice from coconut shells They were innocent, light-hearted, and seemed happy. Their world couldn't have been further from the scene they watched on the television. Their only connection with the TV was the French language, and I knew it would only be a short time before the children would become discontented with their simple lives on the island.

Dora presented us each with handsome hand-carved wooden swords for honoring them with our visit to their home. The deep intricate designs on both sides of the swords were impressive and had probably required hours to carve. I would have loved to have both of them, but didn't feel right in accepting them, because I was sure they had been carved with the idea of being sold as income for the family. Finally, upon her insistence, we graciously accepted one of them. The next day we returned to bring her some Ecuadorian canned goods and a hand embroidered linen towel from St. Thomas. Roger wasn't home when we arrived. He was probably out cutting more copra, but Dora was there and the children were all lined up on the bed just as we had seen them the day before. They were watching French television and getting exposed a little more each day to a life none of them would likely ever have.

DAVID'S BRAIDED BEARD

Back on the boat, we continued to maintain radio contact with Scarlet and Neil on LEBENHO, and subsequently, with David on AFRIGAN QUEEN. When we learned David would be anchoring near us, we arranged to meet him, and I invited him to join us for happy hour at around 5pm, and to stay for dinner that evening. Having never met him before, we weren't sure what to expect, but figured he'd be much like us.

At the appointed hour, a long, black, wooden dinghy rowed away from a pirate-looking sailboat in the anchorage. A scruffy, longhaired character wearing a bright tie-dyed shirt, baggy, cut-off shorts, and a braided beard paddled alongside our boat and said, "Hi, I'm David."

He tied his dinghy alongside our boat and came aboard with a bottle of wine in his hand. I was surprised at his appearance. If I had seen him on the street I might have

Our bearded friend, David, seated on his boat the AFRIGAN QUEEN.

crossed to the other side to get away. He had sounded so gentle and wise on the radio, not at all the way he looked. He saw Tom wince when his dinghy bumped up against our white, fiberglass hull, making a long, black streak along the side. David apologized and immediately moved his dinghy off to the stern where it couldn't mar our boat.

"Haw," he said to his dinghy, while giving it a gentle shove to get it as far off the stern as possible. "Get on out there where you won't be marking up other peoples' boats."

We appreciated his keen sense of humor, and once we settled ourselves in the cockpit and got to know one another, we got used to the way he looked. He was interesting and bright. He made it a point to let us know he did not use drugs, and because he had been to these islands before, he was able to answer some of our questions. It was an enjoyable evening, and after he left, I chuckled at myself. I knew we would see David again, regardless of how he looked. We liked our new hippie friend, and his presence on our boat that night reinforced the statement Tom made long ago about cruisers, which was that "we were all eccentrics, each in our own way."

A PIG IN A SACK AND GOAT STEW

The French Marquesas Islands soon held a wide assortment of boats in its rolly harbors, because this time of year was the perfect weather-window when boats could cross the South Pacific without facing a typhoon, and the French Marquesas was the first stop along the way. Many of the larger, more impressive boats were with a flotilla of boats sailing around the world together. They referred to the group as Europa 92, implying their planned arrival in Europe, in 1992. They spent much of their shore time partying and changing crews while they waited for the smaller, slower boats to catch up with the group. We found them to be a noisy, rowdy group, and often they were lazy about their anchoring, and dragged into other boats at night. Sometimes, late at night, loud arguments would break out on those boats, and it wasn't unusual to see a crewmember of one boat switch to another boat due to peresonality conflicts. One time we actually picked up our anchor and moved to the other side of the anchorage, just to have maximum distance between us.

The smallest boats in the harbors were almost always from France. Often, there was a young couple on board who were cruising on a lean budget, but they were usually skilled sailors, and we didn't mind being anchored near them. The smallest and most pathetic boat we saw was sailed by a skinny, French, single-hander. He was so thin that his ribs stuck out to the point where you could count them. He had no lifelines around his boat, but instead, had wire chicken-coop fencing around his cockpit. He had a tipsy, little wooden dinghy that he rowed back and forth to shore, and one day, as he was returning from shore with a bag of food supplies, we watched him get dumped over in the surf. Down he went, and so did all his supplies. He bobbed to the surface and dove down to retrieve what items he could, but we knew some things could not be salvaged. We watched him climb up onto his boat dripping wet, and looking rather disgusted. He tied his dinghy to his pathetic, little sailboat, and went below. We would have invited him to dinner, but we couldn't speak a word to one another, so I did the next best thing. I put together a little care package consisting of a loaf of home-baked bread and a few other foodstuffs from our larder.

With no arguments or false pride, he graciously accepted my gift. "Merci," he said, and I felt like an angel of mercy.

In the same anchorage the next day, Tom had his opportunity to play a hero by rescuing a dinghy that had gotten loose, and was being tossed by the surf. He waded out, grabbed the painter and pulled it up onto the shore. Just as he finished tying the painter to a rock, a young couple, who were carrying bags of groceries, walked up to him.

The young man demanded, "What are you doing with our dinghy?"

Tom helped this Marquesan put his pig in the sack. Note, the pigs nose is sticking out so it can breathe.

"Rescuing it for you," Tom answered. "Apparently you didn't pull it up high enough, and when the tide came up it was floating out toward sea."

The young man blushed when he realized the tide was indeed a lot higher than when they left their dinghy on shore. He thanked Tom, and then they introduced themselves as Doug and Bobby, from Seattle. Bobby was a pretty blond, with a Farrah Fawcett mouth and a Barbie-doll figure, a lovely young woman with an infectious smile. Doug was a happy-go-lucky sort who even smiled when he was trying to be stern. They were a darling couple, so young and fresh, and we parted on good terms and returned to our own boats.

Over the next several weeks, we visited an assortment of anchorages on many of the islands in the Marquesas. At one anchorage, we heard about a waterfall with a fresh-water swimming site at its base, a short walk across the island, so we decided to check it out. We put on bathing suits, a good pair of walking shoes, plenty of sunscreen wide brim hats, and began our hike.

We came across a man with a pig. He was walking the pig to market, but the pig apparently caught on. It sat down and had no intention of taking another step, so the man was trying to put the pig into a sack so he could carry it the rest of the way. What a scuffle it was! We couldn't understand the words the man was using, but we could understand the tone, and they were angry words directed at the pig, and the pig was squealing with its own displeasure. Tom helped the man get the pig into the sack. The man made sure the pig's nose could stick out so that it could breathe, and then we helped him hoist his heavy load up onto his back, and to tie the long vines around the sack and his shoulders to make it into a type of backpack. Down the road they went, with the man bent over with his heavy load, grumbling at the pig, and the pig squealing and squawking at the man.

There were other cruisers at the waterfall when we arrived, and we enjoyed telling them about the man and the pig. We swam in the fresh water pond that was lined with huge, smooth boulders at the bottom of the waterfall. After, we dried ourselves in the sun and then walked back to the boat.

During the time when we were swimming and helping the man with the pig, AFRIGAN QUEEN and LEBENHO arrived in the anchorage.

David had already bargained with a farmer, trading several .22 shells for a hindquarter of a goat. Because he had been to these islands before, he knew that the government allotted a limited number of .22 shells each year for hunting, and to help keep down the wild goat population. The shells were limited because the French worried that the Polynesians might take up arms against them. Of course, the farmers were always eager to get more than their allotted amount, and David had the foresight to bring shells with him for trading.

"I thought I'd make a big batch of goat stew," David told me, "but I'm not sure if I have a big enough pot for the bones to fit."

"I have a lobster pot on board," I said. "Do you think that's large enough?"

"I'll chop the bones and make them fit," he said. "How about we make up a big batch of it and invite all the boats in the anchorage

That's what he wanted to do in the first place, but he didn't want to come right out and ask, "Can we all come over and cook on your boat?" He was clearly the most social single-hander we had ever met. We liked the social aspect of the moment, also, and we invited everyone on board. I dug deep into the storage under the main salon seat and found our lobster pot that hadn't been used since the Los Roques Islands, and started the water boiling. David hacked the bones down to a size that would fit into the pot, and each of the boats that joined us brought whatever shriveled vegetables they had left on board. They added potatoes, carrots, squash, rice and beans, and we let it all simmer in the pot with the goat meat and bones. David had a wonderful time adding spices from the grand assortment I'd purchased in Ecuador. Neither of us knew what half the spices were, but he smelled each one, and if it appealed to him, he poured some in. The aroma was wonderful and whetted our appetites. When the meat was finally tender and falling off the bones, we were famished, and David announced that his creation was finally ready. None of us had ever eaten goat stew before, but we eagerly gobbled it up. Every last scoop was eaten.

THE NO-SEE-EMS SAW ME

We left the Marquesas Islands the next morning and headed toward the second set of French archipelagos, called the Tuamotus. Our charts indicated they were primarily coral atolls, or rim-shaped islands with central lagoons, and that they accounted for more than half of the French Polynesian Territory. Because they were so low to the water they were difficult to see, making them a hazard to boats.

I had no trouble staying awake during my night watch that night because I found myself itching and scratching at my back all night. By morning, I'd nearly scratched my back raw. Tom looked at it and told me I was full of welts everyplace except where my bathing suit had been.

"It looks like you're still wearing a bathing suit," he laughed. "Apparently the 'no-see-em's liked you on your walk to the waterfalls." I didn't quite see the humor and asked about his bites.

"I didn't seem to get any," he said.

During my radio contact that morning, I learned that several of the other women cruisers were plagued with bites as well, but for some reason, the men were not bothered. How puzzling!

I tried lotions, creams, and baking soda, but nothing seemed to stop the itcing. I knew I had to resist scratching myself any further, and put on a soft t-shirt to help keep my hands off my back, but even that was difficult. I'd still find my hands reaching up under the shirt to scratch, and then I'd chastise myself for doing it. Eventually, the welts shrunk and the sores healed, and luckily, none of them became infected. Apparently, some of the women got really sick due to infection, but I still couldn't figure out why the men didn't get bitten. Was their skin tougher? Could the no-see-em's smell the difference between the male and female hormones? Both Tom and I wore the same sunscreen, so we should have smelled the same. It was very puzzling.

That afternoon, while all was quiet, and we were sailing along at a good clip, Tom's fishing reel began screaming louder that it had ever before. The line raced off the reel at an ear-piercing pitch, and Tom grabbed the rod just in time to see the last of the line whip out through the leads. Behind the boat in the direction of the line, we saw a marlin weighing a hunded pounds or more. It burst straight up out of the water and did a little tail dance on the surface before diving back into the sea. It all happened so fast that neither of us could grab a camera, and we missed the opportunity to capture it on film.

Tom was all excited. "Did you see that? What a sight!"

Not until the excitement of the moment had subsided did Tom come to grips with the actual outcome of the situation.

"There went my white feather lure, a good steel leader, and a whole reel of line," he announced.

BLACK PEARL PRODUCTION

As we neared the first atoll, Tom navigated with great care. He also had to calculate the tide based on our time of day and position of 16 degrees south – 147 west. Each atoll had only one entrance, and we wanted to plan our approach to coincide with either a rising tide, so that the tide could work with us as we entred the narrow passageway, or a slack tide that wouldn't hinder us as we entered. What we wanted to avoid was a falling tide because the current coming out of the atoll would be strong, and against us.

Rangiroa was the largest atoll, but Fakarava was considered to be the most important commercially, because it produced the most coconut. Copra and breadfruit were exported from it, and Fakarava was also heavily involved in black pearl production.

We selected a small, lesser-known atoll, and at slack tide slipped through its narrow entrance, unmarked by any navigation markers, while taking care to read the water and keep a close eye on the depth gauge. Tom took the wheel, and once we were inside, he cautiously motored about the inner lagoon attempting to become acquainted with the various depths. He selected a place to anchor, and after getting the anchor set, he dove into the water to make sure it had dug in securely. We could not take a chance of having the anchor drag, and find ourselves on a reef in the middle of the night. Soon, I was in the water as well, and I discovered the somewhat-protected saltwater lake was teeming with fish and assorted coral. It was like an underwater park! We spent several days at that atoll, which was teeming with fish and coral. We loved our own private aquarium! Tom dove for lobsters and speared coral trout and grouper, all of which we ate with gusto. I mostly did sight-seeing while I snorkeled on top of the water, relishing the opportunity to study the movements of the fish as they zipped in and out of the coral. Every color of the painter's palette could be found on them, and many fish had four or five colors.

One day, we snorkeled over to an area where there was mesh grating on the surface of the water, with long ropes hanging down from it. When we saw each rope had dozens of oysters clinging to it, we realized it was a small black pearl farm, and we swam away from it, because we didn't want to disturb the ecosystem of the production.

LAST CRAYON IN THE BOX

After exploring another atoll for several days, we set sail for Tahiti, one of the Society Islands in the third set of French archipelagos. Tahiti was the antithesis of the Tuamotu Islands. It was busy, loud, and bustling with people. We were told to stern-tie the boat to the large cement quay in front of downtown Papeete, the capital city. The quay was next to a boulevard that vibrated with honking horns, policemen's whistles, and chattering pedestrians. To slide into the assigned slot we needed to drop our bow anchor and motor backward to the quay, where we could tie up. We made sure our bow anchor dug in first. Then, with great difficulty and Tom's skill, we backed up as straight as we could, lining our boat up with the others as if we were the last crayon added to a box.

Once we were secure, we walked over to the port captain with our boat papers and checked in. He was a large Polynesian who had just completed a check-in with a French boat, and we noticed his agitation, and that the French couple was angry when they left the building. "Darn arrogant French think the rules don't apply to them same as everyone else," he grumbled to no one in particular, but he knew we could hear him. We waited for his attention, not wanting to upset him any further.

"See that map on the wall?" he asked us.

We looked at the world map on the wall and nodded. "Do you see how big Polynesia is compared to all of Europe, let alone that little country of France?"

We nodded again.

"Those French people think they're some kind of gods or something. They just don't want to understand that they need to post a bond just like everyone else."

Once he got all that off his chest, he asked to see our boat papers. He found them all in order, and Tom gave him a credit card to pay our bond ($400, that we could collect again when we left the Society Islands). The local government held the bond for all visiting yachts while they were in the country, in case any member of the crew became a problem and the officials wanted to send that person back to their home country. The bond was to cover the expense of the airplane ticket.

KEEPING CARL ERIC'S BOAT OFF OURS

Our first interest was to replenish our empty refrigerator, and we found a large store with more food in it than anyplace we'd seen in a very long time. It was exhilarating to see that much food in one place, but when we began doing the dollar conversion, it became depressing. Chicken was $4.00 a pound, and the artistically displayed fruits and vegetables were worth their weight in gold.

We could easily tell which shoppers were cruisers, even if we hadn't met before. They were the ones with the sticker-shock expressions on their faces, and carrying canvas boat bags so they could carry their purchases back to their boats.

When one of the other cruisers saw us lamenting over the cost of chicken, she said,"You don't even want to think about buying chicken in these islands. Lamb is the deal here. You can buy a whole leg of New Zealand lamb a lot cheaper than a skinny chicken."

Sure enough, she was right. We bought several legs of lamb, and that night I read my *Joy of Cooking* to learn how to cook my first leg of lamb.

A few days later I went on a shopping trip with some of the other lady cruisers in the anchorage. I was interested in buying fabric for *pareos* from one of several fabric shops that sold a wide assortment of wonderful, brightly-colored prints. I thought *pareos* would be cool, comfortable and practical, because the fabric could be folded flat and would take up hardly any space at all on the boat, and it would be the perfect thing to put on after we finished swimming and snorkeling. I had a wonderful time and came back to the boat happy.

Tom was anything but happy, however.

"What took you so long? he snapped. "Get the fender board out and help me rig it."

"What happened? I asked, while acting upon his demands.

"The boat that was next to us left, and this guy came in to take its place. I could see right away that his bow anchor wasn't going to hold, and I told him I didn't think it was set, but 'oh no'. In a cocky little way he said, 'I know my boat, and it's set real good. "But it didn't set, and I've been trying to keep his boat off ours since he left."

I helped Tom rig the fender board, because it took two people to do it, one on each end, and then spent the rest of the afternoon helping him fend off the Swedish boat that kept banging up against us. When the captain, Carl Eric, came back, he was a little tipsy, and couldn't figure out why Tom was so steamed at him.

Tom ended up helping him put out another anchor, and he made sure it was set and dug in well.

WE TOASTED THE UNCLE AT COOK'S BAY

A few days later, the Polynesians held a strike about the high cost of gasoline. It was an angry strike that successfully blocked the major roads, effectively tying up all commerce and movement on the island. The deeper wound was the Polynesian distaste for being under French rule, which dated to 1946, when the islands became a territory of France. From the very beginning, the Polynesians detested the arrogant attitudes of the French and abhorred the nuclear testing the French government blatantly continued on one of their atolls. The population was 78 percent Polynesian, 12 percent Chinese, 6 percent local French, and 4 percent French military assigned to maintain order on the island. From the French point of view, the Polynesians acted like ungrateful children who didn't appreciate all the money France had so generously poured into the islands. France paid for the entire modern infrastructure, and Tahiti prospered, partially due to having paved roads, schools, and an airport. But the Polynesians would have happily given it all back if they could return to their simpler lives without the French. The tension was potentially explosive and had all the promise of problems that we didn't want to deal with, so we sailed across to the next island, Moorea, that was only nine miles away. We anchored in Cooks Bay, a harbor named after the British navigator, and surrounded by greenery that grew up the side of a mountainous volcanic spire. It was a quiet anchorage with very little swell.

Shortly after we got the anchor set, Doug and Bobby, the young couple whose dinghy Tom saved from the surf in the Marquesas, came by and invited us for drinks. When we got there, we learned it was a bit more than drinks. It was the culmination of having buried one of their uncles. Apparently, the uncle had been cremated and wanted his ashes spread in Cooks Bay. We didn't get the whole story, but we learned that he had been a whiskey drinker, and we were invited to toast the uncle with the same brand of whiskey that he drank his whole life. It was a tough job, but somebody had to do it, and we willingly helped out.

CELEBRATING FÊTE

All of Moorea was quiet, slower, and more laid-back than Tahiti. It survived primarily on tourism because of its many white, sandy beaches and blue-and-turquoise lagoons. But for some reason, the reefs were all dead, the coral was gray, and there were only a few fish struggling to survive on them.

We sailed on to Bora Bora just in time to witness and participate in Fête, a national holiday. The excitement was infectious. Individual families set up small food kiosks and decorated them with tropical foliage. Large pots of food with enticing aromas tantalized our nostrils, and as we ate we tried not to think about the poor sanitary conditions under which the food had been prepared.

Sanitation didn't appear to be much of a concern among

Fresh, unwrapped, baguettes are delivered daily in the French Islands, but not the mail.

the locals, but freshness and taste mattered greatly, especially with bread. Many of the homes had an open-ended breadbox in front to which bread was delivered daily, much as we receive our daily mail. The bread, shaped into long narrow loaves called a baguette, was soft and fluffy inside with a crispy crust. To maintain that crispness, the loaves were never wrapped, and because they were so delicious, we overlooked the obvious sanitary concerns.

In the evening, a parade was held with music and huge floats that were carried on the backs of men. Some of the floats were high, with a young girl perched at the very top. All of them were decorated with banana leaves, fresh flowers, and greenery that had been growing on the island, only hours before. Big lights powered by generators, were strung up, giving the whole event a sophisticated tone, and sometimes men were called upon to lift the electric lines even higher to allow a float to pass under them. It was a fantastic night, and we couldn't help but admire the magnitude of the undertaking, considering the limited supplies and resources available for it.

When it was time for us to leave the Society Islands, I knew I'd miss them. I would especially miss our nights when we sat in the cockpit watching the outrigger canoes practice their racing skills; I'd miss watching the colorful bougainvillea petals floating across the water; and I'd miss watching the sun setting behind the mountain peaks. (See Color Photo Insert, page 29.)

SLUGGING A SHARK

A day and a half later we were anchored at Suvorov, one of the Northern Cook Islands. We checked in with the official, a young man named Tocaro. He was a handsome, brown-skinned lad with thick brown hair and a wide smile, and his job was to limit our time to no more than two weeks in his anchorage. But when he learned Tom liked to dive, and that we had a dinghy with a motor, he told us we could stay as long as we wanted *if* he could go diving with Tom. It was a marriage made in heaven for Tom.

There were only 10 people living on the entire island: a pair of grandparents, their two daughters, a son-in-law, the boyfriend of one of the daughters, three grandchildren and their youngest son Tocaro, the island's only official. (See Color Photo Insert, page 28.) They lived primarily on fish and the few goods the supply ship brought them twice a year. Shortly after our arrival, the grandfather rowed out to us and presented us with a large parrotfish. When we went on shore the next morning we saw how the grandfather caught them. He slowly walked along the shore holding a long, stiff sapling sharpened on one end. When he saw a sizable fish, he would, with amazing speed and accuracy, spear it and string it on the long vine tied around his slim waist. He kept the strung fish hanging down on the stringer, opposite from his spearing arm, but periodically he'd have to fend off small sharks that were eager to snap up an easy catch from his dripping stringer. What a gutsy old man!

He and Tocaro kept the family in fresh fish, but the grandmother was the social glue of the family. She seldom left her primitive home, but effectively kept order and peace within her family, most of whom had recently been ill. She was the only one in the family who smoked, and she was greatly disappointed when she learned that neither Tom nor I smoked, and that we didn't have any cigarettes on board. She warmed to me somewhat when I brought her some canned goods, but she would have preferred cigarettes.

But Tom and Tocaro bonded immediately, and they went diving together daily. Tom was proud of his ability to dive to 35 feet, but Tocaro could go to 50 feet or more. While Tocaro hunted for anything he could get to feed his island family, Tom was fairly selective, limiting himself to spearing coral trout or grouper, but when Tom got more fish than we could eat on any given night, he gave the extra to Tocaro. One day while they were hunting, I went along with them and snorkeled. At first, I was edgy about the many three-to four-foot white-tip and black-tip sharks in the lagoon, but neither Tom nor Tocaro seemed bothered, so I tried to become more relaxed around them, also. I saw a white-tip shark approach Tocaro and sort of brush against him near his shoulder, but Tocaro just pushed it away. Then I saw the shark circle toward Tocaro again. That time the shark bumped his head into Tocaro with a little more force. Tocaro turned toward the shark, made a fist, and slugged the shark right on top of its head. That was *enough* for me! I scrambled up into the dinghy just as fast as I could.

MEETING BILL AND GENE

A few days later, after hearing me tell LEBENHO about Suvorov on the radio, several other boats showed up in the tiny harbor. The first of those was FETE-ACCOMPLI with two men on board. At that point we were the only boat in the harbor and there was ample room to anchor, but for some reason, they chose to anchor right next to us. Tom grumbled to me about how close they were, but he left it to me to say something to them. I felt badly when I saw they didn't have a windlass, and had to pull up their anchor by hand, but they were good about it and moved a little further away to allow comfortable swing room for both boats.

Later, we met them. Bill had just left the military service and was between career changes, while Gene, the older of the two, was a medical doctor, an endocrinologist. Gene apparently carried a fairly large number of medications with him, and he generously offered his medical services, free of charge, each place they visited.

During medical rounds, the grandmother told him she had been suffering from shortness of breath, and asked his opinion. He examined her and suggested she quit smoking, but that was not what she wanted to hear. Gene also learned that the entire family had been sick a month earlier. The symptoms included high fevers, tender skin, and extreme weakness, and no one knew what the illness could have been. Luckily, they all recovered, and were, for the most part, feeling fine when Gene examined them.

MOSQUITOES AND RATS

Before long, there were several boats in the tiny harbor: LEBENHO, SKYBOAT, FETE-

ACCOMPLI and GRINGO. Not only did they each contribute supplies to the island people, but one of the boats gave the grandmother a full carton of cigarettes. She was so delighted, she announced there would be a potluck feast that night. The islanders would provide the fish and the hot oil to cook whatever else each of the boats wanted to contribute. It was a nice party, but I could tell Tom was getting itchy to move on.

Later, he told me it looked like there was a good weather window to begin our 445-mile passage to American Samoa. When we mentioned our intended departure, the other boats in the anchorage decided to leave too, a reminder of how yachties tend to herd. While Tom and Neil checked out with Tocaro, Scarlet and I took our trash to their dump where we saw one of the granddaughters chasing rats. The dump also was thick with mosquitoes, and as a result, we hurried back to where we'd left the dinghy.

DENGUE FEVER

Our first day at sea began with 15-knot winds, eight-foot seas and 20-percent cloud cover, a perfect beginning for a passage. But by afternoon, the seas were 10 feet and squalls were gusting to 30 knots. By the next day the seas had built to 12 feet. Again, I *hated* it! But because we were the first boat to leave Suvorov, and because we were the fastest boat in our fleet, we were tied to the pier in American Samoa two days later while the others were still out to sea.

Not long after arriving, I began feeling ill and I couldn't concentrate on what Tom was saying. I just wanted to lie down. When it was my turn to take a shower, I couldn't get up. I had never felt so weak in all my life. I didn't want a shower, and I didn't want dinner, and I didn't want to see friends. I only wanted to sleep, and that's what I did. I crawled into my bunk and slept.

FETE-ACCOMPLI and LEBENHO arrived early the next morning. Scarlet, on The LEBEBHO, had become ill at about the same time I did, and had similar symptoms. The biggest difference, of course, was that we had already arrived in American Samoa when I became sick, but they were still out at sea, which meant Neil had to do everything by himself, plus trying to take care of Scarlet. Then reports were received that Dennis and both of the children on GRINGO were also ill, so Sadie, Dennis's wife, was faced with the task of taking care of her husband, two small children, and sailing the boat by herself. SKYBOAT, which was sailing nearby and in the same direction, encouraged her to use the autopilot several hours at a time and try to rest while they provided a lookout for her. She was to keep her radio on and turn the volume up, so SKYBOAT could alert her of danger ahead. It was a hairy situation, and everyone who knew them monitored their daily progress.

When SKYBOAT and GRINGO neared port, Tom and several other men in the anchorage dinghied out to the mouth of the harbor and led the exhausted Sadie into the harbor. They helped her get the boat tied to the pier, showed her the way to the port captain, and got her secured to the assigned mooring. Gene, on FETE-ACCOMPLI, who was already providing medical visits to Scarlet and me, checked on the sick members aboard GRINGO. The children were already beginning to feel better, but Dennis remained very ill. Gene drew a blood sample from Dennis and took it to the hospital for analysis. The conclusion: Dennis had dengue fever, and that was probably what Scarlet and I had, and what the 10 family members on Suvorov had when they were so ill. Gene figured the disease had more than likely been brought to the island from someone on the last supply ship. The disease was able to stay alive in the rats, and spread to us via the mosquitoes. Only those of us who went to the dump where the mosquitoes were, or those who spent time on the island at night when the mosquitoes were out, had gotten sick.

QUARANTINED

As soon as the American Samoan officials learned of the dengue fever, they quarantined all incoming boats. That meant the cruisers couldn't go ashore for several days after they arrived. Tom, Gene, Bill and Neil were not restricted because the quarantine hadn't been put into effect until after their arrivals. So while Gene tended the sick, Tom took care of the needs of those who were well, but quarantined. He did their grocery shopping, took their trash to shore and even brought them pizza, while I lay in my bunk, weak and only slightly aware of my surroundings.

I didn't care if I lived or died. I had no appetite and was so weak that I could hardly get up to use the head, and when I did use it I didn't have the strength to pump it afterwards. Tom sometimes needed to help lift me back into my bunk because I didn't have the strength to take the two steps from the head to my bunk. My skin was sore and hypersensitive to the touch, and I pleaded with him to smooth the wrinkles out from the sheet I was lying on. Even the smallest wrinkle or tiniest fleck of sand on the sheet was painful. He placed a jug of drinking water next to me and encouraged me to sip from it each time I woke. Just lifting my head to drink from the jug was an effort, but I tried to do as he asked, because I knew it was important to avoid becoming dehydrated. For an entire week I lay there, and just when I thought I couldn't possibly feel any sicker, the wind shifted and brought the gagging odors from the fish-packing plants.

Each day Gene and Bill came to make a medical visit. Gene drew a blood sample from me, and I learned that I did indeed have dengue fever, and that Dennis, on GRINGO, was the sickest of us all, so ill that Gene arranged to move him to the hospital. The children bounced back the quickest and were moved to SKYBOAT to allow Sadie time to be at the hospital with Dennis. His condition worsened, and there was concern that his platelet level might not turn around; and if it didn't, he could die, because the hospital was not equipped to do a blood platelet transfer. The hospital was rather primitive in many ways. There weren't even screens on the windows, and mosquitoes were freely flying about.

The situation was bleak, and when Sadie cried in the hallway that night, Samoan nurses chastised her rather than providing comfort. "Why are you wasting your tears before your husband is dead?" they scolded. "He's either going to live or die, and if he dies then that's time enough to do all that crying." It was the Samoan way.

The next day, Gene arranged for Dennis to be flown to a Hawaiian hospital which could do a blood platelet transfer, if it was required. When I learned about that transfer I knew for the first time that I would not be allowed to die of dengue fever in American Samoa. Gene had earned my total trust, and Tom and I not only gained a better attitude about gay men in general, but we were also deeply grateful for Gene's consistent level of medical care.

By the end of the second week I began to feel my strength returning. Each day I became more aware of my surroundings, and when I thought I was strong enough to get off the boat, Tom took me to shore for lunch. My legs felt as wobbly as a newborn calf, but it felt great to be out in the fresh air and sunshine. The outing was a bit too much for me, however, and I could hardly stay awake to finish eating what was on my plate. Tom had to help me into the dinghy, and I wasn't sure how I was going to muster the strength to lift myself up onto the boat. Somehow, with great effort, I managed, and then I slept through the rest of that day and right through the night. Each day I got stronger, and before long I felt like my old self again. Each of us who had dengue fever got better at about the same time, within days of one another. Even Dennis pulled through, and was out of the hospital and back in American Samoa on his boat.

POPCORN AND PIZZA

Soon I began to notice all the things that I had missed while I was ill. American Samoa had a U.S. Post Office and products that we were familiar with, products with labels and instructions in English. I was thrilled with the grocery store in Pago Pago and got really excited when I found Orville Redenbacher popcorn, something we hadn't seen since having left the American Virgin Islands more than two years ago. Equally impressive was the discovery of some of the American fast food chains, like pizza parlors. We took a bus ride around the perimeter of the island on its only road, and we suddenly found ourselves in a traffic jam. "Where do all the cars come from?" Tom asked the bus driver, while we sat behind a long string of cars and vans.

"From the government," he answered. "Each time a typhoon comes through here and destroys our homes, the government gives us money so we can repair them. We know there will be more typhoons, so the people just cut down a few more trees to make new roof supports, and they weave new mats from coconut leaves and find another piece of tin for a roof. Then they use the money to buy a car, because there ain't no use in wasting the money on a house that's gonna come down in the next typhoon anyways."

It wasn't difficult to see the logic in his statement. What seemed illogical was the fact that our government hadn't caught on, and kept sending the money.

I found myself staring at someone on our bus who carried a woman's handbag, wore a dress and lipstick, but had a five o'clock shadow. Other women greeted the person as if she was a female, and she responded as if she was a female, yet she looked like a male. When she got off, we asked the bus driver about her.

"She's a 'fafafine'," he said. "She is a woman trapped inside a man's body. I know she probably looks strange to you, but she's a kind person, and it's not at all uncommon here. After you know her for a while you sort of forget that she needs a shave."

THE CHIEFS TAKE CHARGE

Many things about Samoa surprised me, and one of them was seeing all the tuna canneries – such as Starkist and Bumblebee – lined up next to one another. It was quite a revelation for me to realize there was probably no difference between the brands because the fish came from the same ocean and were canned at the same port. The fishing fleets from each company were impressive. Each boat had a helicopter on deck so it could search for large schools of tuna, and when crewmen sighted one, they strung out miles and miles of nets. When the nets became heavy with fish, they were gathered, or pursed up, and lifted up onto the boat, thus the term "purse seiners." When I saw the 20-foot high piles of nets on shore that were being repaired before the next trip, I remembered the incident off the Western coast of Colombia on our way to Ecuador. It helped me better understand how we had gotten caught up in the net when the fishing vessel it belonged to was so far away that we couldn't even see it.

While the other Polynesians were large, the Samoans were *huge*! Their heads seemed to sit directly on their enormous bodies, with necks so wide they appeared to be part of their gigantic torsos. We heard rumors about how violent and mean they could be, but they were kind and gentle toward us. Each family had a Chief and whenever there was a problem between families, the Chiefs resolved it. Officially, there was a paid American court system and a paid American police force, but these entities were only a façade to placate the American people back home. So one form of government, funded by U.S. taxes, operated to provide people with jobs. The secondary unfunded form of government consisted of the Chiefs, who took care of all the real issues and politics.

THE BILGE WAS FULL OF WATER

When the winds shifted again, causing the stench of the fish factories to be directed into the harbor, we decided to leave Pago Pago and anchor in one of the other harbors on the island. We sailed for a few hours and found a quiet little cove on the other side of the island, with clear, blue water, and no one else around. In the short time that we'd been in American Samoa, we'd become so accustomed to the dark, bloody water from the fisheries, that we had almost forgotten how pleasant it was to see clean water. Historically, Pago Pago was used as a submarine basin in World War II. When the war was over, the U.S. Government replaced the local jobs that were lost, by subsidizing the building of the fish canneries.

As we motored toward shore, we feasted our eyes on the many shades of blue water around us. I kept a close eye on the depth gauge, and when the blue water gave way to the milky translucent water that allowed the ridges in the sand to become visible, Tom gave me the hand signal indicating that I should switch gears to neutral. He dropped the anchor and I immediately shifted into reverse. The anchor did a remarkable job of catching, and it dug in deep and secure.

Tom didn't need to dive into the water to check on the anchor, because he was confident of the holding power of the rich, sand bottom. As a matter of routine maintenance, he decided to check the engine oil, and when he opened the engine room, he was aghast to see it full of water. The water was warm, which told him right away that we had a problem with the check valve that he had installed in Columbia. The aluminum adapters had become corroded, and for some unknown reason, the automatic water pump had failed just when it should have worked. He shouted for me to begin pumping on the hand pump, and while I pumped, he pulled up the anchor, and we headed back toward Pago Pago as quickly as possible. If we were going to sink, we didn't want it to happen on a side of the island where no help was available.

We happily took our same mooring in the dark, bloodied water of the harbor, and Tom took over the pumping. Once the engine was shut down, no more seawater was needed to cool it, and no more leaked through the exhaust system. When he got all of the water out of the bilge, he searched the town for a copper or bronze three-inch hose adapter. It was the same search he went on in Cartegena. The problem hadn't changed, it was the same then as it was now, but none was available and he had to settle for steel adapters. In an effort to avoid a similar electrolytic corrosion problem, he painted the connectors with epoxy paint.

"WOULD YOU MAKE A BABY WITH ME?"

We went on to Western Samoa which, unlike American Samoa, is an independent nation without the wealth of the U.S. government behind it. Here there were no large, subsidized commercial-fishing businesses to provide jobs for the local people, and no monetary assistance after each devastating act of nature. But the lack of financial support allowed them other freedoms. Apia Harbor, with clean water and no cannery odors, was by far a more desirable harbor. In fact, the entire atmosphere of Western Samoa felt more relaxed, and the lack of American influence made it easier for the people to maintain their own customs.

Each morning at 8, and again at dusk, the uniformed police force held a formal flag-raising ceremony in front of the harbor. The uniforms were blue, but not the royal blue one might think. Instead they were teal and looked more like a woman's business suit, consisting of a fitted long sleeve jacket and a tailored wrap-a-round skirt. Pride could be seen on the face of each policeman who stood at attention in his skirt and jacket. While Western Samoans were not as large as the American Samoans, they were still large, compared to us.

After watching the morning flag-raising ceremony, we walked around the downtown area, and stopped in several of the small shops looking for a newspaper. Luckily, we found a two-day old *USA Today*, a current newspaper by our standards, and Tom eagerly purchased it. We were able to keep abreast on world politics via Radio Free Europe, Voice of America, and the BBC on the ham radio, but finding a two-day-old American newspaper was something special. The young woman behind the counter was nearly as tall as Tom, and as she said "Alofa," the Samoan greeting, while smiling and giving him his change, she asked if he had a son.

"Yes," Tom said. "We have two sons."

"Are they here with you?" she inquired.

"No, they're both back in the United States." He explained that we were visiting her island on a sailboat. She continued to stare at him, and Tom felt she expected him to tell her more, so he told her that one of our sons was working and the other was in college. She smiled and caught him off guard by asking if she could come out to see our boat. Of course he agreed, and later that day when she was off work, Tom took the dinghy in to pick her up. She had a girlfriend with her, so Tom brought both large women out at the same time. He had to motor very slowly because the dinghy sat low in the water due to the extra weight. They struggled to climb on board in their long, loose dresses and there was a moment or two when I wasn't sure if the stanchions they used to pull themselves up with would hold under the ladies' great bulk.

Normally we entertained in the roomy cockpit where we could enjoy the open air, but they insisted on going below to explore the boat. I invited them to sit down and offered them each a soda, and when they finally did sit, they petted the velour sofas while sighing appreciatively. They made themselves perfectly comfortable by stretching out full length, putting their feet up, and placing decorative pillows behind their heads. The friend was silent and communicated only with her eyes and sometimes a guttural sound intended for her companion, but the young woman from the shop made up for her friends silence. She never stopped talking. Mostly it was just idle chatter, but finally she sat up and said there was something she wanted to ask us.

"Since you are my Palagi," (pronounced palangie, with an "n"), she began slowly addressing her question toward Tom. We both must have had a puzzled expression on our faces because then she explained, "A Palagi is a white person." Our expressions must have changed to reflect alarm because she quickly said, "Being a Palagi isn't a bad thing. It's a good thing." We relaxed a little upon hearing that and cautiously waited for her question.

"You see, I'd like to have a baby and I'd really like my first baby to have blond hair, blue eyes, and dimples, but I'd need to find a Palagi to be the father, so....," she paused slightly. Then she looked directly at Tom. "So, I was wondering: Would you make a baby with me?"

Good God! That was some question! Her tone didn't seem to imply it to be a sexual favor, and I never for a moment felt she was trying to be insulting toward me. Instead, it was a straightforward proposal: She liked the way Tom looked, and she wanted her child to look like him.

Later we learned that making a baby with someone in Samoa brought with it extensive financial obligations to the mother's entire extended family, including the woman's parents, siblings, aunts and uncles, nieces and nephews. Thus, fulfilling her request would have been a very expensive transaction. Apparently, the boat gave the appearance that we were wealthy enough to support that expectation.

Tom was speechless, but he recovered amazingly well. He explained that it wasn't something he would feel comfortable doing, and as soon as the sodas were finished, he was quick to offer to return the women to shore. When he returned to the boat, he could not hold in his laughter any longer. His male ego had never been so puffed up or plumped, and he could hardly wait to tell Neil about it on the radio the next day.

WE DRESSED FOR CHURCH BY GOING BAREFOOT

We took a day to walk to the home of author Robert Louis Stevenson, who spent the last five years of his life on the island in the late 1890s. He had visited the chiefs every day when they were locked up by the Germans who then controlled the islands, and as a tribute to his kindness, the current chiefs maintained his home and gravesite as a museum.

The next day we sailed to the other side of the island and found a small harbor that looked protected from ocean swells. We stayed on board that night, but the next morning when we heard church music, we decided to participate, knowing that was where much native life took place. I put on a skirt and Tom surprised me by putting on a navy blue, tailored lava-lava that he had bought in American Samoa while I was ill.

As we approached the shore we were met by a church preceptor who was wearing a white shirt, a tie, and the exact same navy tailored lava-lava that Tom was wearing. The preceptor told us not to come on shore because they didn't like tourists to disturb them on Sundays.

"We just want to go to church," Tom told him.

"You *want* to go to church?" he asked, hardly believing his ears.

We followed him to the church, where there was a pile of shoes outside of the door. We contributed ours to the pile. Inside, we walked barefoot across mats woven from sugar cane leaves. If we had closed our eyes, this could have been any church service in the United States; the songs and the preaching were the same, but the appearance of the parishioners was *not*. The women all had full, fluffy heads of curly black hair and wore white dresses, the men wore lava-lavas, and of course, everyone was barefoot.

"TRY NOT TO POINT YOUR TOES"

After the service, a white woman wearing a plain light-blue cotton dress emerged from the crowd and introduced herself. She was a missionary from Iowa and was married to the head minister there at the Piula Theological College. She explained that most of the men we saw on the grounds were studying to become ministers, with the intention of setting up a church on their home island. The other men were instructors, and the women and children we saw were the wives and family members of the instructors. Only the instructors were allowed to have their families with them.

She invited us to lunch, and we followed her to a *fale*, an open-walled structure with a cement floor, covered by woven mats. Unlike the thatch-roofed structures elsewhere, this one had a red tin roof. Each of the diners used a post that supported the roof as a backrest, which spaced us about four feet apart around the circumference of the *fale*. (See Color Photo Insert, page 28.) We were told to avoid pointing our toes. "Pointing ones toes," she said, "is considered extremely impolite."

We sat cross-legged next to her and tried not to point our toes. Along the floor next to Tom sat the minister and instructors. Everyone looked comfortable except Tom and me. We found sitting in that position extremely difficult. When my anklebone screamed with pain, I switched to sitting with my feet tucked under me on the side, and when the pain in my ankle began to ease up, I switched to the other side while the opposite leg throbbed. I continually rotated my uncomfortable body parts, trying not to call too much additional attention to myself. (See Color Photo Insert, page 30.)

A large, freshly rinsed banana leaf soon was placed before each of us. The server was a young man with a huge tattoo. The upper wings of a black fruit bat wrapped around from his back to his rib cage while the lower wings disappeared someplace below the waist of his lava-lava. Another young man, similarly tattooed, came with a large container of individually wrapped food-pouches roasted in banana leaves. Only the tattooed men served the food. Custom dictated that the Chiefs ate food only from their most trusted servants, and the large fruit bat tattoo was an easy way to identify those men. Because we were eating with the chiefs and the instructors, the same trusted servants served us. Several pouches were placed on each of our banana-leaf plates. When our hosts and hostess opened their pouches and began eating with their fingers, we did the same.

Everything was tasty, but we didn't have a clue what we were eating until Tom found the head of a moray eel in one of his pouches. At first he wasn't going to eat it, but then he realized he'd already eaten some of the other parts of the eel in other pouches. Each pouch had been prepared with shavings of coconut, and that made everything tender and somewhat sweet. We liked the flavor, but when we became full we didn't know how we would be able to eat what was continually being placed before us. Fortunately, the instructors stopped eating, and we could stop as well.

"All this food was placed in the *umu* under ground last night," our hostess told us. "Our Sunday meals are prepared in the old traditional way. Men do all the cooking. First they dig a pit, and stones are then placed in the bottom. They build a fire by rubbing two sticks together and ignite the dry inside fiber of a coconut shell and place it on top of the stones to get them good and hot. Then they cover the hot rocks with wet banana leaves.

The food can be fish, meat, sweet potatoes, or taro, and all are mixed with coconut shavings and rolled into pouches of fresh banana leaves. Then the pouches are placed on the wet leaves, never directly on the rocks so the food isn't burned, and then the pouches are covered with more wet leaves and woven mats. It takes a couple of hours to cook all the food and it must be completed before sunrise because no one is allowed to work on Sunday, not even the smoke of the cooking *umu*."

We didn't think it appropriate to point out that the young servers with the bat tattoos, or the young men who sat and fanned us, were working. When we finished eating, she told us, "Now the others will eat what is left. The elders always eat first in Samoa."

After lunch there was some discussion by the elders, and when one of them spoke to the group they held a "talking staff." As long as he held the staff, no one else could speak. Then it was passed to the next speaker. It was all very civilized and orderly. I was impressed!

While the elders talked, the missionary showed us the rest of the grounds and explained that the word Samoan means "sacred central," implying Samoa was the most central and most sacred of the Polynesian islands. We hadn't thought about it before, but if one were to draw a triangle connecting Hawaii, Easter Island (off the coast of Chile), and New Zealand, this would encompass all of the Polynesian people. And Samoa would be in the center. Our guide also pointed out a breadfruit tree and told us when the breadfruit, or *ulue*, ripens, it becomes the perfect bread dough similar to what we use as Bisquick. "The ripe breadfruit is mashed together with coconut milk and patted into a loaf shape before being rolled into a banana leaf and baked. We also use taro root to make poi. You know it as tapioca," she explained.

A WHITE GOD

We were so grateful for being able to attend church, the tour, the lunch, and for learning so much, that Tom asked if there was anything we might be able to do for them. She asked if he had a camera and could take class pictures, which we did as the class posed formally in multiple groupings on the front steps of the church. Then Tom was asked if he could repair a TV. "Oh, I don't think I can do that," Tom said.

"Well, just have a look at it," the instructor begged.

"Alright," Tom said, "but I really don't know anything about television sets."

He took the back off and noticed that a fuse had been burned out when a moth had gotten into the back of the television. He removed the fried moth and lifted out the fuse, and as luck would have it, he had the exact same size fuse in his tool,kit. He put the new fuse into the television and turned it on for a test. When the television worked, I'm not sure who was more surprised, Tom or the owner of the TV.

After that Tom was considered a kind of white god, and many members of the group came out at odd times of the day to pay us a visit on the boat. Some rowed out in dugout logs, and others came in a beat-up old fishing boat with no motor. They were curious to see how we lived, and one man told us he had lived there for 25 years and he could not remember a single boat that had ever anchored in their harbor before.

THE COCONUT TELEGRAPH

We heard about a wood carver who lived in a village on the other side of the small mountain near where we were anchored, and a few days later we decided to hike to his village. After we had walked for a long time, a gasoline truck came by. Many men hitched a ride by sitting on the top and/or hanging on to the side of the truck. The driver stopped to ask if we wanted to hitch a ride as well, and he made the two men who were riding inside the cab get out and hang on to the outside with the others, thus allowing us to sit inside the cab with him. When we reached the fork in the road leading to the wood carver's village, we thanked the truck driver and the two men whom he ousted from the cab. We continued our walk toward the village. At the first small village we were told the wood carver lived two more villages away, about a mile further down the line. So we continued walking.

Several small boys started tagging along next to us, and with big smiles all across their faces they said with loud, clear voices, "Hello, I kill you." The words were unsettling at first, but their friendly mannerisms made us realize they didn't intend a threat. Those were the only English words they knew and they probably learned them from watching some of our American videos. We smiled back at them and ruffled their hair, not sensing any animosity. As we continued on toward the woodcarver's village, we gathered a larger and larger group of children around us, Pied Piper style.

When we finally arrived at the woodcarver's village, people pointed us in the direction of his *fale* without us having to ask. Everyone in the village seemed to be expecting us. The woodcarver had already killed a chicken and was cooking it for our lunch. The communication system was amazing because clearly there were no telephones or electricity in any of the villages we walked through. Our arrival must have been announced by runners and word of mouth via what's called the Coconut Telegraph.

The woodcarver was putting on a clean lava-lava when we arrived. Three chairs were already placed off to the side of the *fale* where we were invited to sit. He joined us and proudly showed us his current project, a kava bowl with 14 legs. He was polishing it with a boar's tooth to bring out the oil in the wood and provide a smooth finish, our equivalent of using very fine sandpaper. (See Color Photo Insert, page 31.)

Samoans serve food as a sign of respect and wealth before any business can be transacted. So we first ate chicken and rice before we were allowed to purchase the kava bowl. The woodcarver's daughter spoke a little English that she had learned from her job at a bingo club in Apia, and she invited us to stay the night. She said her family would not feel good if we tried to walk up and over the mountain all the way back to Piula College that same day. But we explained that we needed to return to the boat. When she heard we had a boat she said her father would carve us something else, anything we wanted, free of charge if we would just come and anchor in front of their village. Apparently our arrival gave her father great status with the other villagers, and if we brought our boat over, it would enhance him even further. We thanked them and explained that we must leave in order to get back before dark. It was a long walk back, made a little more difficult by carrying our newly purchased kava bowl, but we felt great about the entire experience!

TONGA: THE FRIENDLY ISLAND

Even though it was difficult to say goodbye to our new friends at Piula Theolgical College, we knew it was time. We wanted to be in New Zealand – all the way across the rest of the Pacific Ocean – before typhoon season. We soon set a course for The Kingdom of Tonga, the only remaining monarchy in the South Pacific.

Sailing conditions were comfortable all that day and into the evening, requiring only minor adjustments to the sails from within the cockpit. I was always happy when Tom didn't have to go up on deck. By early afternoon we entered the Vava'u group, a cluster of the more than 170 small islands which make up the Kingdom of Tonga, which has a population of about 20,000 people. Our cruising guideook showed a photo of their huge king sitting on a bicycle. Apparently, he intentionally kept himself fat to signify prosperity.

Everything we'd read about Tonga referred to them as the "Friendly Islands," and visually speaking they did look friendly, grouped like small emeralds and with almost no nautical hazards. The process of getting checked into the country, however, was anything but friendly. One official hinted that we should give him gifts and made suggestions about which items we might give him. Neither of us appreciated his solicitations, but we tried to remain upbeat and positive while ignoring his requests, but when an agricultural official confiscated my precious little lettuce garden, I became really irritated. I had nurtured and cared for that garden all across the Pacific so we could have fresh greens during the largest portion of our crossing, but also so we could eat lettuce in Tonga. We had already been warned not to eat the Tongan lettuce because of the slime left on it from the slugs. I knew my garden was healthier than any garden on that island. I *loved* my little garden. I'd tenderly cared for it, carefully watered it when water was scarce, and watched it the way I would a small child, but they didn't care. They took the plants away, and even the dirt, and I was boiling mad! I remember asking him if he was married. He knew how angry I was and politely responded with a "No ma'm" as he continued dumping my garden soil into his plastic bag. I heard myself snap back, "I can understand why!" I knew the idea was to prevent disease from hurting their agriculture, but my little garden? *Really!*

Tom said he had never seen me so angry before. I certainly didn't think I'd ever feel friendly toward Tonga. But the comfort of the anchorage, the ease of going on shore, and the close proximity of the other islands soon eased my loss.

SEA SNAKES

Tom enjoyed Tonga right away. He appreciated the clear, warm water and having access to a compressor to fill his scuba tanks. Bill and Gene from FETE-ACCOMPLI were there too, and they had a compressor on board, so between their compressor and the one on the main island, Tom had lots of options. The underwater cliffs and coral walls held a lot of interest for him, and he often came back with a bag of fresh oysters or clams for dinner. I had high hopes of finding a perfect pearl in one of the oysters when we cleaned them, but if there was a pearl at all, it was usually ugly and misshapen. We kept a few as souvenirs and tossed most of them back overboard with the shells. The absence of a nice pearl, however, did not in any way diminish the taste of the oysters, and we regularly feasted in style.

With food so plentiful, Tom could take the time to enjoy the beauty of the underwater world without always concentrating on hunting. One day, Bill, Gene, and Tom found an underwater cave that was entered through a passage 10 feet below the surface. Upon investigation, they discovered it opened into a cavern that was lighted by natural sunlight, and shimmered with a rainbow of colors. Not being a SCUBA diver, I wasn't able to go into the cave with them, but I did enjoy snorkeling outside at the mouth of the cave.

While they explored the cave, I practiced diving short distances and picked up some exceptionally beautiful shells from the ocean shore. I'd refrained from collecting seashells for the four years we'd lived on the boat due to limited storage space, but there were so many beautiful shells that I just couldn't resist picking them up. My favorite was the murex. I enjoyed playing and exploring in the warm water until I saw the sea snakes in the water. I wasn't protected by a wet suit like the SCUBA divers, and seeing the snakes, while I was alone, frightened me. I tried to reassure myself by remembering what I had read about them. I knew they breathed air like other reptiles, and that they could stay submerged for up to two hours. They were reported to be shy and would likely try to swim away from fast motion. But most of all, I knew their bite was deadly, and that ruined the snorkeling for me that day.

SHIPS LOG, TOM'S ENTRY:
Tonga, 18°S Latitude, 176°W Longitude, 20 Sept 1991

I did a lot of snorkel diving, but rarely was able to use my SCUBA gear. We had two tanks on board, but no compressor, and sometimes we were close enough to a dive shop to get a commercial fill. This morning I got a commercial fill, and was now cruising on the surface with my SCUBA gear and spear gun. I was just outside a coral reef that surrounded one of the smaller Tongan islands.

I searched the bottom for signs of good fishing. I saw coral and rock formations, and some fish. I blew air out of my BC and started down. There were several large fish down there. I hoped they would be coral trout or another one of our favorites. It seemed that I was descending for a long time, so I checked my depth gauge. Wow, I was at 100 ft., and the bottom was still 20 or 30 ft away. The visibility here is perhaps 150 ft. Incredibly clear. By contrast, the typical visibility off the coast of the U.S. is 10 to 30 ft. I didn't much like diving in 120 ft., because one's "bottom time" is only about 10 minutes, and you have to think about problems with decompression to avoid nitrogen in the blood.

I finished my short dive at 120 feet, and marveled at the water clarity as I bubbled my way to the surface.

A BROKEN COMPASS

One day we were motoring toward our next anchorage, a short trip that required us to navigate down a channel and through some shallows. Tom told me to steer a heading of 240 degrees while he put out his fishing line. I wasn't watching the water as carefully as I should have been, but I did keep my eye on the compass and kept it on 240. When Tom looked up, he shouted at me, "Where the hell are you going? That's a reef up there!" Sure enough, when he pointed it out to me, I saw it too. I was steering us straight into a reef. "I told you to keep it at 240 degrees!"

"I've got it on 240 degrees," I shouted back.

He didn't believe me until he looked at the compass. "What the hell!" he said while turning the wheel. "Just steer anyplace except toward that reef," he said and went below to refigure our course heading.

"What the hell," he said again. "The compass down here doesn't indicate that was 240 degrees. I think the compass is broken." As he spoke I realized the compass indicated we were still heading 240 degrees no matter which direction I steered. It was stuck – frozen in that one spot.

TAPA CLOTH AND THE MISSIONARIES

Tongan women made exceptional crafts, such as sturdy baskets, handsome handbags, and charming baby bassinets. They also made tapa cloth from the bark of the mulberry tree. This was the first cloth used for clothing after the missionaries told the people they needed to cover their bodies. It was decorated in various patterns by using bug juice as a dye. Although they no longer use tapa for everyday clothing, it was still used as ceremonial clothing and wall coverings.

Historically, missionaries all across the Pacific made great efforts to alter the Polynesian culture: by insisting on modest clothing, when the people originally wore very little; by making them feel 'sinful' when certain family members married in accordance with their traditional practice; and by adamantly disallowing the people to speak of their Gods, from the religion they had practiced for many generations. One might think that today, with our more enlightened thinking, that the various religious orders would be more accepting of other people having the right to their own belief system, without outside interference, but that's not what we observed.

On one small island with about 300 inhabitants there were three different churches. Each was competing to convert new souls. On shore in front of one of the Protestant churches were two Jehovah's Witnesses working hard to interest the people in still another religion. I wondered what churches, which claim to value family unity, think happens to families when one member is pulled away from the family unit to join a competitive sect? The irony and inconsistency of it boggles my mind.

At one of the outermost islands, Tom agreed to give a woman named Valanie and her friends a lift to the Saturday market on the main island, a five-mile ride.

While they did their shopping, Tom and I walked around to observe the local culture. We marveled at the vibrant color of an extremely large bougainvillea tree that grew in the center of the town, and we made a few small purchases like potatoes, summer squash, bananas, and papaya. When we returned to the dinghy, all four of the ladies were already waiting for us with huge sacks of roots, vegetables, canned lard, fabric and yarn. Each of them also had a container of cooking fuel, and it required several dinghy trips to load the women and their purchases on board.

They thanked us for the ride, and after we got them and all their stuff safely back to their village, they invited us to join them for lunch the next day after church. At Valanie's house, we sat on woven mats spread across a wooden floor. In the center of the mats were colorful tablecloths, and in front of each of us, Valanie placed a plate. Then the ladies each passed the food they had prepared. The oldest and tiniest of them served octopus that had been cooked in coconut milk. It was delicious, and I asked her where she got the octopus. I wondered if it had come across on the boat with us the day before, but she said no, and told us she caught it with her bare hands from the rocks in front of her house the night before. Amazing! In the Tongan way, we, the guests, were invited to eat first, and when we finished the husbands were allowed to enter and eat. After everyone had finished, the ladies allowed themselves to eat the food they purchased, caught, and prepared.

MAKING ROUNDS WITH THE DOCTOR

Bill and Gene anchored near us and joined us for church, and the ladies had graciously invited them to join us for lunch, as well. Afterward, Gene shared the fact that he was a medical doctor, and he offered his services. Valanie said there were several people on the island who would like to see a doctor, so he arranged to do doctor rounds with her, and he also invited me to come along. Mostly the problems had to do with skin rashes for which Gene was able to provide medicated cream. In one home there was a blind lady who hoped Gene could provide some kind of miracle, but there was nothing he could do for her. In another home, a man was in pain and unable to walk from an injury caused when his wife hit him with a board. I would have liked to know more about that episode, but we didn't feel it was our place to ask. Gene gave him a muscle-relaxing shot and he received immediate relief. Several people had leg and foot pain, mostly from walking barefoot on fallen arches their entire lives. One man's leg bone no longer seated itself into the proper socket and he experienced pain with every step. Only properly fitted shoes with arch supports would have prevented his problem, and on an island where no one ever wore shoes, that wasn't likely to happen.

THE TONGAN WAY

While we were on doctor's rounds, the minister and several people were digging at one of the gravesites. Tom came ashore and asked the minister, "Did someone die?"

"No," the minister said, "it's just the Tongan way."

"I don't understand," Tom said. "What do you mean, the Tongan way?"

"You wouldn't understand," he said. "It's just something Tongan's have always done. It's the Tongan way."

"But what exactly are you doing?" Tom pressed. "I don't understand what it is that you're saying is the Tongan way."

"Well," he reluctantly explained, "you see this man here has been having a pain in his side, and he thinks it's his brother calling to him from the grave to let him know there is something sticking into his side. His brother died last year, you see, so we're digging him up and sort of straightening him out again. It's not something you Christian people do, but it's the Tongan way."

GIVING MONEY TO THE CHURCH

I was beginning to see why Tonga was known as the Friendly Islands in spite of our not so friendly check-in. The people themselves were wonderful. One woman asked if I had any shampoo I could share with her. When I said I did, she asked if she could weave a handbag for me in exchange. She didn't want charity. She wanted to pay for what she needed in her own way. I thought it was a wonderful trade and threw in a bottle of conditioner as well. Another lady asked if we would commission a woven item from her because she needed money for her children. We saw she had a large family, so we ordered a baby bassinet from her, agreeing to pay her $70. We thought that was a lot of money, but felt it was mostly charity for her family. She worked on it for over a week, and when she brought it out to the boat we paid her in cash and asked what she was going to buy first with the money.

"I've decided to give the money to the church," she said.

"The church!" we gasped. "What about your family? Didn't you say your children needed clothing and food!"

"They don't need much food, and I'll weave something else to buy clothes for them," she said. "I want to give this money to the church."

We could hardly believe our ears because we knew she and her children had so little in the way of creature comforts, and they were missing much of what we deemed to be the basic needs of life. I wanted to say that her children needed the benefit of that money a lot more than the church did, and it took great effort on our part not to say anything, because we didn't want to challenge her values. Before leaving that village we went in to say goodbye to Valanie, and with wet eyes she presented us with a large tapa cloth that she made herself. It measured at least 6 by 10 feet and was a gift from the heart. We greatly appreciated her gesture, and knew this would be something we would treasure forever.

A TONGAN PARTY AND FEAST

We anchored at another island that was uninhabited, thinking it would be nice to be by ourselves for a while, but we hardly got the anchor down when a couple of boats from the main island came over and began building something on the island. We learned they were planning on holding a feast for some dignitaries from the capital that afternoon, and they were constructing a temporary structure for the event. Tom saw them struggle with their machetes and brought in his handsaw, a hammer and an assortment of other tools. It didn't take long before he found himself helping them build it. Later we watched them prepare a cooking pit, sharpen green saplings, and string whole raw chickens and pigs on them.(See Color Photo Insert, page 30.) Another boat arrived with entertainers dressed in native costume; servers clad in tuxedos with small woven mats worn as the outermost layers of clothing, bowls of prepared food, and an assortment of elaborate decorations. Then we realized our boat was in the way of all the comings and goings. No one asked us to move it, but as a courtesy we decided to move it off to the side. Since we planned on moving it back after the party, we didn't bother to back down the anchor as securely as we normally did.

After the dignitaries arrived, drinks were served, music began and dancers danced. It was a wonderful Tongan performance, one that was natural to the people and not performed for the benefit of tourists. Because Tom helped, we were offered food just as if we were dignitaries. Everything was delicious, and we had a wonderful time. It was dark when everyone left, and by the time Tom found his tools and we returned to the boat, we were tired and went directly to bed, feeling pleased to have had such a rare opportunity.

Seldom did we stay up after dark, and we had forgotten that we hadn't anchored well. The wind picked up in the middle of the night, and for some unknown reason Tom woke in time to discover we were headed backwards toward a 150-foot-high rocky cliff. The anchor and chain were hanging straight down off the bow of the boat. In another five minutes our fiberglass stern would have crashed into the rocky cliff. We quickly got underway, and with a sky full of stars and a bright moon we found our way back to a good anchorage near where we'd been. In the dead of night we anchored with care, making sure it set well before we went back to bed, but not before Tom cursed himself for being a dummy. By morning the incident didn't seem as bad, but it was early November and the typhoon season would soon be upon us. We needed to move south, well out of the typhoon belt.

Tom brought out the hand-held compass from our man-overboard bag and lashed it to the malfunctioning compass. We would steer by it for our passage to New Zealand. Just when I began to think the compass problem was a bad omen, we saw two whales as we sailed out of port. Both did perfect fluke-ups, as if to say farewell to us, Tongan style.

CHAPTER NINE

Winding Down after the Passage from Hell

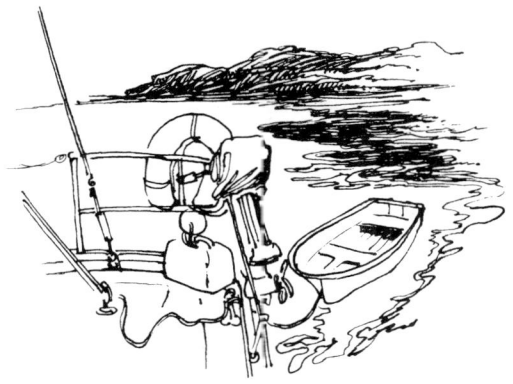

THAT DARN SAT-NAV!

The passage from Tonga to New Zealand started out about the same as all our other major passages. The first day or two Tom was in his typical hyper-captain mode, meaning he was wound up and couldn't sleep. Meanwhile, I was a seasick lump who could hardly stay awake from all the seasick pills I took every four hours. The first day I was awake only long enough to make meals, but by the second day I began to feel a little better and was able to function for longer periods of time. By then, Tom was so tired that he crashed into a deep and deserved sleep, and I was able to stay on watch.

Tom put a fishing line out and on the second morning he hooked a marlin that ran all 300 yards of his 50-lb. test-line right off the reel with his orange squid bait. Wow! That didn't take long! The marlin did a tail dance and away it went.

A few days into the passage we changed our course heading to 224 degrees, a close reach, and when the wind died, we motor-sailed. With less wind it was going to be a tight pinch to get around a worrisome shoaling reef that lurked under the surface. Tom regularly checked our position on the Sat-Nav and carefully charted our position to insure that we did not get to close to the reef. Finally we had to drop off the wind and go around the other side of the reef when it became apparent that we couldn't make it on that tack. Then, just when we needed the Sat-Nav the most, it lost power.

"Could it be confused by the fact that we just crossed the International Date Line?" I dumbly asked, grasping for any explanation at all and trying not to sound as panicked as I felt.

"No," he snapped. "It knows that. I don't know why it lost power!" His nerves were frayed, too. He got the manual out and tinkered with the Sat-Nav until he got it going again.

"What did you do to it?" I asked, trying to sound supportive and calm.

"I'm not sure what I did," he said. "Maybe it was as simple as a loose connection. I don't know, but what ever it was, it's working again."

Thank goodness for that, I thought. We could not afford to be without a satellite navigation system especially with our main compass not functioning. I remembered when the Sat-Nav's first came out on the market. They cost $25,000, which was absolutely out of our budget range. Back then we used the Loran C, which was sufficient while we were in Canadian and U.S. waters, but by the time we reached Florida the price of Sat-Nav's had come down to $800, and that is when we bought ours.

DEAD ENGINE

The winds picked up some on the next day, but they were still moderate. The sea swells were less than four feet and we moved along at a fair clip of five to six knots. It was an uneventful day, and just when I began to think it was going to be a comfortable passage, we saw dark clouds appearing on the horizon. A quick peek at the falling barometer told us a storm front was moving in. We knew we were in for a tough night. Tom shortened sail and we double-checked to make sure nothing was loose either inside the cabin or topsides.

The sky changed from light blue to a dark gray, and the ocean waves looked green, black, and angry. Heavy, ominous clouds could be seen churning and boiling low in the sky. We radioed on the VHF to determine if there were other boats within our radio range. We learned that there were three other boats facing the night with us. They expressed concern as well.

We reported our positions to one another and agreed to monitor channel 16 together throughout the night. We wanted to support one another, plus do everything possible to avoid having our boats collide.

By early evening the storm was upon us, and the wind was strong for about an hour, but then as quickly as it came, it left. When the winds dropped to a comfortable sailing level the sky cleared and the stars lit the sky. We talked with the other boats and could hear the same sense of relief in their voices that we felt.

Most of the time we sailed without the help of the motor, but during that passage we already had to rely on the engine, and after the storm we motor-sailed again. I listened to the comfortable, familiar sounds of the boat cutting through the water and the *thumpity-thumpity-thump* of our friendly diesel engine. I knew Tom did not like using the engine; he was a purist when it came to sailing, but it was a comfort to me. There was something about its deep thundering sound that made me feel secure, but just as I was thinking kind thoughts and appreciation for our engine, it turned itself off. At first I thought the boat motion could have dislodged the key from the ignition, but when I went below to check on it I saw that the key was in its proper place. While I was checking on the key Tom stumbled from his bunk and asked, "What happened? Why did you turn off the engine?"

"I didn't," I answered. "It turned itself off."

He looked at me like I had lost my mind and tried starting it, but he had no luck. The engine refused to start.

"Shit, another thing I have to deal with. Well, I can't do anything about it tonight," he said. "I'll look at it in the morning. You'll just have to do the best you can under sail tonight. Call me if there are any more problems."

With that he went back to his bunk and left me alone in the cockpit. Wow, I thought to myself, that was a change. He had never done that before. He must be really tired.

BECALMINGS WERE ANYTHING BUT CALM

The wind picked up a little bit during the night, enough to keep us moving forward comfortably without missing the engine. By morning I was the one who was tired and as soon as Tom came up on deck I crawled into my bunk without even taking the time to brush my teeth. I hit the pillow and was immediately sound asleep.

While we had wind the disabled engine was not a crisis, but I noticed that Tom was reading the engine manual when I awoke a few hours later. He put the manual away when I came into the cockpit, but I knew he was still pondering the problem. Apparently, this was not going to be one of his quick fixes.

On our fifth day at sea I awoke to find Tom standing in the galley with the manual in one hand and engine parts divided neatly into nearly every soup bowl and saucer from our cupboard. He had placed a board across the entire length of the galley sink and that served as his workbench.

"My gosh," I gasped when I saw he had disassembled the fuel injection pump.

"Yeah, well I figured I had nothing to lose by trying to fix it. It certainly isn't going to run in its present state," he said. "Losing your lettuce garden was not the worst thing that happened to us in Tonga. It looks like Tonga gave us one more little kiss. The fuel they sold us had water in it and the water seized up the fuel injection pump. When we tried to start the engine, the pump shaft twisted off. I wouldn't have believed a shaft the size my thumb could break, but that's what it did. It sure looked like a substantial piece of steel to me."

He was disgusted, but once he understood what the problem was and knew he could not repair it, he put all the pieces back from where he had removed them. I prepared breakfast, and as we ate together I waited for him to explain what his next plan might be, but he said nothing.

By afternoon the wind was down, and there was not enough breeze to prevent the sails from damaging themselves on the rigging, so he took them down. We sat like a child's toy in a bathtub; only our bathtub had big rolling waves that still had not settled down from the storm. They caused the boat to slosh and topple from one side to the other.

One of the sailboats we had been in communication with during the storm motored past us and radioed when they saw us floundering aimlessly.

"VONNIE-T, is everything all right on board?" they asked.

Tom answered them, "Yes, we're fine, we just have a broken engine." And no compass, either, I thought, but he didn't mention that little problem.

"Do you need fuel?" they asked as they motored a loop around us.

"No," Tom said, "We have plenty of fuel but we just can't use it because we have a broken injection pump. Looks like we purchased fuel with water in it back in Tonga."

They looped us a second time and asked if there was anything they could do for us. Tom said, no, but thanked them for asking. "We're a sailboat," he said, "and as soon as we get some wind we'll be on our way again."

So that was our plan. If I had not heard him tell the other boat that we were just going to sit there and bob around until the wind picked up, I might have worried that he had given up. As long as he had a plan, I was OK. We watched them motor away while we sloshed this way and that, back and forth, and up and down. All attempts to move around on the boat under those conditions required hanging on, and attempting to do even the smallest task was tough.

Tom wrote in the ship's log and worked a crossword puzzle in the cockpit while I tried to read a book, but I found it hard to concentrate. I took a seasick pill to calm my stomach, and it made me sleepy, but even the pill didn't seem to take the edge off my nausea. Our situation was more than unpleasant! I almost wished for a storm again; in some ways it was preferable to being becalmed. What a strange word "becalmed". There was *nothing* calm about being becalmed!

THE STEERING BROKE, TOO

Not until early evening did we begin to feel a soft breeze, and as soon as there was enough for sailing, Tom raised the sails. Just having the sails up steadied the boat and made our existence more comfortable. But not for long, as Tom's log entry reveals:

SHIPS LOG, TOM'S ENTRY
32°S Latitude 174°E Longitude, 16 Nov 1991

Dead boat! We had already lost our main compass, our engine and now this.

We were sailing in light air, as close to the wind as we could. The wind was pretty much south, and that was the direction of New Zealand. In sailing close, I used the Autopilot and tried to stay about 50 degrees off of the wind. More than 50 degrees and we were losing progress toward NZ. Less than 50 degrees and the sail would luff up. If we went through the eye of the wind the sails would backdraft, forcing us to do a 360-degree turn. So if the wind shifted slightly towards our bow, I quickly turned off the Autopilot, and steered hard to the leeward. This usually worked if I was quick enough. As I steered hard leeward, the rudder would come up against stops that would prevent it from hitting the hull. I knew that, but never mind, when it came on the stops, I continued to apply a lot of needless pressure on the wheel.

The last time I did that, something snapped, and the wheel turned freely. I had broken the heavy #50 Stainless Steel roller chain that connected the wheel to the cables that turned the rudder! What a dummy!! Now we are hundreds of miles from NZ with no main compass, no engine, and no steering. We are a dead boat. Depression is a mild word for what I feel. The boat began wandering aimlessly, out of control, and the sails flapped all over the place. I gathered a little sense and took the sails down. I sat in the cockpit and looked at LaVonne, with my face nearly falling off. The day was nice with little wind or waves, so we sat there for some time having a think on it.

The two of us liked attacking a problem together. We decided we better dig out the emergency tiller. It fastened directly onto the rudderpost. I had built it from a three-foot piece of oak two by two. It wasn't comfortable to use. LaVonne stood over the place where our stern bunk had been removed, with one end of the tiller in hand. She stuck her head up through the overhead hatch as far as possible. She couldn't see very well, but we were barely moving so it wasn't important for now. This was a <u>big deal</u>. Now we had a way, although clumsy, to steer the boat.

Now we would see what could be done with the broken steering chain. I had repaired roller chain like this before with a new master link, but alas, that was one spare part we didn't have. After more hashing it out between us, I decided to make a master link by destroying two of the regular links to scavenge parts. I chiseled them apart, and fastened a keeper from a washer in our stores. With the chain now whole, we adjusted the length of the cable that was attached to it. The cable ran from the chain around the steering quadrant to the rudderpost. It sounds rather straightforward but each step had to be invented. The whole process took about two hours. Hooray, we are once again a functional sailboat.

ON OUR WAY AGAIN

While we worked on repairing the steering, the wind increased to a comfortable eight to ten knots. After the makeshift repair was working, Tom raised the sails and we were off, once again, heading toward New Zealand.

What, I wondered, would break next. Thank goodness our generator still worked, because that meant we were able to charge our batteries. It also meant we could use our running lights at night, run the microwave, the refrigeration, and the ham radio. Each was important.

Word was out in our cruising circle about our engine problems, and during my morning radio check-in, several of our friends wished us well and said they were following our progress. "Take it easy out there, you two," one of our friends said to cheer us. "When you get here we're going to treat you to some of the best ice cream you've ever tasted. They have a flavor here called Hokey Pokey, and it's really great."

It was comforting to know we had friends rooting for us, and as long as the wind kept blowing we were OK; we just could not afford any more becalmings. I thought the probability of that would diminish, because the farther south we went and the closer we got to New Zealand, two things would happen: the wind would increase and the temperatures would drop. It was not unusual for the winds to blow at 20 to 30 knots that far south and cabin temperature was typically in the low 60s. Both were big contrasts to the gentle winds of Tonga and the hot tropical temperatures.

The days and nights rotated with very little pleasure in either. We just existed and each did whatever we could to keep the other person from going stark raving mad. We needed each other!

The wind became a little stronger each day and I began worrying about how high it might get. I began wishing it would let up a little, and then on November 18th I got more than I wished for: it stopped blowing all together. We were becalmed again, and that feast or famine of wind had gotten really old! We had to drop the sails and that resulted in the boat becoming parallel to the waves where it rolled, pitched and floundered aimlessly. It was miserable!

The only good thing that happened as we waited out that becalming was a sighting of a humpback whale 50 feet from the boat. We heard him breathe and saw him blow. I guess he wanted to check us out, because he sounded once and came up one more time on the other side. Then he disappeared, and we did not see him blow again until he was way off on the horizon.

ENTERING NEW ZEALAND HARBOR WITH NO MOTOR

After being out to sea for 21 days we finally sighted New Zealand, and then we faced a whole new set of problems. Tom studied the charts and began planning how we would sail around the small outer islands and the peninsula that we needed to pass, before entering the country. Normally, we would motor past those obstacles, but without a motor we had to plan our approach more carefully. Before Tom had an opportunity to develop a

Deep cold water diving site off shore from Whangarei, New Zealand called the Poor Knights.

plan, our good friends Janet and Bob on JUBILATION sailed out to meet us, and they guided us in the rest of the way.

Under a reefed jib we tacked this way and that and followed them way into the harbor, and when we came really close to the docking area they tied us along their side, beam to beam. In that manner, they motored to the pier and put us right next to the dock where we needed to check into the country. That was some very impressive boatmanship, and we were grateful!

"SAVE THE EGG SHELLS, I'LL PICK THEM UP TOMORROW"

Every cruiser I met was happy when he or she finally made it to New Zealand, but I doubt there has ever been one happier than me. New Zealand is a country with 3 million people, 7 million sheep, and a million sailboats. Seeing people, putting my feet on solid land, finding a washing machine, taking a hot shower, and going out to a restaurant were pleasures I could hardly wait to indulge myself in, but we could partake in none of those things until we passed inspection with the customs and agricultural people.

Going through customs, other than my lettuce garden experience in Tonga, had always been easy for us because Tom did a good job of keeping all our boat papers in order. We knew that the rules for entering New Zealand were stricter than for many of the other countries, but still we did not anticipate having any problems. We heard from the other cruisers that the agriculture check-in for New Zealand was especially strict, and that part of our check-in did indeed, live up to its reputation. First, the inspector questioned us about any farms we may have been on, and even though we had not been on any, he asked to see our shoes and proceeded to scrape off any dirt that was on the bottom. Then he questioned me about my shells, and confiscated my big Pacific clam.

"Why are you taking that?" I asked.

"Pacific clams are on the endangered species list," he said. "You could actually be fined for having this."

"But I didn't kill it," I explained. "I just found it on the ocean floor and picked it up."

"I believe you because I can see where it's been chipped and probably rolled around empty for a while," he said. "That's why I'm not going to issue a fine, but I still can't allow you to keep it."

He put my large Pacific clamshell that I had struggled to dive for, into his red bag, which already had some dirt or sand in it from our shoes.

"Let's address your food supplies next," he said, and read a long list of items we needed to relinquish to him and his red bag: meat, eggs, fresh vegetables, fruit, etc. Then he asked specifically about any corn or popcorn that we had on board.

"Popcorn? We have some Orville Redenbacher popcorn that we stocked up on in American Samoa. We love it. It's the best as far as popcorn is concerned," I said. "You don't need to take that do you? We've just stocked up on it."

"I'm afraid I do, " he said. "We've had a problem with infected popcorn doing damage to our local crops."

"What do you do with all that stuff?" Tom asked while looking at all the food supplies waiting placement in his red bag.

"We incinerate it," he said.

"Well you'd better stand back when you put those jars of popcorn into your incinerator, because its going to sound like you have firecrackers in there," Tom told him.

He was actually a nice man, and he kept apologizing for all the things he needed to take from us. In some ways I felt sorry for him because I knew he hated playing the role of 'the heavy', unlike the power and pleasure the same job provided for the officials in Tonga.

"Tell you what," he said as he looked at our last couple of eggs, "Will you be cooking these eggs for breakfast in the morning?"

"I would if I had them," I said.

"Well, I'll leave them for you to eat, but save the egg shells and I'll pick them up tomorrow," he said, and with that he was off and we were free to put our feet on solid ground.

True to his word, he stopped by the boat early the next morning to collect our eggshells. He also brought a list of names with phone numbers for Tom to contact concerning our malfunctioning diesel engine and our sick compass. Now that is what I call going the extra mile, and within a few days the engine had a rebuilt injector pump and was working as good as new. The solution for the compass was even easier. It simply had to be recarded for the Southern Hemisphere. When we had begun our trip in Duluth the compass had been tested and worked well, but when it tried to adapt itself to the Southern Hemisphere, it got hung up and stuck.

"YOU CAN ALWAYS TELL A SWEDE, YOU JUST CAN'T TELL HIM MUCH"

Shortly after our arrival at New Zealand, we heard reports of Carl Eric's dramatic arrival. Apparently one of his thru-hull fittings began to leak, and he was taking on water. We knew first hand how frightening that situation could be, but instead of trying to solve the problem, he panicked and called a MAYDAY. One of the New Zealand emergency boats responded to his MAYDAY, and went out to meet him. The leak was found and repaired at sea, so he was able to save his boat from sinking. He sailed the rest of the way into port on his own. When he arrived he was billed for the expenses incurred on his behalf, and we heard the stories about how he became "stomping mad" about it. I guess he thought the act of saving him was a free service.

Carl had already developed quite a reputation within the cruising community. He seemed to think that because he was a single-hander everyone was supposed to cater to him, yet he never went out of his way to reciprocate or show appreciation for any of the kindnesses showed to him. Of course that did not exempt him from having strong opinions about nearly everyone and everything.

Dave, on REBECCA, whom we met back in Venezuela, was Swedish, as was Carl Eric, and one day Dave gave Carl Eric a special T-shirt. On it was printed: "You can always tell a Swede, but you can't tell him much!"

Only Dave could have gotten by with giving him something like that, and Carl Eric loved it. It was the first and only time I saw him pleased about anything. He laughed when he read the inscription and he wore it proudly.

THE GPS (GLOBAL POSITIONING SYSTEM) AND THE LIFE RAFT

New Zealand offered something else that I had forgotten while living on the boat, and that was how much I missed the sounds from birds and other wildlife. All around Whangarie Harbor songbirds could be heard, and the harbor itself was full of quacking mallards. The ducks alone made me homesick for our lake home in Minnesota.

When we discovered we could purchase a GPS in New Zealand and not have to pay tax on it, we ordered one to take the place of our Sat-Nav which had failed us several times. Tom installed it while we were in the quiet Whangarie Harbor. That required him to be hoisted up to the top of the mast , and while he was there he changed bulbs and checked on all the antenna and wiring atop both masts and the spreaders. I would have hated sitting in that canvas bosun's chair 65 feet off the water, but not Tom. He enjoyed it so much that he asked me to send up the camera. Not only did he get several birds-eye-view photos of the entire harbor, he also got an interesting shot of his big toe in the center of the harbor. We laughed when we got the prints back.

We learned there was a shop in the area where we could have our life raft opened and repacked. Since it hadn't been serviced for several years, we thought it time to do it. We struggled to get it off our boat and then we struggled further to push it into the little second-hand car we'd purchased. The axle sat low to the road from the extra weight of the raft, but we managed, uneventfully, to get it to the proper business. They opened the raft, installed new inflation cartridges, and packed it with fresh water and dry food packets. It was labeled as a six-man raft, but when Tom and I crawled into it just to see how it felt inside we wondered where and how the two of us could manage in it, let alone six. There was barely enough room for the two of us to lie down next to each another, and it felt more like a double rubber coffin than a liferaft. Tom said, "If we ever have to get into this thing at sea, we are dead!" It was the one piece of equipment we hoped we'd never have to use.

EMPIRE ROCK

Shortly after Christmas we had guests. Clark came first and nearly scared me to death when he announced he wanted to do a bungee jump. Watching our oldest son jump off a bridge was enough to give me a heart attack. No mother should have to witness that!

Then Mark and Michelle came and they wanted to bungee jump, too. They did their jump together, and at the bottom, Mark proposed marriage to Michelle. I can only surmise that Mark figured if they could endure a bungee jump together they would be able to endure any challenges that marriage might present to them in the future.

On the first night of their engagement we were anchored in one of the many pristine little coves in the Bay of Islands where there was one other local sailboat already anchored.

We had never met the captain of that boat before, but true to New Zealand hospitality, Don Freeman came over in his dinghy and invited us on their boat for cocktails. His wife's name was Di, and he introduced himself as a farmer. His land neighbors were on board as well, and we learned that the neighbors raised deer for meat. There were eight of us crammed into their small cockpit but the warmth of friendship made up for any spatial discomfort. Before we returned, Don gave us his address and phone number, and encouraged us to pay them a visit if and when we got to Masterson.

After all our guests returned home, Tom and I began land traveling. It was typhoon season in the South Pacific and we did not want to be sailing during that time, so we spent the next several months soaking up the New Zealand culture. We met and learned about the Maoris, the indigenous Polynesians of New Zealand. We visited a dairy farm, toured a geothermal plant, saw a sheep-shearing contest, and observed the sulfur geyser at Rotorua. We put our little car on the ferry and continued our land trip on the South Island where we saw spectacular fjords and actually walked on a glacier.

We traveled as inexpensively as possible by renting rooms in the local campgrounds, which included the use of a common kitchen that was fully equipped with pots and pans. We purchased legs of lamb from butchers in the towns we stayed in and had them seasoned with mint, de-boned, and de-fatted at no extra cost. We soon discovered that campground kitchens were the perfect places to meet and talk with other New Zealanders. At one campground a man asked if I had mint sauce to go with my lamb, and when I told him I didn't, he brought us some of his. "You can just bring whatever you don't use back to me when you're finished," he said. He was a total stranger, but he went out of his way to see that our lamb was served with mint sauce that night.

We thought we might have made a mistake staying at one of campgrounds when we discovered a rugby team was staying there. We feared the team would be loud and rowdy all night and that we would get very little sleep, but instead we were pleasantly surprised. After their game, the young men, many of whom were stout and seemed to have no necks, came back to the campground to shower and change into suits in preparation to going out for dinner. They talked with us and were nothing but gentlemen, and they even invited us to come and see them play the next day. What a pleasant surprise! We saw our first rugby game.

At another campground we met two sheep-shearers. One of them told us they had just put in a 10-hour day, and each had sheared several hundred sheep that day. They could hardly stand up after working in a bent-over position day in and day out. Their jobs put new meaning into the saying about working at a "back breaking job." They told us of a shearing competition that had just taken place. A new national record was set: one man sheared 620 sheep in an eight-hour day!

We experienced a few challenges of our own with sheep walking down the road. We had no difficulty getting through a flock that was coming head on, but when the flock was walking in the same direction we were driving, it was nearly impossible to get through them. Just when we would think we had navigated our way through the flock, one of them

New Zealand has many more sheep than people and boasts of having twenty different varieties of sheep.

The national record is 620 sheep sheered by one man in a "back-breaking" eight-hour day.

would begin to run and the whole flock would get excited and run up in front of us again. Worse yet were the trucks transporting them to the market. The sheep were stacked three high, and wet, smelly excrement continually dripped from the truck. It caused a nauseating odor and mess all over the hood and windscreen of the car. We were torn between staying close in order to attempt passing, or dropping back a kilometer or so to avoid the stench.

For the most part, our ugly, little used car was perfect for driving around the country, and we were delighted to learn it was only 400cm in length, qualifying us to be charged the minimum ferry fee to visit the South Island.

When we got near Masterton, we called Don and Di thinking that we would just stop by for a short visit, but they insisted we come and stay with them for several days. It turned out that the "farm" Don referred to was a large sheep ranch that he ran by himself with the help of one hired man and two trained "eye" dogs. It was amazing to see how well the dogs could round up and guide a whole flock of sheep, without uttering a single bark. Don traveled his ranch on a 4-wheeler and signaled to the dogs with a small whistle. The dogs would stare down the sheep and move them into whichever paddock they were to graze in that day. It was an impressive thing to watch. After Don got all his sheep moved to a new paddock he took us to a high point of land to show us his entire spread, and when we returned to the house Di teased him about it.

"Did you take them to your empire rock?" she chided.

"Don't call it that," he said and blushed. "It's just our highest point of land."

"It's where you view your empire, is it not?" she laughed.

PAVLOVA

Di told us she had invited their neighbors to join us for dinner that night as well.

"They are the ones you met on our boat in the Bay of Islands," she said.

When the neighbors arrived we learned more about their deer ranch. The deer were being raised for the meat, and through out the evening meal we could hear the bucks making eerie moaning sounds. The family was in the process of trying to find a consumer-friendly name before they began exporting it. They were reluctant to call it venison because they felt the average consumer would assume it had a strong wild flavor, when in fact, the domestically raised deer meat had a mild delicate flavor.

It was a great evening, and we learned so many interesting things about deer, sheep and some of the day-to-day operational problems the two families had to face. We learned that the eerie moaning the deer were making happened only during rutting season when the does were in heat, and that the darling little black-faced sheep were raised solely for their meat. Some naive part of me wanted to think some of them were raised for their wool, but the reality was that black wool was worth even less than white wool. I didn't know until that evening that most sheep were raised for reasons unrelated to the value of their wool, and that the wool was sold as a means to recoup some of the other expenses.

During our visit, the nighttime temperatures dipped, and there was a prediction of a freezing rain that night. The prediction caused much discussion at the dinner table as the men discussed the merits of rounding up the sheep and putting them in a covered corral. A lot was at risk. The potential monetary loss when sheep did not survive a cold night, were astronomical, but the task of rounding up large herds in the dark and moving them to a protected corral was a laborious task, and that would not be the end of the work. If the sheep spent the night in a corral, they would have to be moved back out to a paddock the next morning, to a place where they could graze. As I listened to the conversation I realized that it was not only sailors who took weather reports seriously. Anyone owning livestock had just as big an interest in the weather.

That delightful evening provided an opportunity to learn something new about a way of life that we would never even have thought about before. After dinner Di served a wonderful dessert that we had never seen nor tasted. She called it Pavlova, and it was as delicious as it was beautiful. It consisted of a firm meringue base topped with whipped cream, fresh kiwi, and strawberries. Yum!

(See Appendix C for Pavlova recipe)

When it was time for us to return to the boat we said goodbye with great reluctance because we had developed such a warm bond with Don and Di. We encouraged them to come and sail with us sometime in the future, perhaps in Fiji, but realistically we did not think they would.

We sailed to Auckland and stayed in the marina for a short time. The America's Cup race was taking place in San Diego, California at that time, and the entire event was covered by New Zealand television. Bars and restaurants all over Auckland had their televisions tuned to the regatta coverage, and we were surprised at the huge interest in it, because in the United States the event barely got a line or two during the sports portion of the news.

THIN HAIR

We took advantage of the many opportunities available to us in Auckland and even had physicals. Tom learned he had some pre-cancerous cells on his face, and the doctor told him to return on Wednesday to have them burned off. That was the day when the magic liquid nitrogen was delivered in a thermos bottle to the clinic. The cost for the doctor's visit and the entire procedure was $5.00.

We treated ourselves to professional haircuts, knowing that any professional job would be better than the ones we tried giving one another. On the day of our haircuts, Tom went first while I stopped into the shop next door to look at some clothes. I ended up not buying anything, and joined Tom a few minutes later. We were seated next to each other, but did not bother to speak because the two women cutting our hair were chatting away. The women had no reason to think we knew one another. When one finished cutting Tom's hair, he handed her a $10 bill and she handed him $3 change.

"I gave you a $10," he said.

"Yes," she said. "It's only $7."

"But, the sign says, $10," he said.

"That's OK," she said. "It's only $7."

He put the change into his pocket and walked out of the shop puzzled.

As soon as Tom left the shop, the girl who cut his hair came back and giggled to the one who was cutting my hair. "Gosh," she said, "that guy's hair was so thin that I just couldn't charge him the whole $10, but he kept trying to give it to me anyway. I didn't want to say, 'Look, mister, you don't have $10 worth of hair'."

She thought it was hysterically funny, and I didn't have the heart to tell her he was my husband. When she finished cutting my hair, I caught up with Tom and he was still puzzled about the proper price. When I told him the story we both had a good laugh about it.

FLYING AROUND THE WORLD – IN ONE DIRECTION

Where had the time gone? Four years had somehow evaporated while Tom and I had been living on the water floating from one adventure to the next. Sara, our youngest daughter, who had just begun college when we left Minnesota, was due to graduate that June, and we needed to make arrangements to get back for the ceremony.

When Tom investigated the cost of airfare from New Zealand to the United States and back, he found all flights extremely expensive. It was disappointing, but just when we began to feel very discouraged we discovered a wonderful deal offered by Air France. They offered an around-the-world ticket that cost the same as going round-trip from New Zealand to the United States. The ticket allowed us one full year to complete our journey, the only restriction was that we needed to progress in only one direction. After giving the option careful consideration for a very few minutes, we booked it.

Tom arranged to put VONNIE-T in a cradle up on land at the marina in Opua during our absence. It was a great opportunity to allow the blisters in the fiberglass to dry out and shrink. We parked our little car under the boat, so it would not be an inconvenience to anyone and left the keys with the owner of the boat yard. Tom told him he was welcome to use the car or loan it to other cruisers during the year we would be gone.

With only a few personal items and our passports, we flew home to Minnesota to attend the graduation and then began an around-the-world land adventure.

Our last stop on our around-the-world trip was at New Caledonia, a small French island in the South Pacific. Because it was a French island, we were surprised to see a huge American flag made of flowers, and embedded in the center of the roundabout on the main street. We learned the American flag was there because the local people appreciated what the Americans had done for them during World War II by stopping the Japanese in the Battle of the Coral Sea. Because of that appreciation, the people warmed to us while we observed a not-so-subtle resentment of the French who were assigned to provide law and order to their island.

BLISTERS AND BARE ASSES

Our Air France airplane ticket would have allowed us to continue traveling for two more months, but after 10 months of living out of a backpack, we had had enough and were eager to return to our boat. We flew directly from New Caledonia to New Zealand, and when we arrived we rented a small apartment, dug out our old work clothes, and began getting the boat ready for the next sailing season.

Tom had both masts pulled and he sanded and painted them as well as the booms and the spreaders. He installed a new anemometer, and checked out our new GPS, and painted the bilge. I sanded and varnished the exterior and interior teak. I even put a fresh coat of varnish on the sole. I worked quickly so the varnish would flow evenly and leave a smooth finish with no brush marks. I started in the V-berth and worked my way toward the hatch. When I finished the last little bit I crawled up into the cockpit without the use of the ladder and looked back at my completed work. I expected to see a glowing floor that was smooth as glass, but instead I saw a floor of bubbling varnish-blisters. I could hardly believe my eyes. What would have caused the varnish to act that way? I leapt down the ladder with tears welling up in my eyes and ran over to where Tom was painting. He looked up at me, saw the devastation on my face and turned off the paint sprayer.

"What's wrong?" He asked.

"I don't know," I told him. "I think I just ruined the sole of our boat, but I don't understand what I did wrong."

He checked out the situation and saw that the varnish was still bubbling, but he didn't understand what caused it either. One of the yardmen had to explain it to both of us.

"Probably means the original varnish was an oil-based varnish," he said. "Yup, when you put a water-based varnish over an oil-based varnish it blisters. That's got to be it. Can't be no other reason."

We had to wait three days for the blisters and varnish to completely dry before I could

After "pulling" our masts Tom sanded and painted them and our booms and spreaders.

begin the painstaking process of sanding it off. Then it took several more days to remove all the dust, because each time I'd wipe it, dust would float all over the cabin and I would have to wait for it to settle before I could attack it again. I was finally able to begin all over and I varnished it with an oil-based varnish. It was a hard way to learn about the incompatibility of water and oil-base varnishes.

New Zealand had lost a lot of its luster for us the second time around. The "wow" was missing, and having a wide variety of foods available did not seem quite so extraordinary after having traveled through Europe and Asia. We also missed our old cruising friends with whom we'd crossed the South Pacific. The new cruisers who had just arrived had established bonds with the cruisers they crossed the Pacific with, and they showed little interest in befriending those who had made the crossing earlier.

But fortunately, not all of our friends had sailed on. Bill and Gene, the doctors who had taken care of me while I had dengue fever in American Samoa, were both there. They had their boat up on land during the same time as we did, but they stayed onboard during that time while they worked on their boat. Carl Eric's boat was in a cradle next to them, and when Carl put a fresh coat of bottom paint on his boat he wanted to paint the entire

VONNIE-T as she looked out of the water and during a bottom paint job.

area under the bow, so he removed one of the supports to dab a little paint there. I am sure he intended to put the support back, but apparently he forgot because sometime during the middle of the night when the wind picked up Bill and Gene heard a deep thud someplace near them in the boat yard.

"I couldn't imagine what would make such a deep loud noise like that," Bill said. "Out of a dead sleep I sat up like a shot and ran up on deck butt naked to check it out. There was Carl Eric crawling out of his v-berth hatch. His boat had fallen off its supports and it was laying on its side on the ground."

"Thank God he didn't knock us over," Gene added.

"That's for sure," I said. "His mistake could have cost you plenty."

I was glad Bill and Gene hadn't received any damage from the fiasco, and in spite of Carl Eric's own stupidity I hoped no permanent damage had been done to him or his boat either. Still, I nearly folded in half laughing at the thought of that childish little man crawling out of his porthole, and after learning he caused the problem himself by removing the bow support, it made it even funnier.

DEPARTURE AND APPREHENSION

Our boat had never been in better shape. Both cosmetically and functionally, it was in pristine condition. Even the cockroaches that we had picked up in Ecuador had been killed during the cold New Zealand winter. With everything shipshape, Tom was eager to sail again. He arranged for the boat to be launched and as soon as it was in the water, we moved back on board.

There were many good feelings about being back on the boat. It was a relief not to be living out of a suitcase, it was great to be able to make a pot of coffee when we woke in the morning, and it was a luxury to sleep with the slight rocking motion of the boat in the water. Life was peaceful and relaxing. While I enjoyed all of those things I still had not lost my distaste for bad weather, and I was not particularly anxious to leave the comforts of New Zealand's harbors. I felt that my dread of facing the wrath of the Pacific was justified after the nightmarish passage we endured getting to New Zealand.

Once the boat was back in the water, I was able to resume radio check-ins. I listened with heightened interest to the weather conditions that other boats in the vicinity had been dealing with. I had no intention of checking out of New Zealand until I had heard there was a safe weather window. Tom didn't relish matching his wits against an angry Mother Nature right away either. He checked the weather-fax daily, watching for a storm-free time on the horizon before making the decision to leave New Zealand.

When everything looked like a "go," we put fresh provisions on board, assembled several microwaveable meals, charted a planned route to Fiji, and did our checkout.

THE PASSAGE FROM HELL

We had not been sailing for 12 months, and on March 23rd we left New Zealand. The weather was good, the winds moderate, and sea swells less than four feet. Sailing conditions were comfortable and we moved along at a fair clip of five to six knots. On the third day the wind lightened, and by the following morning we had almost no wind at all. We turned the engine on and continued on our course heading by motor-sailing. The day was pleasant and the sun glistened brightly on the water, but by noon the sky began to cloud over and the water changed to a steely gray. By 3am dark clouds crept across the horizon causing the day to turn into an abnormally early night. When the barometer took a drastic drop, we knew we were in for a major storm.

Tom removed the whisker pole and shortened the sails. We double-checked everything on deck: the lifeboat, the dinghy, extra fuel, and water jugs to make sure they were secured. I microwaved our dinner, and we ate early, feeling tense and uncertain about what was in store for us.

After dinner, the sky became even more black and threatening. The clouds hung so low that they appeared to be at our level and could reach out and grab us. We knew neither of us would be able to sleep, so we sat in the cockpit and waited. We waited for the wind to howl, for the ocean to begin its rage, and for the night from Hell to begin. It wasn't a matter of *if* we would be hit by a storm — it was a matter of *when*. It seemed we had been in that same situation far too many times before, and repeat performances of storms never improved with experience. Each was an act of endurance filled with emotional and physical exhaustion.

We didn't wait long. The wind built until it screeched through the rigging with an ear-piercing shrill. We had forgotten to take down our American flag, and it sounded like a bullwhip as it snapped and cracked back and forth on the stern. We knew it would be ripped to shreds, but neither of us wanted to risk going up on deck, let alone back to the stern to rescue it. Tom did have to go out on deck to put another reef in the mainsail, and then an eerie shroud of blackness surrounded us. Nothing was visible beyond the perimeter of the boat.

Tom turned on the radar and we checked for other boats that might be near us. He put out a general call on the VHF radio and announced to anyone listening that we were "heaving to" and gave our position. To "heave to," Tom shortened the jib sail and locked the wheel in a position that would keep the bow up-wind. The result was that we had little or no boat speed, but it allowed us both to go below deck into the cabin, and even to put the hatch boards in. There was no low side of the boat while "heaving to" so we each took a side in the main salon, stuffed pillows around us, and tried to rest as much as possible while tossing like a cork in a washing machine. The "heaving to" motion was jerky, violent, and erratic and I could feel my innards slosh and move back and forth. But even that was more tolerable than the noise. Hearing the growling sky, the cracking lightning, the irritating shrill sound of the wind in the rigging, and the snapping of our flag was almost more than I could stand. My nerves were frayed and I wanted to scream. The boat crashed as it fell off each new wave, and the water gurgled as it rushed past our hull. The blocks and sheets groaned under the onslaught of inconsistent demands put upon them. One minute they were expected to work and the next minute all pressure had been taken off of them, as the boat dropped off the wind.

There were sounds inside the boat as well. Spoons and forks slid back and forth in the drawer, pots and pans banged in the cabinet, and plastic dishes thumped from one side of the cabinet to the other. I couldn't stand it! Then I got an idea. I emptied the towels from our linen cabinet and stuffed them into the silverware drawer, the dish cupboard and the pots-and-pans cabinet in an effort to save them from destruction, and stop some of the noise. Still, the teak table in the center of the cabin creaked and moaned under the pressure of the mast that went through its center, and the hull made its own sounds as it flexed under the weight of each powerful wave of the ravaging sea. There was no getting away from the fact that those noises represented danger, and if there ever was a time when we needed to trust the integrity of the boat, it was that night.

Tom checked the radar every 10 or 15 minutes and was relived each time to see no boats in sight. He checked our position on the GPS, thankful that we were no longer relying on our old Sat-Nav.

It took several hours for the storm to blow itself out. When we were finally able to go topside, Tom raised our sails and set a new course. Our American flag had been badly damaged and needed to be replaced before we entered port, but everything else seemed to have survived.

Many of the boaters discussed the storm on the radio the following morning. One boat was missing and there was an "all look out" put out for it. Another boat, REBECCA, with our friends Linda and David whom we knew from Venezuela, had taken damage to their roller-furling sail. We were unclear about how serious their problem was from the initial radio conversation, but we identified ourselves and arranged to go off to another channel to talk with them. On another radio channel we learned they had tucked into Minerva Reef to allow themselves time to think over their situation and contemplate what they should do next. Since we were within a day's sail of the reef, we agreed to meet them there.

Finding Minerva Reef with our new GPS was a piece of cake. The only question that remained was the accuracy of the charts. All the charts we used were made prior to the existence of GPS. We could be certain about where we were, but could we rely on everything else to be where our charts indicated they should be? Even more baffling was how the old mariners managed to prevent colliding with Manerva Reef. It was a coral atoll in the middle of nowhere that barely stuck up a foot above the sea at high tide. Trying to see it with the naked eye was nearly impossible, and if you came upon it unsuspectingly it might not be seen at all until it was too late to avoid a disaster. It was mandatory for any boat near it to know exactly where it was and the exact location of the entrance. There was no room for error.

When we arrived at the reef, Tom checked and double-checked his calculations before we attempted to enter. Even then he stood on the bow to increase his ability to read the water, and by using hand signals he told me where to steer and what speed to use. Once inside, we saw REBECCA looking rather forlorn and lonely off to one side of the inner reef. We motored over and anchored a few yards behind them. They were thrilled to see us and invited us over for a dinner of hot turkey sandwiches. Yum! What a treat after several days of cold weather sailing and feeling rather beat-up.

After dinner Tom and David discussed their problem, and Tom loaned them our hank-on staysail, which was just about the right size for their boat. We hoped the sail would work for them until they could get their other problems repaired. They decided to return to New Zealand where they knew they could buy parts and get the needed work done properly. We didn't know if, or when, we would get the sail back but that didn't matter. Cruisers helped out other cruisers without worry or concern about things like that. The next day we watched as they sailed out of the reef. Everything looked OK.

I thought we would leave that day too, but instead Tom wanted to explore and hunt the inner lake of the reef. It was only about a mile in diameter and when he discovered that it was teeming with fish he relished the challenge of diving for a fresh catch for our evening meal. We stayed for several more days, and sometimes I swam with him in the morning, but a half-day of swimming was enough for me. I puttered away my afternoons while he returned to the water for more hunting.

I always nagged him about the importance of taking the oars with him in the dinghy, and he always ignored me and went off without them. By his way of thinking, the oars were just one more thing in his way inside our small dinghy, and one more thing for him to put away at the end of the day. One day when he was on the other side of the reef, and ready to return to the boat, the dinghy motor refused to start. He began swimming back to the boat with the dinghy in tow, but found himself swimming against the wind. With the added drag from the dinghy, he quickly tired. He yelled across the water for me to toss him a line, but there was no way that I could have thrown a line that far. I should have floated a fender out to him on a polypropylene line, but I didn't know where we had stowed the polypropylene line, and I didn't want to take my eyes off of him to go below and search for it. I quickly tied one of our lightweight fenders to a jib sheet and tossed it in his direction. Of course, the dacron jib sheet immediately sank, preventing the fender from drifting more than a few feet from the boat.

Meanwhile, Tom was fatigued and it became more and more questionable that he would make it safely back to the boat. "Let go of the dinghy," I shouted to him. We could always replace the dinghy and motor.

"No," he shouted back. "Throw me a polypropylene line."

"I don't know where it is." I shouted back.

"Find it!" he demanded.

We were both frustrated and our shouting at one another did nothing to improve what was already a terrible situation. In hindsight I should have known exactly where I could put my hands on a line that would float on top of the water, and Tom should have taken the oars with him in the dinghy. But all the "should have's" did not matter at that moment. It was a fact that neither of us was prepared to deal with the situation. Tom could easily have been washed over the reef and floated out to sea, never to be found. The likelihood of my being able to get the anchor up and navigate my way out through the right opening to look for him would surely have ended up with VONNIE-T crashed on the reef while he continued to float away. He could easily have had a heart attack from over-exertion while trying to swim with the added drag of pulling the dinghy and motor. He and I could have both ended up dead because I could not have rescued him or sailed the boat out of the reef by myself.

Both luck and Tom's sheer determination enabled him to avoid a tragedy. He reached the swim ladder with the dinghy still in his tow. I grabbed the dinghy tether and clipped it to a stanchion and helped pull him up the ladder onto the aft deck of the boat. That was as far as he went. He crumpled onto the deck exhausted, having neither the strength nor desire to even remove his wetsuit.

We barely talked the rest of that day. We were emotionally washed-out although relieved the incident ended as well as it did. We each harbored blame toward what the other person "should have" done to prevent the problem in the first place. A heavy cloud of blame hung between us, and the joy of diving on the reef no longer existed. It was time to move on, so the next day we left for Fiji.

MAKING BEER ON BOARD AT FIJI

Fiji is an independent nation made up of 332 islands. We entered the country at Suva, which is the capital city on the southeast corner of the largest island, and anchored in front of the Royal Suva Yacht Club. The yacht club was a haven for visitors because it offered reasonably priced meals, fresh water showers, laundry facilities, and was located in front of a bus stop that went directly to the downtown area where the port captain's office was located.

With all our boat work caught up, we had plenty of time to explore Suva before our guests began arriving and we took many long walks. One day we walked near the jail, and became puzzled when we saw people lined up in front of the gate. All the people in line held containers of food that they brought to family members inside. Apparently prisoners in Fiji were at the mercy of their family for their total sustenance. On another day we searched for a copy machine to make duplicates of our most recent "Dear Gang" news letter for family members and friends back home. I had typed the letter on colorful, tropical, designer paper. It looked so attractive that I was willing to splurge and print it on a color copier. Were we ever surprised to learn that color copy machines were against the law in Fiji! The concern was that they could be used to print money.

A few days later a boat called GREEN DOLPHIN carrying Linda and Don arrived in the anchorage. We had never met them before, but they radioed to tell us they had just arrived from New Zealand and they had brought the sail we had loaned Linda and David on REBECCA. We dinghied over to meet them and pick up our sail. As a thank-you, we brought them a map of Suva with directions to the port captain's office, and loaned them enough Fijian money to get there by bus. They seemed so appreciative of our small gesture that we decided to do it for every new boat that entered the harbor. It turned out to be a great way to meet new people. Don invited us on board for a cold beer.

"This is really good beer," Tom told Don.

"I'm glad you like it," Don said with a sly grin.

"Did you buy it here?" Tom asked.

"No," Don said, "It's my home brew."

"You've got to be kidding," Tom said. "You made this?"

Don proudly showed Tom his set-up for making beer on the boat. Well, after tasting Don's beer Tom could hardly wait to make his own. We had acquired a new quest for our walks over the next several days. First, we had to locate a store where we could purchase the needed supplies: canned beer mix, a plastic petcock and new bottle caps. Next we made a trip to the open market to buy a six-gallon plastic barrel with a sealable lid and a long-handled plastic spoon. Then came the big search to find empty beer bottles. Tom was so excited when he found the first empties that he just tossed them into the dinghy and began taking them out to our boat. His excitement changed dramatically when he discovered the bottles were full of cockroaches. Apparently cockroaches liked the beer that was left in the bottoms of the bottles, so Tom reached over the side of the dinghy and rinsed each bottle out in the salt water. Man, did those cockroaches hate the salt water! They tumbled out of the bottles, and as soon as they hit the water they swam lickety-split back toward us and walked right up the sides of the dinghy. We had to turn on the motor and speed away from them while we brushed the speedier ones off the side of the dinghy. After that, we made it a point to wash the bottles thoroughly on shore before putting them in our dinghy.

Tom's first batch of beer was a disappointment. He said it tasted "skunky." Don came over to supervise the making of his second batch and found nothing wrong with the Tom's process. He apparently got an old mix for his first batch. With the right mix, all subsequent batches were great.

(See Appendix B for Beer Making Directions)

YOU HAVE A DATE?

Soon our guests began to arrive. Clark was due to arrive in a few days, then after him, the newly weds Mark and Michelle, who planned to spend their honeymoon with us, and finally Don and Di.

Prior to Clark's arrival, we requested permission from the port captain to sail to a small group of islands south of Suva called Kandavu. Our charts indicated that the islands had an interesting diving area protected by the Great Astrolabe Reef. Before permission was granted we were told we would need to bring an armload of kava roots as a gift to the chief of any village we wished to visit. The chief would have the last word as to whether or not we would be allowed to anchor there. It was also respectful, we were told, to keep our heads lower than the chief's head while we talked with him.

During Clark's long airplane ride, he built a friendsip with a young British woman who was returning to her medical job in Suva, after vacationing with her family in England. The airport where they landed was nearly on the opposite side of the island from Suva, where we were anchored, and he shared a two-hour taxi ride with her. Clark seemed quite smitten with her and asked if she could come to the boat to see it with us. After what I thought would be a quick tour neither seemed anxious to leave the other's company, so the four of us sat in the cockpit sipping Tom's new home brew while we made small talk. Not until I invited her to stay for dinner, and she declined, did Clark ask to use the dinghy to return her to shore.

He took his time on shore saying good-by and dinner was all prepared by the time he returned. I thought he would want to go to bed early after his marathon flight, but I couldn't have been more mistaken. "Mom, I've sort of got a date tonight," he said. "Would there be a problem if I took the dinghy in to shore tonight."

I was speechless, but Tom answered for me. "That's no problem, just be sure you lock it up good. You know it's our only transportation to shore."

So, after dinner, after having only a short time with him, Clark left for his date and Tom and I went to bed. I lay awake much of the night listening for him to return, but I never did hear him. When the sun rose we both got up and discovered Clark and the dinghy had still not returned. Tom made coffee and I made breakfast, and still there was no sign of him. Neither of us said what we were thinking, but my thoughts were scarcely short of panic. I reminded myself that he was a 30-year-old man, not a kid, and he certainly did not have to answer to his mom. Still, I wondered and worried about how one would begin searching for a missing tourist in Fiji. Not until we finished eating and I had washed the dishes and emptied the coffeepot of its grounds, did Clark and the dinghy return.

"Hi," he said, looking both sheepish and happy with himself, and completely oblivious of the worry he had caused me.

"We were planning on sailing to a smaller island that has a diving reef," Tom said, trying to be as nonchalant as possible, "but if you would rather stay here we can do that."

"No," Clark said. "Let's go. I came here to dive."

"OK," Tom said. He raised the anchor, hoisted the sails and set a course for Kandavu. We hadn't been sailing more than 20 minutes when Clark said, "I think I'll take a little nap." He crawled up into the V-berth and we did not see him again until we were in the process of dropping the anchor in front of a small village near the Great Astrolabe Reef.

DRINKING KAVA

After anchoring, we took our arm-load of piper methysticum roots, better known as kava, into shore, and asked to see the chief. We were led to a grass-roofed hut by several men who were wearing *sulus*, the Fijian version of *pareoes* and *lava-lavas*. Once inside the hut they invited us to sit with them on the dirt floor and wait. At first it seemed dark but our eyes adjusted quickly, and it was surprisingly pleasant and cool inside. Soon another man entered. He introduced himself as Chief Paul. Like the others, Paul sat down cross-legged opposite us while the others scooted on their seats to form a small circle, being careful to keep their heads lower than their chief's. He signaled for one of the others to bring in a kava bowl which was then set inside the circle. He accepted our gift and brought it up to his nose to sniff it. He smiled and said, "Good." Then he instructed someone to begin the process of making the kava, while we all watched.

First, the roots were mashed with stones. Then the pulverized results were mixed with water until an opaque, gray liquid was formed. The liquid was scooped into a coconut shell and the maker tasted it first. Apparently, it met the taste test because the second cup was given to Chief Paul, the third to Tom, the fourth to Clark, and finally one was given to me. After one sip I knew my feelings would not have been hurt if they had skipped me completely. The stuff tasted *terrible*! But skipping a cup of kava when one was offered did not seem an option. Tradition dictated that we clap three times before being presented with a cup, drink it down all at once, and clap one more time after returning the empty cup. The ceremony was treated with respect, and Fijians considered it an honor to include us. Honor or not, by my third cup I could not feel my lips and found it difficult to swallow. My mouth was numb and I had to concentrate to do that which should have been automatic. I told Tom I needed to return to the boat. He was ready, too, and at the risk of offending Chief Paul, Tom asked if we could remain anchored out in front of his village for a few days. The chief granted our request and when we got up to leave, the rest of them stayed seated and continued drinking the kava we had brought to them. They were happy and relaxed as babies.

WHAT A FISH!

We had many good experiences with the various members of that village. Clark and Tom went diving each day with a young man from Scotland, who operated a dive shop at the Great Astrolabe Reef. While they dove, I taught school at the request of the chief, who asked if I would work with the three 14-year-olds at the village, one of whom was his daughter. All three were scheduled for tests, and their scores would determine which high school they would be assigned to in Suva. There was a simple study guide for the concepts they would be tested on, but they had no idea what a test was like. So with the small computer we had on board I designed

Fijian making traditional drink by mashing kava roots and water until it's a gray opaque liquid.

practice tests for them, covering much of the subject matter they already knew. They learned what a true-false question was, what a multiple-choice question was, and how to format an answer for an essay question. After a few practice tests they thought it was a wonderful game, and they looked forward to the new challenge each morning. It was a joy to have had the opportunity to teach them.

If a man could grow gills from being in the water too long, Clark might have been a candidate. He loved the reef, and he dived several times each day. While Tom had become picky about what he speared, Clark just enjoyed the hunt. The bigger the fish, the more fun it was for him. One day he returned to the boat with a huge smile and so excited that he was visibly shaking.

"Get the camera, Mom! This one's worth a little film." (See Color Insert, page 11.)

Wow! He could hardly lift the fish up long enough for me to snap a picture. His trophy fish was a 46-inch wahoo, and we figured it had to weigh at least 50 pounds.

He told us what a fight it had been to bring it to the surface. "What a blast. That fish took me for a ride and dragged me all over down there. I felt like a rag doll on a sleigh ride. Up and down we went and there was a point when I wasn't sure if I was going to be able to hang on to him, but if I let go I would have lost my spear gun and everything, so I just kept riding him out. I have to admit I was pretty tired by the time he gave up, and then lifting him into the dinghy was a major struggle. God, what a kick!"

We discussed what would be the best thing to do with a fish that size. It was way too large for us to eat, so he decided to take it in and give it to the chief, for the village. Ironically, on that particular day another chief and elders from the "pig" village were visiting with Chief Paul. Custom dictated that a gift of that magnitude would have to be given to the visitors. The visitors then needed to reciprocate with something of equal value. Ordinarily, it would have been a pig but since they didn't bring a pig with them,

Uniformed school children walking to school on the island of Kandavu, a seven-hour sail from Suva, Fiji.

they gave Chief Paul cash. The visitors cooked the fish for dinner that night and a big kava ceremony was held afterwards, with Clark invited as the honored fisherman. Clark sat with the two chiefs, the most distinguished men of both villages, and drank kava with them well into the wee hours. Everyone was happy, especially Clark. He had the exhilaration of spearing a huge fish, as well as photographs to prove its size, and the experience of sitting with two Fijian chiefs in a traditional kava-drinking ceremony. What a day!

A TOOTH-BRUSHING DEMONSTRATION

When Clark's vacation came to an end and it was time to take him back to Suva to get his plane, Chief Paul asked if we would be willing to take two passengers with us. A mother and son needed to see a doctor in Suva and they dreaded making the crossing in one of the open taxi boats. It was a four-hour crossing, and we did not ordinarily like taking local passengers on a trip that long because they always had the potential of getting seasick. But if we were to return to this village with Mark and Michelle we could not say no. "That would be O.K.," we said, "but we'll want them to take a seasick pill. Will that be O.K.?" Not only was that O.K., they liked the idea and eagerly swallowed the pill.

They had a bundle of stuff that I presumed was a combination of food and clothing they would need in Suva, and as Tom lifted the bundle up onto the side of the boat, I saw a bug scurry back into it. I got a large black garbage bag and put the bundle inside and Tom tied it to the base of the mizzenmast. We figured it would be safe there and hoped the bugs would remain inside the bag.

Both mother and son were large, heavy people, and during the passage we learned that it was the son, Ben, who was seeing the doctor. He was 28 years old and I told the mother that her son looked very healthy to me.

"He is most times," she said, "but sometimes he gets those fits."

"Fits?" I asked.

"I think the doctor called them seizures," she said.

"Epileptic seizures? Is that what he called them?" I asked.

"Yes, I think so," she said.

"Oh, my gosh!" I thought to myself. What would we do if he had had a seizure while we were under way?

It was no wonder they didn't want to make the trip in an open boat, in spite of the fact that the open boats went faster and would have gotten them to Suva in less time than our sailboat. Having a seizure in an open boat could result in a drowning. I did not particularly want to see a seizure on our sailboat, either, but fortunately the seasick pill made both of them sleepy and soon they were leaning on each other and sound asleep. They slept through the entire passage and awoke as we entered the Suva harbor. Tom took them and the bundle into shore and they made their way up the street to wait for their bus. They disappeared and we never heard from them again.

Our next set of guests was Mark and Michelle, who were on their honeymoon. As always, they brought lots of other goodies with them and this time they brought toothbrushes for all the school children. Michelle, who is a dental hygienist, gave a tooth-brushing demonstration. The children liked getting their gift and enjoyed the entertainment aspect of her demonstration, but it was doubtful that any of them grasped the importance of dental hygiene. Very likely neither they, nor their parents, had ever seen a dentist or a hygienist before. When teeth got diseased they were allowed to rot in the mouth until they fell out, and when that finally happened it was considered good riddance.

Mark and Michelle enjoyed the village, but after all it was their honeymoon, so we anchored in some of the private coves where they could take the dinghy and go off on their own. They usually went to one of the tiny uninhabited islands, and returned after being gone for several hours. Tom began referring to the island as Conception Island.

Our third set of guests was Don and Di from New Zealand. During their visit the village was putting a roof on their new church. When the last peak was finished, the village held a big celebration with food, kava, and singing and dancing by the school children. We were invited to participate just as though we were members of the village. It was a happy, rich experience and we knew we were lucky to have had the opportunity to participate.

WHAT'S NEXT?

We had enjoyed each of our island experiences, but after six years some of the thrill had begun to diminish. After our guests had all returned home we talked about how much longer we were going to continue with the cruising life.

Tom thought it might take us two years or more to sell the boat, and as we got older, the demands of cruising had become increasingly difficult. We talked about the possibility of trying to sell the boat and return to land life.

SHIPS LOG, TOM'S ENTRY,
Fiji, 20°S Latitude 171°?E Longitude, 24 June 1993

How much longer are we going to do this? We are over six years into our adventure now. Some of it was scary, but most of it was rich, tasting of the cultures of the world, and fascinating marine life. It was now that we realized that each new set of Islands was "wow". Some time back, each new set was "WOW". We discussed our future. Our loose plan was to visit New Caledonia, and then spend the typhoon season in Australia. Following the typhoon season we would enter the North Pacific, perhaps to Guam, Japan, and Hawaii. That sounded like several years to us, so the next logical question was "How much longer are we going to do this?" The answer was: not the rest of our lives. We knew that boats took a couple of years to sell, depending on where you were, and how much loss you were willing to take. We knew the VONNIE-T was in excellent shape, so we thought it was time to start the process.

CHAPTER TEN

How Much Longer Do We Tempt Fate?

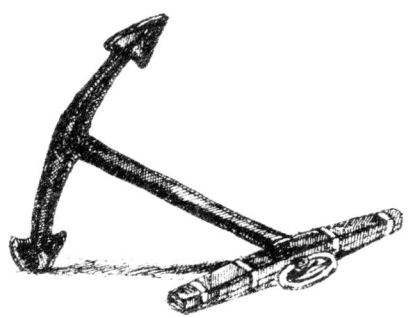

A HOLE IN THE BOW OF THE BOAT

After bringing the last of our guests back to Suva to catch their airplane, we checked out of the country and began our passage toward New Caledonia. It was a several-day passage, and unlike other passages that had at least begun pleasantly, this one was miserable from the start. The seas were lumpy, with eight-foot swells and the winds were gusty and varied. One moment they were 20 knots, the next we had a gust of 30 knots. There seemed to be nothing either of us could do to get comfortable. It was one of those passages we each had to endure silently, because complaining to one another could not improve it.

As a coping mechanism, I took a daytime nap in the main cabin where there was the least motion, while Tom stayed on watch up in the cockpit. The bunk where I slept was narrow, and my arm automatically hung off the side, with my hand touching the sole of the boat. When I awoke, I was surprised to discover my hand was in water, and I sat up with a start. I swung my feet to floor and found them in water, too. Water was coming up from the floorboards in the main cabin of the boat!

"Tom," I yelled. "We've got a big problem here!"

"Geezs!" he exclaimed, when he saw the water slosh across the teak from one side of the boat to the other. "Get pumping on the hand pump!"

He crawled into the engine compartment and checked our hoses and through-hull fittings. We had thirteen of them, and some hoses branched into Y's. Any one of them could have been leaking. But none of them seemed to be the culprit, and panic heightened. If the bilge pump could not keep up with the amount of water coming in, we would surely sink. As a frantic last resort, Tom opened the chain locker in the bow, and he saw the problem. Seawater was entering the boat from a hole where there should have been a running light, and each time the boat crashed down into another wave, a quart of water gushed through the hole. The brass screws that should have held the running light in place, had apparently become weak and could no longer hold the light in its socket. The light was hanging by its wires inside the boat. Normally that light would be three feet above the water line, but not in the heavy seas we experienced. So, each time the boat slammed into another wave, the running lights became buried in the forceful water.

As part of our emergency preparation seven years earlier, Tom had purchased an assortment of tapered wooden plugs, and he dug deep into the bottom of his tool compartment to find them. He stripped off his clothes, put on a lifeline, and crawled to the bow of our heaving deck with a hammer and his entire stash of wooden plugs. The bow of the boat heaved from water to air and back with each pounding wave, and his movements had to be timed to correspond with those brief moments when the bow was airborne. When he was as far forward as he could go, he spread out on his stomach and reached over the side until he could touch the hole. Once he located the hole, he used the hammer to pound one of the wooden plugs into it. He got the plug in the hole on the first try and had to hang on tight when the bow crashed down into the next wave. His entire body got a cold saltwater bath with each crashing wave, and I could see that he started to slide and needed to struggle to hang on. When the bow rose out of the wave and became airborne again, he reached back over the side to check on the status of the plug. Thank goodness, it withstood the power of the previous wave. Tom gave the plug another quick tap with the hammer to give it a snug fit. Again, the boat crashed down into a wave, and again, he was immersed in frothing, gurgling saltwater. When the bow came up out of the water the next time he pushed himself backward toward the cockpit. I opened the flap of the cockpit enclosure to help him enter and relieved him of his extra plugs and the hammer. He was soaked, salty, and freezing, and I handed him a towel. "You'd better keep pumping," he said. "I don't know how long that plug will last."

For the rest of that passage we kept the chain locker door propped open so we could see if the plug was still in place. We had been very fortunate to catch that leak before the boat had reached its capacity and sunk. We could never allow that much water to ever enter the boat again!

With all the boat motion and worrying about the wooden plug in the bow, neither of us was able to get much rest. The next night we could see a glow on the horizon. Our charts indicated they were likely city lights far off in a distance from the Loyalty Islands. Shortly after that, we saw a similar glow from the island of Mare', and by dawn we rounded the tip of Ile Des Pins. By the time we were safely tucked in behind the New Caledonia reef, we were both exhausted. We knew it still required several more hours of sailing before we would arrive at Noumea where we needed to check into the country. We felt we could go no further without first getting some rest, so we motored over to a small cove and dropped our anchor. We showered, ate breakfast, and crawled into our bunks for naps.

We were awakened out of a sound sleep when we heard shoes stomping onto our deck. It was frightening to think people were so brazen as to come aboard without asking permission. When I saw a uniformed man standing over Tom, I froze with fear. He was yelling at Tom in what sounded like French, but neither of us could understand a single word. He sounded almost as angry as I was frightened.

I wanted to get up but I was not wearing anything, and when he saw my situation, he had the decency to turn his head while I grabbed some clothes and dressed. Three other uniformed men were already down below decks searching the main cabin. One shuffled through our food lockers, another dug into the vertical lockers, and the man in our cabin lifted the mattresses to look under the very bunks we had slept on. The lead-ranking officer spoke a little English, and had already begun looking through our boat papers that were sitting on the chart table ready for our check-in. He demanded an explanation from Tom as to why we neglected to check in at Noumea before anchoring. Tom tried to explain that we had just arrived and planned to check in as soon as we had gotten a little sleep, but the officer was not pleased, and I could only suppose he considered it to be a rather lame excuse. Tom tried to tell him about the problem we faced while taking on water. He pointed to the wooden plug in the running light, and tried to show him what had happened, but he was not interested. He could not comprehend how very different it was to be facing ferocious waves, as opposed to being anchored in the calm, quiet water behind the reef.

Meanwhile, the other men continued searching the boat for something. They took out drawers and looked underneath and behind each one. They went through all the clothes lockers. They looked in the engine compartment, the lazarette, and all through Tom's tools and spare parts. They searched through the spice cabinet, smelling each bottle, and looked under the sinks, and around both heads.

"What are you searching for," I asked. "If I knew what you were looking for, maybe I could just show it to you." They pushed me out of their way, gently but with authority, and continued their search.

They returned each drawer as they finished with it, not caring that the contents were all jumbled. We assumed they were looking for drugs or guns, and we hoped they would not find the two guns or the ammunition that we had hidden away. I didn't even want to think about the consequences if they found them.

After they finished their search, the lead officer told Tom, "You go check in *now!*" That was pretty clear. They got off the boat, Tom pulled up our anchor, and we motored into Noumèa for our official check-in.

FAREWELL VONNIE-T

We checked in at Nouméa on the southwestern end of New Caledonia Island, and much to our relief, everything went smoothly. We wondered if we might experience some repercussions from not having checked in immediately, but it did not appear that one department had talked to the other.

A few days later, GREEN DOLPHIN arrived. They wisely called ahead on the radio, and were told to stern-tie to the pier, because the officials wanted to bring a new drug-sniffing dog onboard. They did exactly as they were told and laid a two-by-ten plank from their boat to the pier. The officers and the dog walked the plank toward the boat several feet above the water. It was a simple oversight, but Linda and Don neglected to mention the fact that they had a cat on board. When the dog got a sniff of the cat, he lunged toward it and fell off the plank into the harbor, nearly pulling its trainer in with him. Linda said it was one of the funniest things she had ever seen, and couldn't stop laughing; of course, the officers didn't see any humor in it at all. "Imagine seeing a big police dog getting all shook up over our little pussy cat," Linda said. "Gosh, old Bligh (the cat) never caused so much excitement in his life before."

The next day was Bastille Day. A large parade was held with bands, color guards, military machinery, and French uniformed units of men marching down main street. It was an impressive display of power, and spectators lined both sides of the street. As part of the crowd, we overheard discussions about how the French military had been concerned about a potential uprising from the indigenous (Kanaks) people prior to the parade. There was also much discussion about the tight security measures that were implemented shortly before our arrival to the island. It was then that we began to understand what our boarding had been all about. When they saw our boat anchored off to the far corner of the reef, they probably thought we were bringing in guns to instigate a potential coup. It was good that they did not find our two handguns. It did make me wonder though, if Tom and I were able to hide two handguns so well that they were not found after such a thorough search, just think of how much smarter real gun-runners probably were.

That night, we talked again about hanging up the cruising life and selling the boat. There were still many aspects of the lifestyle that we enjoyed, but the big *wow* had become less and less with each new island country. For the most part, Tom still enjoyed the sailing, but even he was shaken by the water episode of our last crossing. How long were we going to tempt fate?

Lavonne and Tom sitting together within the center cockpit enclosure on VONNIE-T.

Knowing that it could take years to sell the boat, Tom placed a 'For Sale' ad in the local New Caledonia newspaper. He made arrangements to take a slip at the dock the following Sunday, and we readied the boat for an open house. We hosed off the hull, polished the stainless steel, vacuumed the interior, and made everything look neat and tidy. Even the bilge looked clean and fresh with the nice paint-job Tom had given it when we were in New Zealand, and after its saltwater bath from the prior week.

Many people came on board. A few asked questions, and nearly everyone complimented us on how nice the boat was, but it appeared to us that there were no serious lookers.

On Monday, we relinquished our slip and returned to the anchorage out in the harbor. Several other women and I went to town to visit the used bookstore, and go out for lunch. Rather than my taking the dinghy into shore, Tom brought me in so he could still get back and forth during my absence. There were several things he wanted to do, and he suggested that I call him on the two-meter radio when I needed a ride back to the boat.

SHIPS LOG, TOM'S ENTRY
Nouméa, 22°S Latitude 168°E Longitude, 18 August 1993

Someone said "The two best days of boat ownership are the day you buy, and the day you sell". My love affair with VONNIE-T ended today.

She was in excellent shape, this beautiful girl of ours. Writing of what I did today brings tears to my eyes, even as I sit in her bosom at the chart table.

On arrival in Nouméa, we put out the word that VONNIE-T was for sale. We visited a boat broker, and entertained a number of lookers, who probably were only curious to see what she looked like. We even made FOR SALE signs. We placed an ad in the Sunday paper with the help of one of our French-speaking friends.

I thought it might take two years to sell. Boats do not sell easily. Most are usually sold at a loss after too long, particularly if they sit unattended for any length of time, and begin to appear neglected. We would probably sail out of here to pass the typhoon season in Australia, and then sail into the North Pacific.

On Saturday, while LaVonne was off to a ladies lunch, a friend brought a prospect to see this fine lady, the VONNIE-T. They were Dr. Robert De Malet and his pretty wife, Therese. Robert had practiced medicine for several years in France, and wanted to escape the grinding pressure of big city medicine. Here in Nouméa, his patient load was only one third of that in France. They were happy people living in this island paradise. Robert had been looking for a suitable boat for some time. Out to the boat we went in the dinghy. I saw them softly smile as they first looked from the water line to the masthead, and then from bow to stern. I circled VONNIE-T, the precious dear, for them to have a better look. We approached the port side, and mounted the wood and rope ladder that I had made. We sat in the cockpit for a while and discussed VONNIE-T's history. Then I led them on a tour topsides and below, as I described in warm terms each piece of the lady's equipment. Robert and Therese went on a second round by themselves, and returned to the cabin and promptly said, "We'll take her".

Now the emotions started as I thought "Do I really want to sell my beautiful lady?" Well yes. LaVonne and I had discussed it thoroughly, and we knew it was the right thing to do. My next thought was "What the hell do I do now?" I had experience buying and selling real estate, so I figured I could draft a purchase agreement. I had a hard time asking what their offer was, without risking any hint that we had price flexibility. Somehow, Robert said they would pay the asking price. They were worried that if they tried to bargain, and the time dragged on to Sunday, that we might receive other offers. So, I drafted up a purchase agreement using carbon paper, and listed all of what was, and was not, included. We all signed the dastardly document, and I got a security deposit check. We shook hands, and did French-style cheek kisses. All of us were very pleased. We boarded the dinghy, and I again circled VONNIE-T before returning them to the pier.

I shoved off from the pier and headed back to that fine lady, who was gently swinging on her anchor. Gentle breezes softly pushed the waves caressing her waterline. On approach, I once again circled her in a salute of respect. I tied up the dinghy, and as soon as I touched the stanchion, the tears started to flow. I could scarcely see as I climbed on board. I walked the entire length of her decks apologizing for having sold her. We had sailed some 20,000 miles together. I had maintained lights at her masthead, and scrubbed the depths of her bilge. She had delivered us safely through numerous storms, and captain error. Then, in the end, she had returned to us more money than we had paid for her eight years ago. I said I was sorry, out loud.

I felt really bad.

APPENDIX A

Growing Leaf Lettuce On Board

Why would anyone want to grow leaf lettuce on board their boat? While living aboard our sailboat for six and a half years, we found it difficult to find lettuce in most places. This was particularly true in the South Pacific. Even in the few areas where lettuce was available, we questioned the safety of eating it.

I found growing our own lettuce was the answer. This way we had all the lettuce we wanted for fresh salads, and we did not have to second-guess its safety. Our fresh salads were especially enjoyable during our longest South Pacific passage when we heard our radio friends complain of the boredom from eating canned goods.

Growing lettuce on board is easy. Just follow these simple steps.

■ **STEP ONE:** Purchase TWO plastic dishpans for EACH garden you wish to have and be sure they can nestle inside one another easily.

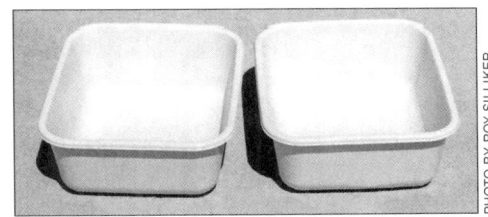

■ **STEP TWO:** Use a soldering iron to melt holes in the bottom of ONE dishpan. This will be the dishpan into which you will plant your garden. The holes will allow proper drainage while the bottom dishpan will catch run-off water. This keeps your garden healthy and your boat clean from garden dirt.

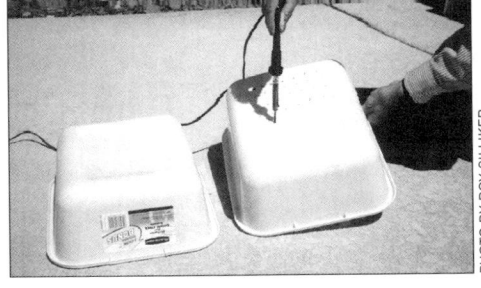

■ **STEP THREE:** Cut a rectangle of fiberglass screen to fit into the bottom of the dishpan with the holes. The screen will prevent the garden dirt from clogging the holes.

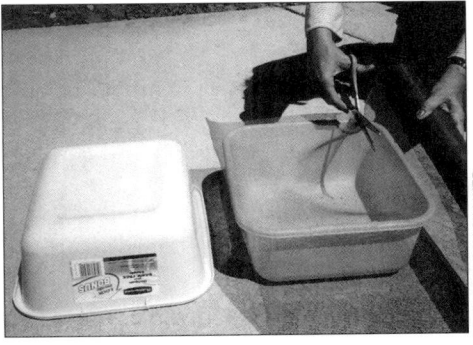

■ **STEP FOUR:** Assemble the dishpans in their proper order by placing the screen in the bottom of the pan with the holes. Then place this dishpan inside the dishpan without the holes. Fill the dishpan with potting soil to three-fourths full. If you wish to use fertilizer, do so at this stage. Mix in well.

■ **STEP FIVE:** Now you are ready to plant. There are many varieties of leaf-lettuce seeds for you to choose from. (I based my selection of seeds upon the shortest germination period, usually seven to fourteen days. This insured we could be eating from our garden during the third week.) Space the seeds according to the package directions. Water your new garden with about a half-cup of water. Water ONLY where you planted seeds. With a small garden like this you will use very little water because you can put the water exactly where it is needed.

■ **STEP SIX:** Select a place for your garden.
(A) Your garden must be secured so it does not move around.
(B) It needs to be out of the way of normal sailing activies.
(C) It needs a place where it will get plenty of sunshine.
(D) It needs to be protected from salt spray.

Seal the rest of your package of lettuce seeds, storing them in a dry, cool place. As your lettuce grows, start picking it from one end of your small garden, replanting as you go. This will ensure a continuous source of fresh lettuce for as long as you have seeds.

I had two gardens going at all times on our boat, one on each side of the cockpit hatch. I used bungee cords to tie them in, thus meeting all the above criteria.

APPENDIX B

Making Beer On Board

One warm day while at anchor in front of the Fiji Yacht Club in the South Pacific, some friends invited us on board for one of their home brews. In the name of sociability we accepted but we didn't anticipate much of a taste treat. We couldn't have been more wrong! The beer had full-bodied taste, not the watered down flavor of so many pasteurized store beers.

We were hooked! The next day we searched for empty bottles and set up our own home brewery.

Like us, you will find much pleasure in having your own brewery. Just think, no more carrying cases of heavy beer back to the boat. No more concern about cost (beer, along with most other things, was expensive in the French islands of both the Caribbean and the South Pacific). No more concern about how much alcohol was on board when we checked into new countries (The kits waiting to be made up are not alcohol. Not until the bottles have gone through the last fermentation stage are they considered alcohol). Besides, having your own brewery is ecologically friendly because the bottles are used over again, thus eliminating the problem of disposing cans or bottles.

Once our own home brewery was established, we looked forward to rewarding ourselves with a cool one immediately after setting our anchor in a new port. We also enjoyed having the luxury of inviting others on board for a cold beer without posing a hardship on supplies. We were often a popular boat in the anchorage.

BEGIN BY GATHERING UP THE FOLLOWING:
- **A six-gallon plastic fermenting barrel with a sealable lid.** The opening must be large enough so that you can clean the inside.
- **A plastic petcock** that will be fitted into a bunghole near the bottom of the barrel.
- **An airlock** that needs to be fitted into the top of the fermenting barrel. This will allow carbon dioxide to escape during fermentation and prevent bacteria from entering the brew.
- **Long handle plastic spoon** for stirring.
- **Empty bottles.** (My husband uses 22 ounce beer bottles. He fills 36 bottles per batch. Some cruisers use the plastic soda bottles with screw on lids. You will want to have enough bottles for 2 or 3 batches.
- **Bottle caps.**
- **Measuring spoons.**

Tom is in the galley filling the sterilized beer bottles from the fermenting barrel.

- **Funnel.**
- **Can opener** for opening Brew Kit.
- **Brew kit**, which is a one-liter can containing the hops and brew syrup and a separate package of yeast. Coopers brand is our favorite, but there are many others to choose from. Coopers is made in Australia but is readily available in the United States. They produce different kits, including stout, draft, lager, and ale.

Home brewing has become increasingly popular in the United States. Check the yellow pages of the city nearest you for a store dealing with brew equipment and kits. Any supplies you don't already have can be purchased there.

NOW LET'S BREW

Sterilize all equipment with a chlorine bleach solution of 1-Tablespoon bleach to 1-quart water. Completely wet down all surfaces with the bleach solution. Rinse well to get rid of bleach.

- Place brew kit in boiling water 5 minutes to help liquefy it.
- Open brew kit with clean can opener and pour into sterilized fermenting barrel. Add 4 1/4 cups sugar.
- Add most of one gallon of boiling water and stir well with sterilized spoon to dissolve all sugar and syrup from the brew kit.
- Pour remaining boiling water into empty brew kit container to rinse out the remaining ingredients. Pour this into the fermenting barrel.

- Top off the fermenting barrel with cold water and stir in the yeast.
- Cover barrel and check air lock periodically. Once bubbles stop (usually 4 to 8 days, but may be longer in colder climates), beer is ready for bottling. Caution: Be sure this first fermentation process has stopped or you might end up with broken bottles. Fermentation has basically stopped when there is one bubble or less per minute.

BOTTLING

- Sterilize all equipment, including the bottles with the bleach solution.
- Add 1/2 Tablespoon sugar to each bottle and then add the beer. (Be certain the sugar is added before the beer. The amount of sugar determines the amount of carbonation. It is better to err on the side of less sugar rather than risking having too much. You don't want any exploding bottles in the bilge).
- Cap each bottle.
- Store the beer in a dark place. Slow fermentation during the second fermentation period gives a better flavor. Wait about two weeks before tasting.

ENJOY

Now, choose that perfect warm sunny afternoon when you are sitting in the anchorage and invite a few friends over. Pull out a few bottles of your chilled home brew and pop the lids. Pour carefully so the "dregs" in the bottom of each bottle don't get in the glass when you are pouring. Offer your guests their first glass of home brew and watch them smile.

Caution: I suggest you make sure you have extra time on your hands during the next few days because your guests will want you to help them get started making their own home brew after tasting yours.

First fermentation takes place in the barrel, second fermentation takes two weeks in the filled bottles.

APPENDIX C

Recipe for Pavlova

PAVLOVA

New Zealand recipe given to LaVonne from Di Freeman

Ingredients:

4 egg whites
3 cups sugar
1 teaspoon vinegar
1 teaspoon cornflour *(known as corn starch in USA)*
Few drops vanilla essence
8 Tablespoons boiling water

Directions:

Whip egg whites till frothy. Add sugar gradually. Then add vinegar, cornflour, vanilla essence and lastly add boiling water.

Beat 10 full minutes with electric beater.

Spread onto oiled cookie sheet.

Bake 15 min at 350° then drop temperature to 200° for one full hour. Leave in oven to cool.

Decorate with whipped cream and assortment of fruit; kiwi and strawberries are most common.